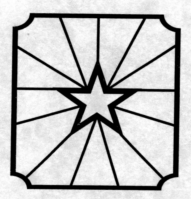

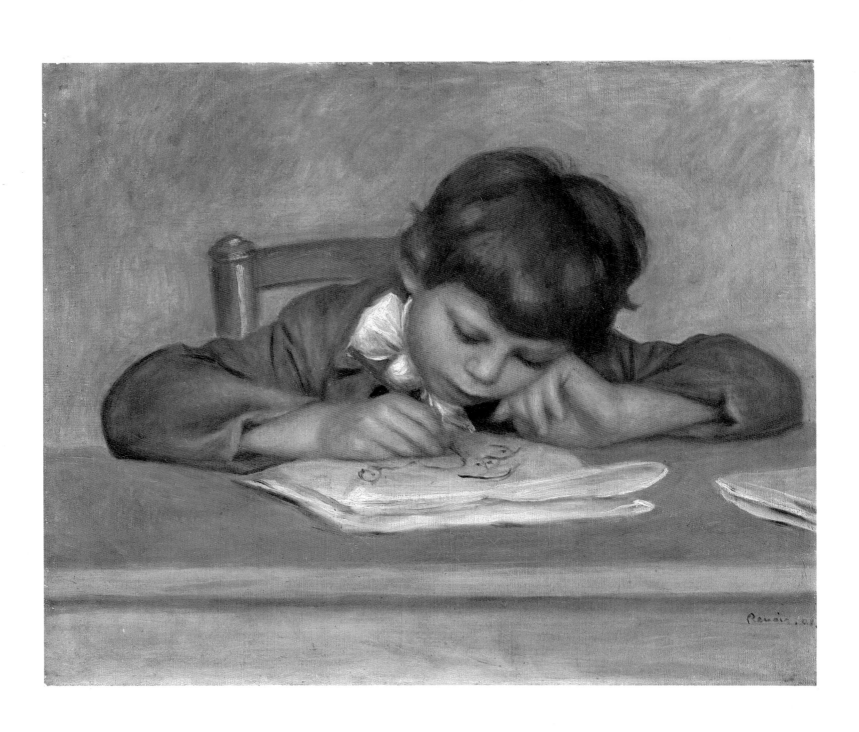

Edited by Michael Howard

The Impressionists *by Themselves*

A selection of their paintings, drawings and sketches with extracts from their writings

Conran Octopus

For Bill & Jean and Martin & Maureen

First published in 1991 by
Conran Octopus Limited
37 Shelton Street, London WC2H 9HN

Reprinted 1992

This paperback edition first published in 1995

British Library Cataloguing in Publication Data
The Impressionists by themselves
   1. France, Paintings, Impressionism
   I. Howard, Michael 1954–
   759.4

ISBN 1–85029–755–X

This book created by
Amazon Publishing Limited, 96a Albert Street, London NW1 7NE

Design: Derek Birdsall RDI
Editors: Mary Trewby, Andrew Kerr-Jarrett
Picture research: Amanda Baker
*Thanks to Julia Allen for translation, Bernard Denvir for reading the
manuscript, Peter Maloney for proofreading and Barry White for
indexing.*

Typeset by August Filmsetting, Haydock, St Helens
Colour separations by Landmark Fotographic
Printed in Hong Kong

The illustration on page 2 is Renoir *The Artist's Son Jean Drawing*,
1901.

Contents

Editor's Acknowledgements

Working on *The Impressionists by Themselves* has been a fascinating and rewarding experience and I would like to thank the many people whose help and enthusiasm have been instrumental in the completion of this project.

The wealth of material related to the Impressionists is so vast as to present any editor with an *embarras de richesses*. Going through a rigorous process of selection and organization has been the only way to bring everything into shape, not only to allow the individual pictures and texts to work in their own right, but also by their selection and juxtaposition to articulate a clear set of ideas.

I hope that this collection of letters and other texts will do justice to the artists, all but one of whom exhibited at one time or another in the Impressionist exhibitions held between 1874 and 1866, and to their works.

The term 'Impressionism', though helpful in some respects, has often hindered a deeper appreciation of the artists' individual and collective achievements. I have tried to emphasize the individuality of each of their personalities and the diversity of their artistic aims; I have also sought to give a sense of the times in which they lived.

Some writers need endless cups of coffee, or the sounds of Vivaldi or Bach, to keep the words and ideas flowing. I need the daily inspiration of living with my wife, whose work is a constant reminder of the realities of artistic production. Our children, Maxim and Cordelia, have also played their part; their very existence has kept the project in its proper perspective – I hope the text does not owe too much to their burgeoning editorial skills.

After the support of my family, I owe most to the examples set by Richard Kendall and Bruce Bernard, the editors of the companion volumes – books that show such wisdom and flair in their marriage of text and images. I also want to thank Sarah Snape and Ian McLellan at Amazon and my editors, Mary Trewby and Andrew Kerr-Jarrett, whose professional expertise and sympathetic understanding were invaluable. Others crucial to the production of the book were the picture researcher, Amanda Baker, and the designer, Derek Birdsall, whose layouts and choice of typography have given visual form to the ideas around which the book was organized. Another debt is to Julia Allen for her translations from French sources. I would also like to thank my sister Kate Howard and my friend Arianne Lawson for help at times when it was needed most.

A book of this nature is built upon the achievements of others: the artists themselves and the scholars, curators and collectors who, over the years, have organized and safeguarded the precious material. Like other writers in this field I am indebted to the magisterial work of John Rewald. My discussions with Richard Kendall and Richard and Belinda Thomson, who gave selflessly of their time and knowledge, were crucial in forming the structure of the book. I must also note my gratitude to Christopher Lloyd, J. Kirk Varnedoe, Richard Shone, Nancy M. Mathews, John Bensusan-Butt and Barbara Ehrlich White.

Finally, I would like to express my appreciation of the invaluable assistance given to me by Gaye Smith and the other librarians at Manchester Polytechnic.

Michael Howard
Glossop 1991

Editor's Note

Where known, the place of writing and date of a letter appear in *italics* at the head of the letter. Suggested places and dates, where any of this information is not known for certain, are given in roman type in square brackets.

Biographical details of the leading figures in, or connected with, the Impressionist movement appear at the back of the book (*Guide to Principal Personalities*, pages 322–325). Brief details of other figures are given in square brackets at the point where they first appear in the text.

Introduction

'Impressionism', with its brilliantly coloured, vibrant pictures of contemporary life in town and country, has achieved an unmatched position in the affections of art lovers throughout the world. Even though many of its finest works were painted over 100 years ago, its appeal has proved itself enduringly fresh and modern.

This selection of the works of the Impressionist circle of painters and of their writings, taken from the vast collection of correspondence, aphorisms and reminiscences of the artists themselves and those close to them, provides a detailed and in some ways surprising picture of the way in which the Impressionists worked as a group. For while it is true that they shared aims and ambitions and together confronted the antagonism and sometimes hostility of their critics, it is also true that the artists drawn together in the Impressionist exhibitions from 1874 to 1886 were often sharply at odds with one another, and their ideas, techniques, subject matter and sympathies could be startlingly diverse.

Over the last few decades our awareness of the achievements of Claude Monet, Pierre-Auguste Renoir, Edgar Degas, Paul Cézanne, Camille Pissarro and Alfred Sisley has been enriched by reassessments of the work of other Impressionist painters working at the same time, such as Berthe Morisot, Gustave Caillebotte and Mary Cassatt. This book charts the progress of these artists, who worked together in a loose and constantly changing association, and reveals their shared ambition to create an art that would be equivalent in stature to the art of the past yet would respond to the challenge presented by the modern world.

The letters and memoirs reveal the frustrations – practical and otherwise – of making art: the difficulties of setting up and sustaining an artists' co-operative with participants as diverse and troublesome as Monet, Degas and Cézanne; the irritations of *plein air* painting ('In a boat ... it rocks, there is an infernal lapping of the waves; you have the sun and the wind, the boats change position every minute,' Berthe Morisot complained to her sister); Monet's obsession with the weather ('another spell of bad weather would spoil everything I have begun'), and the self-confidence and uncertainties inherent in their chosen occupation (Cézanne's 'I am beginning to consider myself stronger than all those around me' and, later, '... if I were a great painter, a great painter!').

We witness their quarrels and friendships, and their family histories. There is something immensely touching in the way Frédéric Bazille writes to his parents about the birth of Monet's eldest child and Camille Pissarro encourages the artistic ambitions of his son Lucien, as there is in the sad letters of Alfred Sisley from his deathbed. Equally fascinating are the homely aspects of their existence: Monet writing to his gardener ordering plants for the gardens at Giverny, Renoir joking with his dealer Vollard, Pissarro agonizing over his lack of financial security, Degas lamenting a day lost trying to compose a 'blasted sonnet'.

Such insights are as revealing in their own way as the Impressionists' relatively few forays into aesthetic discussion. They rarely wrote to each other about theories of art: they spent evenings in cafés discussing such matters and felt little need to put their deliberations down in black and white. When they did, the results can sound astonishingly simple and straightforward or – as in the case of Cézanne, for example – highly ambiguous. For most of these artists painting was first and foremost a matter of doing, not theorizing. None of the Impressionists was as theoretically engaged as Gauguin and Van Gogh were. Monet, in particular, deliberately exaggerated the instinctive nature of his art: 'Paintings aren't made up of doctrines.... I have always been repelled by theories. My only merit lies in having painted directly in front of nature, seeking to render my impressions before the most fleeting effects, and I remain deeply sorry to have been the cause of a name given to a group, most of whom had nothing of an Impressionist about them.'

The term 'Impressionist' had been used before it was applied to these painters, and it has been used since to describe the work of many other, very different artists. However, the popular image of Impressionism remains so strong that it resists all attempts to be modified. There was never any Impressionist manifesto as such (although Pissarro did suggest a charter based on that of his local bakers' union), nor was there, except in the most prosaic sense, a group attitude. Those involved only accepted the term grudgingly, and some never accepted its use at all. Like so many artistic terms it was invented by an outsider, a journalist, initially as a piece of good copy in a satirical review of the first exhibition of the group who showed their work outside the accepted venue, the Salon.

The extracts presented in this selection raise certain questions. What is the relationship between the creator and the thing created? Do the opinions artists express concerning their own work have any more significance than those the viewers gain through their own understanding?

The link between a work of art and its creator remains a fascinating and, ultimately, a mysterious one. There is something elusive about the business of making art that no amount of elucidation can completely eradicate. Despite many volumes written on the subject, we remain little closer to the truth concerning artistic creativity than when Giorgio Vasari wrote his famous *Lives of the Artists* in the middle of the sixteenth century. A painting, print or sculpture quickly outgrows its progenitor and takes its place in the outside world where it is mediated by the circumstances in which it is found: in a gallery, palace or church, reproduced in a book or hidden away in a Swiss bank vault. Meanings are generated culturally, and to regard a painting solely from the artist's point of view is to present only one of many possible interpretations. At the same time, these texts allow us to chart the development of a number of artists from their beginnings to their extreme old age and, for most of them, from a time when their works were found to be problematic, even subversive, to their late years when they themselves were seen almost as state institutions.

It should not be forgotten that the Impressionists were painting during a very complex period of European history in which artists and writers, as well as scientists, philosophers, politicians and others, were seeking to give form to an age that seemed to have lost certain long-established values.

France was a country under shadow. At the beginning of the nineteenth century painters had had the opportunity to create an art worthy of their Renaissance and Baroque counterparts in representing the exploits of Napoleon Bonaparte: 'the greatest man since Caesar'. For a few short years, the nation could view herself as the most powerful in the world, until Napoleon's defeat at Waterloo in 1815. France had not recovered from that humiliation by the middle of the century.

In the years covered by this volume the country experienced revolution and dictatorship; she met defeat at the hands of the Prussians, and endured the suffering and terrors of civil war. Then, in the early part of the twentieth century, France found herself the theatre of one of the most bloody and pointless wars of modern history. From his gardens at Giverny, the elderly Monet could hear the cannons of the First World War battlefields. On the social front, Paris was transformed into the city we recognize today, with the modern world of high capitalism given visible form in the smart new department stores that flanked the boulevard Haussmann. Many artists felt that the accepted means of representation no longer equipped them to deal with this new world.

In 1855 the Emperor Napoleon III inaugurated the Exposition Universelle, a world fair that was intended to prove to the rest of the civilized world that his regime, although only three years old, had given back to France her stability and prosperity and had restored to the country her traditional place at the forefront of western and, by implication, world culture.

Included in the Exposition was that year's Salon, the State-sponsored event which was a public arena for the major French artists, who vied with each other for preeminence within their profession and, of course, for lucrative church, State and private commissions. Acceptance at the Salon was governed by a jury made up of artists representing various aspects of the artistic world. Conservatives and progressives were included, but compromise was the order of the day. Deals of one kind or another were common, and there was a vast range of work on show in any one year.

Art was considered to be an essential and important part of the fabric of France, intimately, though obscurely, tied in with the moral health of the nation. The Establishment used art as a means to preserve the status quo and to make visible the cultural values it held dear. The best-known representatives of high art were the by-then ageing Jean-Dominique Ingres and Eugène Delacroix. Although their work was very different, both painters looked to past traditions and were supported by the State and the Establishment.

Although by the mid-1850s Eugène Delacroix was acknowledged to be a great artist, his manner of painting was held to be too individualistic to be used as a model by the students of the State-sponsored Ecole des Beaux-Arts. For his own part, Delacroix viewed the age he lived in as decadent and was deeply pessimistic about the art of the day. In 1857 he began to work on a 'Dictionary of the Fine Arts' in the hope of providing the framework for a revival of great art. Although his notes remained unpublished until 1893, thirty years after his death, the artist's comments make interesting reading and suggest what the young Impressionists may have seen in his life and work:

Academies. What Voltaire says of them that they have never produced the greatest men.

Tradition. (Continuous until the time of [Jean-Louis] David).

Cohesion. The effect of the atmosphere and reflections that brings objects of the most incongruous colours into one whole.

Reflections. Every reflection contains green, and the edge of every shadow contains violet.

Grey and Earth Colours. Grey is the enemy of all painting ... Banish all earth colours.

Touch. Touch [ie, the brush stroke] is merely one of the several means that contribute towards rendering thought in painting. No doubt it is possible to paint a very beautiful picture in which touch is not apparent, but it is childish to imagine that in doing so you are getting closer to nature ... At a certain distance everything blends into the whole effect, but gives an accent to the picture which the blending of colours alone cannot produce . . .

On his visit to the Exposition Universelle of 1855 Delacroix wandered into the pavilion set up by Gustave Courbet next to the large building dedicated to the fine arts. Courbet had opened this independent exhibition because a number of his paintings had been rejected by the Exposition's jury, and he showed his *Burial at Ornans, L'Atelier* and over thirty other works. Delacroix wrote in his journal entry for 3 August: 'Went to the Exposition where I noticed the fountain that spouts artificial flowers. . . . I think all these machines are very depressing . . . Afterwards I went to the Courbet exhibition. He has reduced the price of admission to ten sous. I stayed there alone for nearly an hour and discovered a masterpiece in the picture they had rejected [*L'Atelier*]; I could scarcely tear myself away. . . . The only fault is that the picture, as he has painted it, seems to contain an ambiguity. It looks as though there were a *real sky* in the middle of the painting. They have rejected one of the most remarkable works of our time, but Courbet is not the man to be discouraged by a little thing like that.'

Courbet felt that his exhibition, made possible through the support of a private patron, would introduce his artistic ideals to a wide public. In a written statement he advocated the independence of the artist: 'The title of realist was imposed upon me . . . I have studied, not in any systematic spirit and without pre-conceived ideas, the art of the ancients and of the moderns. I have no more wish to imitate the former than to copy the latter; neither has my thought been to arrive at the lazy goal of ART FOR ART'S SAKE. No! I have simply wished to draw from the accumulated wisdom of tradition a reasoned and independent sentiment of my own individuality. To know in order to do, this was my thought . . . to be not only a painter, but a MAN, in a word, to make a living art, that is my aim.'

Thirteen years later, Edouard Manet, a painter from a very different background, having followed and developed some of Courbet's ambitions in his own way, repeated Courbet's strategy. He held a one-person show in 1867. His friend Zachérie Astruc wrote a pamphlet outlining the 'Reasons for Holding a Private Exhibition':

From 1861 onwards, M. Manet has exhibited or tried to exhibit.

This year he has decided to put the whole of his works directly before the public.

When first he exhibited at the Salon, M. Manet obtained an honourable mention. But afterwards, the repeated rejection of each work by the jury convinced him that, if the first phase of

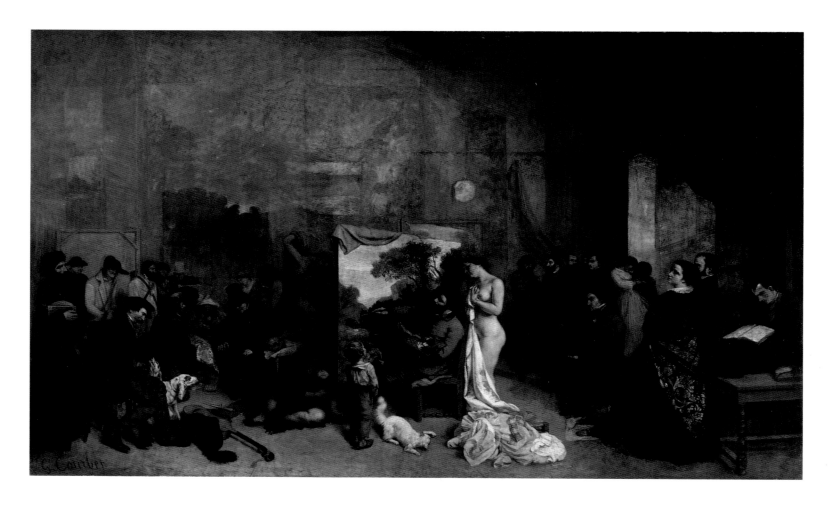

an artist's career is inevitably a kind of warfare, it is at least necessary to fight on equal terms – that is to say, to be able to secure publicity for what he has produced.

Without that, the painter too easily suffers an isolation from which egress is difficult. He is compelled to stack his canvases, or roll them up in a garret.

It is said that official encouragement, recognition, and rewards are, for a certain section of the public, a guarantee of talent; they are informed what to admire and what to avoid, according as the works are accepted or rejected. But, at the same time, the artist is assured that it is the spontaneous impression which his works create upon this same public that is responsible for the hostility of the various juries.

Under these circumstances, the artist has been advised to wait.

To wait for what? Until there are no more juries.

The artist does not say today, 'Come and see faultless works,' but, 'Come and see sincere works.'

The effect of sincerity is to give works a character that makes them resemble a protest, when the only concern of the painter has been to render his impression.

M. Manet has never wished to protest. On the contrary, the protest, quite unexpected on his part, has been directed against himself, because there exists a traditional teaching as to form, methods, modes of painting, and because those who have been brought up in this tradition refuse to admit any other. It renders them childlishly intolerant. Any work not done

Courbet *The Artist's Studio* 1855

Contemporary photograph of Courbet's *'Pavillon du realisme'* 1855

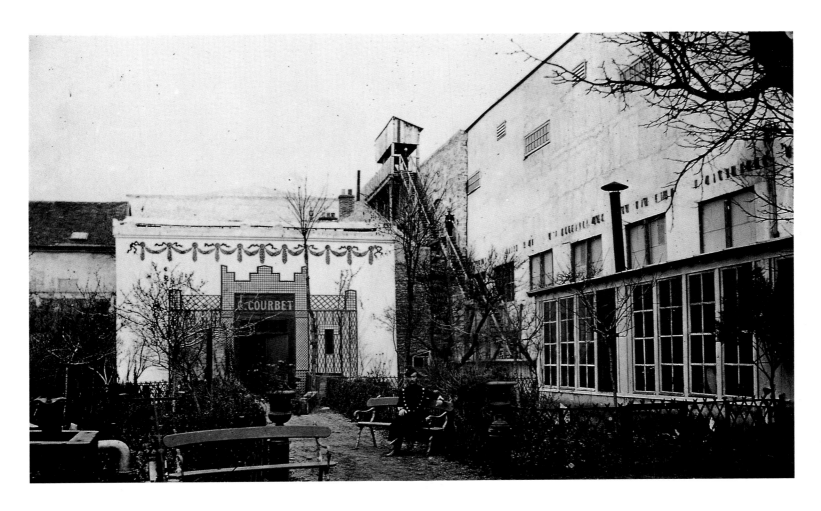

according to their formulas they consider worthless; it provokes not only their criticism, but their active hostility.

The matter of vital concern, the *sine qua non* for the artist, is to exhibit; for it happens, after some looking at a thing, that one becomes familiar with what was surprising, or, if you will, shocking. Little by little it becomes understood and accepted.

The challenge for ambitious young artists could not have been set down more succinctly. This event was a call for a distinctly modern art, one appropriate for the age. Here, in the works of Courbet and Manet, and technically in those of Delacroix, were the tools by which a contemporary art could be forged.

Paradoxically, the further model for a sincere and independent art was the landscape painting of Corot and the Barbizon school characterized by the work of Daubigny, Rousseau and Millet. By the middle of the century, from being a minor genre, landscape was well on the way to

Manet *Luncheon in the Studio* 1868

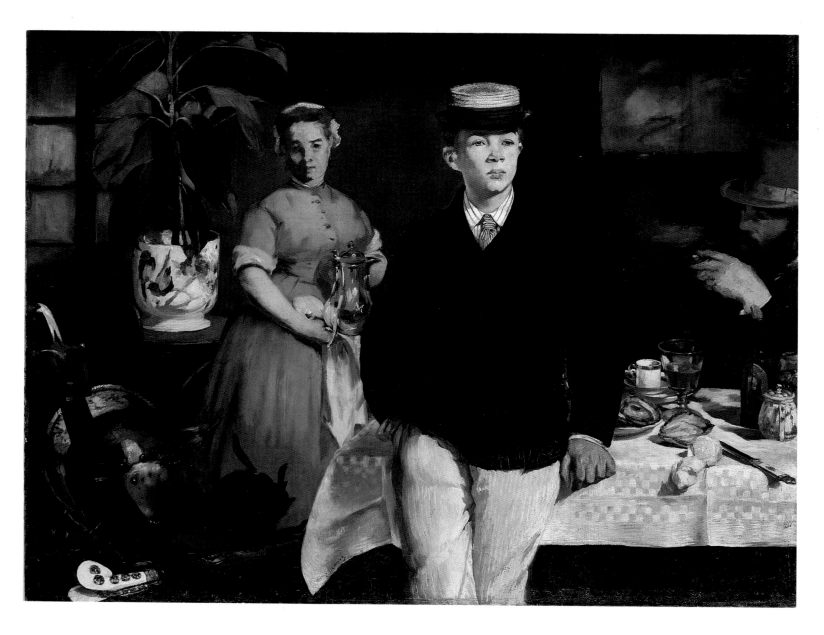

becoming the officially sanctioned art of the Establishment. There was also a discernible trend towards what could loosely be described as a more realistic art. A visitor to the Salons of the time would be surrounded by all kinds of paintings; there was confusion in the diversification of art and in its meaning, for artists, critics and the public alike.

* * *

For some time, artists had been dissatisfied with the restrictions of the Salon system. In 1863, more than half of the 5,000 works submitted were rejected. The jury was widely condemned for its severity, and an exhibition of rejected pictures, the Salon des Refusés, was instituted by Napoleon III. But far from advertising the shortcomings and corrupt practices of the Salon system, the exhibition of rejects was presented to the public in such a way as to uphold the status quo. The majority of the Press responded accordingly and the public visited the exhibition with the express purpose of ridiculing the exhibits. Singled out for particular abuse were Edouard Manet's *Déjeuner sur l'herbe* and James McNeill Whistler's *White Girl*. The respected writer Maxime du Camp declared in the *Revue des Deux-Mondes* that, 'Never have the jury's labours received more striking ratification, and we are grateful to it for having attempted to spare us the sight of such lamentable things.'

Despite the unfortunate reception of the Salon des Refusés, many artists realized that such events were their only hope of breaking the near-monopoly of the Salon and, over the years, many tried to have it reinstated; however, the government steadfastly ignored their requests. In the Establishment's view, one Salon des Refusés was enough. It had done what it was meant to do and there was no further need to show the liberality of the Second Empire administration or to further public support for the jury as arbiters of taste.

But the examples of Gustave Courbet and Edouard Manet had shown that it was possible to exist outside the Salon system. In 1874 a group of painters, printmakers and sculptors banded together to show their own works. They exhibited as independent artists in an attempt to find a more direct way of reaching the public than that offered by the official Salon, which over the years had shown itself hostile to their work.

From the beginning, there was a sense of identity among the key members of the *Societé anonyme* [limited company] *des artistes, peintres, sculpteurs et graveurs:* Camille Pissarro, Claude Monet, Pierre-Auguste Renoir, Alfred Sisley, Paul Cézanne, Berthe Morisot, Gustave Caillebotte and Edgar Degas. Their origins were as diverse as their artistic aims, although, in their different ways, they were all fired by the

examples of Courbet and Manet. Neither of the two older artists joined the venture or exhibited at any of the seven subsequent group shows, despite their friendship and admiration for many of the artists of the co-operative.

One of Berthe Morisot's letters makes clear that their first show was not an unmitigated disaster, although sales and critical approbation were slight. A witty review of the show by the critic Louis Leroy resulted in the work of the more avant-garde exhibitors being labelled 'Impressionist', from the title of a study by Monet: *Sunrise – an Impression.* The writer described a reverie in which he accompanied M. Vincent, an imaginary painter of academic landscapes, around the exhibition. This august personage, a 'recipient of medals and decorations under several administrations', was not pleased with what he saw.

' "Ah, here he is, there he is!" he shouted in front of No. 98. "I recognize him: Papa Vincent's favourite! What *does* it depict; have a look at the catalogue." '

' "*Sunrise – an Impression.*" '

' "Impression; I was certain of it. I was just thinking that as I was impressed, there had to be some impression in it. And what freedom! What ease of handling! A preliminary drawing for a wallpaper design is more highly finished than this seascape." '

* * *

Each of the subsequent exhibitions was accompanied by much wrangling and dissent within the group. Of the so-called Impressionists, only Pissarro exhibited at all eight events (held between 1874 and 1886), and an examination of what was displayed at the various shows makes it very clear how differently each of the artists viewed the enterprise. Even the most casual glance through this book will reveal the diversity of styles, subject matter and media employed by the central figures of Impressionism, although certain traits were held in common.

Their view of art was essentially anti-academic, a rejection of the official position that the artist should improve upon nature and present an idealized view of the subject, whether it be a nude or landscape. Academic art was founded upon the premises that drawing was the basis by which nature should be idealized; that colours should be subordinated to the expression of the idea, and that tonal rather than colouristic values should be stressed. Hence, before the 1870s, landscapes were still painted using a relatively restricted palette and, if they did not contain any 'elevating' elements, were usually restricted in size.

The images of modern life favoured by Monet, Renoir and the rest kept the brevity, freshness and apparent spontaneity of the sketch in the finished work. Their subject matter was mundane, modern and casual, bringing to mind the 'outrageous' pictures of Courbet and Manet rather than the model artists held up to the students of the Beaux-Arts, artists such as Alexandre Cabanel and Thomas Couture, painters patronized by the Emperor, nourished by the State and upholding the notion that traditions stemming from the work of the Renaissance artists should be at the heart of art teaching.

The Impressionists were quick to exploit recent technical developments within their own craft. At the same time, many artists were obsessed – or at least intrigued – by the supposed 'secrets' of the old masters now lost to the present age. Degas and Renoir were haunted by the achievements of the past: their letters and recorded statements are full of references to technical matters and are tinged with a sense of the loss of inherited ways of painting, which they could have employed and thereby continued the Grand Tradition, as they perceived it.

The day-to-day experience of living in a modern city, a knowledge of photography, popular prints and readily available art and artefacts from other cultures, all allowed the Impressionists to reinterpret their own cultures, and so produce a new vibrant art in keeping with their personal experiences. Intimately connected with such concerns were the technical improvements of painting materials and the availability of ready-made canvases and, from the 1840s, easily portable tubes of ready-mixed oil-paint, all of which facilitated the already well-established practice of painting in the open air. Equally important for these artists was the fact that modern forms of transportation enabled them to travel freely into the countryside and to the sea.

In his 1879 review of the Impressionist exhibition, Joris-Karl Huysmans remarked: 'In a new age, new techniques. It's a simple matter of good sense.' Edmond Duranty had discussed this earlier in his 1876 pamphlet, 'The New Painting', published about the time of the Impressionists' second show at Durand-Ruel's gallery in 1876 and written very much with Degas' work in mind:

The idea, the very first idea, was to eliminate the partition separating the artist's studio from everyday life, and to introduce the reality of the street ... It was necessary to make the painter come out of his sky-lighted cell, his cloister, where his sole communication was with the sky – and to bring him back among men, out into the real world.

Now these new painters [are aware] that our lives take place in rooms and in streets, and rooms and streets have their own special laws of light and visual language.

And as we are solidly embracing nature, we will no longer separate the figure from the background of an apartment or the street. The individual will be at a piano, examining a sample of cotton in an office, or waiting in the wings for the moment to go on stage, or ironing on a makeshift table ... She might be

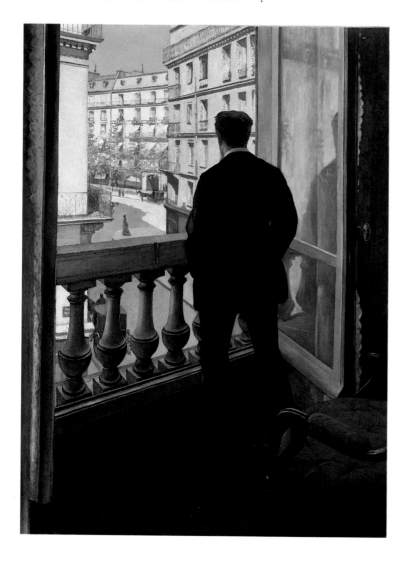

Caillebotte *The Man at the Window* 1876

avoiding carriages as she crosses the street or he might be glancing at his watch as he hurries across the square ... From indoors we communicate with the outside world through windows. A window is yet another frame that is continually with us during the time we spend at home, and that time is considerable. Depending whether we are near or far, seated or standing, the window frames the scene outside in the most unexpected and changeable ways, providing us with constantly changing impromptu views that are the great delights of life.

*   *   *

The Impressionist painters, while rebelling against the academic traditions of their time, nonetheless strove to create works that would be the equal of those found in the museums. This ambition to make a public art can be seen in Claude Monet's series of paintings of the station of St-Lazare and his *décorations* at the Orangerie, in Cassatt's decorative panels for the 1893 Chicago Exposition, in Degas' frustrated desire to paint on a large scale and, most obviously, in Manet's unsuccessful *Ventre de Paris* proposal to the Prefect of the Seine for a decoration in the newly rebuilt Hôtel de Ville: 'I would show the Paris of the public markets, bridges, subterranean activities, race courses and parks ...' Even their smaller works, the apparently casual observations of varied aspects of modern life, may be seen as a continuation – in visual terms – of the fiction of Balzac and, later, of Zola, in their attempts to capture the epic quality of contemporary life, an age of shifting values and crass materialism.

Creativity, sensitivity and sincerity had become the hallmarks of the independent painter, rather than adherence to a particular set of values.

In 1883 the young writer Jules Laforgue gave an account of Impressionism that may serve as a benchmark for discussions about the complexity of those artists' chosen goals: 'forgetting the pictures amassed throughout the centuries in museums, forgetting his optical art-school training – line, perspective, colour – by dint of living and seeing frankly, and primitively in the bright open air ... outside his poorly lit studio – [the artist] has succeeded in remaking for himself a natural eye, and in seeing naturally and painting as simply as he sees.'

These letters and reminiscences make very clear the shortcomings of such an analysis, but it is a description that many of those represented in this book would have been happy to embrace.

There is a danger that the existence of these painters as individuals who worked together, albeit for a relatively short period of time, may be forgotten in the desire to straitjacket them into their respective slots in the 'development of modern art'. By bringing together material in this unique way we can watch the drama of their lives unfold and bring to life the wonderfully rich and evocative images that were created by artists who, for most of their careers, were unaware of the place that history would allot to their works.

I: The Student Years 1856—1871

In late 1862 a group of young artists, all in their early twenties, met in the Paris studio of Charles Gleyre, a Swiss painter who produced rather mannered works, yet presided over a studio that was decidedly liberal in outlook and sympathetic to the development of individual talent. Pierre-Auguste Renoir, the son of a tailor, had been a student in the *atelier* for at least a year, when three new students enrolled: Claude Monet, Parisian-born and raised in Le Havre, Alfred Sisley, the son of a British-born silk merchant, and Frédéric Bazille, whose wealthy Montpellier family assumed that their son's artistic interests were secondary to his medical studies. The four artists, who were to form the nucleus of the group of painters known as the Impressionists, were soon working together, with Bazille helping out his poorer colleagues with money and accommodation when occasion demanded.

Renoir's lively classical interpretations of the nude owed much to his master's example. He recalled that it was under Gleyre that '*j'apprenais le métier de peintre*'; as late as 1890 he identified himself in the Salon *livret* (catalogue) as a 'student of Gleyre'. Monet played down this aspect of his career, claiming that he had only remained in Gleyre's studio for a matter of weeks; in fact he was associated with the *atelier* for two years and some of his early work seems related to the Swiss master's genre pieces. The mentor whom Monet did acknowledge was Eugène Boudin, a marine painter who specialized in bravura sketch-like paintings of the upper classes enjoying the Normandy coastal resorts. Following the examples of Boudin and his colleague Barthold Jongkind, Monet had been painting in the open air since the late 1850s, and later noted: 'Boudin, with untiring kindness, undertook my education. My eyes were finally opened and I really understood nature; I learned at the same time to love it.'

In 1863, the year of the notorious Salon des Refusés, Monet introduced Camille Pissarro and Paul Cézanne to the group. Cézanne was from Aix-en-Provence and, on the advice of his childhood friend, the critic and future novelist Emile Zola, he had come to Paris to study art at the Académie Suisse, the same *atelier* where the thirty-three-year-old Pissarro had been a student some years earlier.

Studio in the rue de la Condamine, which Bazille painted in 1870, is a candid and relaxed representation of the artist and his close colleagues, a deliberate reprise of Courbet's vast *allégorie réelle*, *L'Atelier* of 1855. Bazille's painting emphasizes the central role played by Edouard Manet, who is shown standing before the easel. The tall figure of Bazille, which was painted by Manet, stands to one side, palette in hand, surrounded by his friends: Edmond Maître at the piano, with Zola and Renoir (or possibly Monet and Sisley) chatting by the stairs. Around the walls hang works which declare in no uncertain terms the shared interests and ambitions of the young artists. Bazille, who was to be killed in the last days of the 1870—1871 Franco-Prussian war, was an artist of real promise whose essays in avant-garde painting were as daring as those of his friends.

From the first, Monet had assumed some kind of authority over his colleagues. He valued his artistic independence and, although for the next fifteen years or so he painted a considerable number of scenes of contemporary Parisian life, his letters make clear his preference for a more natural environment. By the end of the decade he and his friends — often in each other's company — were painting in the French capital and the surrounding countryside.

Renoir's brother Edmond later recalled: 'In those days ... art students would go in a group to the forest of Fontainebleau ... the inns of Chailly, Barbizon or Marlotte would welcome them all, well-known and unknown, and they would go and work outdoors with their knapsacks. This is where my brother met Courbet, who was the idol of the young painters, and Diaz [Narcisse Diaz de la Peña], who won their admiration to an even higher degree ... it was Diaz who told him "no self-respecting painter should ever touch a brush unless he has the model before his eyes."'

However accurate or otherwise such accounts may be, the students shared an ambition to paint landscapes out of doors — *en plein air* — and many of their letters refer to the organizational and artistic problems involved in such a project.

Other painters were following a similar path. Berthe Morisot was from a different social milieu, a member of the *haute bourgeoisie* like Edouard Manet. Her brother Tiburce has left an amusing account of Morisot's teacher, the Lyonnais academic painter Joseph-Benoît Guichard, recognizing the talent of Berthe and her sister Edma and warning their mother of the dangers of further education: 'Given your daughters' natural gifts, my instruction will not endow them with petty drawing-room results; they will become painters. Do you realize what this means? It will be revolutionary — I would say catastrophic — in your bourgeois milieu. Are you sure that one day you will never curse the art, once allowed into your household, now so respectably peaceful, that will become the sole master of the fate of your two children?' Guichard's regime was traditional, centred around 'lessons before the masters' in the Louvre. After two years, Berthe decided to follow a different path, to Guichard's great sorrow. Her parents' friend Corot and the artists of the Barbizon school were a great influence on her, and she had work accepted for four Salon exhibitions between 1864 and 1870. But in 1868, while she was copying a work by Rubens in the Louvre, the painter Henri Fantin-Latour introduced her to Edouard Manet. Six years later she married Manet's brother Eugène and through him met Monet and like-minded artists.

Edgar Degas came from a similar social environment to Morisot. He had been thoroughly grounded in the academic art practices of the day by his teacher Louis Lamothe, who was a former winner of the prestigious Prix de Rome and a pupil of Ingres. In 1855 Degas had entered the Ecole des Beaux Arts and, through a family friend, had met the great guardian of academic principles, Ingres. He never forgot the advice the great master gave him – 'Draw lines, many lines' – and years later he playfully suggested that he might donate one of the Ingres that he owned to the nation so that he could sit before it and think about what a noble deed he had done.

In the late 1850s, Degas and his friend Gustave Moreau had journeyed around Italy and neither forgot their experiences of that country and its artistic heritage. Moreau went on to paint latter-day mythological constructions of intricate detail, laden with literary and mystical references. But within a few years Degas found that he could not follow that route; he spent the next thirty years finding an appropriate way of reconciling aspects of a modern, scientific age with the lessons he had learnt from the past: 'Oh Giotto! Let me see Paris and you, Paris, let me see Giotto!'

Back in Paris Degas began to frequent the Café Guerbois, which was situated on one of the new boulevards in the Batignolles quarter at the foot of Montmartre. There he met Cézanne, Monet, Sisley and the other painters of their circle (Berthe Morisot's sex and position in society barred her from such informal gatherings). History has given to their early careers a coherence and order that tends to separate the future Impressionists from the wider social and artistic milieu in which they operated; the truth is, their association with each other was much looser than is often suggested. At the Café Guerbois they shared tables with academic painters, successful modish painters such as Alfred Stevens and Carolus-Duran, and, most importantly, artists and writers associated with the realist school, including Emile Zola, Edmond Duranty and Théodore Duret. Discussions were often heated and usually centred around the charismatic figure of Edouard Manet whose paintings had

shocked and scandalized the public and Establishment a decade earlier.

From the late 1860s the ambitions of these young artists were to set them on a course that would result in the establishment of an independent organizing body that was to become known as 'Impressionists', despite the diversity of characters and aims of those involved. The beginnings of a recognizable Impressionist style may be found in the painted sketches of La Grenouillère, a bathing and boating resort on the Seine, where Monet, Renoir and Pissarro spent time in the summer of 1869 painting out of doors, attempting to develop a living modern art by building on the achievements of Gustave Courbet and Edouard Manet. The Grenouillère paintings present a fascinating insight into the obvious similarities and striking differences between the paintings of Renoir and of those of his friend Monet. Every aspect of Renoir's work reveals a real interest in the individuals that populate his landscapes: people talk, and by their distinctive poses they reveal their characters and concerns. Monet is much more summary in his indication of the figure and, it would appear, less interested in human relationships.

One member of the Guerbois circle preferred other means of capturing *la vie moderne*. The writers Edmond and Jules de Goncourt noted in their Journal in 1874: 'Yesterday … spent the whole day in the studio of a strange painter called Degas. After a great many essays and experiments and trial shots in all directions, he has fallen in love with modern life, and out of all the subjects in modern life he has chosen washerwomen and ballet-dancers. When you come to think of it, it is not a bad choice.'

I: The Student Years 1856–1871

In Gleyre's Studio

Frédéric Bazille to his mother

[Paris], *1 December 1862*

... You ask for details of my lifestyle, I'm going to give you very precise ones. Every morning between eight and nine Alfred Parlier [a friend] wakes me up on his way to school. I get up and go to the studio where I stay until eleven. I then get lunch at a student *pension* not far from the rue Serpente, as I have given up eating at the Café Caron, it's too expensive. The food at this *pension* is plentiful and good. Lunch costs 16 sous, dinner 25, without wine. These figures must seem extraordinarily low to you, nevertheless, I'm very well fed. ... I have also the pleasure of being with medical students, some of whom are old school friends.

After lunch, I go back to the studio until three or four, then I go on to my anatomy class on the days when there is one.

The studio is open only four days a week. The other days I get up a bit later, or go to the Hôpital de la Charité. In the evening, I have dinner at my *pension* or with Frat and Teulon, then we play billiards, take a stroll on the boulevard, or go to the theatre ...

Frédéric Bazille to his father

[Paris], *Sunday,* [1863]

... I recently made the acquaintance of Monsieur le Vicomte Lepic, son of the Emperor's *aide de camp*. He's taken up painting, and although already quite good, comes to our studio in order to improve his technique. He showed me his apartments in the Louvre, where his father has set him up with a splendid studio. This young man, and another from Le Havre, by the name of Monet ... are my best friends among the art students. I did my first daub a few days ago, a copy of a Rubens in the Louvre. It's terrible, but I'm not discouraged. Some of the other copyists are just as bad as I am.

Frédéric Bazille to his father

[Paris], *Tuesday evening,* [1864]

I nearly forgot to tell you that we put on a performance of *Macbeth* at the studio last week. I accepted a part rather reluctantly, but didn't waste any time learning it as I played a ballerina – we'd introduced a *pas de deux* into the banqueting scene.

I had a pink lustrine costume made consisting of a bodice and a very short skirt, and petticoats of stiff muslin, the kind used by decorators to back wallpaper. I borrowed silk tights, dancers' shoes and paste necklaces and bracelets – all very effective. Needless to say it was a huge success. Our play bills and invitations are to be published in some kind of a newspaper, and someone is doing our caricature which I'll send you. ...

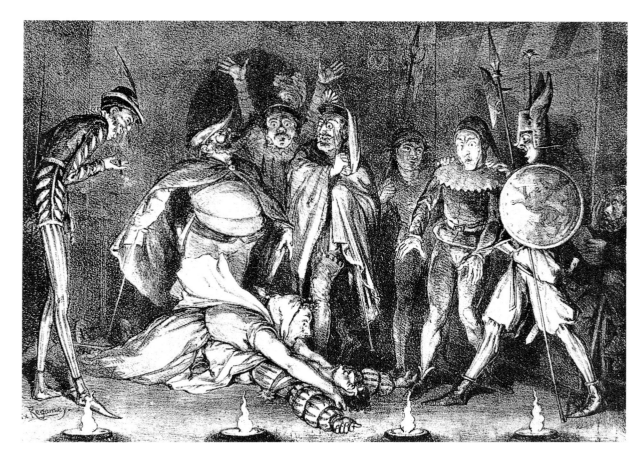

Contemporary lithograph of a production of *'La Tour de Nesle'* at Gleyre's studio 1863

From 'Art in a democracy' by Jean-François Raffaëlli, in *La Nouvelle Revue*
(15 October 1896)

The students sang stupid obscene songs and acted out shameful and demeaning
masquerades. Depraved louts talked with wretched women posing in the nude,
sometimes exposing their pathetic diseased private parts in the midst of all those brutish
young men with their barrack-room jokes. — Oh! the awful weeks I spent there, my
cheeks flaming!

And the horrors went on around me. I looked on while the new students were
stripped naked and plastered with filth. In this room with its colourless walls, orgies
ran riot! ...

And not once, in this gathering of young men supposed to be future artists, was
there a discussion about art! Never a generous word. Never a lofty idea. Nothing but
obscene, stupid banter, nothing but filth.

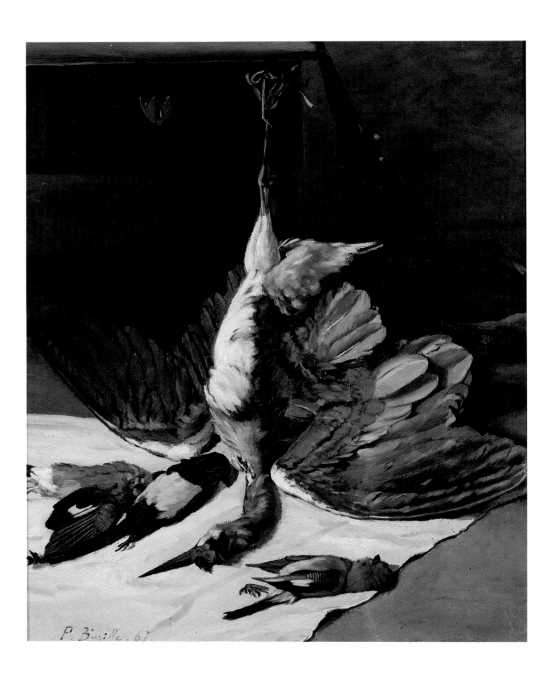

Bazille
Still-Life with Heron
1867

Frédéric Bazille to his father

[Paris, 1864]

My reason for going so long without writing to you, dear Papa, is, I have to admit,
that I didn't dare tell you about my exam and give you the details of why I failed. There
was not much other news and I see from your letter that you were annoyed with me.
As I told you, I was failed on my dissection, although it wasn't too bad. . . .

I take some comfort from the fact that my painting has improved since I took it up
again. I work all day either in Gleyre's studio or in my own. I paid 75 francs rent out of
the last lot of money you sent me, and since you promised to reimburse this sum, I'd
appreciate it if you'd do so as soon as possible because I'm completely broke after making
this payment.

I'm afraid, dear Papa, that you're displeased at my devoting myself to painting.
I wish you'd tell me how you really feel about this . . .

Frédéric Bazille to his mother

[Paris], *Wednesday*, [1866]

... The news from rue Visconti is that Monet has arrived from out of the blue with a collection of magnificent canvases, which will be highly successful at the Exposition. He will stay with me until the end of the month. Along with Renoir, I am giving shelter to two needy painters. My apartment is a regular infirmary and I'm delighted. I have plenty of room, and they are both so cheerful.... Many people have seen my paintings and liked them. If I had them to do over they would be much better. But that will be for next year.

Frédéric Bazille to his parents

Paris, 1867

I don't think I've told you yet that I'm giving hospitality to one of my friends, a former pupil of Gleyre's, who has no studio at the moment. Renoir is his name and he's a hard worker. He works from my models and even helps me in part to pay for them. It is pleasant for me not to spend my days entirely alone. At the moment I'm doing the portrait of one of my friends [Sisley?], which I shall send in to the exhibition together with the picture of [the village of] Méric.

Sisley
Still-Life with Heron
1867

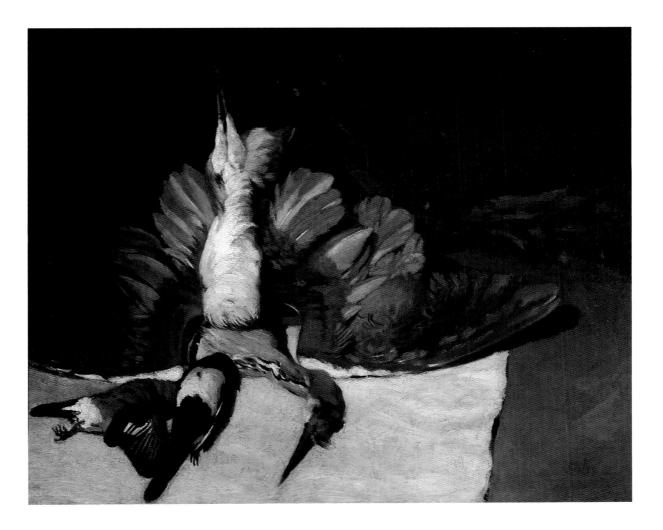

Pierre-Auguste Renoir from *Renoir, My Father* by Jean Renoir (1962)

The [Dutch] Ambassador had a daughter who wanted to learn to paint. Gleyre was very impressed. His powerful figure shifted from one foot to the other, as he made little bows and friendly gestures of welcome [to his *atelier*]. In his thick accent he exclaimed rapturously:

'A bubil from Remprant's and Rupen's native gountry. Vot an honour for de School!'

His pupils, as though quite by chance, had left in full view the pictures of the male model, whom they had deliberately portrayed without his drawers. They had even equipped the gentleman with attributes of a size to make Karagueuse sick with envy. Gleyre flushed and hastened to turn the canvases to the wall, edging his visitors to the safety of his private office. This office was at the far end of a little garden, and had three stone steps in front of it. One of the students, a bit of a wag, would occasionally place a bit of glazed faience in the shape of human excrement on one of the steps. Gleyre never paid much attention to it but usually pushed it aside with his foot when he went in. The Ambassador and his wife and daughter were dumbfounded when they beheld the unsavoury object blocking their way.

'Don't bay it any nodice,' Gleyre begged them, apologetically. 'It's only a choke.' And he picked up the offending piece with his hand to show the Ambassadress that it was only imitation. However, by some mystery which was never explained, that day it turned out to be the real thing!

From *Renoir* by Albert André (1919)

Gleyre sarcastically commented to Renoir, 'You no doubt paint merely to amuse yourself.' To which the young artist replied, 'I certainly do. If painting didn't amuse me, I can assure you I wouldn't be doing it.'

Degas' Journeys in Italy

From the notebooks of Edgar Degas (Numbers 5 and 6)

18 January 1856

... It is essential – one must never make bargains with nature. One certainly needs courage if one is to approach nature head-on in its grand planes and lines and it is cowardly to do it by means of facets and details. It is a struggle ...

It seems to me that if one wants to be a serious artist today and create an original little niche for oneself, or at least ensure that one preserves the highest degree of innocence of character, one must constantly immerse oneself in solitude.

From the notebooks of Edgar Degas (Number 11)

24 July 1858

...I leave Rome 6.45 arriving at a height beyond Ponte Molle – superb plain, the Italy of our dreams! Yellow plain, corn cut – mountains grey with night falling at their feet, hazy mountains truly azure blue ...

I would rather do nothing than do a rough sketch without having looked at anything. My memories will do better. ... I am going to return to the bustle of Paris – who knows what will happen – but I shall always be an honest man.

... 10 o'clock in the evening. I leave for Orvieto – moonlight. I can make out the landscape and the mountains. Superb terrain – Montefiascone – mountains – daybreak. Fog over the plain – we descend into the plain of Orvieto – the Cathedral appears above the fog – we climb up the steps, a real eagle's nest ...

Sublime Cathedral, I am quite startled – façade so rich and so tasteful. The mosaics too fresh – one so dreadfully decadent – I recognize the sculptures – I go in and run to Luca Signorelli.

It always seems that there must be, in the most beautiful monuments, this mixture of tastes ... I don't know what to say – I am in a dream which I don't know how to recall.

... I walk on the ramparts. Everywhere in the streets medieval houses. The sun behind Monte Cimino.

I don't feel like going out to draw from nature. Luca Signorelli fascinates me. I must think about figures above all else, or at least I must study them when thinking only about backgrounds ... I must not forget the beautiful effect I saw on the way between the Carmine and Sole gates – the clouds covered the plain in shadow and only the hill of Assisi was lit by the sun ...

Everything breathes an atmosphere of prayer.

Everything is beautiful, the details, the whole.

Degas
View of Naples 1860

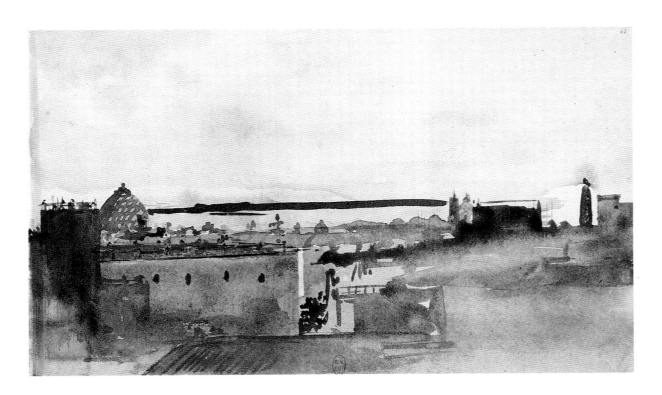

Edgar Degas to Gustave Moreau

Florence, 27 November 1858

... My family are looking after me too well for me to work the way I would like to. I am busy with a portrait of my aunt and my two little cousins. I will show you this on your return. I am doing it as if I were making a *picture*; it must be like that, I want to leave this souvenir and I have an inordinate desire to fill canvases, so that everything revolves around the picture, which is a very forgivable dream for a child, as you call me. I have had to give up my studies at the Museum, and I don't budge from the house any more. Once I am back in Paris I promise not to give into the family as I've been doing here....

... I have two little cousins coming for a meal. The older one is a real little beauty; the little one has the disposition of a devil and the kindness of a little angel. I am painting them in their black dresses and their little white aprons which make them look charming. Backgrounds keep running through my head. I would like a certain natural gracefulness with a sort of nobility which I don't know how to define. Van Dyck is a great artist, Giorgione also, Botticelli also, Mantegna also, Rembrandt also, Carpaccio also....

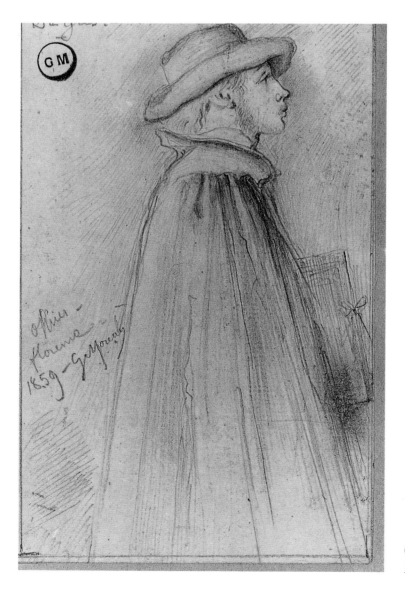

Gustave Moreau
Portrait of Degas 1859

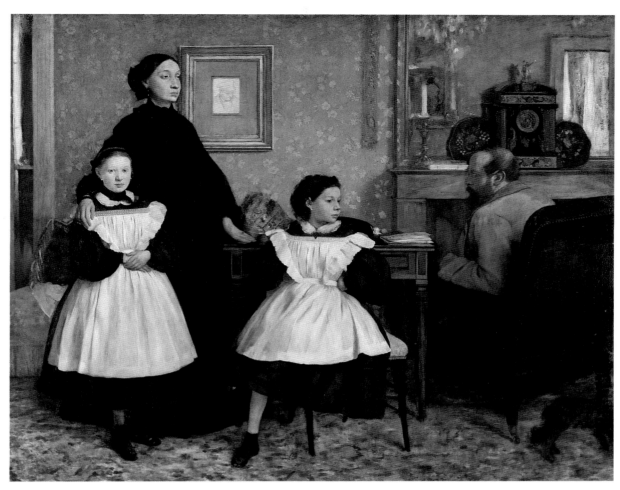

Degas *Portrait of the Bellelli Family c.*1858–60

From the notebooks of Edgar Degas (Numbers 22 and 23)

[Paris, late 1860s]

... Oh Giotto! Let me see Paris, and you, Paris, let me see Giotto!

Make of the *Tête d'expression* [an academic expressive study of the head] a study of modern feeling – it's like Lavater, but a more relative Lavater in a way. – Study Delsarte's observations on those movements of the eye inspired by feeling. – Its beauty must be nothing more than a specific physiognomy. Work a lot on the effects of, say, a lamp, a candle etc. The point is not always to show the source of light, but its effect. This aspect of art can become immensely important today. Is it possible not to see it?

Draw a lot. Oh! the beauty of drawing!

Think about a treatise on ornament for or by women, according to their way of observing, combining, sensing the way they dress and everything else. – Every day they compare a thousand more visible things with one another than a man does....

... Make portraits of people in typical, familiar poses, being sure above all to give their faces the same kind of expression as their bodies. Thus if laughter typifies an individual, make her laugh. – There are, of course, feelings which one cannot convey, out of propriety, as portraits are not intended for us painters alone. How many delicate nuances to put in.

The Young Cézanne

Paul Cézanne to Emile Zola

Aix, 29 [?] *1858*

A certain inner sadness has me in its grip and, dear friend, I dream only of that woman I spoke to you about. I'm so stymied by her I can't help sighing, but not with sighs that betray themselves externally, these are mental sighs...

That morsel of poetry you sent gave me great joy, I was very pleased to see that you remember the pine tree which shades the banks [of the River Arc] at Palette [a village near Aix]. ... My dear friend, I reveal for your eyes a picture representing:

Cicero
striking down Catilina
after having discovered the conspiracy
of that citizen lost to honour. ...

The weather improves, I'm not sure if it will go on doing so. One thing is sure – and that's that I'm burning to go:

Like an intrepid diver
To furrow the liquid substance
Of the Arc
And in its limpid waters
Catch the fish offered me by chance. ...

Paul Cézanne to Joseph Huot [childhood friend]

Paris, 4 June 1861

Ah, my good old Joseph, so I'm forgetting you, *morbleu!*, as well as our friends... and the good wine of Provence; you know that the stuff here is execrable. I don't want to wax nostalgic in these few lines – all the same, *can't be denied*, I'm not exactly blithe of heart. I fritter away to left and right my little existence; [the Académie] Suisse keeps me busy from six in the morning until eleven. I eat in keeping [with his status as a student] at 15 sous a meal; it's not a vast amount; but then what can you expect? On the other hand, I'm not dying of hunger.

I imagined when I left Aix that I was leaving that *ennui* that always dogs me far behind. All I've done is to change places and the *ennui* has followed me. I've left my parents, my friends, the odd habit or two – that's all. And to think, though, that I spend just about the whole day wandering around. I've seen – it's a little naive to tell you all this – the Louvre and the Luxembourg and Versailles. You already know this, of course, but the titbits contained in these *admirable monuments – they're tremendous, astonishing, overwhelming*. Don't think that I'm becoming Parisian...

I've also been to the Salon. For a young heart, for a child born for art, who says what he thinks, I believe that it's there that you'll find what is really best – because it's there that all tastes, all styles come together and collide. I could now give you a series of fine descriptions and send you to sleep. Be grateful to me for sparing you. ...

Emile Zola to Baptistin Baille

10 June 1861

To try to convince Cézanne of anything would be like trying to persuade the towers of Notre-Dame to perform a quadrille. He might possibly say yes, but he wouldn't budge an inch. And bear in mind that age has only made him more stubborn, without giving him any rational grounds for digging his heels in. He's all one, rigid and hard to the touch; nothing bends him, nothing can wring a concession from him.

Paul Cézanne to Emile Zola

[Aix, *c.* 19 October 1866]

. . . As for me, I am sunk in idleness – in the last four or five days I haven't done a thing. . . . But, you understand, no painting done inside, in the studio, will ever be the equal of things done out of doors. When representing out-of-door scenes, the contrasts of the figures against the terrain behind are astonishing, and the landscape is magnificent. I see wonderful things, and I must make a resolution only ever to do things out of doors. . . .

The Café Guerbois Group

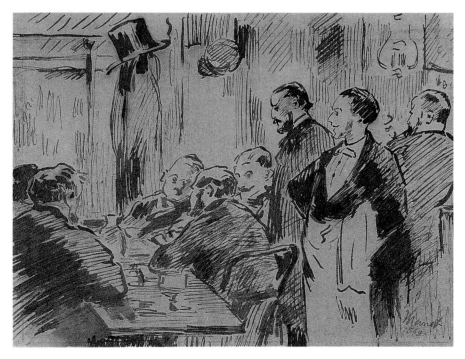

Manet *Interior of the Café Guerbois* 1869

From *En écoutant Cézanne, Degas et Renoir* by Ambroise Vollard (1938)

In 1863 Cézanne made the acquaintance of Renoir. One day the latter saw one of his friends, Bazille, come into his studio with two unknown men whom he presented to Renoir: 'I'm bringing you two first-class recruits!' They were Cézanne and Pissarro. About that same period Cézanne met Manet . . . Cézanne was struck at once by Manet's power of realization. 'He spits out the colour!' exclaimed Cézanne. Then thinking awhile, he added: 'Yes, but what he lacks is harmony, and temperament as well.'

Claude Monet from an article in *Le Temps* (November 1900)

'The two seascapes that I sent [to the 1865 Salon] were received with the highest approval and were hung on the line. It was a great success. The same unanimity of praise was accorded in 1866 to the *Woman in Green*. The papers even carried my name back to Le Havre. My family at last began to take me seriously, and with this my allowance started to come in again. I floated in my wealth – temporarily at least, for later we started to quarrel again. I threw myself body and soul into *plein air* painting.

'It was a dangerous innovation. Till then, nobody had indulged in it; not even Manet who attempted it only some years later, after me. His painting then was still very classical, and I have never forgotten the contempt he showed for my painting at the time. It was in 1867; my style had become definite, but it was still not really revolutionary in character. I was still a long way off adopting the principle of subdivision of colour that set so many against me, but I was beginning to make some attempts at it, and I was experimenting with effects of light and colour that flouted conventions. The Salon jury, which had once been so favourable to me, turned against me, and I was blackballed when I presented this picture to them.

'Still I found a way to exhibit elsewhere. Touched by my entreaties, a dealer in rue Auber agreed to display in his window the seascape which the Salon had rejected. One evening when I had stopped in the street amongst a group of onlookers to hear what was being said about my picture I saw Manet coming along with some of his friends. They stopped to look, and Manet, in a contemptuous tone, remarked, shrugging his shoulders, "Just look at this young man who tries to do *plein air* painting. As if the old masters would have thought of such a thing!"

'Manet, moreover, had an old grudge against me. At the Salon of 1866 he had been received, on entering the *vernissage* [varnishing day], by a chorus of acclaim. . . . He was delighted. Then imagine his consternation when he discovered that the picture about which he was being congratulated was actually by me! It was my *Woman in Green*. The saddest part of all was that on leaving the building he came across a group which included Bazille and me. "How goes it?" one of them asked. "Awful," replied Manet; "I am disgusted. I am being complimented on a picture that is not mine."

. . . 'It was only in 1869 that I saw him again, and then we at once became firm friends. At our first meeting he invited me to join him every evening at a café [Guerbois] in the Batignolles district, where he and his friends gathered at the end of the day to talk. There I met Fantin-Latour, Cézanne, Degas, who had recently returned from Italy, the art critic Duranty, Emile Zola, who was then making his first foray into literature, and several others. For my part I used to take Sisley, Bazille and Renoir there. Nothing could be more interesting than the discussions we had, with their perpetual clash of opinions. They kept our wits sharpened, encouraged us to press ahead with our own experiments, and provided us with enough enthusiasm to keep at it for weeks on end until our ideas became clear and coherent. From then on we emerged more finely tempered, our wills firmer, our thoughts clearer and less confused.'

From *Au pays des souvenirs* by Armand Silvestre (1892)

The Café Guerbois ... is in a working-class area, a world in which people, in Rabelais' words, 'scratch a poor living as best they may'.... Manet was not the leader of a school – nobody ever had a temperament less suited for such a role, for I have never known anyone so free of the least touch of solemnity – but ... his influence ... was considerable. He was one of the first to brighten the French palette and bring light back into it. Less intense, less magisterial than Baudelaire, but with a much surer taste ... a sense of modernity, which ... had not till then seen light of day ... This revolutionary – the word is not too strong – had the manners of a perfect gentleman. With his often gaudy trousers, his short jacket, his flat-brimmed hat, always wearing immaculate suede gloves, Manet did not look like a Bohemian, and in fact had nothing of the Bohemian in him. He was a kind of dandy. Blond, with a sparse, narrow beard which was forked at the end, he had in the extraordinary vivacity of his gaze, in the mocking expression on his lips, his teeth irregular and uneven – a very strong dose of the Parisian urchin. Although very generous, and very good-hearted, he was deliberately ironic in conversation, and often cruel. He had a marvellous command of the annihilating and devastating phrase. But at the same time his expression was benevolent, the underlying idea always absolutely right ... Among the other figures to be detected in the gaslight of the Café Guerbois against the clicking of the billiard balls on the table, I would like to pick out the painter Degasz [sic], who never used to stay seated for very long. Degasz, with his very Parisian, very original looks, infinitely mocking and witty ... The contemporary school owes a great deal to Degasz, and even the traditionalists, though grudgingly, have to admire the incontestable qualities of his draughtsmanship and the quality of his painting ... He is a parlour revolutionary, the ironic modesty of his appearance saving him from the hate which firebrands draw upon themselves

Pierre-Auguste Renoir from *En écoutant Cézanne, Degas et Renoir* by Ambroise Vollard (1938)

'I saw a lot of Courbet. He was one of the most astonishing fellows I ever came across. I remember in particular one detail about his exhibition in 1867. He had had a sort of closet built from which he could keep an eye on his exhibition. When the first visitors arrived, he was getting dressed. To miss nothing of the enthusiasm which the public was bound to feel, he went out in a flannel waistcoat, without pausing to slip on the shirt which he was still holding in his hand. And Courbet himself, gazing at his own pictures, commented: "How fine they are! They look magnificent! So fine it's really ridiculous!"

'And he kept repeating: "Yes, it's really ridiculous!" ...

'His admiration was of course reserved for his own painting. One day he wanted to pay a compliment to his friend Claude Monet: "Oh, it's pretty bad, what you're sending into the Salon. But just think how it will annoy them!"'

Pierre-Auguste Renoir to unknown recipient

[undated]

I painted two or three canvases with the palette knife, as Courbet was so fond of doing, and then I painted some with a full brush. A few of them came off, I suppose, but I found this a nuisance when I wanted to work them over again. I had to use a knife to scrape away whatever I was dissatisfied with, and once I had put a figure in I couldn't move it without scraping the canvas. I tried painting in tiny dabs, which makes it easier to run tones into one another, but then the surface is so rough – that rather puts me off. Everyone has his likes and dislikes. I like to fondle a picture, run my hand across it. But damn it all, when they're painted like that, I feel more inclined to strike a match against them. Then there's the dust that settles in the crevices and mars the tones.

Frédéric Bazille to his father

[Paris], *1 January 1870*

I have had to interrupt my letter because two painters just arrived to see my painting which finally returned from being relined. They are even now complimenting me highly for it. I have been amusing myself recently with painting the interior of my studio with my friends. My own figure has been painted in by Manet, and I may send it to the exhibition in Montpellier.

    This picture has retarded the one that I meant to do for the Salon, but I'm tackling it now and it won't take long to complete.

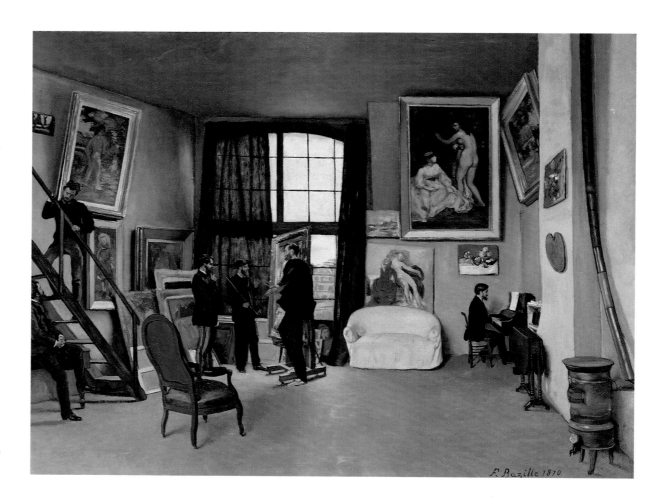

Bazille
*The Artist's Studio,
9 rue de la Condamine*
1870

A World Apart

Edouard Manet to Henri Fantin-Latour

Boulogne-sur-Mer, 26 August 1866

... the Morisot girls are charming. What a nuisance it is that they aren't men. However even as women, they might serve the cause of painting by each marrying an academician and sowing discord in the camp of those old fogeys. But that is asking a great deal of self-sacrifice. Meanwhile present my compliments to them.

Berthe Morisot to Edma Pontillon [sister]

[Paris, March] *1869*

... Monsieur Degas seems greatly pleased with his portrait. It is the only thing he has done for the exhibition. He talked about you to me last night: he finds you very strange ... He came and sat beside me, pretending that he was going to court me, but this courting was confined to a long commentary on Solomon's proverb, 'Woman is the desolation of the righteous'....

Berthe Morisot to Edma Pontillon

[Paris], *19 March 1869*

... this painting, this work you mourn for [Edma had given up painting on her marriage], is the cause of many griefs and many troubles. You know it as well as I do, and yet, child that you are, you are already lamenting that which was depressing you only a little while ago.

Come now, the lot you have chosen is not the worst one. You have a serious attachment, and a man's heart is utterly devoted to you. Do not revile your fate. Remember that it is sad to be alone; despite anything that may be said or done, a woman has an immense need for affection. For her to withdraw into herself is to attempt the impossible.

Oh, how I am lecturing you! I don't mean to. I am simply saying what I think, what seems to be true....

Berthe Morisot to Edma Pontillon

[Lorient, 23 April 1869]

I am not any more cheerful than you are, my dear Edma, and probably much less so. Here I am, trapped because of my eyes ... I was not expecting this, and my patience is very limited ... Men incline to believe that they fill all of one's life, but as for me, I think that no matter how much affection a woman has for her husband, it is not easy for her to break with a life of work. Affection is a very fine thing, on condition that there is something besides to fill one's days. This is something I see for you in motherhood.

Do not grieve about painting. I do not think it is worth a single regret ...

Berthe Morisot to Edma Pontillon

[11 May 1869]

Now that I am free from all anxiety, and am taking up my plans for travel, which in truth I had never really given up, I am counting definitely on my stay in Lorient to do something worthwhile. I have done absolutely nothing since you left, and this is beginning to distress me. My painting never seems to me as bad as it has in recent days. I sit on the sofa, and the sight of these daubs nauseates me. I am going to do my mother and Yves [sister] in the garden; you see I am reduced to doing the same things over and over again ... Yves has certainly made a conquest of M. Degas. He asked her to permit him to paint a portrait of her. He is always talking about you, asking about you, and is indignant at my keeping you posted about his new infatuations ...

Berthe Morisot to Tiburce Morisot [brother]

[May] *1869*

Do you know that Monsieur Degas is mad about Yves' face, and that he is doing a sketch of her? He is going to transfer on to the canvas the drawing that he is doing in his sketch book. A peculiar way of doing a portrait!... I certainly do not find his personality attractive, he has wit, but nothing more. Manet said to me very comically yesterday, 'He lacks spontaneity, he isn't capable of loving a woman, much less doing anything about it.' Poor Manet, he is sad; his exhibition, as usual, does not appeal to the public, which is for him a source of wonder. Nevertheless he said that I had brought him luck and he had an offer for *Le Balcon* [Morisot was one of the models]. I wish for his sake that this were true, but I have grave fears that his hopes will be once again disappointed....

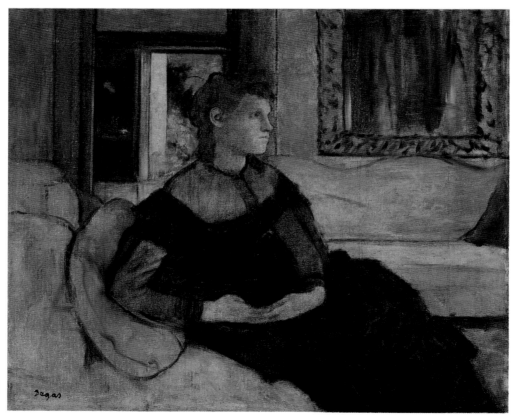

Degas
Portrait of Mme Gobillard
1869

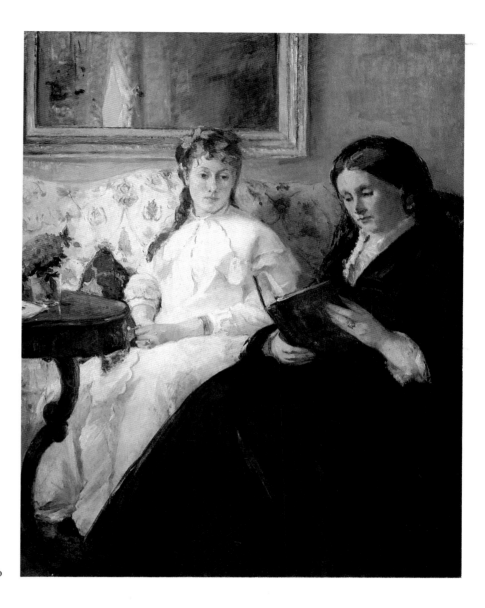

Morisot *The Mother and Sister of the Artist* 1869–70

Berthe Morisot to Edma Pontillon

[Paris, early 1870]

... Tired, unnerved, I went to Manet's studio on Saturday. He asked me how I was getting on, and seeing that I felt dubious, he said to me enthusiastically: 'Tomorrow, after I have sent off my pictures, I shall come to see yours, and you may put yourself in my hands. I shall tell you what needs to be done.'

The next day, which was yesterday, he came about one o'clock. He found it very good, except for the lower part of the dress. He took the brushes and put in a few accents that looked very well: Maman was in ecstasies. That is where my misfortunes began. Once started, nothing could stop him: from the skirt he went to the bust, from the bust to the head, from the head to the background. He cracked a thousand jokes: laughed like a madman, handed me the palette, took it back: finally by five o'clock in the afternoon we had made the prettiest caricature that was ever seen. The carter was waiting to take it away [to the Salon]: he made me put it into the handcart, willy-nilly. And now I am left confounded. My only hope is that I will be rejected. Maman thinks this episode funny, but I find it agonizing. I put it in with the painting I did of you at Lorient. I hope they take only that.

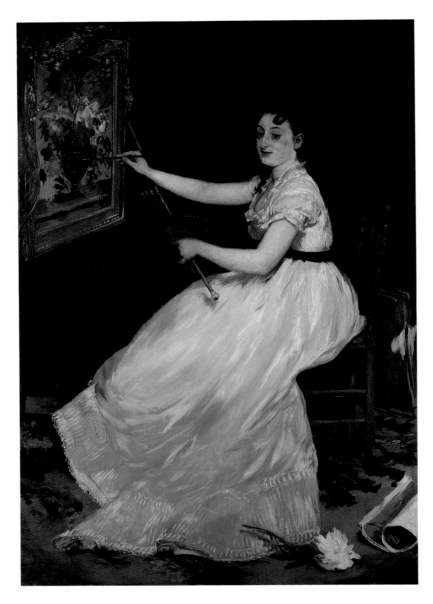

Manet
Portrait of Eva Gonzalès 1870

Berthe Morisot to Edma Pontillon

[Paris], *13 August 1870*

Manet lectures me, and holds up that eternal Mademoiselle Gonzalès as an example; she has poise, perseverance, she is able to carry an undertaking to a successful issue, whereas I am not capable of anything. In the meantime he has begun her portrait over again for the twenty-fifth time. She poses every day, and every night the head is washed out with soft soap. This will scarcely encourage anyone to pose for him!

Berthe Morisot to Edma Pontillon

[Paris, September or October 1870]

The Manets came to see us Tuesday evening, and we all went into the studio. To my great surprise and satisfaction, I received the highest praise: it seems that what I do is decidedly better than Eva Gonzalès. Since I have been told that without knowing it I produced masterpieces at Lorient, I have stood gaping before them, and feel myself no longer capable of anything . . .

Painting in the Country

Frédéric Bazille to his mother

Wednesday, 1863

I've just had a very pleasant week, dear Mother. As I told you, I spent a few days in the village of Chailly near the forest of Fontainebleau. I went with my friend Monet from Le Havre, he's good at landscapes and gave me some very useful tips. I did a lot of work and will be able to show you my first paintings in August, six or seven of them. Two or three are unfinished and I shall spend a few more Sundays at Chailly to finish them. We stayed at the Auberge du Cheval Blanc, where excellent food and lodging can be had for 3 Fr 75 a day.

Parts of the forest are magnificent; you never see such oaks in our part of the country. The rocks are famous but are less fine, there are more impressive ones near Montpellier. I'm resolved to do a great many studies these holidays. You may be surprised to find that I'm not nearly as lazy as I was last year.

Claude Monet to Frédéric Bazille

Honfleur, 15 July [1864]

I wonder what you could be doing in Paris in such beautiful weather, for I imagine it must be as lovely down there. It's simply adorable here, my friend, and each day I find something even more beautiful than the day before. It's enough to drive you crazy, I so want to do it all my head is bursting. Damn it man, come on the 16th, get packing and come here for a fortnight, you'd be far better off; it can't be easy to work in Paris.

Today I have exactly a month left in Honfleur; and what is more, my studies are almost done, I've even got some others on the go. On the whole, I'm quite content with my stay here, although my studies are very far from being as I should like. It really is appallingly difficult to do something which is complete in every respect, and I think most people are content with mere approximations. Well, my dear friend, I intend to battle on, to scrape off and start again, since one can do something if one can see it and understand it, and when I look at nature I feel as if I'll be able to paint it all, note it all down, and then you might as well forget it once you're working ...

All this proves that you must think of nothing else. It's on the strength of observation and reflection that one finds a way. So we must dig and delve unceasingly. Are you making any progress? I'm sure you are, but I'm also sure you don't work enough and in the right way. You can't hope to work with playboys like your friend Villa and the others. One's better off alone, and yet there are so many things that are impossible to fathom on one's own. In fact it's a terrible business and the task is a hard one.

Have you done your life-size figure? I've some wonderful things lined up for myself. It's quite awesome what I've got in mind for this coming winter in Ste-Adresse and Paris. . . .

Frédéric Bazille to his mother

Honfleur, Wednesday, [1864]

I left Paris with my friend Monet in the middle of last week. Our journey was delightful, we took a day to get here, stopping off at Rouen for a few hours. We saw the splendid Gothic buildings of this great city and visited the Museum which has a fine Delacroix.

We took the steamboat down the Seine to Honfleur, the banks are very beautiful. As soon as we got here we looked for landscape subjects. They were easy to find because this countryside is a paradise... The sea, or rather the Seine which is exceedingly wide at this point, provides a delightful backdrop for these waves of greenery.

We are staying right in Honfleur and have rented a couple of small rooms from a baker. We eat at the St-Siméon farm which stands on the cliff not far from Honfleur. That's where we work and spend our days. As you can imagine I'm fascinated by the port of Honfleur and the Norman costume with its cotton bonnets... I get up at five every morning and paint all day till eight at night. But you mustn't expect me to bring back any good landscapes, I'm improving, that's about all. But that's enough for me, I hope I'll be satisfied with myself after painting for three or four years.

I'll have to go back to Paris and that dreadful medical school which I hate more and more. We're not dissecting at the moment so I shan't get any better at it. If I pass, I'll have the pleasant prospect of having to spend at least six months in the hospital preparing for the next exam. Six repulsive months, to say the least....

Pierre-Auguste Renoir to Frédéric Bazille

[Paris], *3 July 1865*

M. Henri Sisley [Alfred's older brother], little Grange [a young male model from Manet's studio] whom you know from our dinner, and I are leaving on Thursday for a long trip by sailboat. We are going to see the regattas at Le Havre. We plan to stay there for about ten days and the whole expense will be about fifty francs... I am taking my paintbox in order to make sketches of the places I like. I think it may be charming. There's nothing to keep you from leaving a place you don't like, nor anything to keep you from staying on in an enjoyable one. Very frugal meals. If you want to come, I'll tell you later what we intend to do. We have figured out the expenses more or less exactly. We'll have ourselves towed as far as Rouen by the *Paris et Londres*, and from there on we're on our own. You don't have to feel embarrassed about refusing. The truth is, I'd be very glad to have you with us, but take this invitation as a simple offer if you like the idea....

Frédéric Bazille to his father

[Paris, 1865]

... I need about another fortnight to finish off the paintings, then I have to go to Chailly for five or six days as a favour to Monet. He's doing a big picture in which I'm to appear and he needs that much time to paint me. After that I shall leave for Montpellier. Let me know at once what you think of my plans....

Claude Monet to Frédéric Bazille

[Chailly, July or early August 1865]

I'm writing to you again, as you didn't let me know whether my pictures were ready in time to be sent. . . . I'm angry with you in fact, for not having written; you appear to have forgotten me completely. You promised to help me with my picture, you were supposed to come and pose for some figures and my picture depends on it: so I hope you will keep your promise, but time is passing all the same and no sign of you. Please, my dear fellow, don't hold me up like this. All my studies are progressing admirably, it's only the men that are missing now. So come right away, there can't be anything serious keeping you in Paris. Here it's as agreeable as ever, we are quite a pleasant little group of artists. So come, but above all write and tell me at once; I'm very worried, I know how fickle you are, my dear fellow, I think only of my painting, and if I were to drop it, I think I'd go crazy. Everyone knows what I'm doing and I'm getting a lot of encouragement, so it must be done, and well, I'm counting on the kindness that you've shown in the past to come quickly and help me out.

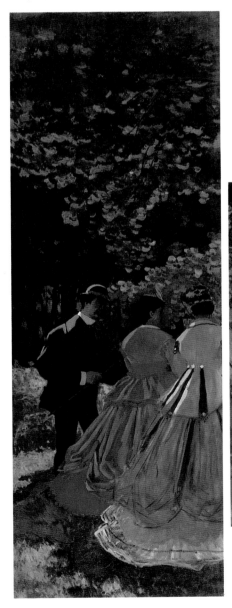
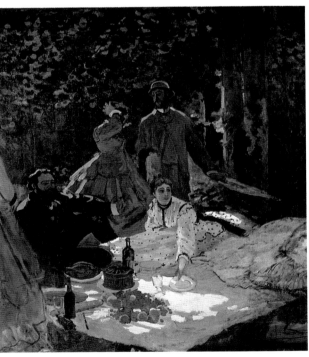

Monet *Le Déjeuner sur l'herbe, left and central panels* 1865–6

Frédéric Bazille to his mother

[Paris], *Friday,* [1865]

... Tomorrow, I mean to finish off the portraits of uncle.

Once I've done the last brush stroke, that is to say tomorrow, I'm leaving for Chailly, where Monet is awaiting my coming as if I were the Messiah. I hope he'll keep me for only four or five days ...

Monet has fallen out with the Auberge Paillard, so please write to me at the Auberge du Lion d'Or, c/o Monsieur Barbey, Chailly, near Melun ...

Claude Monet to Frédéric Bazille

[Etretat, December 1868]

As I told you in my little scribble, I'm happy, very happy, very delighted. I'm setting to like a fighting cockerel, for I'm surrounded here by all I love. I spend my day out of doors on the shingle when the weather's stormy or when the boats go out fishing; otherwise I go into the country which is so lovely here that I perhaps find it even more agreeable in winter than in summer; naturally I'm working all the time, and I think this year I'm going to do some serious things. And then in the evening, dear fellow, I come home to my little cottage to find a good fire and a dear little family. If only you could see how sweet your godson [Monet's son Jean] is now.

... Thanks to a gentleman from Le Havre who is coming to my aid, I'm enjoying the most perfect tranquillity ... I assure you that I don't envy you being in Paris, and scarcely miss the gatherings, even though I'd be glad to see some of the *habitués*, but frankly I don't think one can do anything good in such surroundings: don't you think that face to face with nature and alone, one can do better? I'm sure of it, myself. Moreover I've always thought so, and what I've completed in such conditions has always been better.

One is too taken up with all that one sees and hears in Paris, however strong one is, and what I do here will at least have the merit of being unlike anyone else, at least I believe so, because it will simply be the expression of what I, and only I have felt.

The further I get, the more I regret how little I know, that's what hinders me the most. The further I get the more I notice that one never dares give frank expression to what one feels. It's strange. That's why I'm doubly glad to be here and I don't think I will spend much time in Paris now, a month at the very most, each year ...

Claude Monet to Frédéric Bazille

25 September 1869

Here I'm at a halt, from lack of paints ... Only this year I will have done nothing. This makes me rage against everyone. I'm jealous, mean; I'm going mad. If I could work, everything would go all right. You tell me that it's not fifty or a hundred francs that will get me out of this; that's possible, but if you look at it this way, there's nothing for me except to break my head against a wall, because I can't lay claim to any instant fortune ... I have a dream, a finished picture [*tableau*] of the bathing place of La Grenouillère, for which I've done some bad sketches [*pochades*], but it is a dream. Renoir, who has been spending two months here, also wants to do this picture.

Troubles at the Salon

Frédéric Bazille to Marc Bazille [brother]

[Paris], *Sunday*, [1865]

... my picture for the Salon is coming along well and has earned me compliments from maître Courbet, who called by to look at Monet's picture, which he was delighted with. More than twenty painters have come to look at this picture and they've all admired it very much, even though it's still far from finished (naturally, I'm not talking about my work). This picture will cause a big stir at the Exposition....

Marie Le Coeur [daughter of one of Renoire's patrons] to unknown recipient

6 April 1866

M. Renoir, poor man, has been rejected. Just imagine, he had done two pictures: a landscape with two figures — everyone says that one is good, that it has defects and virtues — the other was done at Marlotte in two weeks, he calls it a sketch, and he only sent it to the exhibition because he had the other one that carried more weight, otherwise he would have decided that he shouldn't exhibit it.

On Friday, since nobody could tell him whether he'd been accepted or rejected, he went to wait for some members of the jury at the exit from the exhibition and when he saw MM. Corot and Daubigny coming out, he asked them if they knew whether the paintings of a friend of his, Renoir, had been accepted. Whereupon M. Daubigny remembered the work and described Renoir's painting to him, telling him: 'we're very sorry about your friend, but his painting was rejected. We did all we could to prevent that, we asked for the painting to be reconsidered ten times, without being able to get it accepted, what could we do, there were six of us in favour against all the others. Tell your friend not to get discouraged, there are great qualities in his painting; he should get up a petition and ask for an exhibition of rejected paintings.'

So in his misfortune he has the consolation of having been congratulated by two artists whose talents he admires.

In the evening he went into a café and overheard some artists talking about the exhibition, and one of them said: 'There's a painting by someone named Renoir that is very good and was rejected.'

Now what annoys him most is that he learned yesterday that his Marlotte painting was accepted. The other having been rejected, he would have preferred that this one be rejected too.

Paul Cézanne to M. de Nieuwerkerke [Superintendent of the *Beaux-Arts*]

Paris, 19 April 1866

Sir, I recently had the honour of writing to you with regard to two paintings of mine which the jury has just turned down.

Since you have not yet replied, I feel that I must stress the motives that led me to write to you. Moreover, as it is certain that you received my letter, I do not need to repeat here the arguments that I thought it necessary to submit to you. I restrict myself to telling you once again that I cannot accept the unauthorized judgement of colleagues to whom I have never given the task of assessing my work.

I am writing, therefore, in order to insist on my demand. I wish to appeal to the public for judgement and still want to be exhibited. What I desire does not seem to me to be excessive, and, if you were to question all the painters who are in my position, they would all reply to you that they disown the jury and that they wish to take part in one way or another in an exhibition that should preforce be open to any serious worker.

So let the Salon des Refusés be re-established. Even if I were to find myself there alone, it would be my ardent wish that people should at least know this: that I no more desire to be mixed up with these gentlemen of the jury than they appear to wish to be mixed up with me.

I trust, sir, that you no longer wish to continue in silence. It seems to me that any polite letter deserves a response.

Paul Cézanne to Camille Pissarro

[Aix, 23 October 1866]

My dear friend, here I am with my family, among the foulest beings in the world, those who compose my family being more *emmerdants* than anyone else. Don't let's talk any more about all that. . . .

I'm still working a little, but paints are rare here and extremely expensive – depression, depression! Let us hope, let us hope that we manage to sell. We shall sacrifice a golden calf over that. – You aren't sending anything to Marseilles, oh well, nor am I. I have no desire to send anything any more – all the more so because I haven't got any frames, because that means incurring expenses that would be better dedicated to painting. I speak for myself in this, and then damn the jury . . .

Frédéric Bazille to his mother

[Paris, May 1867]

The pictures I submitted for the Exposition have been turned down. Don't take it too hard, it's nothing to be discouraged about – far from it. I'm in the same boat as all the best entrants to this year's Salon. A petition demanding an Exposition des Refusés is going around, it's being signed by every decent painter in Paris. But it won't come to anything.

In any case I've seen the last of this kind of unpleasantness as I shall never again submit anything to the jury. It's absurd for anyone in his right mind to lay himself open to the whims of the Establishment, especially when one attaches no importance to their medals and prizes.

A dozen or so talented young people agree with me on this matter. We've therefore decided to rent a large studio each year and to exhibit as many of our pictures as we wish. We'll invite the painters we like to send their work. Courbet, Corot, Diaz, Daubigny, and many others whom you may not know, have all promised to send pictures and are strongly in favour of the idea. With these people, and with Monet, who is stronger than all of them, we can't fail. You'll see, as we shall be talked about . . . Don't worry, I assure you I'm being perfectly reasonable, we are certainly in the right, this is in no sense a student revolt. . . .

Frédéric Bazille to his parents

[1867]

... Paris is overflowing with painters at the moment. The Ingres exhibition is interesting and it would be a great pity to miss it ...

Nearly all the portraits are masterly, but his other paintings are rather boring. I've never seen so dull a Salon, there are twenty or so beautiful Millets and Corots at the Exposition Universelle. Courbet and Manet have one-man shows opening shortly, I'm longing to see them.

In one of my last letters I told you about our plan of staging a separate exhibition. We bled ourselves white but all we managed to raise was 2,500 Frs and this was not enough. We've therefore had to give up the idea. We've no choice but to return to the bosom of the Establishment ... which rejects us. . . .

Frédéric Bazille to his mother

[Paris], *Thursday,* [1868]

... both my canvases have been accepted by the Salon. Most of my friends were turned down. Monet was among those who had only one out of two paintings accepted. Mine must have slipped through, I can't think how, perhaps there's been some mistake. . . .

Frédéric Bazille to his father

[Paris], *Friday night,* [1869]

... I simply must go to the Salon at least three or four times. The jury has massacred the entries of the four or five young painters with whom we see eye to eye. Only one of my canvases has been accepted, that of the woman. Apart from Manet, whom they no longer dare turn down, I am one of the least badly treated. Monet was turned down flat. What pleases me is that we've aroused real animosity. The source of the trouble is M. Gérôme, he says we're a bunch of madmen and has declared that he considers it his duty to do all he can to stop our paintings being seen. There's no harm in that, when I do a really good picture people will look at it. I was amazed that Cabanel [a very successful academic painter] should take my part ...

Frédéric Bazille to his father

[Paris], *Sunday,* [May 1869]

... As you can imagine I've been to the Salon. My picture could hardly be in a worse position, but at least I'm in with the other Bs and not, like last year, in one of the large rooms at the back. I'm fairly pleased with the overall effect of my picture, but I'm hoping those I paint this year will be much better. I've received a number of highly flattering compliments, notably from M. Puvis de Chavannes [a respected muralist].

Most of the works on show are lamentably poor. The only really fine ones are the Millets and Corots. The Courbets, which are far from his best pictures, stand out like masterpieces amid the general mediocrity. Manet is beginning to be a little better appreciated by the public ...

Berthe Morisot to Edma Pontillon

[Paris], *2 May 1869*

The first thing we beheld as we went up the big staircase [at the Salon] was Puvis' painting. It looked well. . . . I don't have to tell you that one of the first things I did was to go to Room M. There I found Manet, with his hat on in bright sunlight, looking dazed. He begged me to go and see his painting, as he dare not move a step.

I have never seen such an expressive face as his; he was laughing, then had a worried look, assuring everybody that his picture was very bad, and adding in the same breath, that it would be a great success. I think he has a decidedly charming temperament, I like it very much.

His paintings, as they always do, produce the impression of a wild or even somewhat unripe fruit. I do not in the least dislike them, but I prefer his portrait of Zola.

In *Le Balcon* I am more strange than ugly. It seems the epithet of *femme fatale* has been circulating among the curious . . .

Manet
*The Balcony c.*1868–69

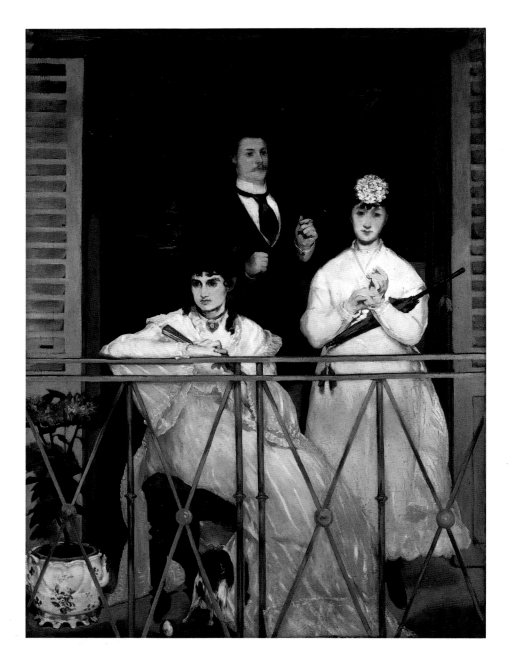

Berthe Morisot to Edma Pontillon

[Paris], *5 May 1869*

... Corot is poetic, as usual. I think he spoiled the *étude* we admired so much when we saw it at his home, by re-doing it in the studio.

The tall Bazille has painted something that I find very good. It is a little girl in a light dress seated in the shade of a tree, with a glimpse of a village in the background. There is much light and sun in it. He has tried to do what we have so often attempted – a figure in outdoor light – and this time he seems to have been successful.

Here I stop to laugh at myself for passing this judgement. It seems to me that our friends would laugh even more if they could hear me dealing out censure and praise. I met Bracquemond, who was very amiable, paid me compliments on my exhibits last year, and reproached me for not showing this year....

Financial Woes

Claude Monet to Frédéric Bazille

Ste-Adresse, 14 October 1864

I received your fine letter which gave me a great deal of pleasure; I never doubted that you would be ready to do anything to help me out and I'm very grateful to you.

Next Monday I'm going to put a box on the express train containing three pictures with frames which I've just had made, since you know well enough how a picture gains a hundred per cent in a fine frame. One of these is a simple study which you didn't see at the outset, it's done entirely from nature. You might find it bears a certain relationship to Corot, but if this is so, it is not because of any attempt to imitate him on my part. It is due entirely to the motif and above all to the calm and misty effect. I did it as conscientiously as possible and did not think of any painting whatsoever. Besides, you know it's not the way I do things... I'm going to get down to a still-life on a size 50 canvas of a rayfish and dogfish with old fishermen's baskets. Then I'm going to turn out a few pictures to send wherever possible, given that now, first and foremost (unfortunately) I have to earn some money.

Claude Monet to Frédéric Bazille

Ste-Adresse, 12 August [1867]

I really don't know what to say to you, you've shown such pig-headedness in not replying, I've written letter after letter, a telegram and nothing has got through to you; yet you know me better than anyone and my situation too. Once again I had to borrow and received snubs from people I don't know, and I'm really angry with you; I didn't think you would abandon me like this, it really is too bad. It's almost a month since I asked you first: since then, in Paris as here, I've waited for the postman and every day it's the same. For the *last* time I am asking you for this *favour*, I'm going through the most terrible torments, I had to come back here not to upset the family and also because I didn't have enough money to stay in Paris while Camille was in labour. She has given birth to a big and beautiful boy and despite everything I feel that I love him, and it pains me to think of his mother having nothing to eat. I was able to borrow the strict minimum for the birth and my return here, but neither she nor I have a penny of our own.

It's all your fault, so hurry up and make amends and send me the money right away to Ste-Adresse: as soon as you get my letter, send word by telegraph as I am terribly worried.

Really Bazille, there are things that cannot be put off until tomorrow. This is one of them and I'm waiting.

Frédéric Bazille to his mother

[Paris], *Monday*, [1867]

... Monet is staying here at the moment, unhappier than ever. His family has been shamefully mean with him, he's probably going to marry his mistress [Camille Doncieux]. The woman's family are quite decent parents, they've agreed to see her again and to help her if she gets married. This is not so wonderful, but their child has to eat somehow....

Claude Monet to Frédéric Bazille

Paris, 29 June [1868]

A hasty note to ask you to come speedily to my rescue if you can. I must have been born under an unlucky star. I've just been turned out, without a shirt to my back, from the inn where I was staying. I have found somewhere safe in the country for Camille and my poor little Jean to stay for a few days. As for myself, I arrived here this morning and I leave this evening, very shortly, for Le Havre, to try and see if my patron can help me.

Don't fail to write as soon as you receive this if you can do anything more for me, in any case, I expect a word from you.

Write to me at Le Havre, *poste restante*, as my family refuses to do anything more for me, so I don't even know yet where I'll be sleeping tomorrow.

[P.S.] I was so upset yesterday that I was stupid enough to hurl myself into the water. Fortunately no harm was done.

Claude Monet to Frédéric Bazille

St-Michel, 9 August [1869]

Dear friend, do you want to know in what situation I am, and how I live, during the week I have waited for your letter?, well ask Renoir who brings us bread from his mother's house so that we don't die of hunger. For a week, no bread, no wine, no fire for cooking, no light. It's terrible....

Pierre-Auguste Renoir to Frédéric Bazille

Ville d'Avray, [late August 1869]

I'm coming from Les Batignolles... I can't find the pawn ticket for your watch; tell me exactly where it is. I'm in Ville d'Avray and come to Batignolles only very rarely and only to get some little things. In order for what you ask me to be done, and if you have some money, you'd better send it to me right away, just so that you won't eat it up. You don't have to worry about me, since I have neither wife nor child and am not about to have one or the other. Drop me a line so that I'll know whether I have to take care of carpentry work immediately, which would upset me a lot since first of all I'm working and also I don't always have enough to eat in Paris and here I get along all right. I'll write you more some other time, because I'm hungry and I have a plate of turbot with white sauce in front of me. I'm not putting a stamp on the letter, I have only twelve sous in my pocket, and that's for going to Paris when I need to.

Pierre-Auguste Renoir to Frédéric Bazille

[Paris, late August or early September 1869]

... I'm waiting for your masterpieces. I intend to criticize them mercilessly when they arrive. I haven't seen anybody. I'm staying with my parents and I'm almost always at Monet's, where by the way they're getting rather old. [Baby Jean was two.] They don't eat every day: but I'm happy just the same because as far as painting is concerned, Monet is good company. I'm doing almost nothing because I don't have many colours. Things may go better this month. If they go better, I'll write to you....

War

Edmond Maître [friend of the artist] to Frédéric Bazille

[mid-August] 1870

My dear and only friend, I've just received your letter; you are mad, stark raving mad, I embrace you with all my heart. God protect you, you and my poor brother! Ever yours E. Maître.

[P.S.] Why not consult a friend? You have no right to go ahead with enlistment. Renoir has just come in. I'm giving him my pen. E.
Triple shit, stark raving bastard! Renoir.

Berthe Morisot to Edma Pontillon

[Paris], *18 September 1870*

I am writing to you, my dear Edma, though I do not think this letter will reach you ...

I have made up my mind to stay, because neither Papa nor Maman told me firmly to leave; they want me to leave the way anyone here wants anything — weakly, and by fits and starts.... the militia are quartered in my studio, hence there is no way of using it. I do not read the newspapers much any more; one day is enough for me. The Prussian atrocities upset me, and I want to retain my composure ...

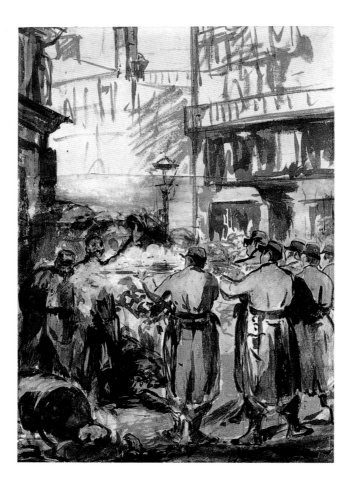

Manet *The Barricade* 1871

Madame Morisot to Edma Pontillon

[Paris], *18 October 1870*

Each day we hear the cannonading – and a great deal of it. All the fighting is taking place near us – so far without any important results. It is impossible to keep still; Berthe and I got as wet as water spaniels when we went to see where the fighting was taking place ...

Monsieur Degas was so affected by the death of one of his friends, the sculptor Cuvelier, that he was impossible. He and Manet almost came to blows arguing over the methods of defence and the use of the National Guard.

Frédéric Bazille to his parents

6 November 1870, 11 at night

... This time it really seems as if we're going off to fight. We thought it was all over and that the armistice had been signed, but the order has just come to shoulder our packs tomorrow morning at 4.30. We're being sent to Dole, probably to join Garibaldi. We'll be spending tomorrow night at Orchamps if all goes well. We are part of the 2nd division and of the 2nd brigade of the 7th Armoured Corps. Our regiment is in the advance guard with two light infantry squadrons ...

My sergeant-major hasn't been commissioned, but it won't bother me not getting my stripes until I've fired a shot or two.

Before we leave tomorrow morning we shall have to witness a sad sight, a poor wretch goes before the firing squad. He shot at a sergeant who jeered at him for arresting a sniper he'd mistaken for a Prussian. My whole battalion will be there. It will teach us all a lesson about discipline. . . .

This morning, 7th November, there's been a complete change of plan. We set out and had not gone one kilometre when the order was countermanded and we're back where we were yesterday. It's disgraceful, you can't maintain discipline with orders like that. We're probably going to be shut up in Besançon, shut up like rabbits, then taken prisoners.

Frédéric Bazille to his parents

Beaune-la-Rolande, Tuesday, 16 November 1870

On Sunday we arrived in Chagny, or rather on the outskirts, for I didn't see the town. We found large numbers of troops. The positions we're occupying would be beautiful if it were not for the triangle formed by the Saône and the Canal du Centre behind us . . . if there's a move towards the Loire, we'll probably go along, but as reservists we'll be the last to leave and may well have the Prussian vanguard on our heels. . . .

Thanks to my great height, I'm the best known man in the regiment. The officers are very nice to me.

There's no time to tell you what I'm going through or how I feel about everything I see and hear. I'm storing it all up, I don't know whether I'll ever manage to bring myself to say what I think of the men, but I'm in a hard school. On the physical side I have no complaints. Fatigue doesn't bother me. I get plenty to eat and plenty of sleep, that's all I need. I shan't be wanting any money for some time.

I am sickened and disgusted. I now can't wait to fire a shot or two to pass the time . . .

Madame Morisot to Yves Morisot and Edma Pontillon

[Paris], 8 January 1871

My dear Yves, my dear Edma, I have not had the courage to take up my pen for a week. We celebrated the birth of the New Year in sadness and tears. Berthe's health is visibly affected . . .

The bombardment never stops. It is a sound that reverberates in your head night and day . . .

One does not lose courage. I find it superb, and yet what suffering, what dire need. It is heart-rending.

Berthe Morisot to Edma Pontillon

[Paris], 27 February 1871

. . . Do you know that all our acquaintances have come out of the war without a scratch, except for that poor Bazille, who was killed at Orléans, I think . . . Manet spent his time during the siege changing his uniform. His brother writes to us today that in Bordeaux he recounted a number of imaginary exploits.

Edouard Béliard [painter] to Camille Pissarro

22 February [1871]

I have no news of your house at Louveciennes! Your blankets, suits, shoes, underclothes, you may go into mourning for – believe me. Your sketches, since they are generally admired, I like to think will be ornaments in Prussian drawing rooms. The nearness of the forest no doubt saved your furniture. . . .

Félicie Estruc [Julie's sister] to Julie Pissarro

10 March [1871]

I went to Louveciennes yesterday and saw your house and M. Ollivon [neighbour and landlord] who returned two days ago. The railroad only began operating yesterday . . . The houses are burned, the roofs broken, your front door, staircase and floor – all that has disappeared . . . I didn't even recognize your house. I went to see M. Ollivon who reassured me a little. He was able to save some things; your two beds but no mattresses, your wardrobe, wash stand, desk, about forty paintings, the small wooden bed. The Prussians lived for nearly four months in the house and searched it thoroughly. . . the horses were kept on the ground floor and the Prussians lived upstairs . . .

Madame Ollivon to Julie Pissarro

27 March [1871]

. . . You are asking about your house; that is not the right word for it, you should say stables. There was a good two cart-loads of manure in your place. In the small room, next to the living room, there were horses; the kitchen and your cellar were sheep-pens, and the sheep were killed in the garden . . . I was forgetting to tell you that we have some paintings well preserved. Only there are some which these gentlemen, for fear of dirtying their feet, put on the ground in the garden to serve as a carpet. My husband picked them up and we have them too.

Camille Pissarro to Monsieur Retrou [neighbour]

Westow Hill, Upper Norwood, at Canham's Dairy, [late March 1871]

. . . You tell me that Monsieur Ollivon has saved . . . forty-odd out of between twelve to fifteen hundred: pictures, studies, sketches, the work of twenty years. I believe that if property can be called sacred it is that which is produced by the intelligence and made by our own hands. . . .

Berthe Morisot to Edma Pontillon

[St-Germain-en-Laye, March or April 1871]

. . . Everyone is engrossed in this wretched business of politics. We can hear the cannon throughout the day; we can even see the smoke on Mount Valérian from the terrace. From time to time we meet people who have got out of Paris. Their accounts are very contradictory: according to some, people are dying of starvation; according to others, the city is perfectly peaceful. The only thing certain is that everyone is fleeing from it . . .

Gustave Courbet to his parents

[Paris], *30 April 1871*

Here I am, thanks to the people of Paris, thrown into politics up to my neck. President of the federation of artists, a member of the Commune, a municipal-authority delegate, a Public Education delegate; the four most important jobs in Paris ... Paris is a real paradise: no police, no nonsense, no expectations of any kind, no disputes. Paris is running itself, like clockwork. That's the way it should be allowed to stay....

Claude Monet to Camille Pissarro

27 May 1871

You have doubtless learned of the death of poor Courbet shot without trial [an error in dispatches: Courbet confused with Cournet]. What shameful conduct, that of Versailles, it is frightful and makes me ill. I don't have the heart for anything. It's all heartbreaking....

Madame Morisot to Berthe Morisot

[Paris], *10 June 1871*

... It's unbelievable a nation destroying itself! Going down by boat, I saw the remains of the Cour des Comptes, of the Hôtel de la Légion d'Honneur, of the Orsay barracks, of part of the Tuileries. The poor Louvre has been nicked by projectiles ... I also noticed that half the rue Royale is demolished, and there are so many ruined houses, it is unbelievable ... Tiburce has met two Communards, at this moment when they are all being shot ... Manet and Degas! Even at this stage they are condemning the drastic measures used to repress them. I think they are insane, don't you?

Edouard Manet to Berthe Morisot

Paris, 10 June 1871

... What terrible events and how are we going to get to the end of them? Everyone puts the blame on his neighbour and, in short, we have all been accomplices in what has happened....

Camille Pissarro to Théodore Duret

London, [early June 1871]

I am to return to France as soon as possible ... it is only when you are abroad that you realize how beautiful, grand, and hospitable France is. What a difference here! ... Oh! how I hope everything will be all right and that Paris recovers her supremacy!

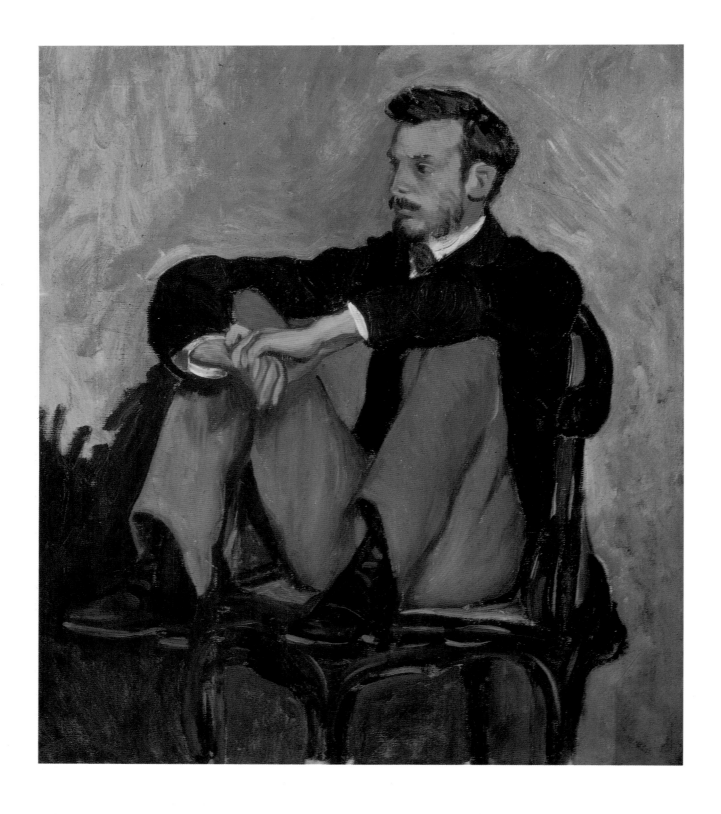

Bazille *Portrait of Renoir c.*1867

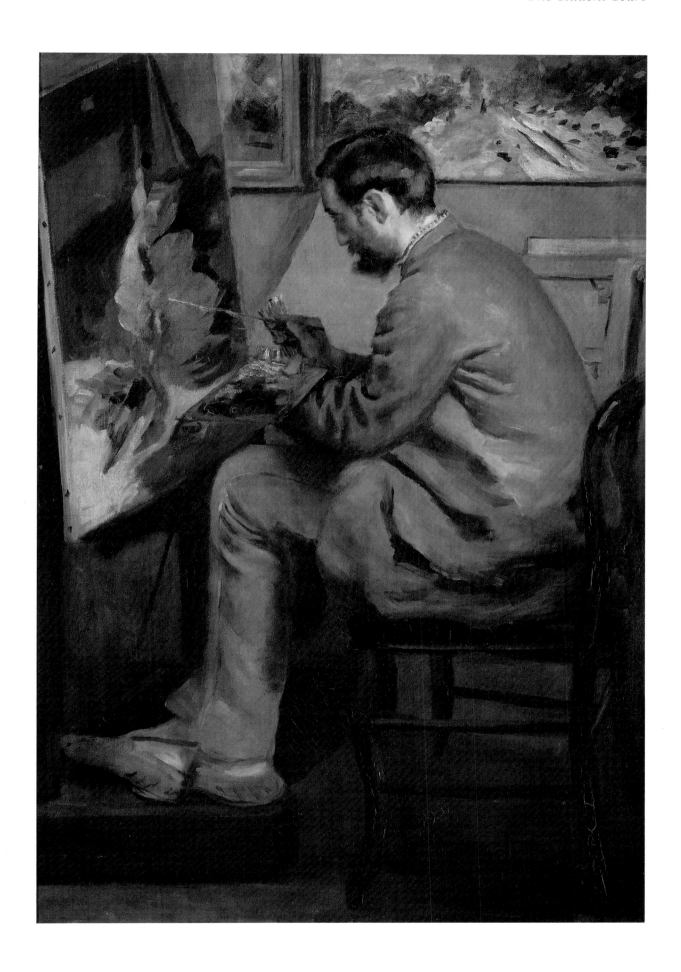

Renoir *Portrait of Bazille* 1867

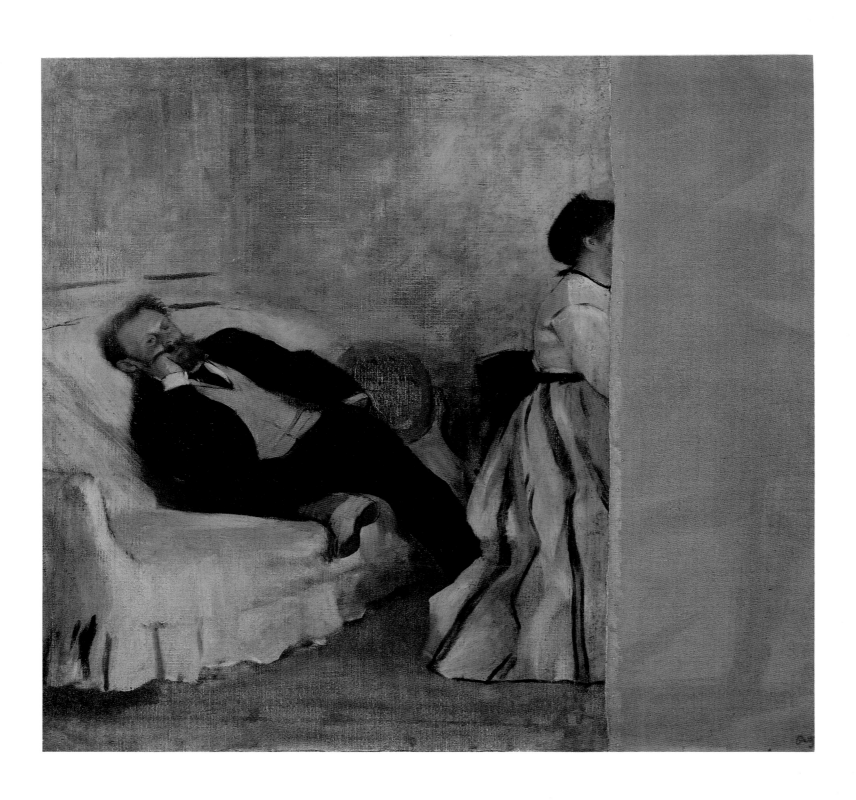

Degas *Manet and his Wife* 1868–9

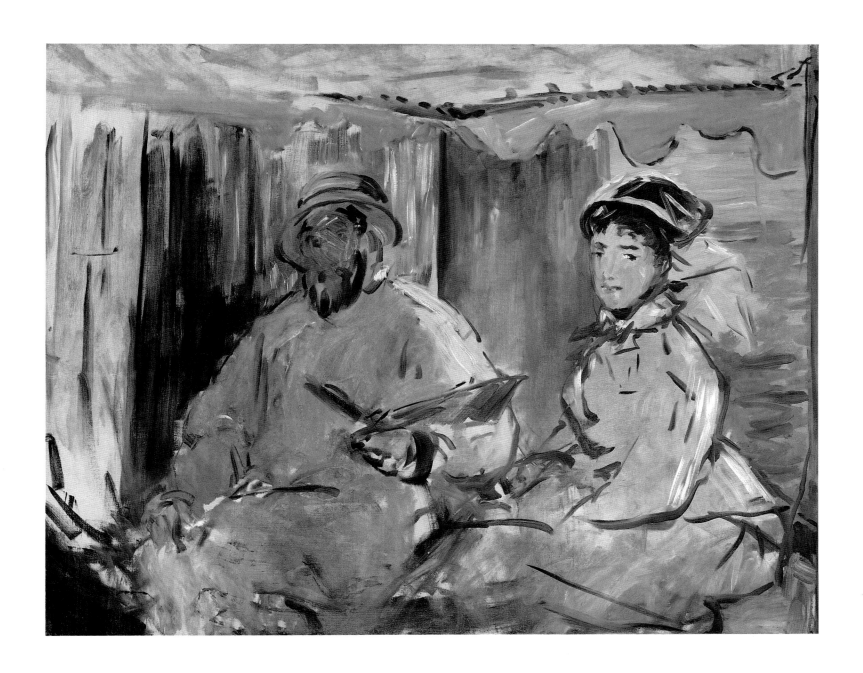

Manet *Monet Painting in his Studio Boat* 1874

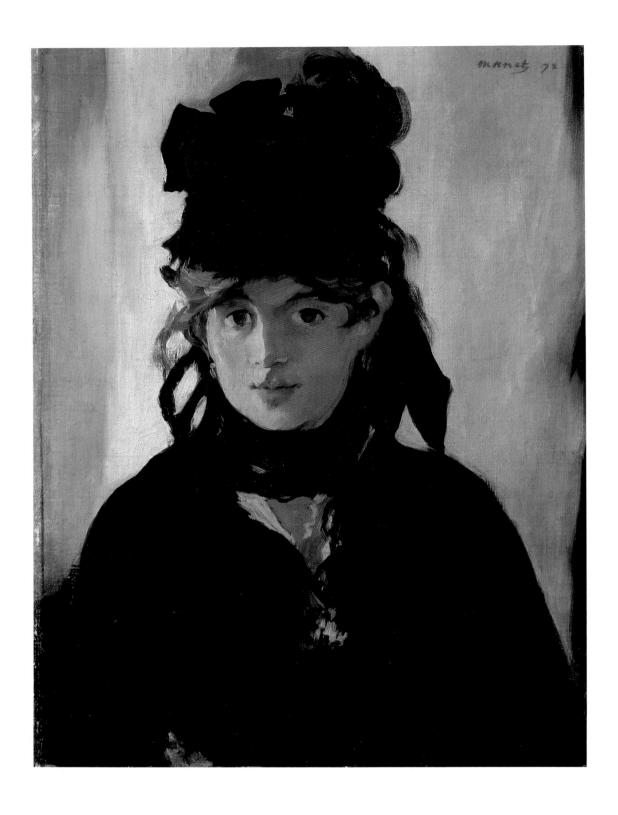

Manet *Berthe Morisot with a Bouquet of Violets* 1872

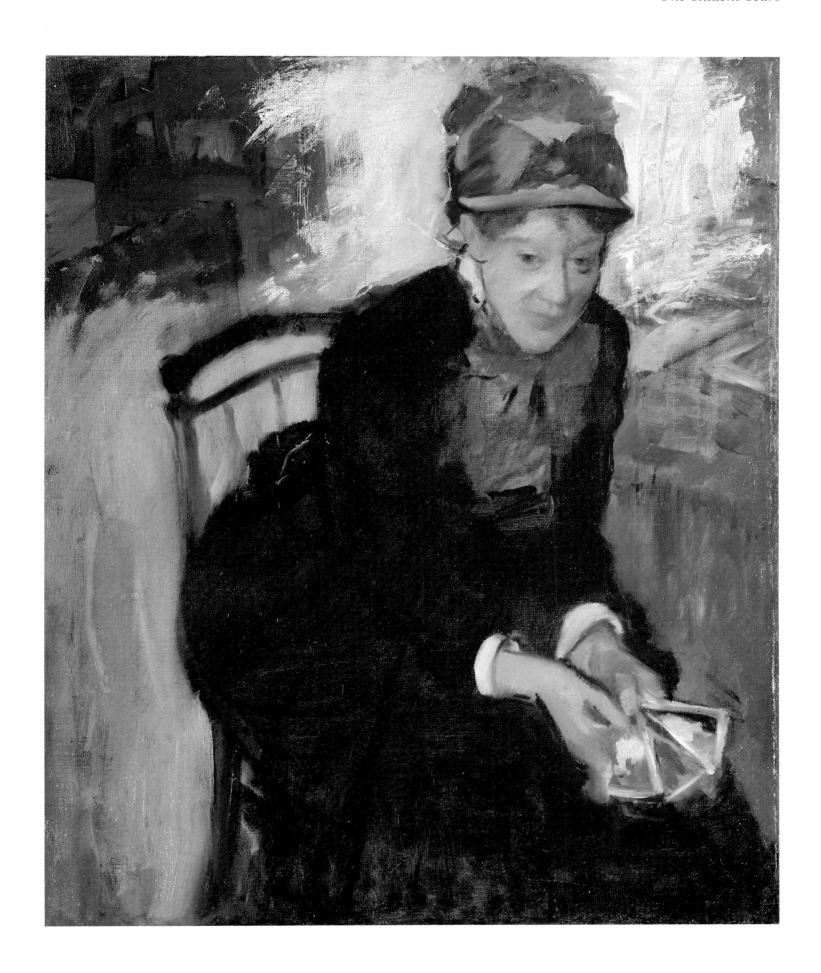

Degas *Portrait of Mary Cassatt* c.1880–4

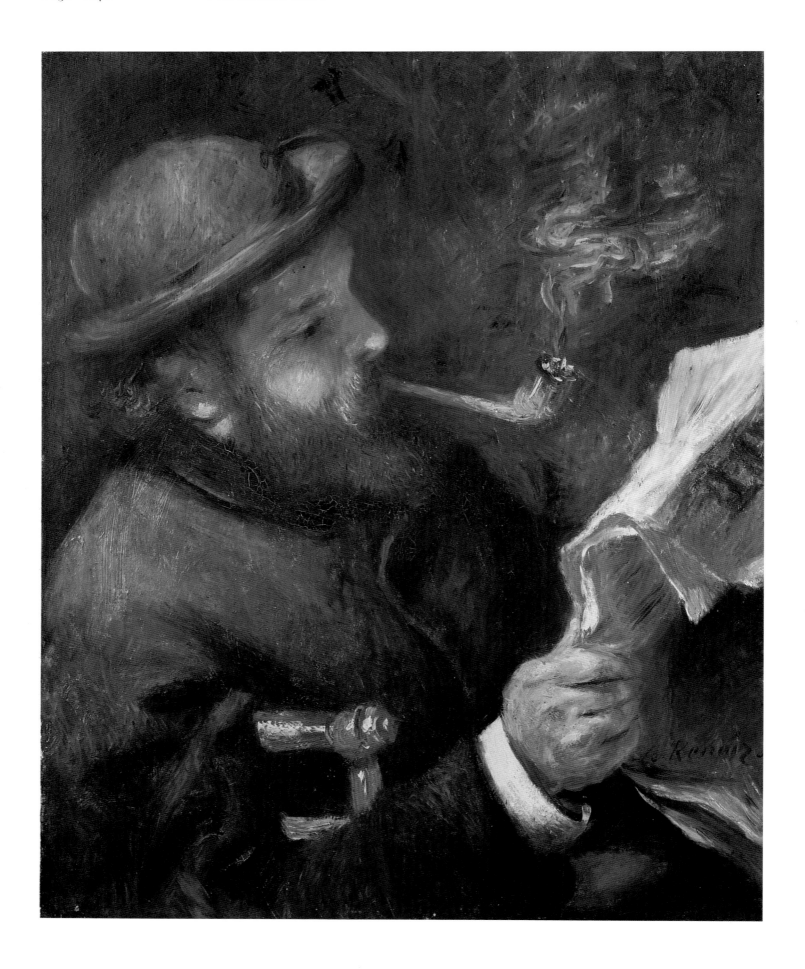

Renoir *Portrait of Monet* 1872

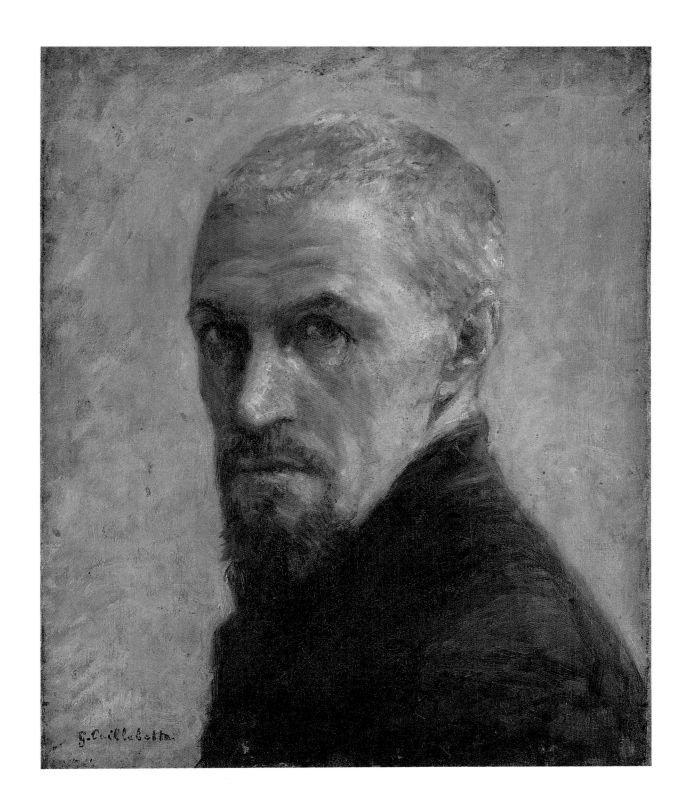

Caillebotte *Self-Portrait c.*1889

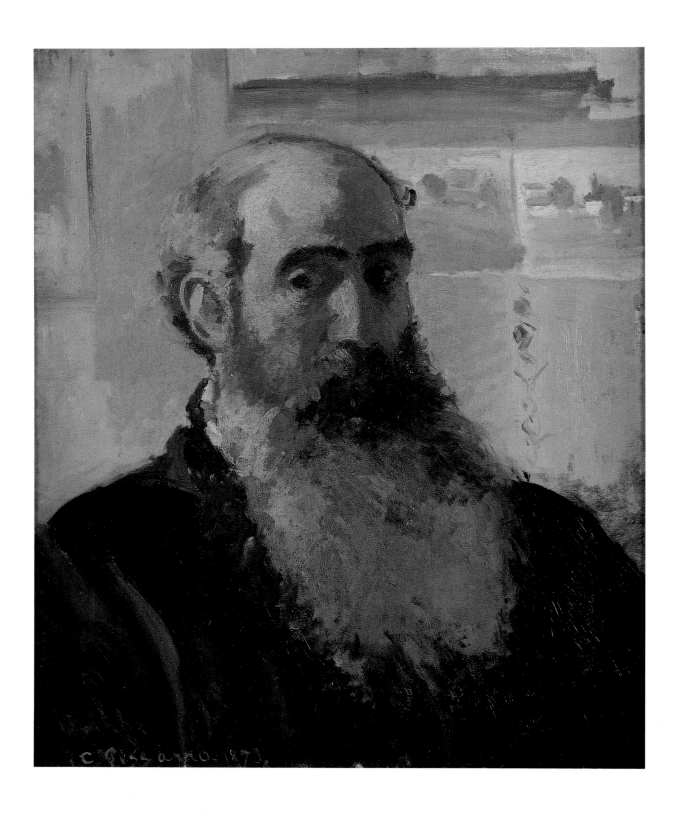

Pissarro *Self-Portrait* 1873

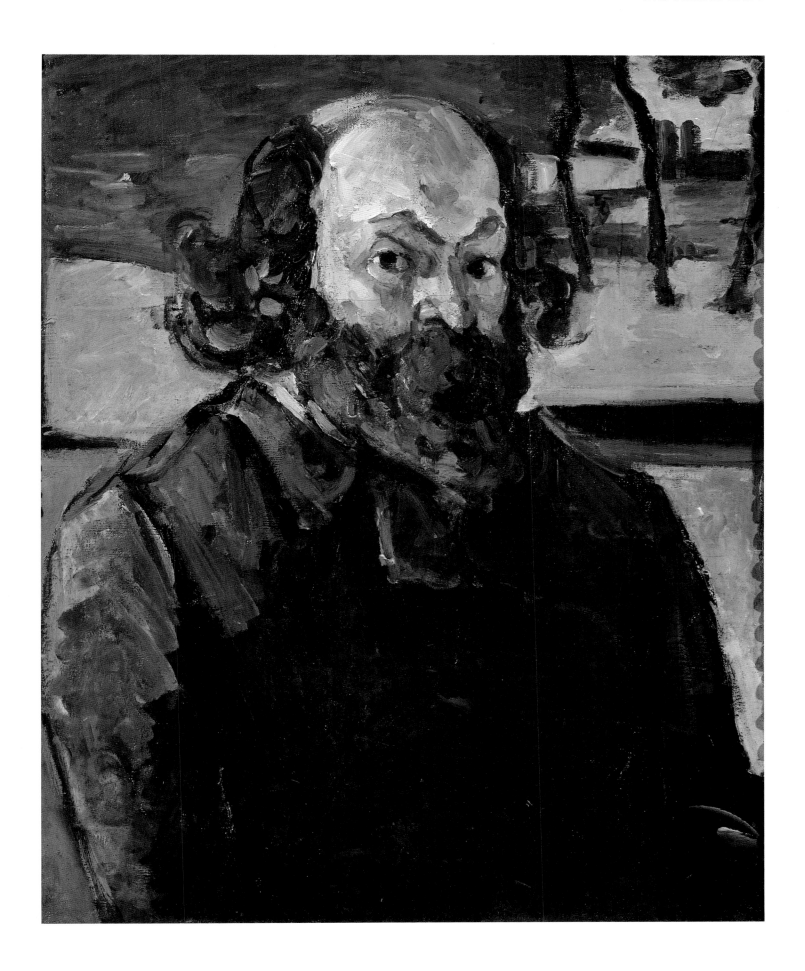

Cézanne *Self-Portrait* c.1872

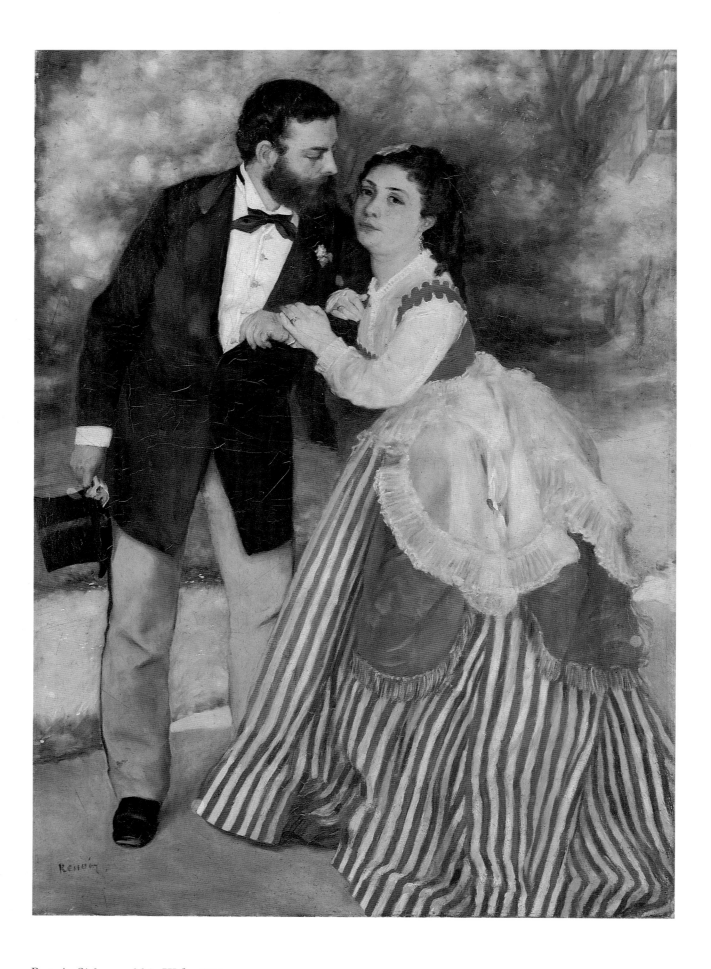

Renoir *Sisley and his Wife* 1868

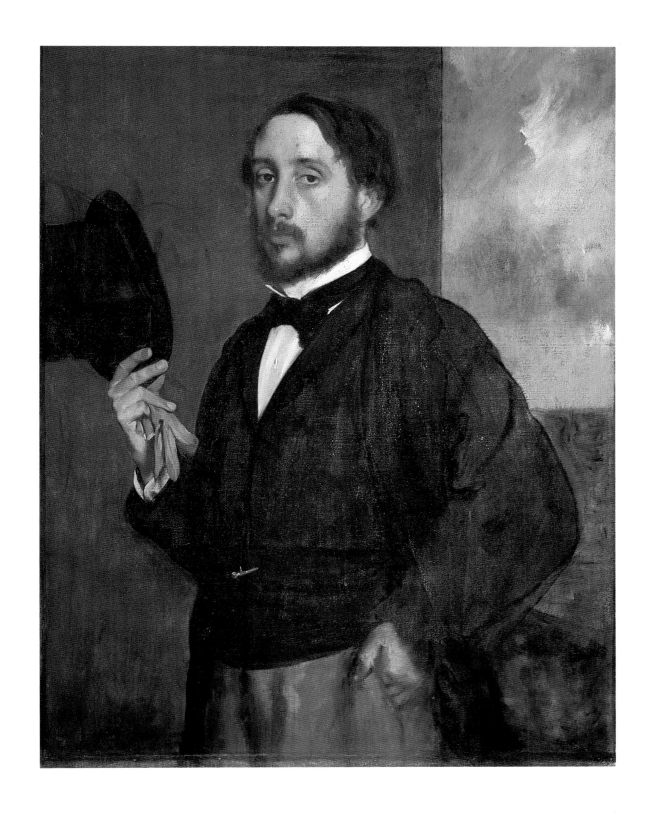

Degas *Self-Portrait* c.1863

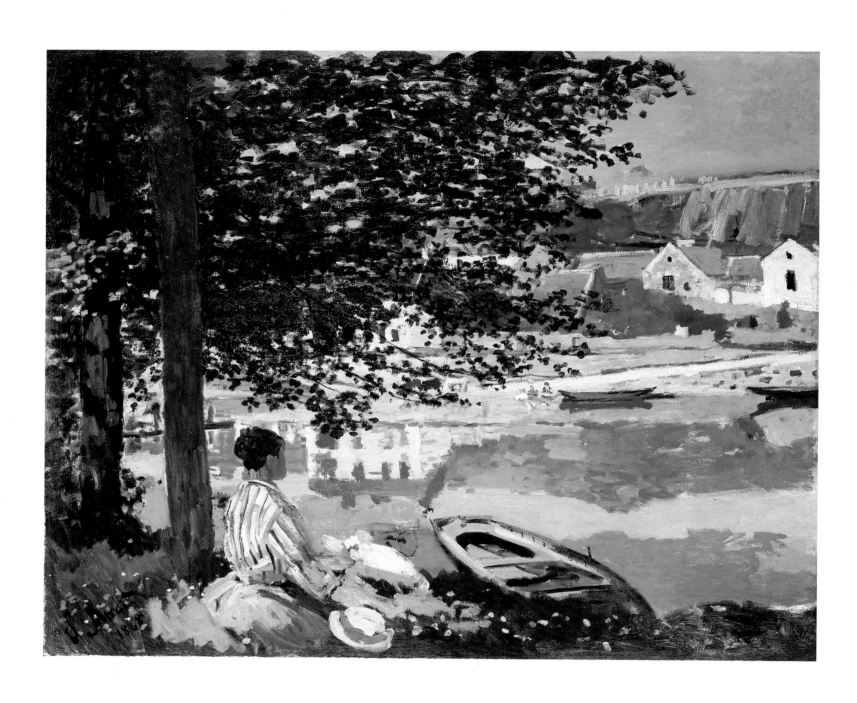

Monet *On the Seine at Bennecourt* 1868

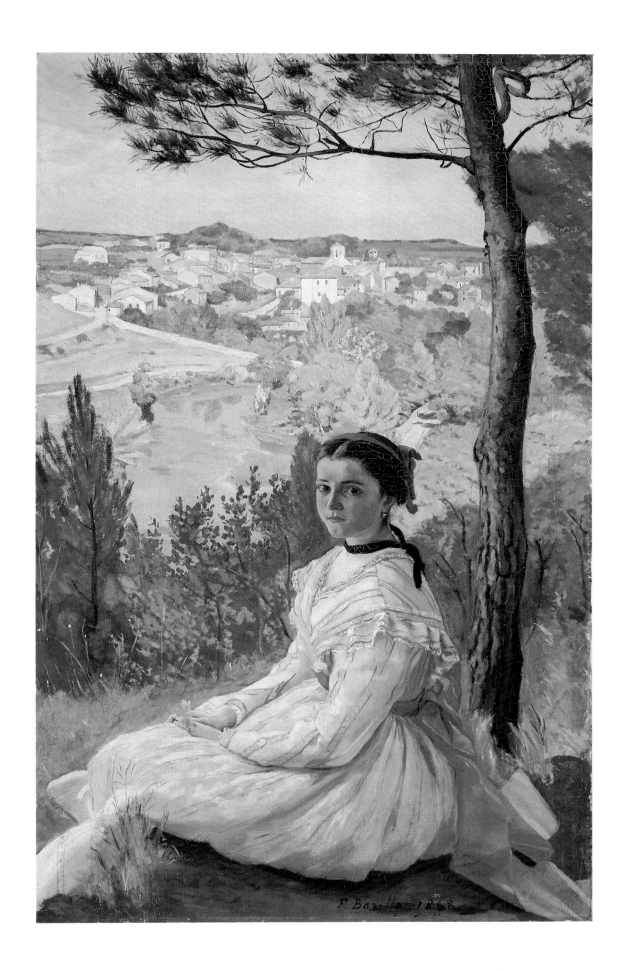

Bazille *View of the Village* 1868

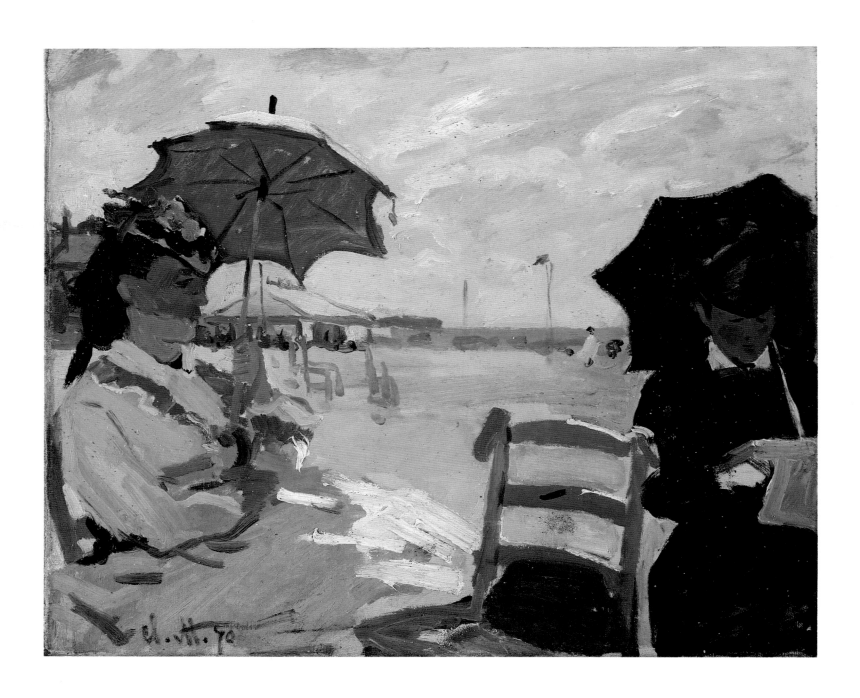

Monet *On the Beach at Trouville* 1870

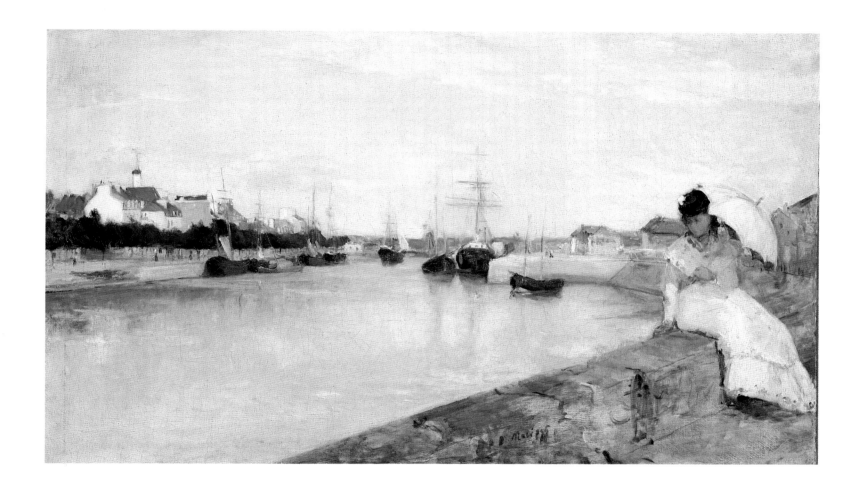

Morisot *The Harbour at Lorient* 1869

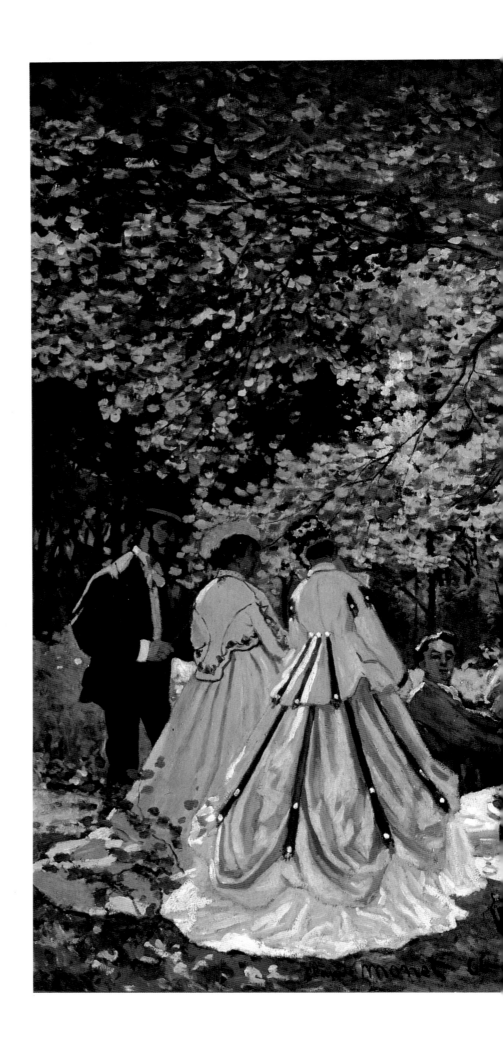

Monet *Le Déjeuner sur l'herbe* 1865–6

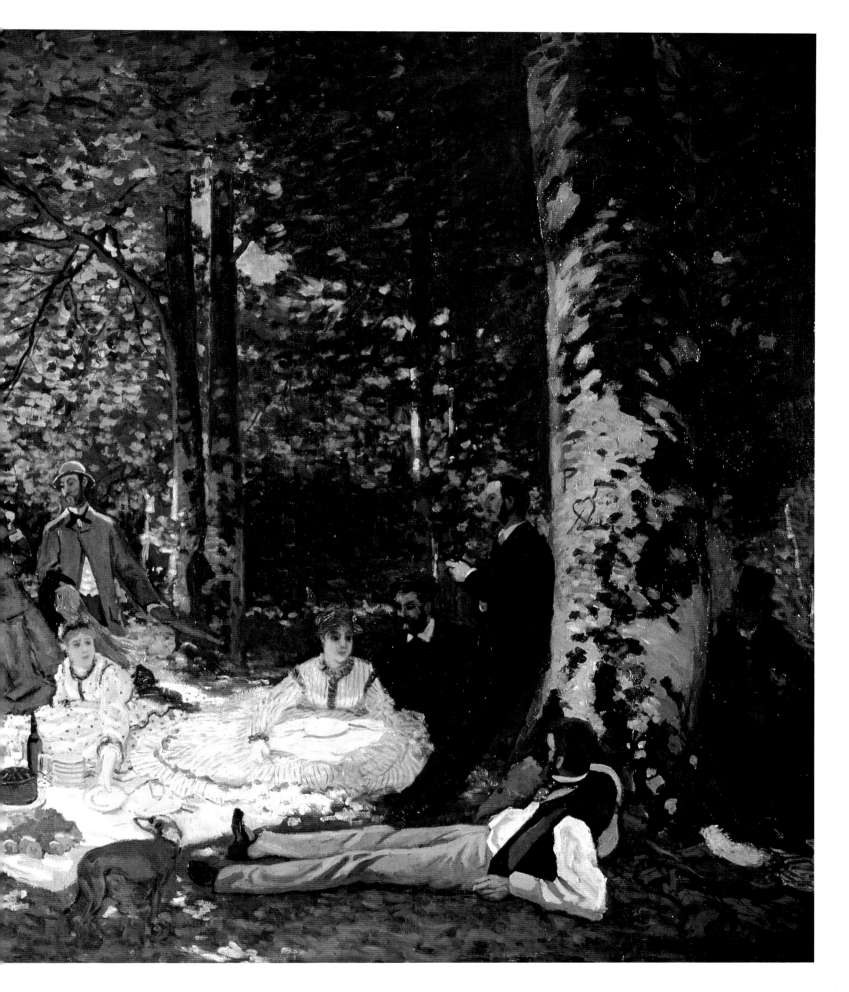

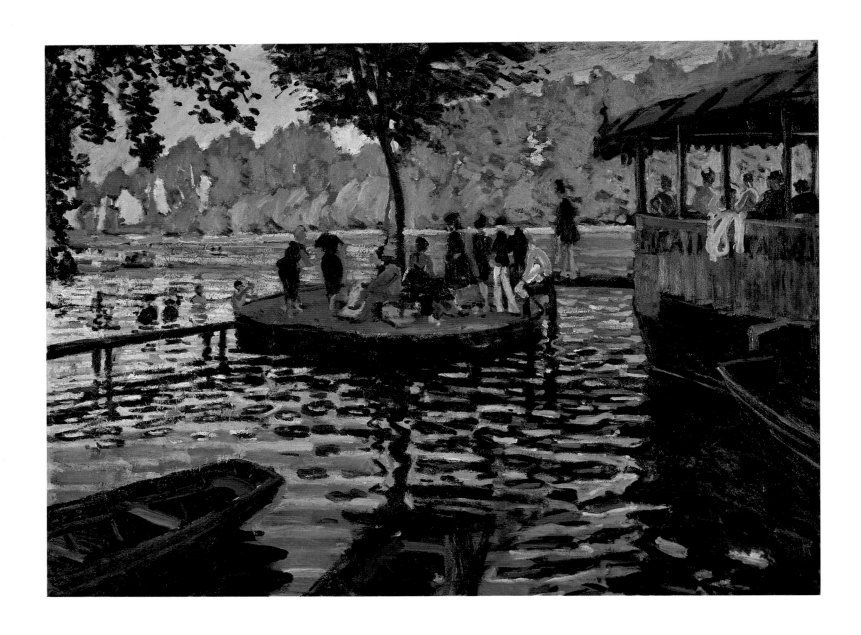

Monet *La Grenouillère* 1869

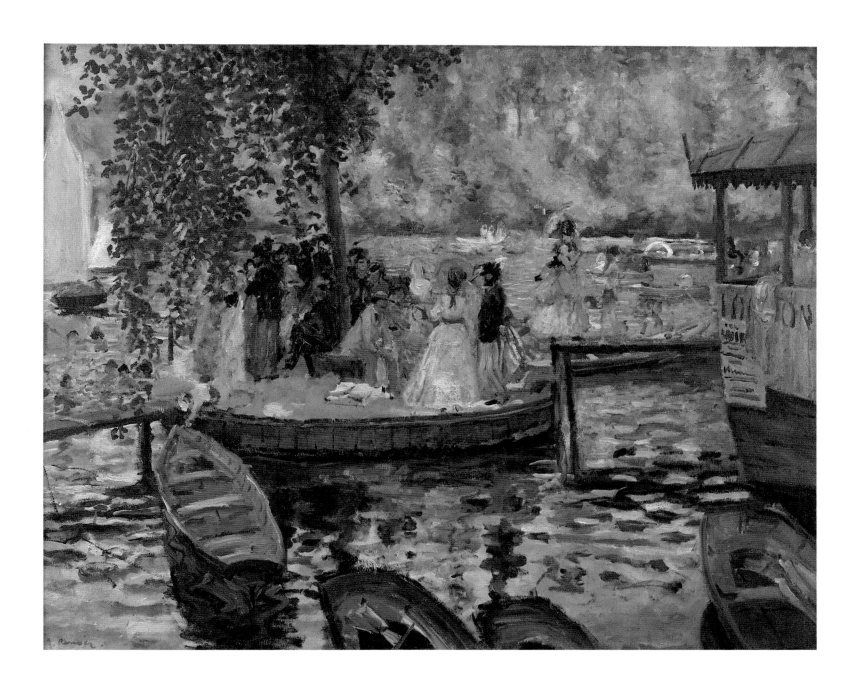

Renoir *La Grenouillère* 1869

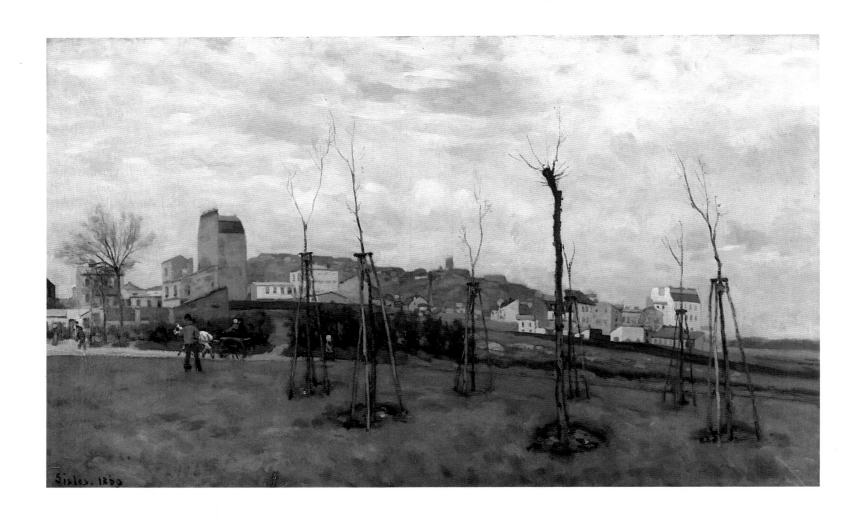

Sisley *View of Montmartre from the Cité des Fleurs* 1869

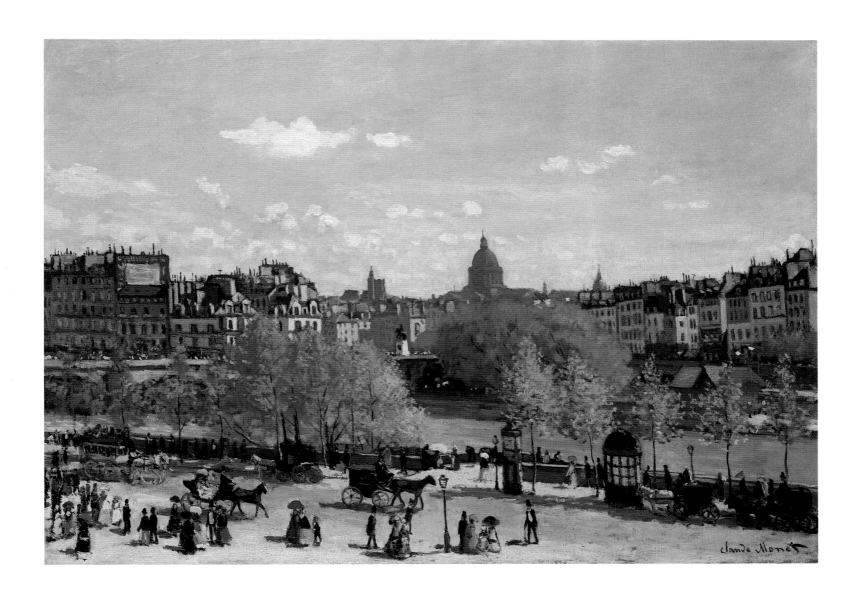

Monet *Quai du Louvre* 1867

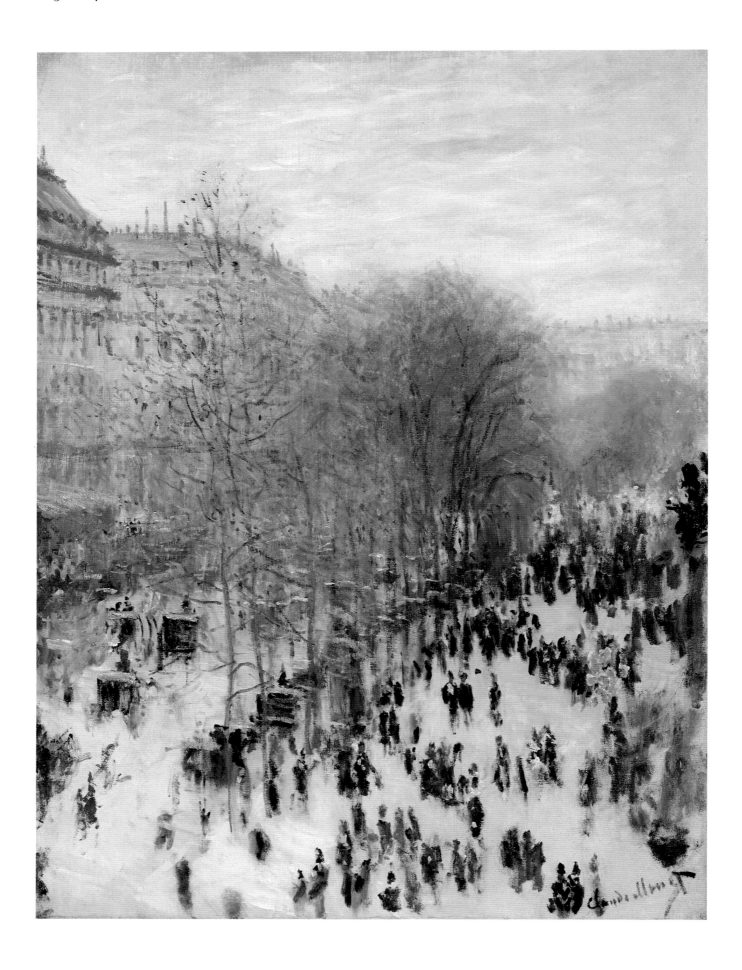

Monet *Boulevard des Capucines* 1873–4

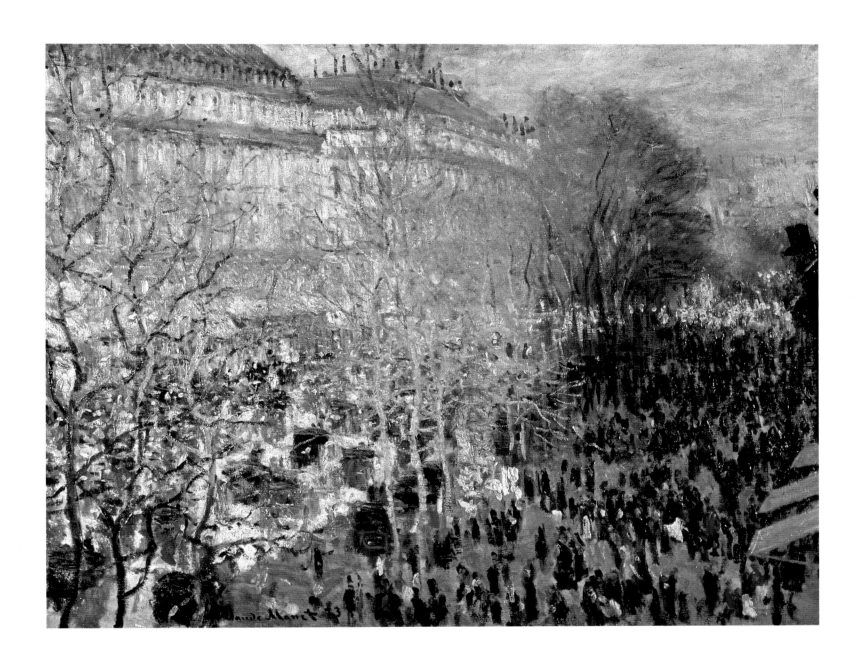

Monet *Boulevard des Capucines* 1873

II: The Impressionist Years
1871–1880

Cézanne *Portrait of Victor Chocquet c.*1877

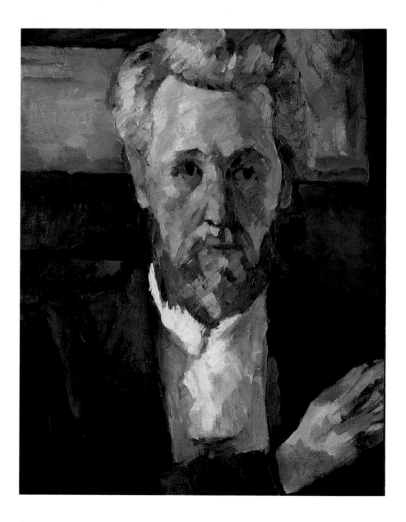

The first Impressionist exhibition took place in 1874, only three years after '*l'année terrible*', as Victor Hugo christened the devastating months of 1870 and 1871 in which France suffered a humiliating defeat at the hands of the Prussian army and the subsequent and disastrous siege of Paris by French government forces. It has been estimated that some 20,000 French people were killed by their own countrymen.

The Salon of 1872, the first held after these events, was looked upon as an opportunity to prove that France was still the centre of European culture. Manet, ever hopeful of official recognition, had sent a painting recognizably influenced by a seventeenth-century Dutch work by Frans Hals. Manet's painting was a portrait of a friend relishing a tankard of beer and smoking a clay pipe – it enjoyed a popular and critical success. Monet, Pissarro and Sisley did not submit. They were aware that in such circumstances there was little chance of their unconventional work being accepted. Renoir sent in one painting, which was rejected. Of the young group, only Morisot was successful in her submission to the Salon. It was a sign of the times that their friend and sometime mentor, Gustave Courbet, who had played a highly visible part in the 'revolutionary' Paris Commune, had been excluded from exhibiting and, a little later, was forced to shoulder the entire cost of the reconstruction of the Vendôme column, which had been destroyed during the siege of Paris.

Despite the support of about half a dozen private individuals – including the customs official Victor Chocquet, who befriended Renoir and Cézanne, the famous opera singer Jean-Baptiste Faure, the Romanian Georges de Bellio, the eccentric Dr Paul Gachet and his friend, novelist and *pâtissier* Eugène Murer, who supported the artists and bought their work – the outlook was bleak.

Little wonder, then, that the group spent many hours at the Café Guerbois discussing the possibilities of a separate exhibition. Courbet and Manet had held successful one-man shows and the Salon des Refusés of 1863 had shown that such events were possible, if not necessarily profitable. Gustave Caillebotte was at the centre of these discussions. A wealthy engineer and yachting enthusiast, Caillebotte's contribution to Impressionism, both as painter and organizer, has been seriously undervalued until relatively recently. His daring experiments with perspective and his radical choice of subjects paralleled the work of the older Degas, whom he much admired, although, as his correspondence reveals, he found the latter's awkward personality very difficult to come to terms with.

By 1873, the need to find new buyers was even more pressing. A major financial crisis meant that the market for paintings and other luxury goods had dwindled. The dealer

Paul Durand-Ruel, whose patronage had briefly provided Sisley, Pissarro and others with a good livelihood, found himself over-stocked with unsaleable canvases and withdrew his support. Caillebotte, Degas and Morisot still had private incomes, although later in the decade with the collapse of his family's banking firm, Degas found himself obliged to work hard for sales.

On 22 April 1873 the first public proposal was made for an independent show in a radical journal, *L'Avenir National*. It was written by Emile Zola's protegé, Paul Alexis, and appeared on the eve of the opening of the official Salon. Monet's prepared reply was published in the same journal on 12 May.

During the summer of the same year, Pissarro formulated a charter, based upon that of his local baker's union in Pontoise: 'The purpose of the society is first to organize independent exhibitions, without jury or juries, where each member could exhibit his work. No honours, no prizes, no awards.'

It was not until almost a year later that thirty artists gathered together formally in a co-operative. Pissarro recruited Berthe Morisot but, despite the best endeavours of Degas and others, the prize catch, Edouard Manet, remained unimpressed; his recent success at the Salon suggested that official recognition was not far away. Publicly, he let it be known that the reason for his abstention was the inclusion in the group of the surly, brusque and deliberately vulgar friend of Zola and Pissarro, the Provençal, Paul Cézanne. Another absentee was 'Papa' Corot, respected by the Establishment and the avante-garde alike, whose presence in the group would have lent a certain respectability to the proceedings. Although he flirted with the idea, the older artist recognized the gap that separated his work from that of Monet and his friends, felt the enterprise was doomed, and in the end did not forsake the Salon. He wrote to Antoine Guillemet, a successful young landscapist and friend and supporter of Cézanne: 'You have done very well to escape from that gang.'

From the first, opposing ideas were in evidence and factions emerged. Degas' influence was strong. His ambition was to found a *salon* of realist artists, whereas most of the others wanted a much freer association of individuals. Pissarro, whose political sympathies lay with the left wing, desired a co-operative that was ideologically sound and politically aware, ideas that found little favour with either Renoir or Degas. More discord was to arise out of the inclusion of additional artists, who were invited primarily as a means to defray the obvious expenses. 'Bold and bighearted like Christ, you even invite your enemies to the feast,' Ludovic Piette wrote to Pissarro. Such artists as James Tissot, Henri Rouart, Jean-Louis Forain, Jean-

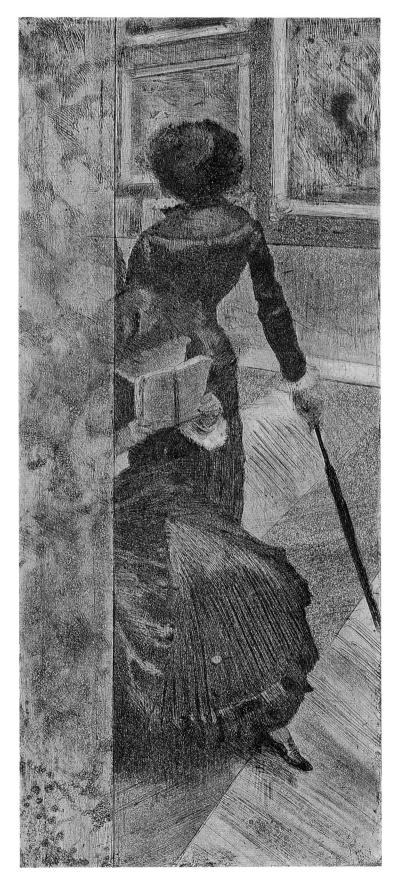

Degas *Mary Cassatt at the Louvre* 1879–80

Baptiste Guillaumin and Piette himself were generally accepted, but the later inclusion, at Degas' insistence, of Jean-François Raffaëlli, was to cause much bitterness. The artists who have since come to be known as the 'Impressionists' were in a minority.

The small clique had become a loose grouping of artists working outside the State-supported system for their own benefit. They hoped that, by by-passing the Salon and dealers, they could attract new patrons. Their choice of exhibition space reflected such concerns. The venue was the former studio of their friend, the fashionable photographer Nadar, who lent it to them without charge. His well-known premises were situated on the corner of rue Daunon facing the chic boulevard des Capucines (Degas had suggested facetiously that the group call themselves the Nasturtiums [*capucines*]), within sight of the centrepiece of Baron Haussmann's glittering new Paris, the almost-completed Opéra.

The first exhibition of the *Société anonyme des artistes, peintres, sculpteurs et graveurs* opened in April 1874, two weeks before the Salon. It ran for a month, the premises were open from ten until six and from eight until ten in the evening, and the paintings were hung on red-brown walls. The admission charge was kept deliberately low but, although 3,500 attendances were recorded, sales and good publicity were singularly lacking.

Of course the mere existence of the show had political overtones, and it is no surprise that such an anti-Establishment event opened in a hostile atmosphere. A letter from Berthe Morisot to one of her aunts reveals one of the reasons for the exhibition's lack of success: although mentioned in more than fifty articles or notices, most of those favourably disposed to the show or to individual artists appeared in left-wing periodicals and not in the journals that the picture-buying public was likely to read. A witty critique of the show by the critic Louis Leroy resulted in the more avant-garde exhibitors being given the title 'Impressionists', a term only grudgingly accepted by the artists. Pissarro preferred *Intransigeants*, a term associated with the Left; Degas wanted something apolitical, such as *Indépendants*.

On 14 December, six months after the show closed, a sorry group met in Renoir's studio. The *Société anonyme* had liabilities of 3,713 francs and holdings amounting to just 278 francs. Each exhibitor owed the co-op precisely 184.50 francs. There was no alternative but liquidation.

Nevertheless, despite the difficult times in which they lived and wide differences of opinion and character within the group, another seven 'Impressionist' exhibitions were held between 1876 and 1886, although Pissarro was the only painter of significance from the original group who

Nadar's photographic studio

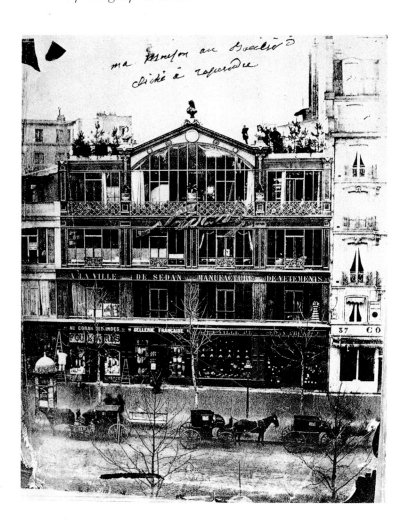

exhibited at all eight. Berthe Morisot only missed one show: that of 1879, the year her daughter Julie was born.

Several one-off ventures were organized by Renoir: the Hôtel Drouot auction in 1875, where his works were sold alongside those of Sisley, Monet and Morisot, became one of those typically French *scandales*, and police were mobilized to deal with the demonstrators. When financial conditions allowed, Durand-Ruel began to market their works again and to encourage the artists to develop their reputations on an individual basis through his gallery, as opposed to group exhibitions, although he continued to support these.

Once the reputations of the Impressionists began to be established through the hard work of the dealer and their own enterprising efforts, the idea of exhibiting as a group became less attractive. The exhibitions became battle-grounds where the rivalries of the participants as much as the reactions of the critics and public were exercised. Degas remained convinced that the proper nature of their exhibiting body should be to present a realist art. Monet, Pissarro and Caillebotte regarded the shows merely as personal exhibitions of like-minded artists; they were convinced that some of the artists Degas had introduced – in particular, Raffaëlli – had been planted 'to bring them all down'.

Degas found a kindred spirit in the American painter and printmaker Mary Cassatt. 'Here is someone who thinks as I do,' he is recorded as exclaiming on seeing her works for the first time. Mary Cassatt's importance to the group cannot be overestimated. She was from a wealthy American family and enjoyed complete financial independence. She had first arrived in Europe in 1851, spending four years in Italy. She returned in 1866 to study with the fashionable painter Charles Chaplin and wrote enthusiastic letters home about Paris, where she settled for good in the early 1870s. Degas admired her work at the Salon of 1874 and asked her to join the Impressionists. Cassatt's role within the Impressionist camp was at least two-fold: she was an independent artist of the first rank, and she was willing and able to sell the Impressionists to wealthy friends, such as Louisine Havemeyer and Mrs James Stillman, in the United States, thus complementing Durand-Ruel's moves in the same direction.

Mary Cassatt impressed all her colleagues with her genius for printmaking. In 1879 she was one of a small group – which included Degas, Pissarro and Marie and Félix Bracquemond – who invested their small profit from the fourth show in a venture to produce a journal of etchings, which they named *Le Jour et La Nuit*. Although the journal was never published, the enterprise set these artists on the road to producing some of the finest prints of the last 150 years.

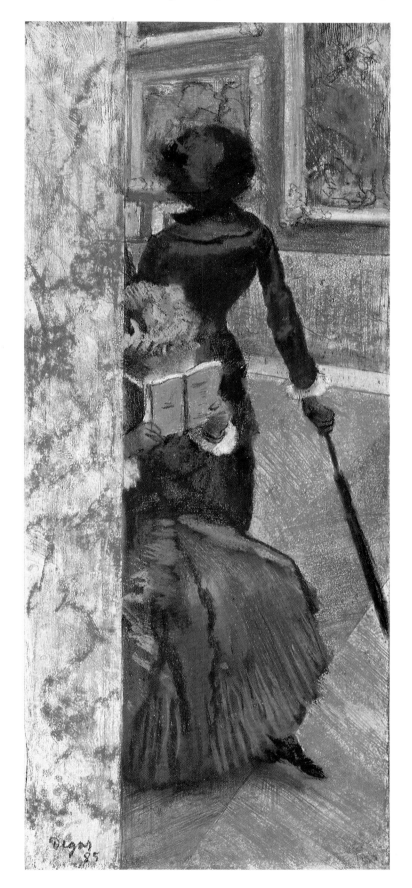

Degas *Mary Cassatt at the Louvre* 1885

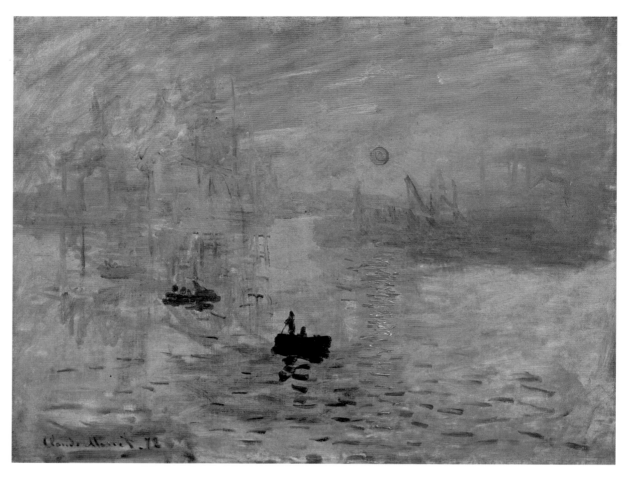

Monet *Impression: Sunrise* 1873

II: The Impressionist Years 1871–1880

Société anonyme

Ludovic Piette to Camille Pissarro

[Montfoucault, Spring] *1873*

Here are my impressions. You are trying to bring about a useful reform, but it can't be done; artists are cowards ... I would say nothing against an association restricted to people of talent who work, are loyal and inspired by enlightened audacity, such as you and some of your friends around you. I would foresee good results from an association of this kind and I do believe that it would be profitable and just to establish it, but I am distrustful of the mass of the idle and treacherous colleagues without moral or political convictions who only want to use others as stepping stones ...

Pierre-Auguste Renoir from *En écoutant Cézanne, Degas et Renoir* by Ambroise Vollard (1938)

'Société anonyme des artistes, peintres, sculpteurs et graveurs – Such was the name of our group. It gives no clue to the tendencies of the exhibitors. But I was the one who refused to accept any name with a precise signification. I was afraid that if we were called merely "Some" or even "The Thirty-Nine", critics would immediately begin to talk about a "new school", whereas all we wanted was, so far as possible, to show painters that it was time to return to the ranks; otherwise it looked as if painting would go under for good. And returning to the ranks meant, of course, relearning a craft that no one was any longer familiar with.'

Claude Monet to Camille Pissarro

Argenteuil, 22 April 1873

... You will tell me if you have seen Béliard and if we are getting ready to gather together again to bring things to a close. I also have a subscriber, and he will not have a place at the exhibition. It is my brother [Léon] ... Definitely, everyone approves very much, only Manet is opposed.

From an article by Paul Alexis in *L'Avenir National* (5 May 1873)

... The [Salon] jury is innocent, because in art matters no jury can be other than ignorant and blind. Instead of attacking it – which doesn't help – let's be practical and abolish it. ... This powerful idea, the idea of association, is growing not only in the passionate and lively environment of artists, it is beginning to suffuse new blood into the anaemic old world. The contemporary artist, to be truly worthy of his name, can no longer shut himself up in an ivory tower. He must descend from it.

Claude Monet to the Editor of *L'Avenir National*

[Paris, May 1873]

A group of painters assembled in my home have read with pleasure the article which you have published in *L'Avenir National*. We are happy to see you defend ideas which are ours too, and we hope that, as you say, *L'Avenir National* will kindly give us assistance when the society which we are about to form will be completely constituted.

Edgar Degas to James Tissot [painter]

Friday, 1874

Look here, my dear Tissot, no hesitations, no escape. You positively must exhibit at the boulevard [des Capucines – Felix Nadar's studio]. It will do you good, you (for it is a means of showing yourself in Paris from which people said you were running away) and us too. Manet seems determined to keep aloof, he may well regret it. Yesterday I saw the arrangement of the premises, the hangings and the effect in daylight. It is as good as anywhere. And now Henner (elected to the second rank of the jury) wants to exhibit with us. I am getting really worked up and am running the thing with energy and, I think, a certain success. The newspapers are beginning to allow more than just the bare advertisement and though not yet daring to devote a whole column to it, seem anxious to be a little more expansive.

The realist movement no longer needs to fight with the others – it already *is*, it *exists*, it must show itself as *something distinct*, there must be a *salon of realists*.

Manet does not understand that. I definitely think he is more vain than intelligent.

So exhibit anything you like. The 6th or 7th is the deadline but unless I am very much mistaken you will be accepted after then. So forget the money side for the moment. Exhibit. Be of your country and your friends . . .

My eyes are bad. The oculist . . . has allowed me to work just a little until I send in my pictures. I do so with much difficulty and the greatest sadness.

Edgar Degas to Berthe Morisot

[Paris], *April 1874*

I do not know whether you have been notified that this is the moment for sending your pictures. The opening will be Thursday morning, the 30th of this month. It is therefore necessary that you send in your work on Monday or Tuesday, and that you come if possible to take care of the placing. We are planning to hang works of each painter in a group together, separating them from any others as much as possible.

I beg of you, do come to direct this. . . .

Joseph-Benoît Guichard [artist and teacher] to Madame Morisot

[Paris, April or May] *1874*

Madame, the kind welcome you gave me this morning touched me deeply. I felt younger by fifteen years, for I was suddenly transported back to the time when I guided your delightful girls in the arts, as teacher and friend.

I have seen the rooms at Nadar's, and wish to tell you my frank opinion at once. When I entered, dear Madame, and saw your daughter's works in this pernicious milieu, my heart sank. I said to myself: 'One does not associate with madmen except at some peril; Manet was right in trying to dissuade her from exhibiting.'

To be sure, contemplating and conscientiously analysing these paintings, one finds here and there some excellent things, but all of these people are more or less touched in the head ... How could she exhibit a work of art as exquisitely delicate as hers side by side with *Le Rêve d'un Célibataire?* The two canvases actually touch each other! ...

As a painter, friend and physician, this is my prescription: she is to go to the Louvre twice a week, stand before Correggio for three hours, and ask his forgiveness for having attempted to say in oil what can only be said in watercolour ... she must absolutely break with this new school, this so-called school of the future....

Camille Pissarro to Théodore Duret

[Paris], *5 May 1874*

Our exhibition goes well, it's a success. The critics are devouring us and accusing us of not studying. I'm returning to my work – this is better than reading their comments. One learns nothing from them....

Pierre-Auguste Renoir from 'Le peintre Renoir et le salon d'automne'
in *La Revue démocratique* No. 10 (15 October 1904)

'If a few patrons [of the 1875 Hôtel Drouot sale] came to our aid, it is much more because of the violence with which the public attacked us than because of their admiration for our work.... This sale was a disaster. The Fine Arts students even paraded by in single file to demonstrate against our painting, and the intervention of the city police was necessary. From that day on, we had our defenders and, even better, our patrons.'

Berthe Morisot to her aunt

[Paris, April or May] *1876*

If you read any Parisian newspapers, among others *Le Figaro*, which is so popular with the respectable public, you must know that I am one of a group of artists who are holding a show of their own, and you must also have seen how little favour this exhibition enjoys in the eyes of the gentlemen of the press. On the other hand, we have been praised in the radical papers, but these you do not read. Anyway, we are being discussed, and we are so proud of it that we are all very happy. My brother-in-law [Edouard Manet] is not with us. Speaking of success, he has just been rejected by the Salon, he takes his defeat with as great good humour as possible.

Paul Cézanne to Camille Pissarro

l'Estaque, 2 July 1876

...too many exhibitions in a row seem to me to be bad, and on the other hand, people who believe they are going to see the Impressionists only see co-operatives...

I will conclude by saying like you, that since there seems to be a common drift among some of us, let us hope that necessity will force us to act together, and that self-interest and success will strengthen the bond that very often goodwill has not seemed sufficient to consolidate....

Paul Cézanne to his parents

[Paris], *Saturday morning,* [10] *September 1876*

I went to Issy [-les-Moulineaux] to see my friend Guillaumin. I found him there and had dinner with him last Wednesday. – I learnt from him that the exhibition organized by painters from our group last April was a great success. .... And already artists from the official exhibition, when they got to know about our little triumph, came to book the room, but it had already been booked for next year by the people who exhibited there this year.

According to what Guillaumin told me, I am one of the three new members who must take part in it, and I was very warmly defended by Monet during a meeting over dinner, which took place after the exhibition, a certain Lepic having taken a stand against my admission.

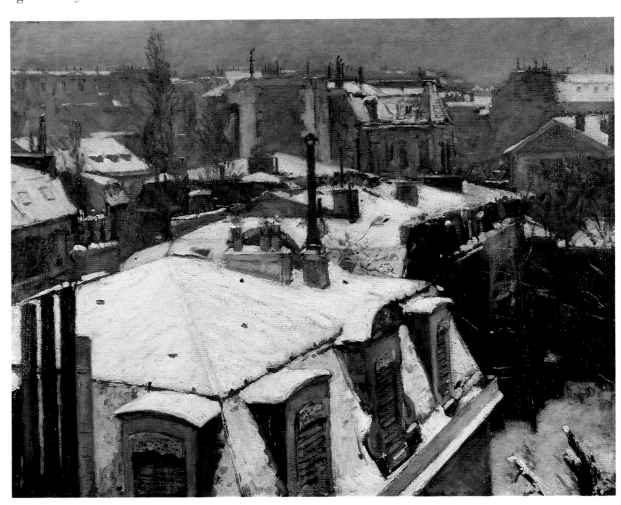

Caillebotte
Rooftops under the Snow
c.1878

Pierre-Auguste Renoir from *Renoir* by Ambroise Vollard (1920)

'At Argenteuil I also met the painter Caillebotte, the first "patron" of the Impressionists. There was no idea of speculation in the purchases he made from us. All he wanted was to do a service to his friends. He went about it very simply: he only bought the pictures that were considered unsaleable.'

From 'Chroniques Parisiennes: Les Indépendants' by Jules Montjoyeux in *Le Gaulois* (18 April 1879)

... Caillebotte, the youngest of the good ones. Scarcely thirty. Former student of [Léon] Bonnat, whose studio he was still in when, three years ago, he exhibited his *Raboteurs* at Durand-Ruel's. I confess this canvas stemmed rather a little from his master's school ... The Impressionists welcomed him with warmth as a precious recruit ... He entered the fray like a spoiled child. Assured against misery, strong with a double strength; well served by fortune. He had another courage, which isn't the most common, of hard-working wealthy folk ... His apartment on the boulevard Haussmann, which could be luxurious, has only the very simple comfort of a man of taste. He lives there with his brother, a musician ...

Gustave Caillebotte to Camille Pissarro

Wednesday, [1877]

Will you come to dinner at my house next Monday? I am returning from London and would like to discuss certain matters with you relative to a possible exhibition. Degas, Monet, Renoir, Sisley and Manet will be there. *I count absolutely on you.*

    Monday at seven o'clock....

Gustave Caillebotte to Camille Pissarro

[Paris], *January 1877*

The exhibition will take place; it must ...

Ludovic Piette to Camille Pissarro

24 January 1877

Yesterday ... I was approached by Sisley who was talking with Monet and Degas, and I extended my hand which he shook. At the same moment Degas held out his hand to me and mechanically I took his, but it was a reflex gesture, done quickly before I could think and against which I reacted immediately by my coldness ... I regret having even taken his hand because beyond that you are right. I have found and have said that his phrase was sadly deplorable ... I think the expression betrayed the thinking of M. Degas.

Ludovic Piette to Camille Pissarro

[Montfoucault], *1877*

The gentlemen of our association have not appeared (except for Cézanne and Guillaumin). If you had been here, I am sure you would have come [to Piette's one-man show]. Why? Because independent of your friendship, a feeling of solidarity would have prompted you to do so. Since we fight against a common enemy, we should enter into a sincere pact. You are doing this, but neither Renoir nor Monet see anything in the annual association but a means to use others as rungs of a stepladder.

Edgar Degas to Berthe Morisot

[Paris, Spring] *1877*

Caillebotte and Renoir must have already written to you that the premises are rented and that on Monday (tomorrow) there will be a general meeting ... at no. 20 or 22 rue Laffitte (next door to the optician). But I am writing this anyway, just for the pleasure of doing so and of sending you my best wishes ...

The meeting is at five o'clock. A momentous question is to be discussed: is it permitted to exhibit at the Salon as well as with us? Very important!

Degas *Woman with a Dog* 1875–80

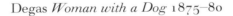

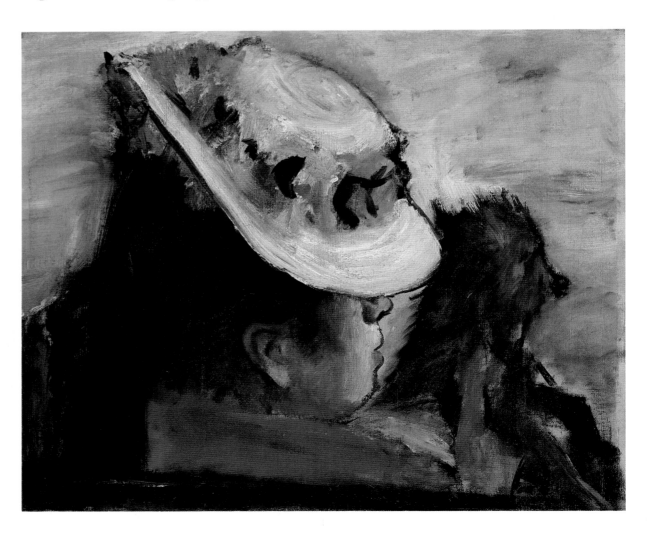

Edgar Degas to Gustave Caillebotte

[Paris], *Sunday,* [1877]

Well, Master Caillebotte, so things aren't working out so well? Seriously, tell me!??!
Sisley has renounced. I saw Pissarro this morning, Cézanne is arriving in a few days, and
Guillaumin will follow him. Monet only knows one thing and that is he won't send
anything to the Salon. Manet has persuaded a woman who is sitting for Forain, that the
place for her portrait is not with us. . . . Amen for little Forain. Mlle Cassatt will see Mlle
Morisot tomorrow then we will know her mind. . . .

Mary Cassatt from *Mary Cassatt* by Achille Segard (1913)

'It was at that moment [1877] that Degas persuaded me to send no more to the Salon
and to exhibit with his friends in the group of Impressionists. I accepted with joy. At last
I could work with complete independence without concerning myself with the eventual
judgement of a jury. I already knew who were my true masters. I admired Manet,
Courbet and Degas. I hated conventional art. I began to live.'

Degas *Place de la Concorde* 1875

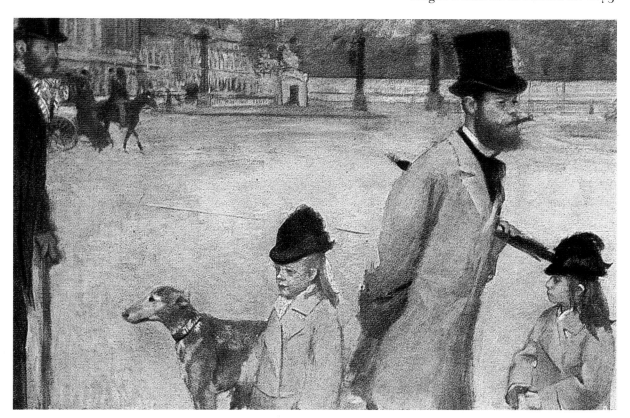

Paul Cézanne to Emile Zola

[Paris, August] *1877*

...it seems that a profound depression reigns in the Impressionist camp. Streams of gold are not exactly flowing into their pocket, and people's work goes into decline...

Mary Cassatt to J. Alden Weir [American artist]

[Paris], *10 March 1878*

Your exhibition [the first held by the Society of American Artists, in New York] interests me very much. I wish I could have sent something, but I am afraid it is too late now. We expect to have our annual exhibition here, and there are so few of us that we are each required to contribute all we have. You know how hard it is to inaugurate anything like independent action among French artists, and we are carrying on a despairing fight and need all our forces, as every year there are new deserters.

Edouard Manet from *Edouard Manet, Souvenirs* by Antonin Proust (1913)

[On leaving the Exposition Universelle of 1878]: '... Really, to ridicule people like Degas, Monet and Pissarro, to make jokes at the expense of Berthe Morisot and Mary Cassatt and fall about before the Caillebottes, Renoirs, Gauguins and Cézannes, when they produce works like that!

'I have done my best to find some good in them. But I can't and then there are some things that really upset me. One of them is Gustave Moreau. I have a real sympathy for him, but he's barking up the wrong tree ... [his work] will have a terrible effect on our times. He is dragging us back towards the incomprehensible, when what is needed is a move towards clarity.

'... if Corot is admired today, it is not for the correctness of his studies of nature; but for the ambiguities of his studio pieces.'

Claude Monet to Georges de Bellio

10 March 1879

... I am giving up the struggle as well as all hope; I don't have the strength to work any more under these conditions. I hear that my friends prepare a new exhibition this year; I renounce taking part in it, not having done anything that's worth being shown....

Alfred Sisley to Théodore Duret

Sèvres, 14 March 1879

I am tired of vegetating, as I have been doing for so long. The moment has come for me to make a decision. It is true that our exhibitions have served to make us known and in this have been very useful to me, but I believe we must not isolate ourselves too long. We are still far from the moment when we shall be able to do without the prestige attached to the official exhibitions. I am, therefore, determined to submit to the Salon. If I am accepted ... I think I'll be able to do some business....

The Business of Art

Claude Monet from an article in *Le Temps*, 27 November 1900

'War was declared on Germany. I had just married. We went to London, where I met Pissarro... I endured much poverty, for my works were not popular there. Life was difficult. Quite accidentally I met Daubigny, who had formerly shown some interest in me. He was then painting scenes on the Thames, which were having a considerable success. He was moved by my distress. "I know what you need," he said. "I'm going to get you a dealer." The next day I met M. Durand-Ruel.'

Pierre-Auguste Renoir from *Renoir, My Father* by Jean Renoir (1962)

'We needed a reactionary to defend our painting, which the Salon crowd said was revolutionary. He was one person at any rate who didn't run the risk of being shot as a Communard! ... Old Durand is a fine man ... Without him we wouldn't have survived.... Enthusiasm is all very well, but it doesn't fill an empty stomach.... He was intelligent enough to sense that something could be done in this direction. And I believe he really liked our painting; Monet's especially.'

Mary Cassatt to Louisine Havemeyer [American collector]

[undated]

... I went and flattened my nose against that window [of the Durand-Ruel gallery] and absorbed as much as I was capable of. It changed my life. I saw art such as I wished to see it....

Camille Pissarro to Julie Pissarro

Paris, Monday evening, January [187?]

... I went to see Durand-Ruel and he talked about my pictures, he was most encouraging and said he'd like to buy some, large and small. He said that if I didn't live so far away he'd have come out to choose what he wanted. I am delighted with the way things went.

I'll show him my best things. He's bought five or six large pictures from Manet and wants some from Monet. Latouche [dealer] has sold my picture of the du Parc farm. So far I haven't managed to sell the ones I brought along with me – they are not my *best* work – but don't fret, I'll make a few sous in the end ...

Camille Pissarro to Théodore Duret

Pontoise, 31 October 1873

... Last time I saw Monet he asked me to ask you to let him have the 200 francs you owe him, he is having a hard time and the money would be a great help to him. Also the sooner you get this little matter cleared up the better.

I'm extremely sorry that this business should have caused a rift in our camp. I think very highly of Monet, so I feel torn between the two of you and regret my inability to bring you together and make you forget a moment's bad humour. Also I think too highly of you to believe for one instant that you'll remain inflexible. Why not forget the whole thing and concentrate on art? . . .

Claude Monet to Edouard Manet

[Argenteuil], *Monday morning, 28 June* [*1875*]

It's getting more and more difficult. Not a penny left since the day before yesterday and no more credit at the butcher's or the baker's. Even though I believe in the future, you can see that the present is very hard indeed.

So could you send something then, on whatever terms, to a broker? Only be careful as to whom you choose to deal with, in case some harm comes of it.

You couldn't possibly send me a twenty-franc note by return of post, could you? It would help me out for the time being.

Edouard Manet to Théodore Duret

[Paris], *1875*

I went to see Monet yesterday. I found him in a sorry state, completely broke. He asked me to find someone who would take any ten to twenty of his works, and pay 100 francs apiece for them. What about it? Would you be willing to join me and we would each give him 500 francs?

Of course, we would have to hide from him the fact that we are the actual buyers. I had thought of applying to a dealer or some art-lover; but I foresee the possibility of a refusal.

Unfortunately one has to be a good judge of painting like ourselves in order to make this excellent purchase, however reluctant one may be, and at the same time render this service to a man of talent. Do let me know as soon as possible and let me know when we can meet.

Camille Pissarro to Théodore Duret

Pontoise, 1 October 1875

I am extremely short of money, as always at this time of year, and would be very grateful if you could send me what you owe me – it's all I have to live on until the customers get back to Paris and I can sell a picture.

I have a bill that falls due on the 10th of the month and there's my rent and I don't have a sou!

I've done a lot of work and hope to make myself secure from want this year, at least during the slack season.

I'm busy painting a shepherdess and sheep, if I'm pleased with it, I'd be delighted to find a buyer.If you know someone who might like it do please try and sell it for me . . .

Camille Pissarro to Théodore Duret

Pontoise, 21 October 1875

I got your letter containing the 100-franc note, on account of the 250 still due to me – many thanks, I needed the money very badly and still need a great deal more. I hope to manage by selling two or three pictures.

All you owe me now is one hundred and fifty francs ...

Eugène Manet to Berthe Morisot

[Paris], *September 1876*

The entire tribe of painters is in distress. The dealers are overstocked. Edouard [Manet] talks of cutting down expenses and giving up his studio. Let us hope the buyers will return. The present moment, it is true, is unfavourable. Developments are taking place in Europe that would enable France to recover her rightful place, if it were not for the fact that we have been governed since 1870 by ... [script illegible].

Eugène Murer from *Pissarro* by Aldolphe Tabarant (1924)

[Wednesday evening, 1877]: 'Over the dessert Renoir told us that all day long he had been about from place to place with a picture under his arm trying to sell it. Everywhere he had been bowed out with the words: "You have come too late. Pissarro has just been here. I've taken a picture from him as a matter of common humanity. You know. Poor chap, with all those youngsters." This "poor chap", repeated at every door he knocked at, exasperated Renoir, who was very much put out at not having sold anything.

' "What", he cried, with that good-natured ogre's voice of his, and rubbing his nose nervously with his forefinger – a familiar gesture with him – "because I am a bachelor and have no children, am I to die of starvation? I'm in just as tight a corner as Pissarro; yet when they talk to me, no one says, 'that poor Renoir'."

Gustave Caillebotte to Camille Pissarro

[Paris], *28 January 1878*

Here are the 750 francs. Please excuse me if I can no longer continue to send you 50 francs a month at the moment ...

Camille Pissarro to Eugène Murer

Paris, Wednesdy, 1878

I have received the 20 francs you sent me by my boy [Lucien, who was now 15]. Many thanks.... Art is a matter of a hungry belly, an empty purse, of poor, luckless devils.... I am still waiting for the thing that shall deliver me out of this hell of inaction. Mlle Cassatt paid me a visit.

Desboutin and the Italian man of letters [Diego Martelli] came to see me. The

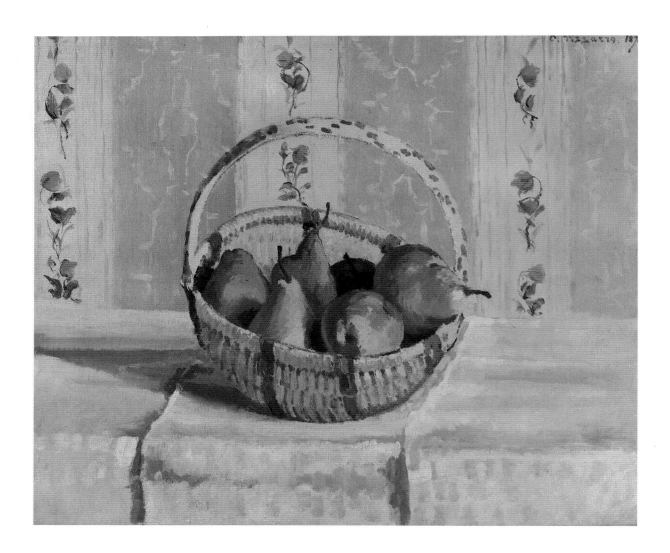

Pissarro
*Still-Life: Pears in a
Round Basket* 1872

latter is so enthusiastic about this style of painting. He thinks so highly of my art that I am confused and can hardly bring myself to believe what he says. I don't understand how a stranger has a clearer insight than myself. Strange.... I want to take him to see Guillaumin, I am certain he will like his work a great deal.

Paul Cézanne to Emile Zola

[Aix], *4 April 1878*

Would you be so kind as to send Hortense [Cézanne's mistress, later wife] sixty francs at the following address? – Mme Cézanne, rue de Rome 183, Marseilles. In spite of his promises, I've only been able to get 100 francs out of my father, and I was even afraid that he'd give me nothing at all. He's had it from various people that I have a child, and he's using all the means at his disposal to try and catch me. He wants to deliver me from the burden of him, he says. – I shall say no more. – It would take too long to try to explain the fellow to you, but appearances are deceptive where he is concerned, you can take my word for it. – When you can, if you can drop me a line, you'd give me great pleasure. I'm going to try to get to Marseilles, I managed to get away without being noticed on Tuesday, a week ago, to go [and see] the little one, he's better now, and I was obliged to come back on foot to Aix, since the railway train shown in my guide was wrong, and I was supposed to be back for dinner – I was an hour late...

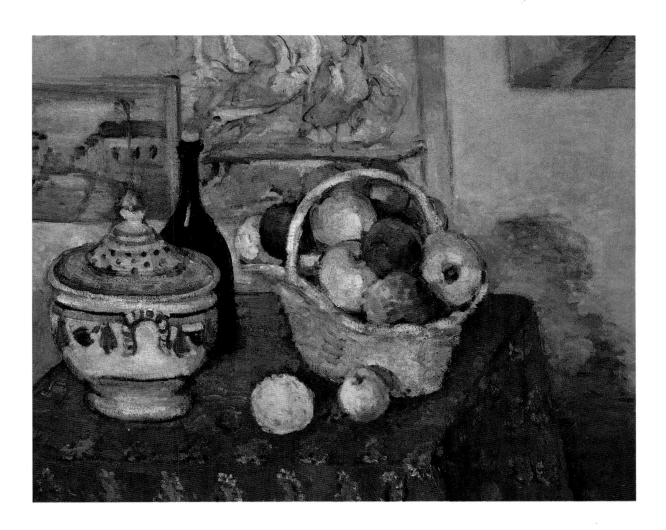

Cézanne
*Still-Life with
Soup Tureen c.*1877

Camille Pissarro to Eugène Murer

[Paris, July 1878]

I am in the greatest need of money ... What hard times these are! I don't know where to put my head.

Pierre-Auguste Renoir to Dr Paul Gachet

[Paris], *January 1879*

Please go tomorrow to see Mlle L ... [Alma Leboeuf, his model], 47 rue Lafayette.

She has broken out in pimples and when she scratches them, a white blister appears.

I think it's acute. And she writes to me that it's very painful, she has been waiting for you since Tuesday, you can imagine how much fun she must be having.

As for myself, I don't know what to think, and I'm afraid she'll decide to go and see her doctor who could make the pimples go back inside.

It may be smallpox.

Well, I'm very impatient to know, so impatient that I've done nothing all day while waiting for you....

I count on you to get in touch with me and relieve my anxiety, which is very great.

I'm almost at the point of waiting for you at your door.

Encouragements and Criticisms

From *Confessions of a Young Man* by George Moore (1886)

Ah! The morning idleness and the long evenings when life was but a summer illusion, the grey moonlight on the Place [Pigalle] where we used to stand on the pavements, the shutters clanging up behind us, loath to separate, thinking of what we had left unsaid, and how much better we might have enforced our arguments ... I can hear the glass door of the café [de la Nouvelle-Athènes] grate on the sand as I open it. I can recall the smell of every hour. In the morning that of eggs frizzling in butter, the pungent smell of cigarettes, coffee and bad cognac; at five o'clock the fragrant odour of absinthe; and soon after the steaming soup ... and as the evening advances, the mingled smells of cigarettes, coffee and weak beer. A partition ... separates the glass front of the main body of the café. The usual marble tables are there, and it is there we sat and aestheticized till two o'clock in the morning. . . .

These two young men [Degas and Manet] are the leaders of the Impressionist School. Their friendship has been jarred by inevitable rivalry. 'Degas was painting Semiramis when I was painting modern Paris,' says Manet. 'Manet is in despair because he cannot paint atrocious pictures like Duran, and not be fêted and decorated; he is an artist, not by inclination, but by force. He is a galley-slave chained to an oar,' says Degas. Different, too, are their methods of work. Manet paints his whole picture from nature, trusting his instinct ... this extraordinary oneness of nature and artistic vision does not exist in Degas, and even his portraits are composed from drawings and notes.

From *Notes et Souvenirs* by Joseph de Nittis (1895)

Manet: 'My dear fellow, if there were no honours and awards, I would not invent them. But there are. And when you can, you had better take anything that sets you apart from the crowd. That brings you one stage onward, and it is also a weapon. In this dog's life of ours, which is a daily struggle, you cannot be too well armed. I have received no awards. But that is not my fault, and I assure you that if I can get them then I will! And I'll do whatever is necessary for that.'

　　Degas (breaking in angrily and shrugging his shoulders): 'Of course you will. I haven't waited until now to find out what a bourgeois you are!'

From *Growing up With the Impressionists: the diary of Julie Manet*
Wednesday, 20 November [1895]

Arrived at M. Degas' house. We met Zoë [Degas' housekeeper] on the stairs and she let us in – M. Mallarmé, M. Renoir and M. Bartholomé were there, and M. Degas was very busy arranging a lamp he had just bought, which gave off a brilliant light. I admired the portrait of my Uncle Edouard by him, which I hadn't seen before.

This had been the cause of an argument. [About 1869] Monsieur Degas had painted Aunt Suzanne at the piano and Uncle Edouard on the sofa listening [*Manet listening to his wife playing the piano*]; the latter, thinking that his wife looked ugly, cut her off. Monsieur Degas quite reasonably became angry with this conduct and took back the canvas, which he now has in his drawing room.

From *Souvenirs d'un marchand de tableaux* by Ambroise Vollard (1936)

'But, Monsieur Degas, wasn't it Manet himself who cut down the portrait you did of him and his wife?'

The painter, sharply:

'By what right, sir, do you presume to judge Manet? Yes, it's true. And after all, maybe he was right to do so. I was the fool in that business, for at the time I got angry and took down from my wall a small still life that Manet had given me: "Sir, I wrote to him, I send you back your *Plums.*" Ah, what a pretty canvas that was! And I did a fine thing that day. For when I was reconciled with Manet I asked him to give me back "my" *Plums*, and well, do you know, he had sold them!'

Berthe Morisot to Edma Pontillon

[Paris, July or August 1871]

I did not go to Manet's last Thursday evening ... The previous Thursday he was so nice to me. Once more he thinks me not too unattractive and wants to take me back as his model.... Out of sheer boredom, I shall end up proposing the very thing to him myself....

Eugène Manet to Berthe Morisot

[Autumn or Winter 1874]

... you overwhelm me. A letter bearing compliments, without periods or commas – that indeed is enough to cause a stronger man than I to lose his breath ...

Berthe Morisot to Tiburce Morisot

[Paris], *January 1875*

... I have found an honest and excellent man [she had married Eugène Manet the previous month], who I think loves me sincerely, I am facing the realities of life after living for quite a long time in chimeras that did not give me much happiness ...

Berthe Morisot from *Edouard Manet, Souvenirs* by Antonin Proust (1913)

'During the course of the year 1879, Manet has been haunted by two fixed ideas, doing a work about the out of doors but about the entire out of doors, where people's features dissolve, according to their expression, into a shimmering atmosphere, something even more vibrant than *Skating* or the *Boat in Argenteuil*, and dashing off my portrait on a white unprimed canvas in one sitting . . . After having used seven or eight canvases, the portrait came at one sweep.'

From *Edouard Manet, Souvenirs* by Antonin Proust (1913)

When on Sundays, one called on Manet in the rue de St-Pétersbourg studio, his one thought was to sing the praises of all the painters who, improperly as it happens, have come to be known as the school of Batignolles. He would set their canvases in a good light, so anxious to find purchasers for them that he forgot all about his own works. During these drawings, he would express the most passionate admiration for Claude Monet, whose portrait he had painted in a boat, a canvas he particularly liked and called *Monet in his boat. . . .*

Manet had this to say of Monet: 'There is not one painter in the whole School of 1830 who can paint a landscape as he can. And then his water! He is the Raphael of water.'

From *En écoutant Cézanne, Degas et Renoir* by Ambroise Vollard (1938)

Looking at Monet's canvases Degas said:
'I'm leaving. All these reflections on the water hurt my eyes!'

Camille Pissarro to Théodore Duret

Pontoise, 2 May 1873

. . . Don't you think you may be mistaken about Monet's talent? In my opinion it's considerable; true, it's very pure, a far cry from the sentiment that drives you: but his art is highly studied, based on observation; the feeling is completely new, it's poetry through the harmony of true colours, Monet is a worshipper of real nature.

This summer I shall try to paint a field of ripe corn. Nothing *colder* than the full glare of the summer sun; whatever the colourists may say, nature is colourful in winter and cold in summer. You can therefore expect to find my picture to be very pale, whitish, etc. . . .

From *Auguste Renoir* by Ambroise Vollard (1920)

Manet said to Claude Monet [*c.*1874]: 'You are a friend of Renoir's. You should advise him to give up painting. You can see for yourself that he's not very good at it.'

Camille Pissarro to Antoine Guillemet [landscape painter]

Pontoise, 3 September 1872

... Guillaumin has just spent a few days with us, he's still working by day at his painting and at night on his cess-pits – what energy! Cézanne gives us reason to hope and I've seen some pictures. At home I have a painting of remarkable force and vigour. If, as I hope, he stays some time in Auvers, where he is going to live, he will end by astonishing quite a few artists who were too ready to write him off.

Camille Pissarro to Théodore Duret

Pontoise, 8 December 1873

... I'm sorry you couldn't have the *Ploughed Fields*, but on the other hand, as an artist, I'm enormously flattered that Degas liked this picture ...

Thanks for your advice, you must realize that I've listened to what you say for some time now. What has long prevented me from painting from life is simply the lack of models, not just for the actual pictures but also for serious studies. All the same I shall try again soon; it will be very hard, for as you no doubt know these pictures can't always be done from life, in other words, out of doors, so it will be far from easy.

If you are looking for something out of the ordinary, I think Cézanne's the man for you; he has some very strange studies, his vision is unique.

Paul Cézanne to Camille Pissarro

[Aix], *24 June 1874*

Thank you for having thought of me while I'm so far away and for not holding it against me that I wasn't as good as my word, according to which I promised to go and say hello to you at Pontoise before leaving. – I started painting the minute I arrived, which was on a Saturday evening at the end of May. ... I'd like it if you could give me news of Mme Pissarro, after her confinement, and if you could let me know if there are any new recruits to the *Société coop*. But not, of course, if it will in any way disturb you in your own activities.

... During these last few days I've seen the director of the Musée d'Aix, who, spurred on by a curiosity encouraged by the Parisian papers which have spoken of the co-operative, wanted to see for himself the extent of the danger to Painting. But when I pointed out that seeing my productions would not give him a very accurate idea of the progress of the evil and that he ought to see the works of the great criminals in Paris, he told me: 'I shall be perfectly able to form an idea of the dangers that threaten Painting be seeing your outrages.' Upon which, he came, and when I told him, for example, that you replaced modelling with the study of tones, and when I tried to make him understand all this from nature, he closed his eyes and turned his back. – But he said he understood, and we went our different ways quite happy with each other.

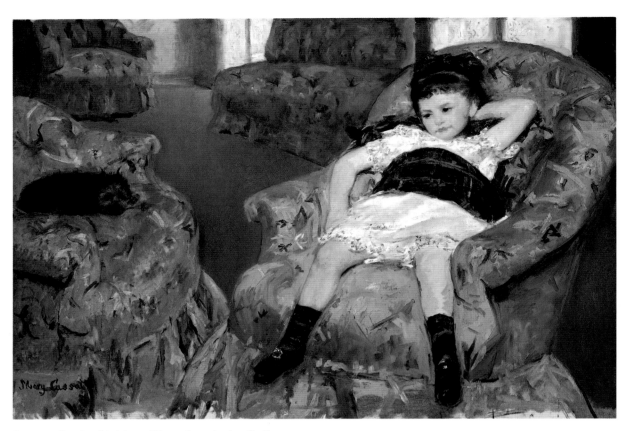

Cassatt *Little Girl in a Blue Armchair* 1878

Mary Cassatt to Mrs James Stillman [American collector]

[*c.*1894]

[Cézanne] is like the man from the Midi whom Daudet describes: 'When I first saw him he looked like a cut-throat, with large red eye-balls standing out from his head in a most ferocious manner, a rather fierce-looking pointed beard, quite grey, and an excited way of talking that positively made the dishes rattle.' I found later that I had misjudged his appearance for, far from being fierce or a cut-throat, he had the gentlest nature possible, *comme un enfant*, as he would say.... I am gradually learning that appearances are not to be relied upon over here. Cézanne is one of the most liberal artists I have ever seen. He prefaces every remark with *pour moi* it is so and so, but he grants that everyone may be as honest and as true to nature from their convictions; he doesn't believe that everyone should see alike.

Mary Cassatt to Louisine Havemeyer

[undated]

When he [Degas] saw my *Boy Before a Mirror* he said to Durand-Ruel, 'Where is she? I must see her at once. It is the greatest painting of the century.' When I saw him he went over all the details of the picture with me and expressed great admiration for it, and then, as if regretting what he had said, he relentlessly added, 'It has all your qualities and all your faults – it is the infant Jesus with his English nurse.'

Mary Cassatt to Ambroise Vollard

Mesnil-Beaufresne, Tuesday, [1903]

I wanted to come back to your place yesterday to talk about the portrait of the little girl in the blue armchair. I did it in '78 or '79 – it was a portrait of a child of a friend of Degas – I had done the child in an armchair, and he had found that to be good and advised me on the background, *he even worked on the background* – I sent it to the American section of the Gd. exposition '79 [in fact Exposition Universelle 1878], but it was refused. Since M. Degas had thought it good I was furious especially because he had worked on it – at the time it seemed new, and the jury consisted of three people, one of whom was a pharmacist!

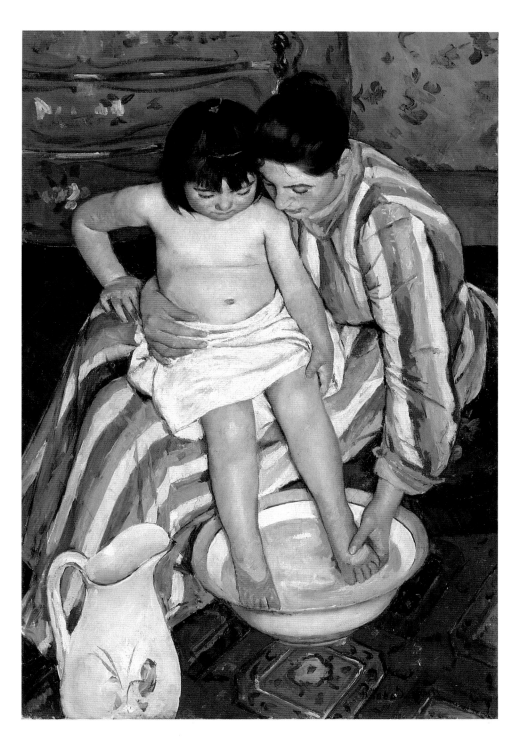

Cassatt *The Bath* 1891–2

Gustave Caillebotte to Camille Pissarro

24 January 1881

Degas spends his time talking at the Café de la Nouvelle-Athènes or in society. He would be better advised to do a little more painting. How right he is a hundred times over, in what he says, how witty he is and knowledgeable about painting, no one can have any doubt about that (and is this not the brighter side of his reputation?). But the fact remains that a painter's truest arguments are his paintings, and however right he may be in all he says, he is at his truest in his work.

Les Indépendants

Edgar Degas to James Tissot

De Gas Brothers, New Orleans, 19 November 1872

What do you say to the heading? It is the firm's note paper. Here all they speak of are cotton and exchange. Why do you not speak to me of other things? You do not write to me. What impression did my dance picture make on you, on you and the others? – Were you able to help in selling it? And the one of the family at the races, what is happening to that? Oh, how far from so many things one is here.

Villas with columns in different styles, painted white, in gardens of magnolias, orange trees, banana trees, negroes in old clothes like the junk from *La Belle Jardinière* [a shop in Paris] or from Marseilles, rosy white children in black arms, charabancs or omnibuses drawn by mules, the tall funnels of the steamboats towering at the end of the main street, that is a bit of local colour if you want some, with a brilliant light at which my eyes complain. Everything is beautiful in this world of the people. But one Paris laundry girl, with bare arms, is worth it all for such a pronounced Parisian as I am. The right way is to collect oneself, and one can only collect oneself by seeing little. I am doing some family portraits; but the main thing will be after my return . . .

Edgar Degas to Henri Rouart

New Orleans, 5 December 1872

. . . You see, my dear friend, I dash home and I commence an ordered life. . . . I am thirsting for order. – I do not even regard a good woman as the enemy of this new method of existence. – A few children for me of my own, is that excessive too? No. I am dreaming of something well done, a whole, well-organized (style Poussin) and Corot's old age . . .

Edgar Degas to Henri Rouart

Paris, 8 August 1873

. . . I cannot stop putting the final touches to my pictures, pastels, etc. How long it is, and how sad to see my last good years trailing off into mediocrity! I often weep over my poor life. . . .

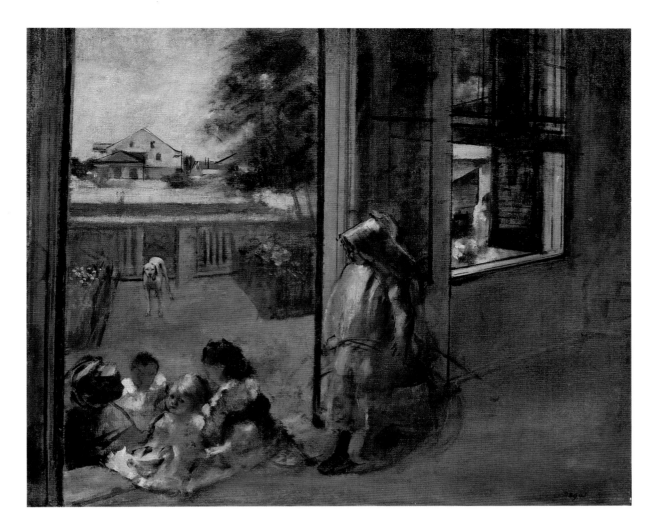

Degas
Children on the Steps,
New Orleans 1872–3

Paul Cézanne to his mother

[Paris], *26 September 1874*

Pissarro hasn't been in Paris for about a month and a half – he's in Brittany, but I know he has a high opinion of me, who have a pretty high opinion of myself. I'm beginning to look upon myself as more gifted than all those around me, and you know that the good opinion I have when it comes to myself is the result only of careful deliberation. I have to work the whole time, not in order to reach that degree of perfection which is what wins the admiration of imbeciles. – And this thing that people commonly set so much store by is no more than the product of craftsmanship, and it means that every work resulting from it is unartistic and banal. I must only seek to complete a work for the truer, wiser pleasure of doing. And believe me, there is always a time when one wins recognition, and one has admirers who are a good deal more fervent, more convinced than those who are only drawn by a vain appearance.

It's a very bad time for selling, the middle classes are all distinctly reluctant to let go of their sous, but that state of affairs will come to an end ...

Camille Pissarro to Théodore Duret

Pontoise, 20 October 1874

This is to let you know that I'm off to stay with my friend Piette and I shan't be back before January. I'm going there to study figures and animals in the real country ...

be able to carry them ... g
anything. – But there are some motifs that would require three or four months' work, which one might be able to do, for the vegetation doesn't change here. There are olive trees and pines which always keep their leaves. The sun here is so tremendous it seems to me that when things stand out in silhouette it's not just in black or white, but in blue, in red, in brown, in violet. I may be mistaken, but it seems to me to be the very opposite of modelling. Wouldn't our gentle landscapists from Auvers be happy here! ...

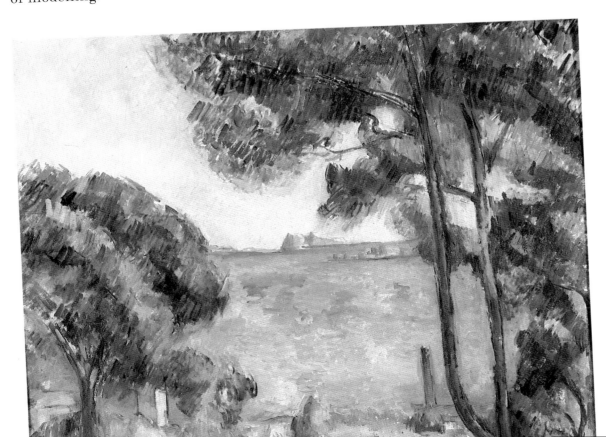

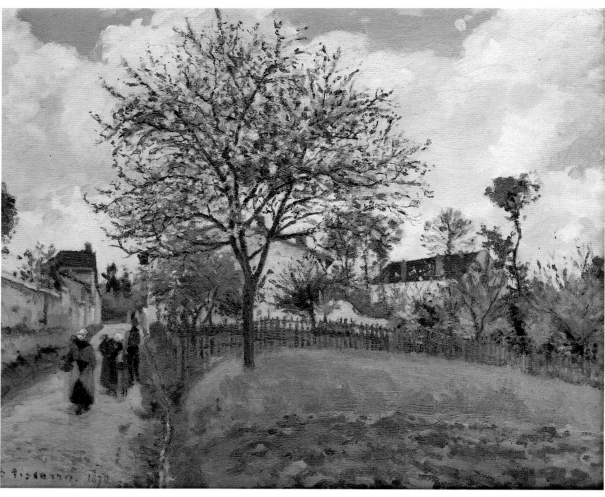

Pissarro *Landscape at Louveciennes* 1870

Camille Pissarro to Théodore Duret

Montfoucault, 11 December 1874

... I have done quite a lot of work here and got going on figures and animals. Although I have a number of ideas for genre paintings I'm embarking with some trepidation on this style which has been employed by artists of the first rank. Perhaps I'm being foolhardy and I'm afraid it may prove a complete disaster. ...

Camille Pissarro to Théodore Duret

Pontoise, 12 June 1875

Paul Cézanne from *Paul Cézanne* by Joachim Gasquet (1921)

'I, too, have been an Impressionist. Pissarro had an enormous influence on me, but I wanted to make of Impressionism something solid and lasting like the art in a museum.'

Camille Pissarro to Eugène Murer

Pontoise, Wednesday, 1878

... It is no longer bearable. Everything I do ends in failure ... When will I get out of this mess and be able to give myself with tranquillity to my work? My studies are made without method, without gaiety, without spirit because of my feeling that I must abandon art and try to do something else – if it is possible to serve a new apprenticeship. Sad!

Claude Monet to Ernest Hoschedé

Vétheuil, 14 May 1879

I don't know if the weather in Paris is the same as here, though it's quite likely it is, so you can imagine how dispirited I am. My heart is heavy and I have to share the burden of my disappointments with you. For almost two months now I have been struggling away with no result. You may have some reason to doubt this, perhaps, but it's a fact. I didn't waste an hour and would have reproached myself for taking even one day off to go and see our exhibition, for fear of nothing more than the loss of one good working session, an hour's sunshine. No one but myself knows the anxiety I go through and the trouble I give myself to finish paintings which do not satisfy me and seem to please so very few others. I am utterly discouraged and can no longer see or hope for a way ahead. I have just been jolted into this realization; I have to come to terms with the fact that I cannot hope to earn enough with my paintings to live in Vétheuil. That is the sad fact of the matter. Moreover, I can't imagine that we are very good company for Madame Hoschedé and yourself, with me becoming increasingly bitter ...

From *Renoir, My Father* by Jean Renoir (1962)

From Louveciennes to La Grenouillère it was only an hour's walk. Renoir had made friends with the Fournaise family [...]

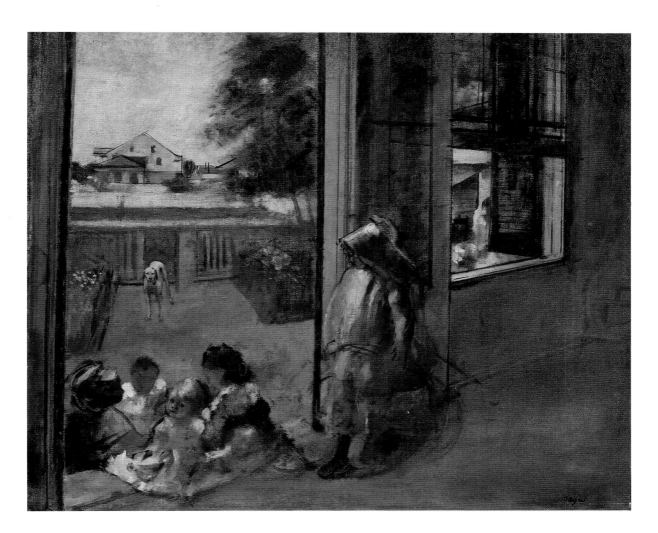

Degas
Children on the Steps,
New Orleans 1872–3

Paul Cézanne to his mother

[Paris], 26 September 1874

Pissarro hasn't been in Paris for about a month and a half – he's in Brittany, but I know he has a high opinion of me, who have a pretty high opinion of myself. I'm beginning to look upon myself as more gifted than all those around me, and you know that the good opinion I have when it comes to myself is the result only of careful deliberation. I have to work the whole time, not in order to reach that degree of perfection which is what wins the admiration of imbeciles. – And this thing that people commonly set so much store by is no more than the product of craftsmanship, and it means that every work resulting from it is unartistic and banal. I must only seek to complete a work for the truer, wiser pleasure of doing. And believe me, there is always a time when one wins recognition, and one has admirers who are a good deal more fervent, more convinced than those who are only drawn by a vain appearance.

It's a very bad time for selling, the middle classes are all distinctly reluctant to let go of their sous, but that state of affairs will come to an end . . .

Camille Pissarro to Théodore Duret

Pontoise, 20 October 1874

This is to let you know that I'm off to stay with my friend Piette and I shan't be back before January. I'm going there to study figures and animals in the real country . . .

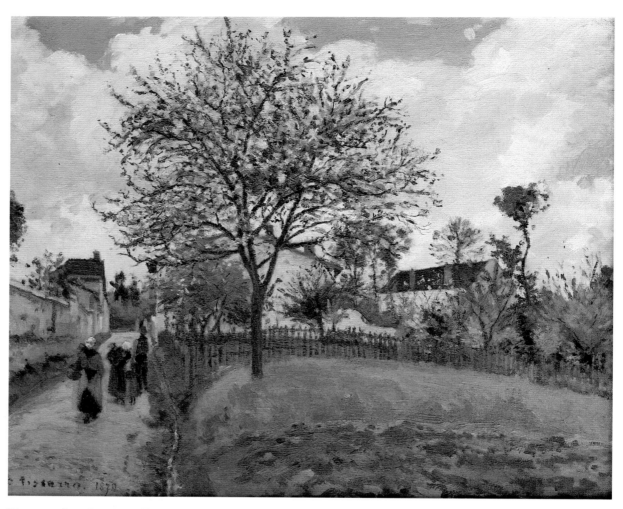

Pissarro *Landscape at Louveciennes* 1870

Camille Pissarro to Théodore Duret

Montfoucault, 11 December 1874

... I have done quite a lot of work here and got going on figures and animals. Although I have a number of ideas for genre paintings I'm embarking with some trepidation on this style which has been employed by artists of the first rank. Perhaps I'm being foolhardy and I'm afraid it may prove a complete disaster....

Camille Pissarro to Théodore Duret

Pontoise, 12 June 1875

... I've been wanting to do a large picture of figures out of doors, as you suggest, but wanting isn't enough. There's no dearth of subjects, the hardest thing is finding a suitable model who is willing to pose. Alas, it would only take money and that is just what I don't have. One should never think of doing a serious picture without models, especially the kind of picture I'm interested in. Don't worry though, when the occasion arises I'll seize it and carry out my plan. Meanwhile I'm working on it.

In preparation I did a little genre painting for Faure, things seem to be going well for him ...

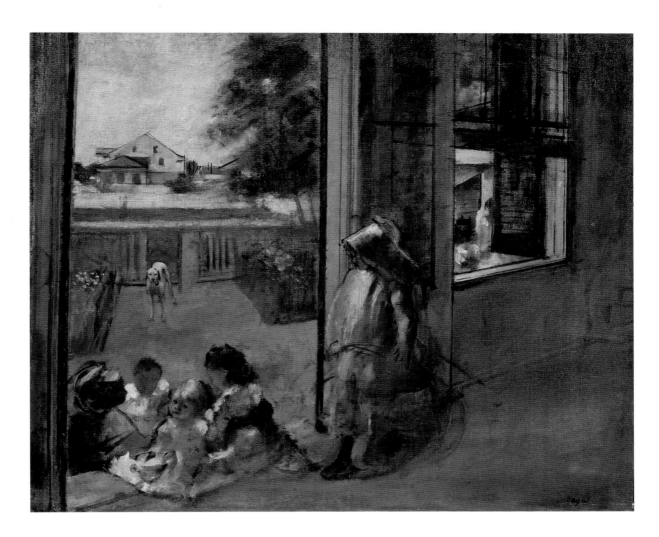

Degas
Children on the Steps,
New Orleans 1872–3

Paul Cézanne to his mother

[Paris], *26 September 1874*

Pissarro hasn't been in Paris for about a month and a half – he's in Brittany, but I know he has a high opinion of me, who have a pretty high opinion of myself. I'm beginning to look upon myself as more gifted than all those around me, and you know that the good opinion I have when it comes to myself is the result only of careful deliberation. I have to work the whole time, not in order to reach that degree of perfection which is what wins the admiration of imbeciles. – And this thing that people commonly set so much store by is no more than the product of craftsmanship, and it means that every work resulting from it is unartistic and banal. I must only seek to complete a work for the truer, wiser pleasure of doing. And believe me, there is always a time when one wins recognition, and one has admirers who are a good deal more fervent, more convinced than those who are only drawn by a vain appearance.

It's a very bad time for selling, the middle classes are all distinctly reluctant to let go of their sous, but that state of affairs will come to an end . . .

Camille Pissarro to Théodore Duret

Pontoise, 20 October 1874

This is to let you know that I'm off to stay with my friend Piette and I shan't be back before January. I'm going there to study figures and animals in the real country . . .

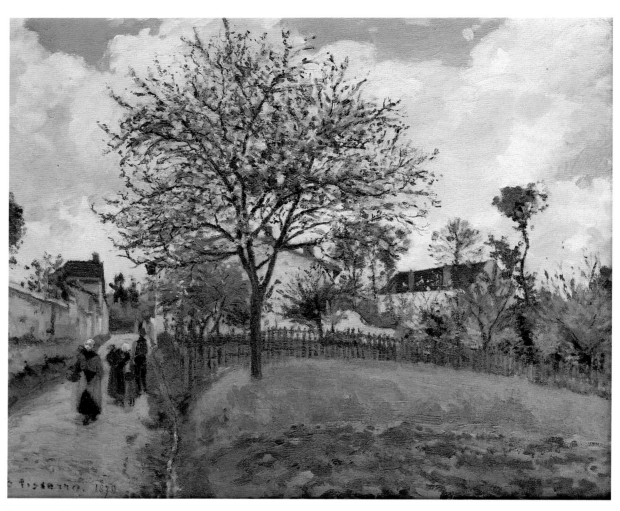

Pissarro *Landscape at Louveciennes* 1870

Camille Pissarro to Théodore Duret

Montfoucault, 11 December 1874

... I have done quite a lot of work here and got going on figures and animals. Although I have a number of ideas for genre paintings I'm embarking with some trepidation on this style which has been employed by artists of the first rank. Perhaps I'm being foolhardy and I'm afraid it may prove a complete disaster....

Camille Pissarro to Théodore Duret

Pontoise, 12 June 1875

... I've been wanting to do a large picture of figures out of doors, as you suggest, but wanting isn't enough. There's no dearth of subjects, the hardest thing is finding a suitable model who is willing to pose. Alas, it would only take money and that is just what I don't have. One should never think of doing a serious picture without models, especially the kind of picture I'm interested in. Don't worry though, when the occasion arises I'll seize it and carry out my plan. Meanwhile I'm working on it.

In preparation I did a little genre painting for Faure, things seem to be going well for him ...

Paul Cézanne to Camille Pissarro

l'Estaque, 2 July 1876

I'd very much like not to talk about impossibilities, and yet I'm always planning to do things that have very little likelihood of being achieved. I imagine the countryside I'm in would be just the kind of thing you like most.... I've started two little motifs which include the sea in them, for M. Chocquet, who'd spoken to me about it. – It's like a playing card. Red roofs against the blue sea. If the weather turns favourable, maybe I'll be able to carry them through to completion. With things as they are I haven't yet done anything. – But there are some motifs that would require three or four months' work, which one might be able to do, for the vegetation doesn't change here. There are olive trees and pines which always keep their leaves. The sun here is so tremendous it seems to me that when things stand out in silhouette it's not just in black or white, but in blue, in red, in brown, in violet. I may be mistaken, but it seems to me to be the very opposite of modelling. Wouldn't our gentle landscapists from Auvers be happy here!...

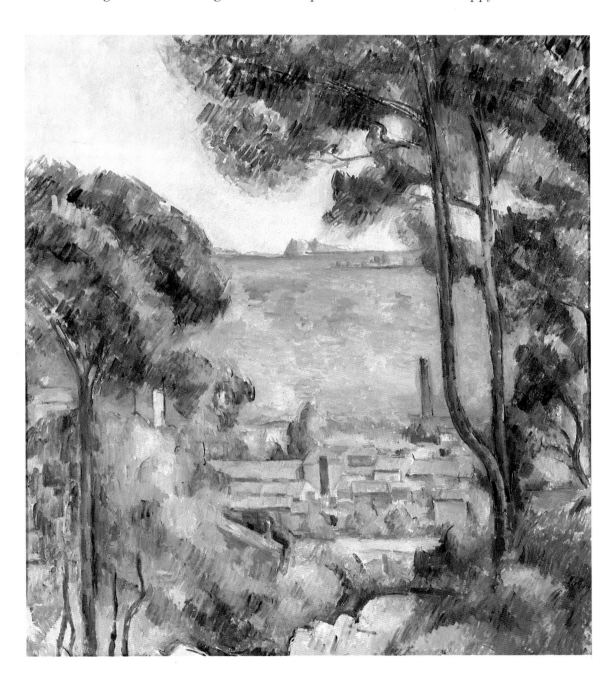

Cézanne
View of L'Estaque
1882–85

Paul Cézanne from *Paul Cézanne* by Joachim Gasquet (1921)

'I, too, have been an Impressionist. Pissarro had an enormous influence on me, but I wanted to make of Impressionism something solid and lasting like the art in a museum.'

Camille Pissarro to Eugène Murer

Pontoise, Wednesday, 1878

... It is no longer bearable. Everything I do ends in failure ... When will I get out of this mess and be able to give myself with tranquillity to my work? My studies are made without method, without gaiety, without spirit because of my feeling that I must abandon art and try to do something else – if it is possible to serve a new apprenticeship. Sad!

Claude Monet to Ernest Hoschedé

Vétheuil, 14 May 1879

I don't know if the weather in Paris is the same as here, though it's quite likely it is, so you can imagine how dispirited I am. My heart is heavy and I have to share the burden of my disappointments with you. For almost two months now I have been struggling away with no result. You may have some reason to doubt this, perhaps, but it's a fact. I didn't waste an hour and would have reproached myself for taking even one day off to go and see our exhibition, for fear of nothing more than the loss of one good working session, an hour's sunshine. No one but myself knows the anxiety I go through and the trouble I give myself to finish paintings which do not satisfy me and seem to please so very few others. I am utterly discouraged and can no longer see or hope for a way ahead. I have just been jolted into this realization; I have to come to terms with the fact that I cannot hope to earn enough with my paintings to live in Vétheuil. That is the sad fact of the matter. Moreover, I can't imagine that we are very good company for Madame Hoschedé and yourself, with me becoming increasingly bitter...

From *Renoir, My Father* by Jean Renoir (1962)

From Louveciennes to La Grenouillère it was only an hour's walk. Renoir had made friends with the Fournaise family [who ran a restaurant]. Mme and Mlle Fournaise figure in several of his pictures. He also did a portrait of M. Fournaise.

The Fournaises would rarely give Renoir a bill.

'You've let us have this landscape of yours,' they would say.

My father would insist that his painting had no value: 'I'm giving you fair warning; nobody wants it.'

'What difference does that make? It's pretty, isn't it? We have to put something up on the walls to hide those patches of damp.'

My father smiled as he thought of those kind people again.

'If all art-lovers were like that!'

He was to give them a number of pictures which later became immensely valuable.

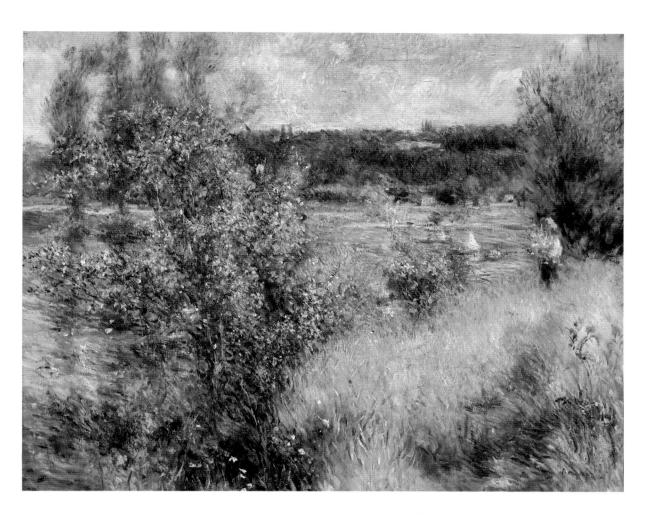

Renoir
The Seine at Chatou
c.1881

Pierre-Auguste Renoir from *Renoir* by Ambroise Vollard (1920)

'It was a perpetual holiday – and what an assortment of people! You could still enjoy yourself in those days! Machinery didn't take up the whole of life; there was a time for living, and we made the most of it. The only unpleasant thing about the Seine at that time (nowadays it's so clean) was the dead animals which came floating down. . . .
I used to spend a lot of time at Fournaise's, I found as many magnificent girls to paint as I wanted; in those days one wasn't reduced to following a little model around for an hour and then being treated as a disgusting old man at the end of it. . . .'

Le Jour et La Nuit

Edgar Degas to Félix Bracquemond

13 May 1879

I spoke to Caillebotte about the journal. He is willing to guarantee for us. Come and talk it over with me. No time to lose! . . . We must be quick and make the most of our gains boldly [each exhibitor to the Fourth Impressionist show had made a profit of 440 francs] . . . Do find time to spend a day with me. There are a number of things to be fixed . . . for our journal so that we can show the capitalists some definite programme.

From the notebooks of Ludovic Halévy

16 May 1879

Visit to Degas. I met him in the company of *l'indépendante* Mlle Cassatt, one of the exhibitors of the rue de la Paix [where the Fourth exhibition was held]. They are excited. Each has a profit of 440 francs from their exhibition. They are thinking of launching a journal; I ask to write for it.

From the notebooks of Edgar Degas (Number 30)

[May 1879]

For the *Journal* – Crop a great deal – do a dancer's arms or the legs, or the back – do the shoes ...

Do in aquatint a series on *mourning* (different blacks) – black veils of heavy mourning flowing over the face – black gloves – mourning coaches, carriages of the Funerary Association – vehicles comparable to Venetian gondolas. . . .

Do all kinds of objects in use, placed, associated etc. corsets ... violinists' hands etc. . . .

Edgar Degas to Henri Rouart

[Autumn 1879]

. . . always articles to fabricate, the last is a monochrome fan for Monsieur Beugniet. I think only of prints and make none. . . .

Edgar Degas to Félix Bracquemond

[1879 or 1880]

How I need to see you, Braquemond, and how badly I let you down!

. . . We must discuss the journal. Pissarro and I together made various attempts of which one by Pissarro is a success. At the moment Mlle Cassatt is full of it. Impossible for me, with my living to earn, to devote myself entirely to it as yet. So let us arrange to spend a whole day together, either here or at your house. – Have you a press at your place? Your wife is still preparing her exhibition, is she not?

Edgar Degas to Camille Pissarro

[Paris, 1880]

. . . Mlle Cassatt is trying her hand at etching engravings, they are charming. Try and come back soon. I am beginning to advertise the journal on all sides. With our issues of proofs before letters we will cover our expenses. That's what several print collectors have told me. . . .

Edgar Degas to Camille Pissarro

[1880]

I compliment you on your enthusiasm; I hurried to Mlle Cassatt with your parcel. She congratulates you, as do I in this matter.

Here are the proofs; the prevailing blackish or greyish shade comes from the zinc, which is greasy in itself and retains the printer's black. The plate is not smooth enough. I feel sure that you have not the same facilities at Pontoise as at the rue de la Huchette. In spite of that you must have something a bit more polished.

In any case you can see what possibilities there are in the technique. . . .

Mrs Cassatt [artist's mother] to Alexander Cassatt

Paris, 13 ave Trudaine, 9 April [1880]

. . . Degas, who is the leader, undertook to get up a journal of etchings and got them all to work for it so that Mary had no time for paintings and as usual with Degas when the time arrived to appear he wasn't ready, so *Le Jour et la Nuit* (the name of the publication) which might have been a great success has not yet appeared. Degas is never ready for anything. This time he has thrown away an excellent chance for all of them. . .

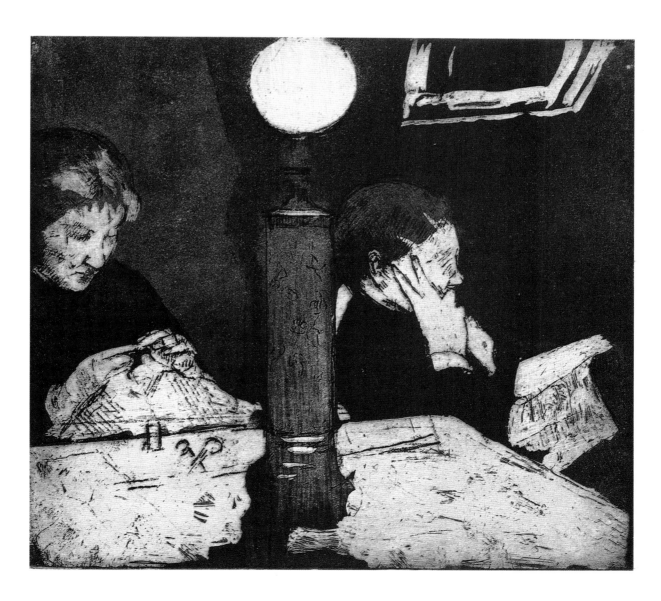

Cassatt
Under the Lamp 1875

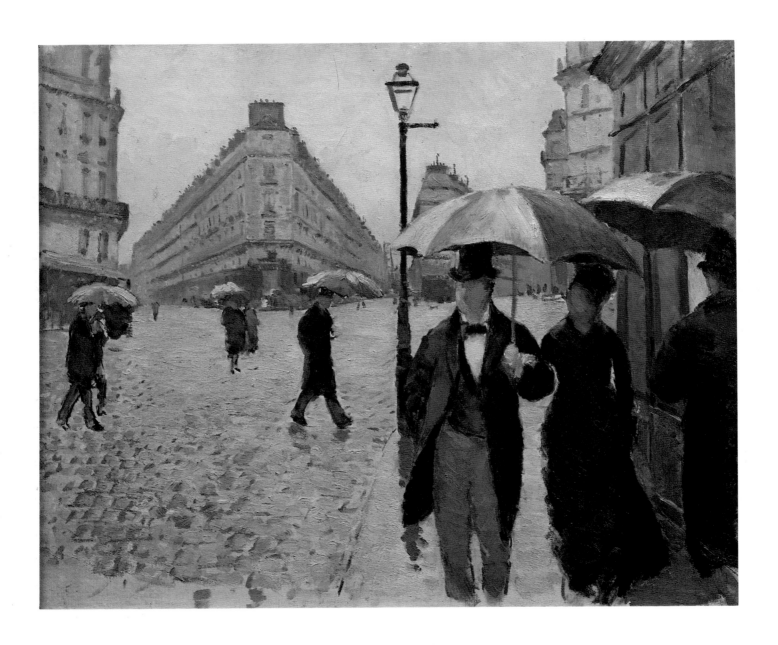

Caillebotte *Paris, A Rainy Day* 1877

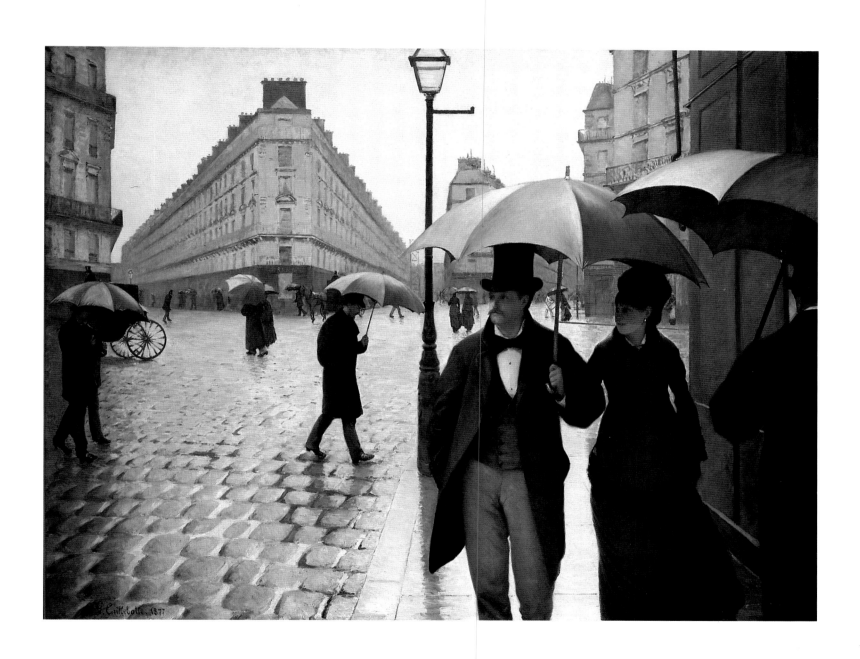

Caillebotte *Paris, A Rainy Day* 1876–77

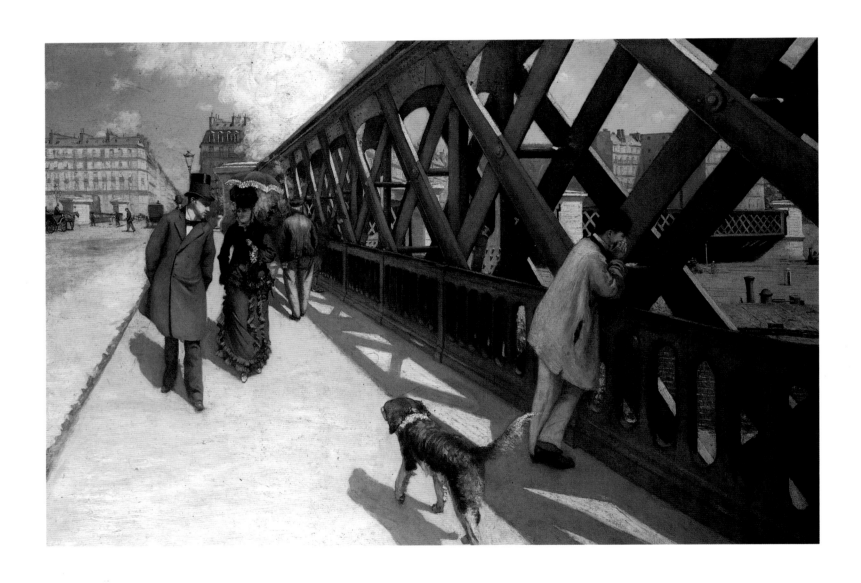

Caillebotte *Le Pont de l'Europe* 1876

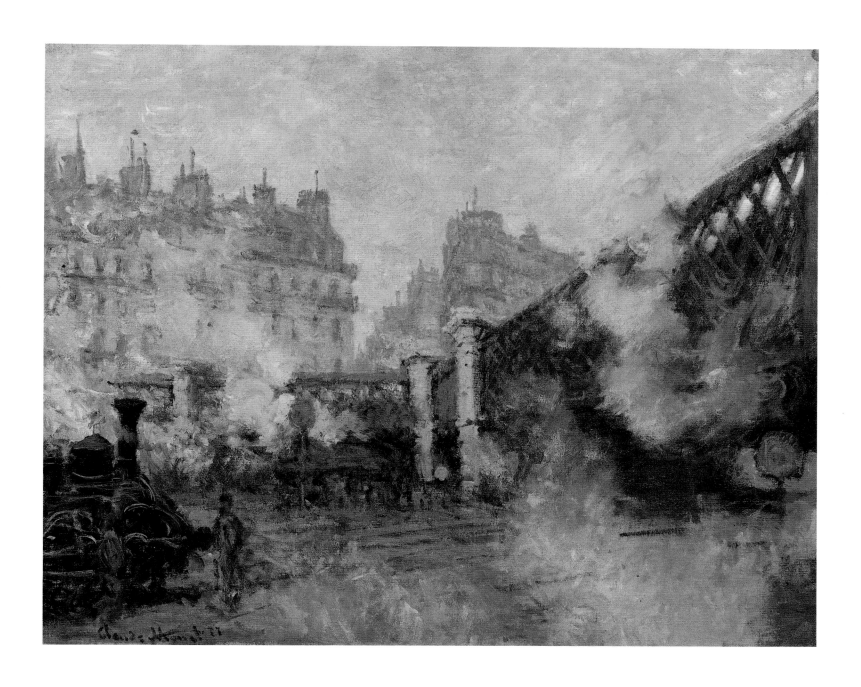

Monet *Le Pont de l'Europe, Gare St-Lazare*, 1877

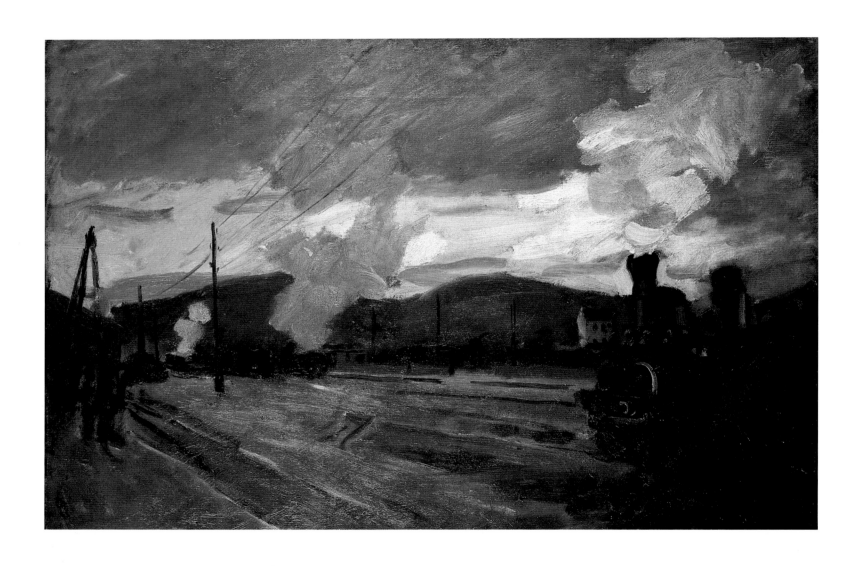

Monet *The Station at Argenteuil c.*1872

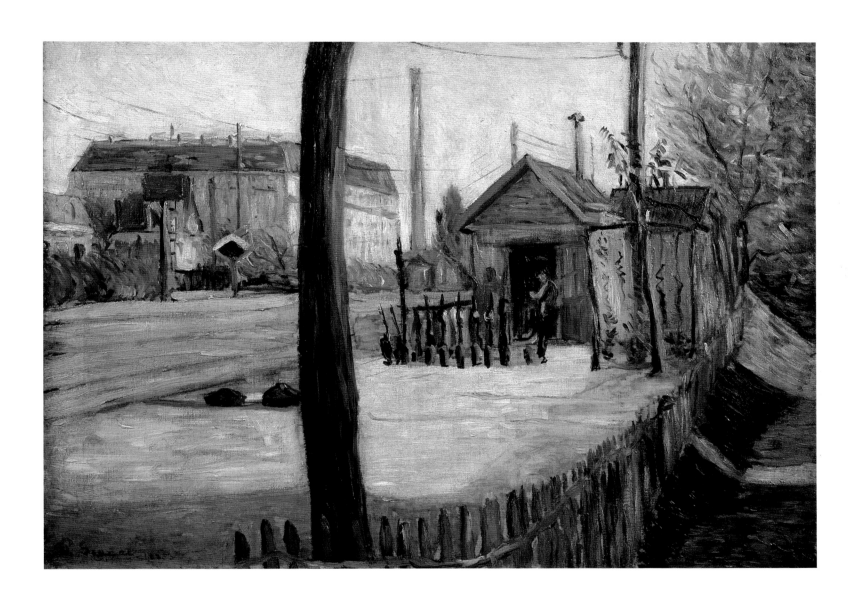

Signac *The Railway Junction at Bois-Colombes* 1886

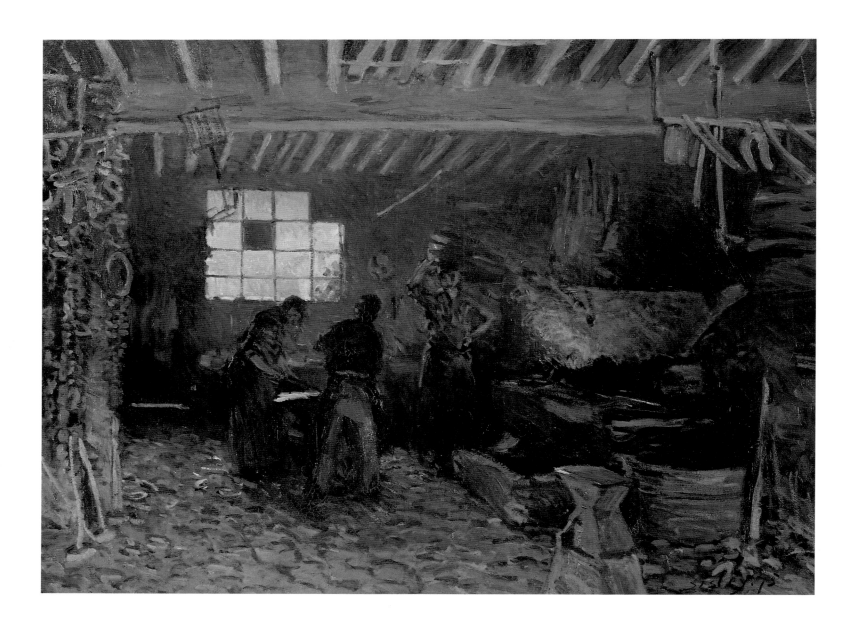

Sisley *The Forge at Marly* 1875

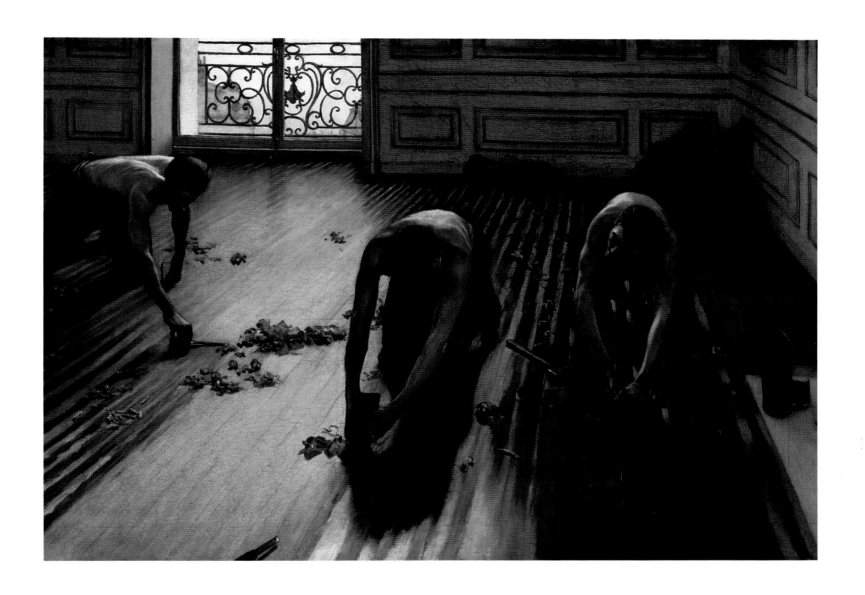

Caillebotte *The Floorscrapers* 1875

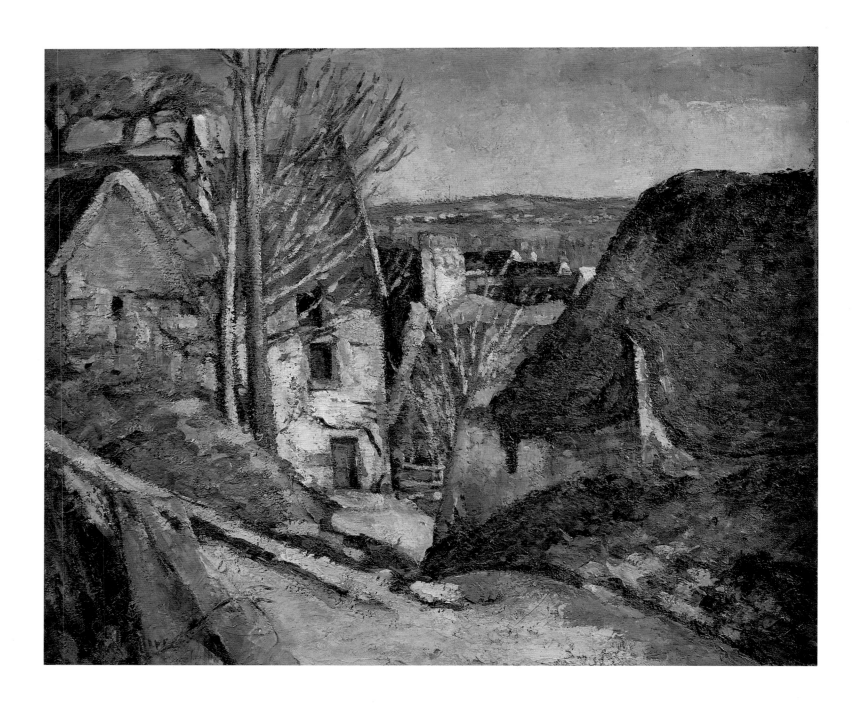

Cézanne *The House of the Hanged Man* 1873

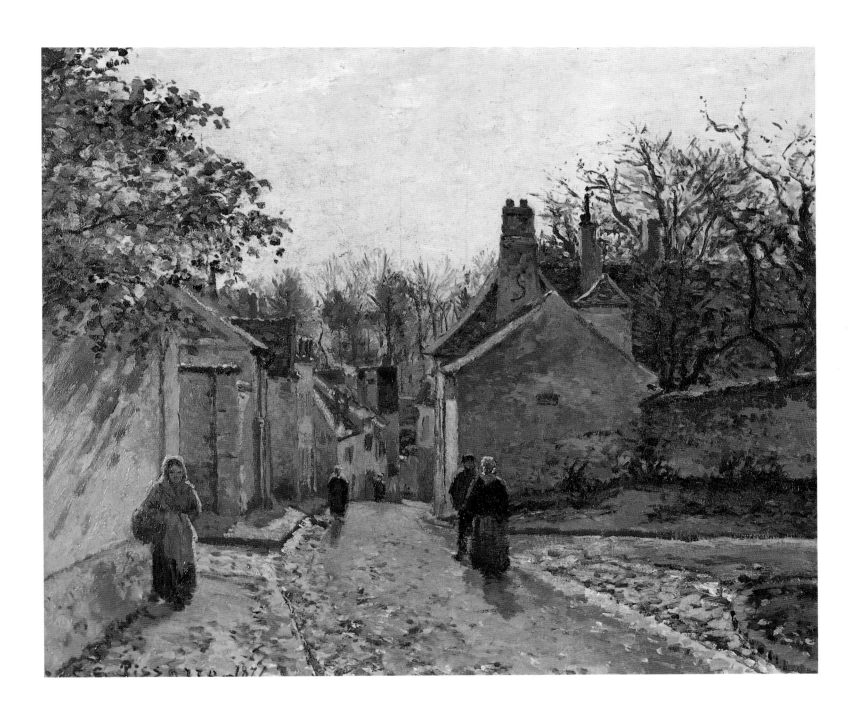

Pissarro *A Village Street, Louveciennes* 1871

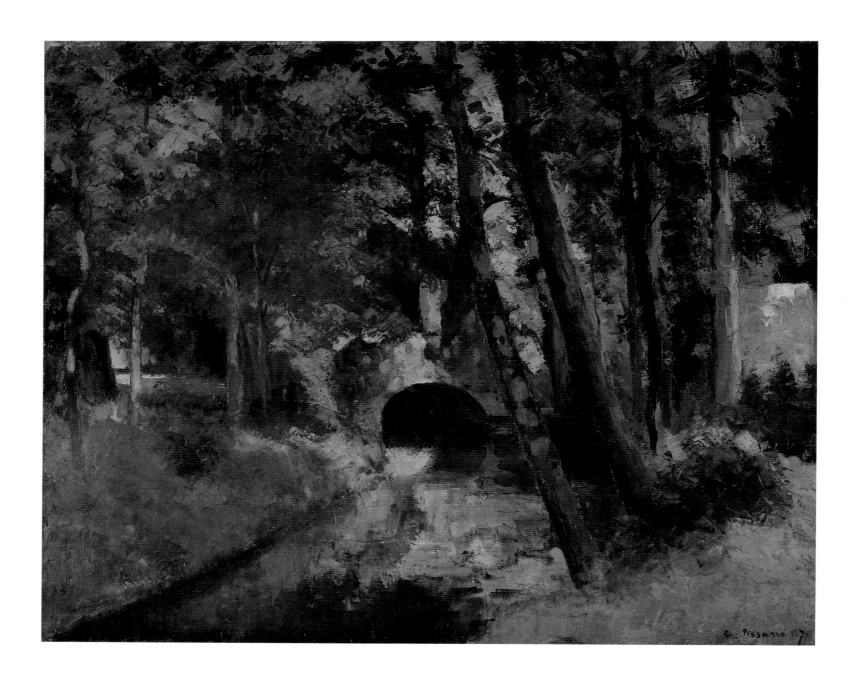

Pissarro *The Bridge at Pontoise* 1875

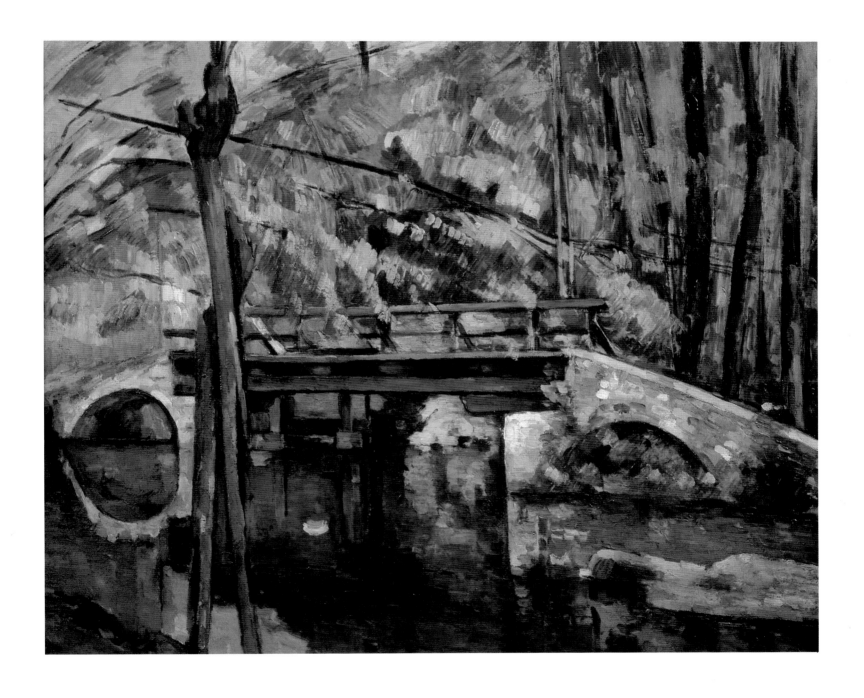

Cézanne *The Bridge at Maincy* 1875–9

Renoir
Coup de vent c.1872

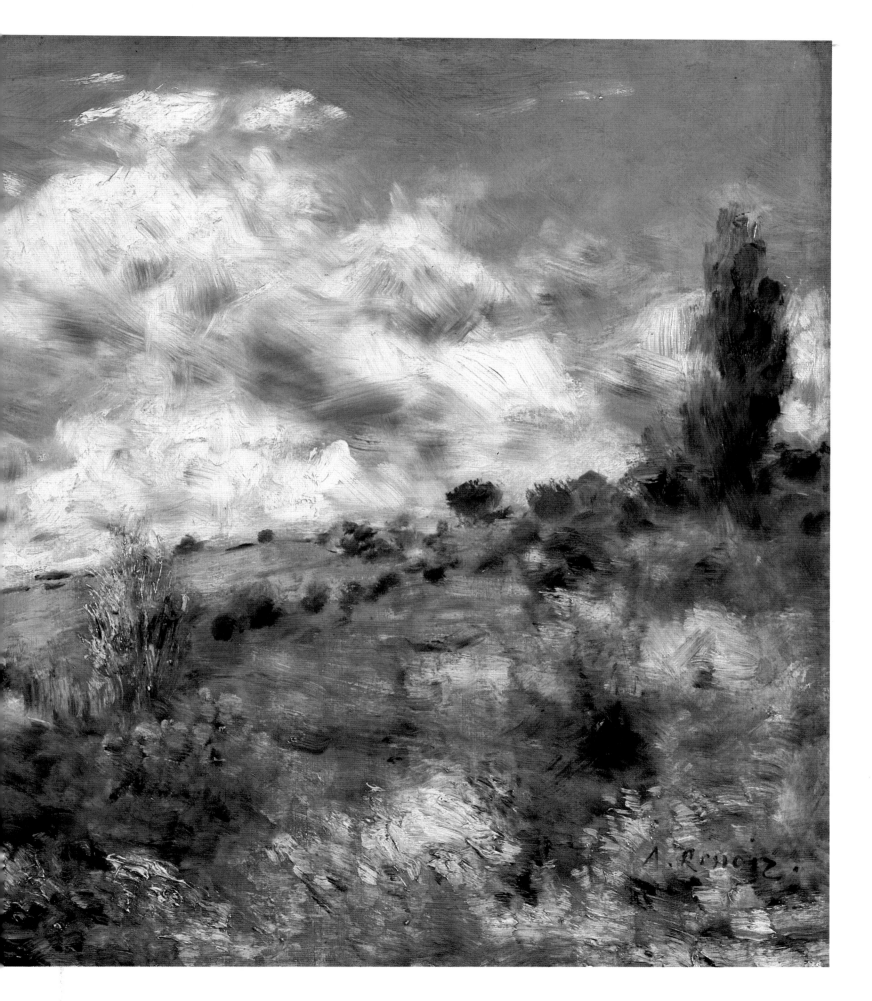

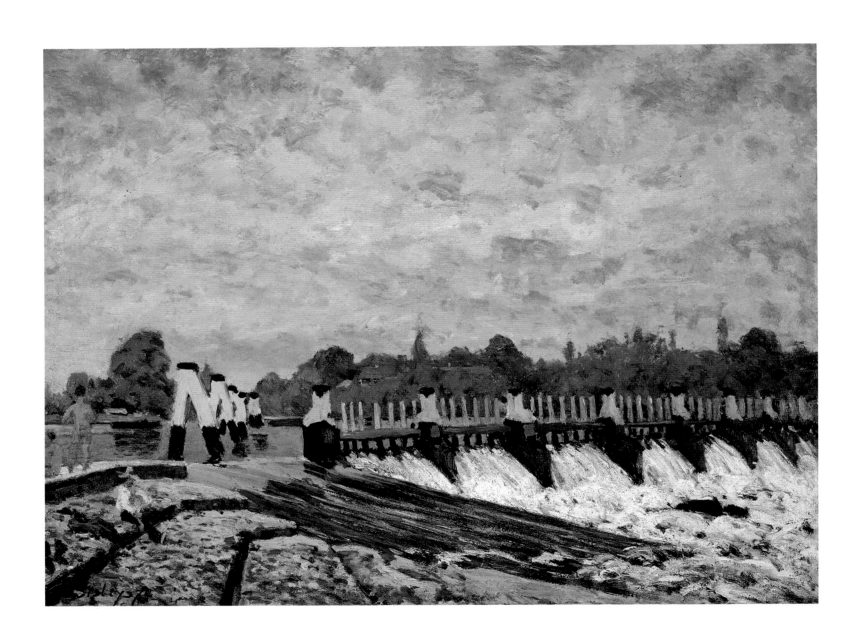

Sisley *Moseley Weir* 1874

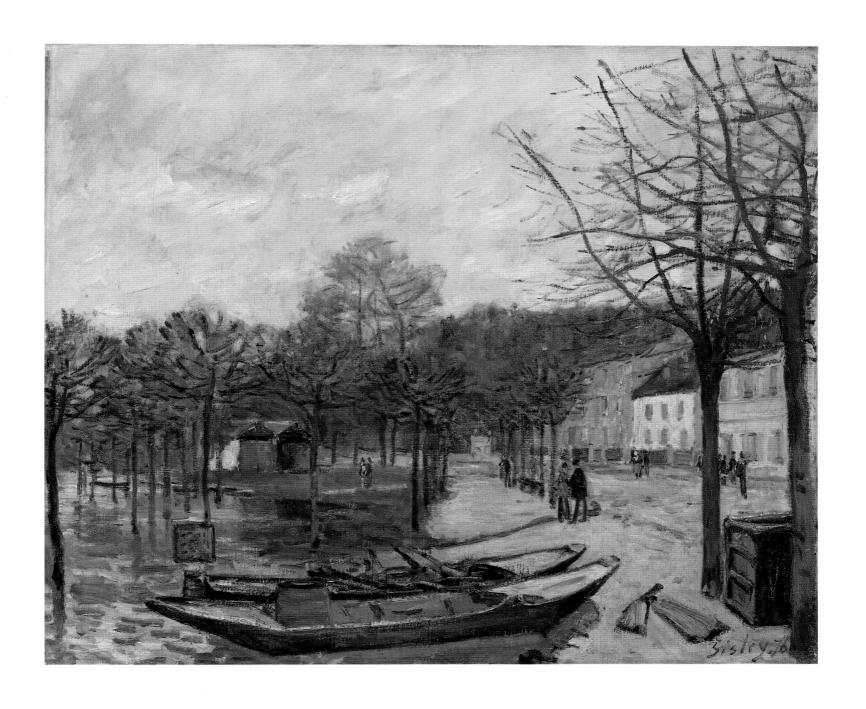

Sisley *Flood at Port Marly* 1876

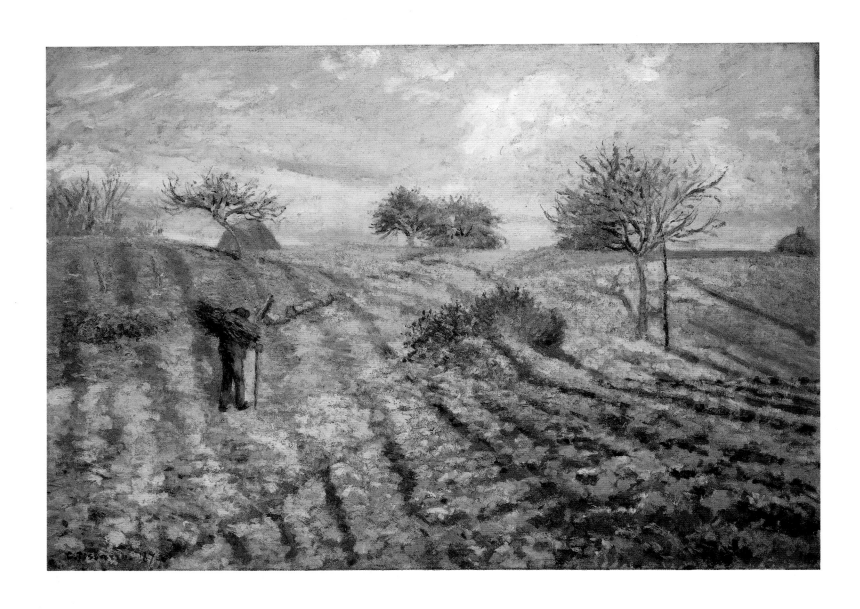

Pissarro *Hoarfrost* 1873

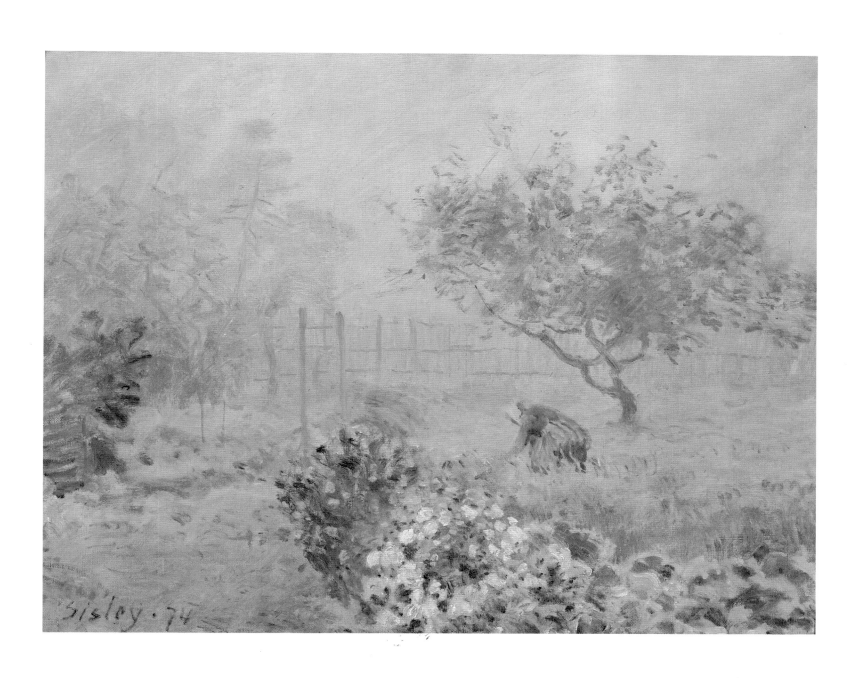

Sisley *Misty Morning* 1874

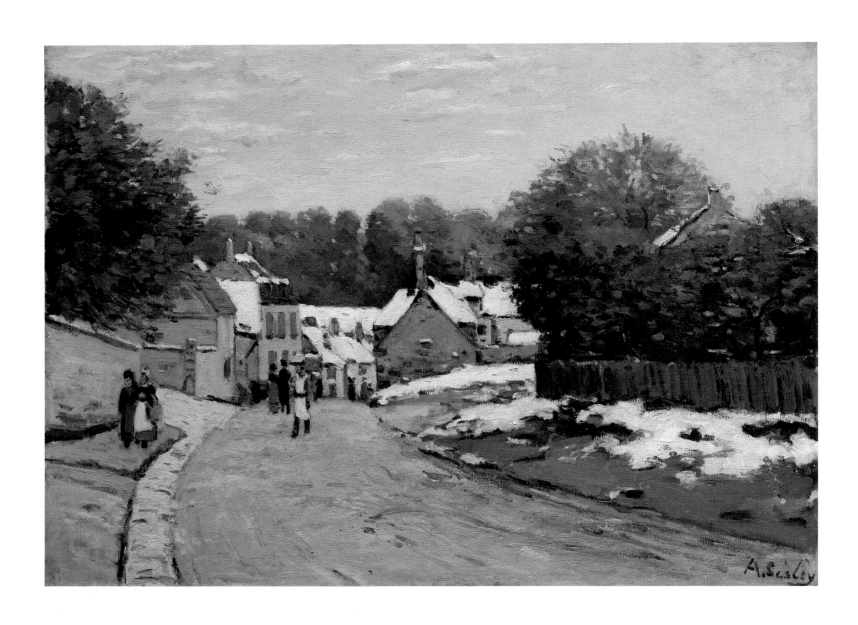

Sisley *Early Snow at Louveciennes c.*1871

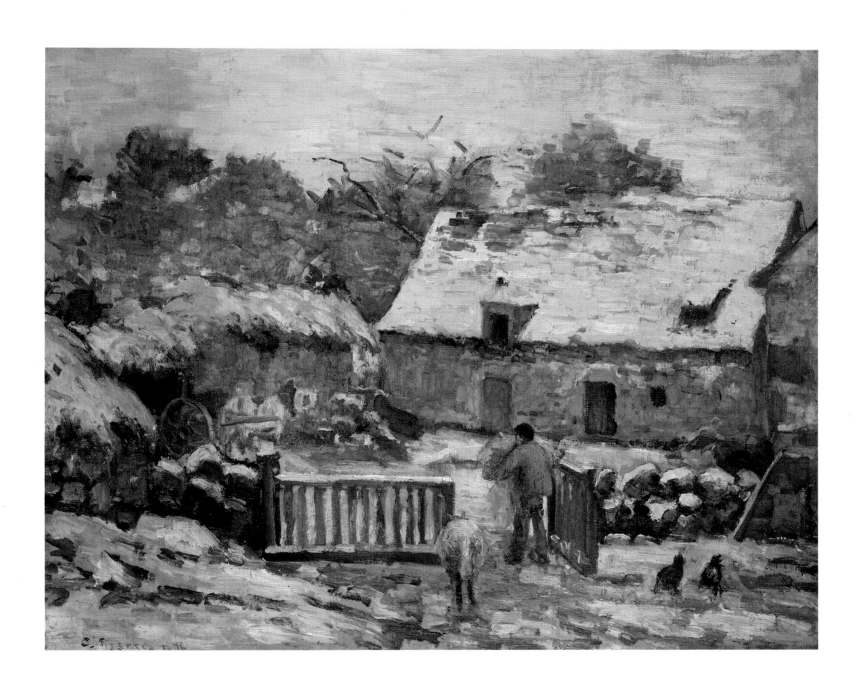

Pissarro *Farm at Montfoucault* 1876

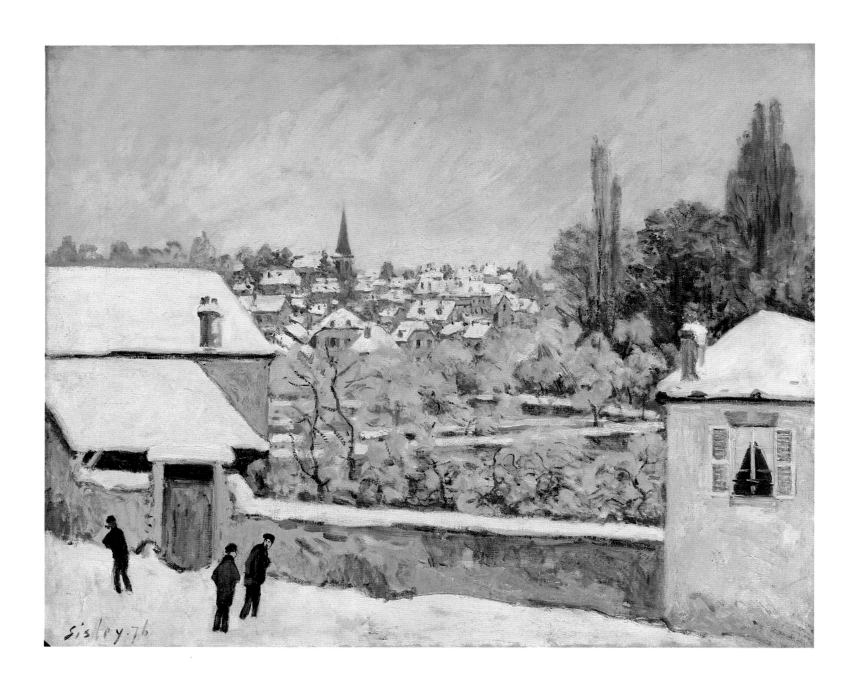

Sisley *Winter, Louveciennes* 1876

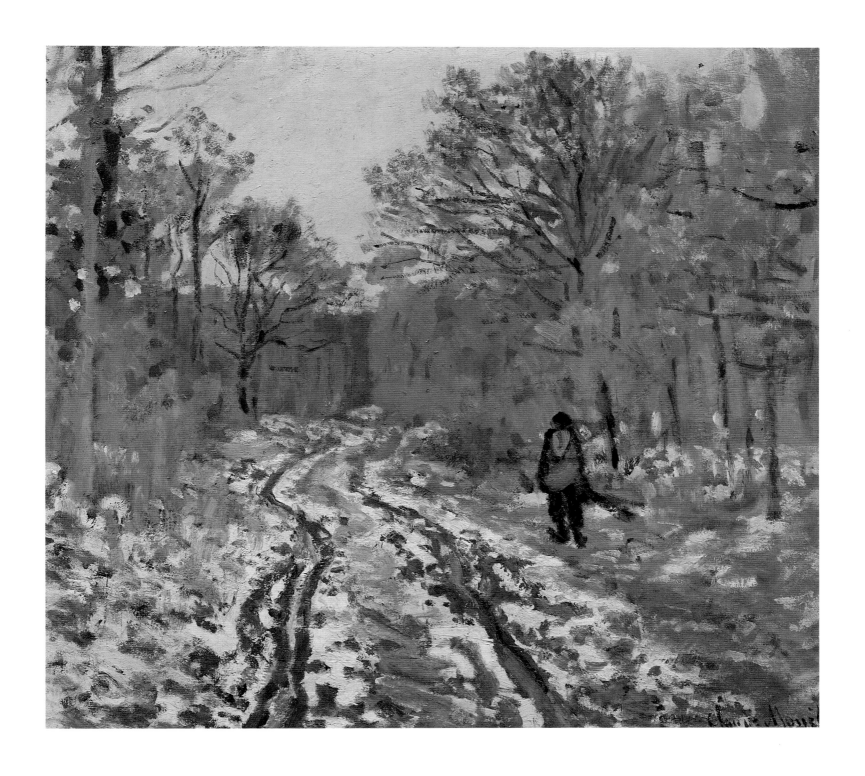

Monet *La forêt neige* 1869

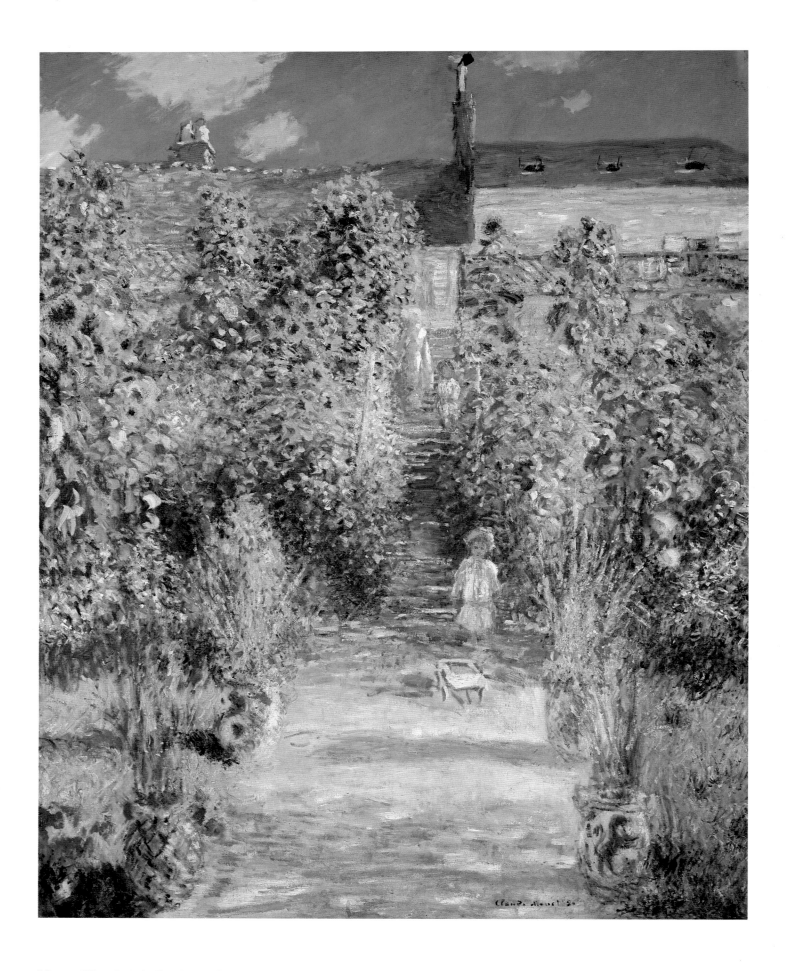

Monet *The Artist's Garden at Vétheuil* 1880

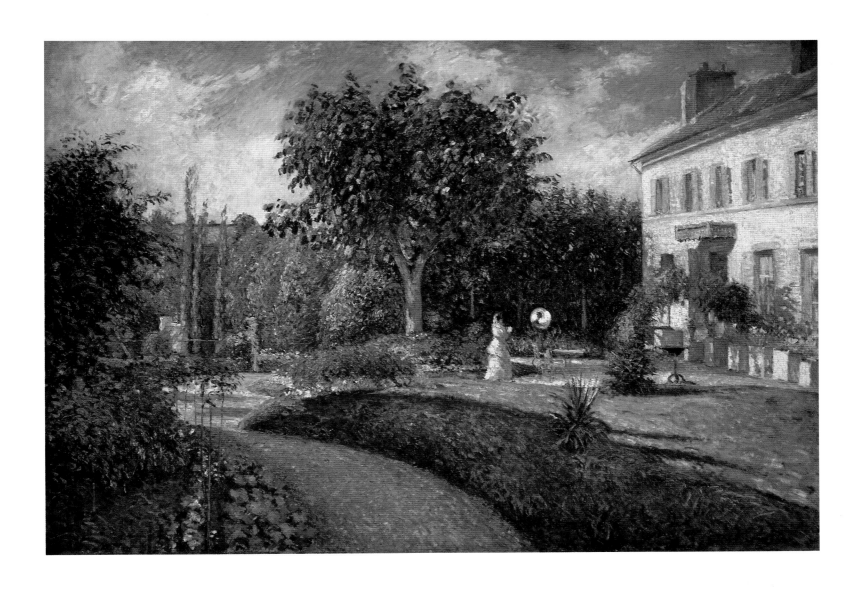

Pissarro *Garden of Les Mathurins at Pontoise* 1876

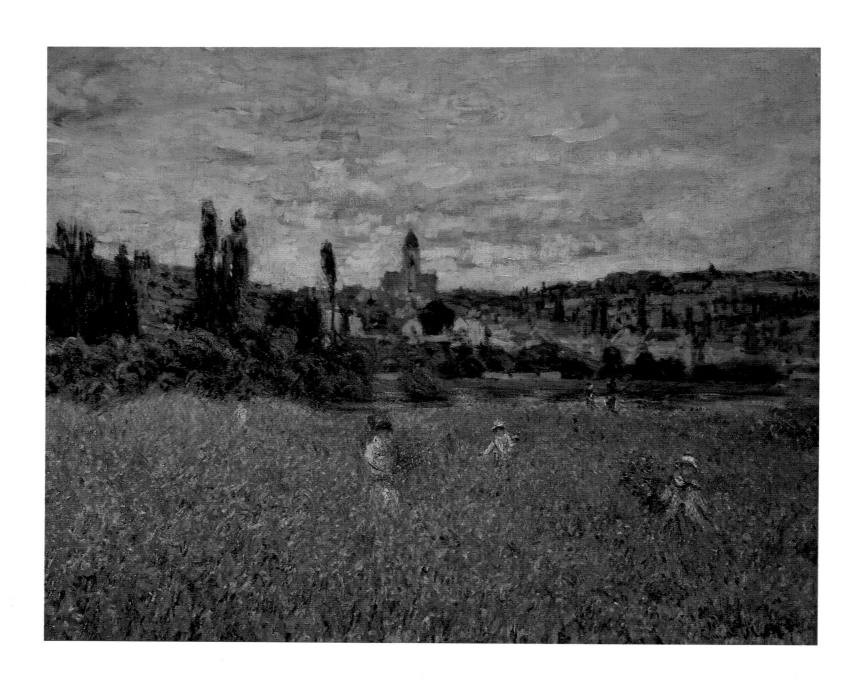

Monet *Poppyfield near Vétheuil c.*1880

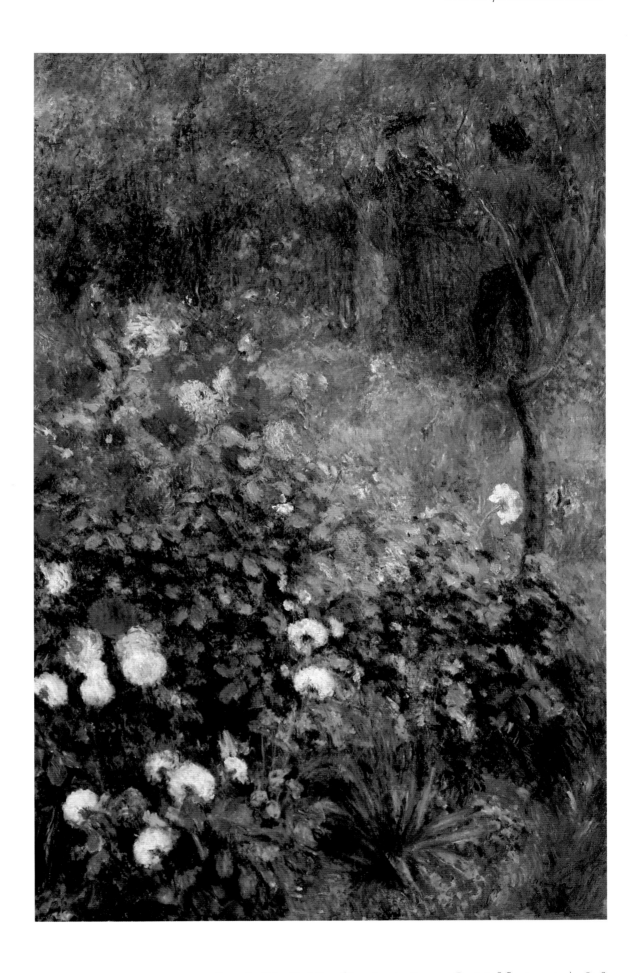

Renoir *The Dahlias (Garden in the rue Cortot, Montmartre)* 1876

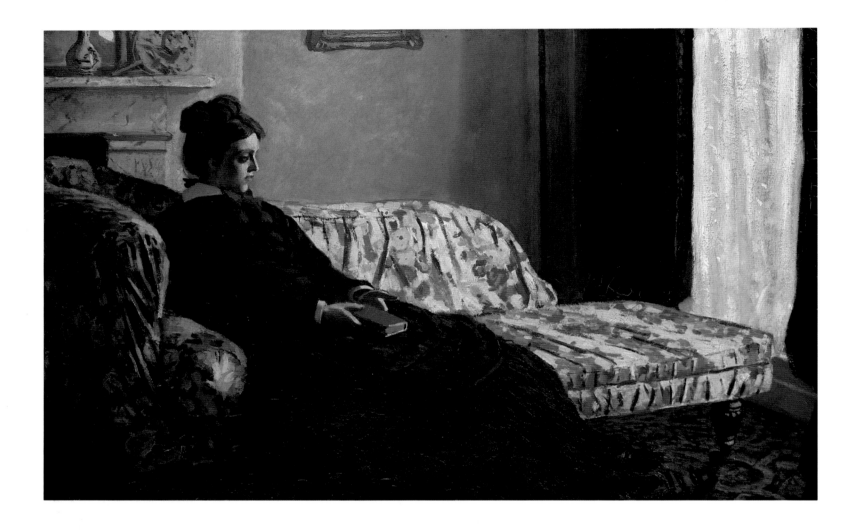

Monet *Mme Monet au canapé* 1871

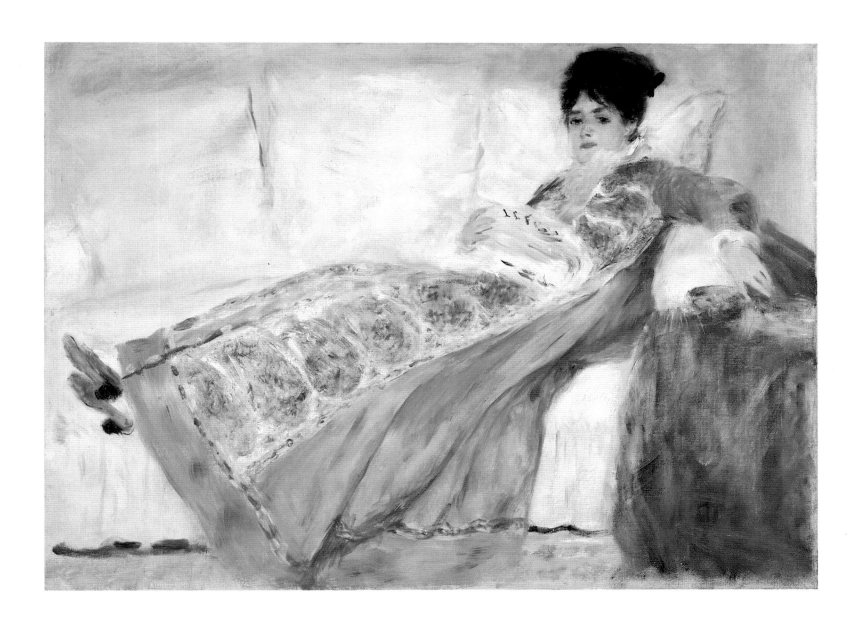

Renoir *Mme Monet reading Le Figaro* 1872

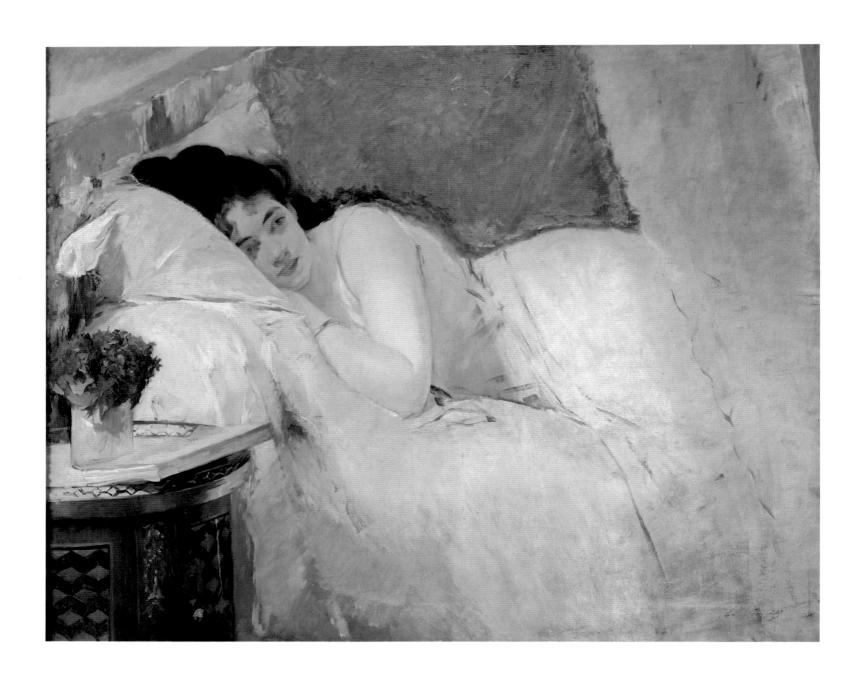

Eva Gonzalès *Morning Awakening* 1876

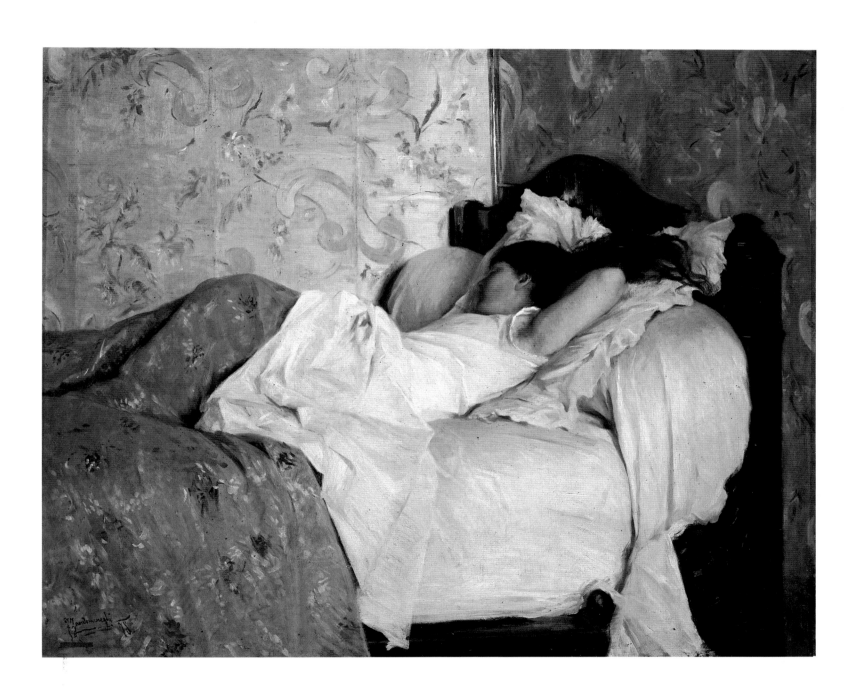

Zandomeneghi *In Bed* 1878

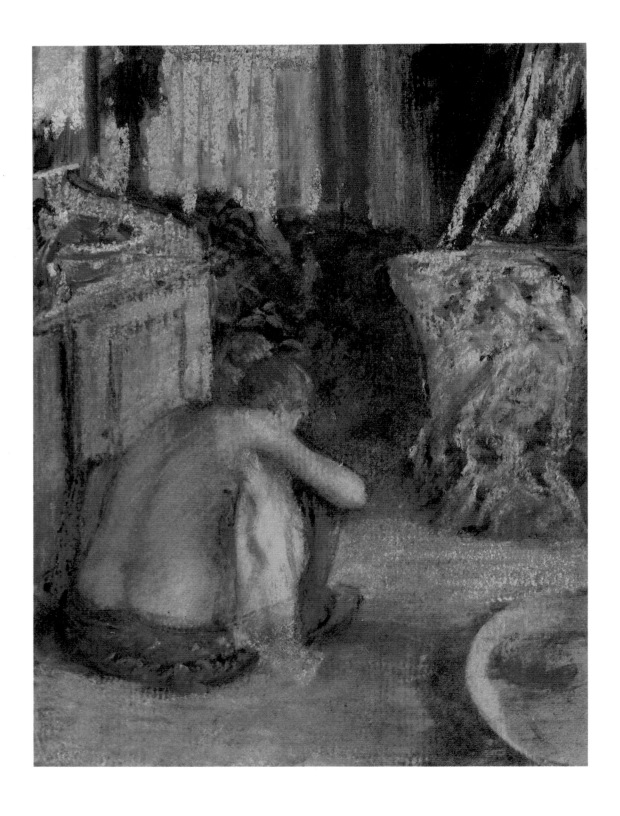

Degas *Squatting Nude* c.1876–7

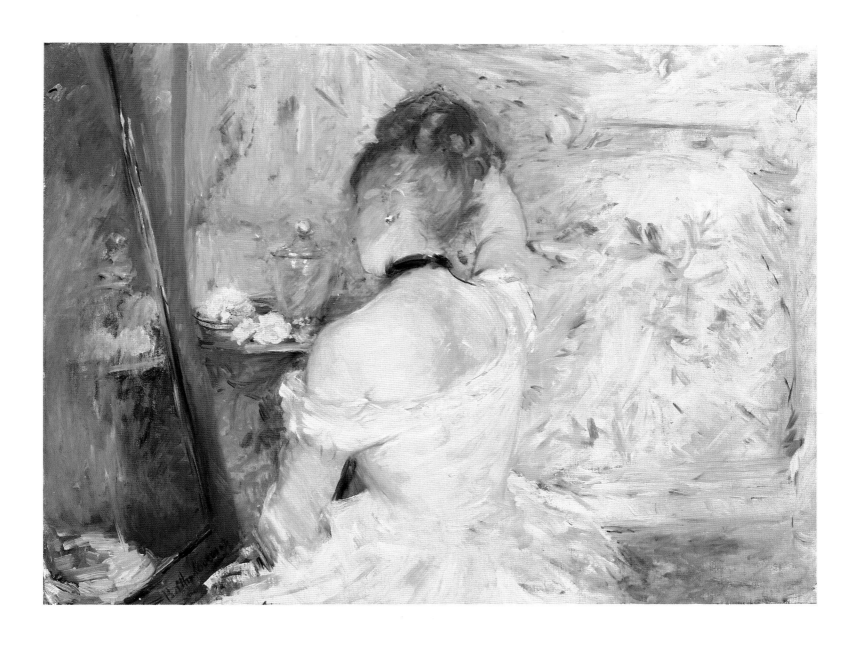

Morisot *Lady at her Toilette* c.1875

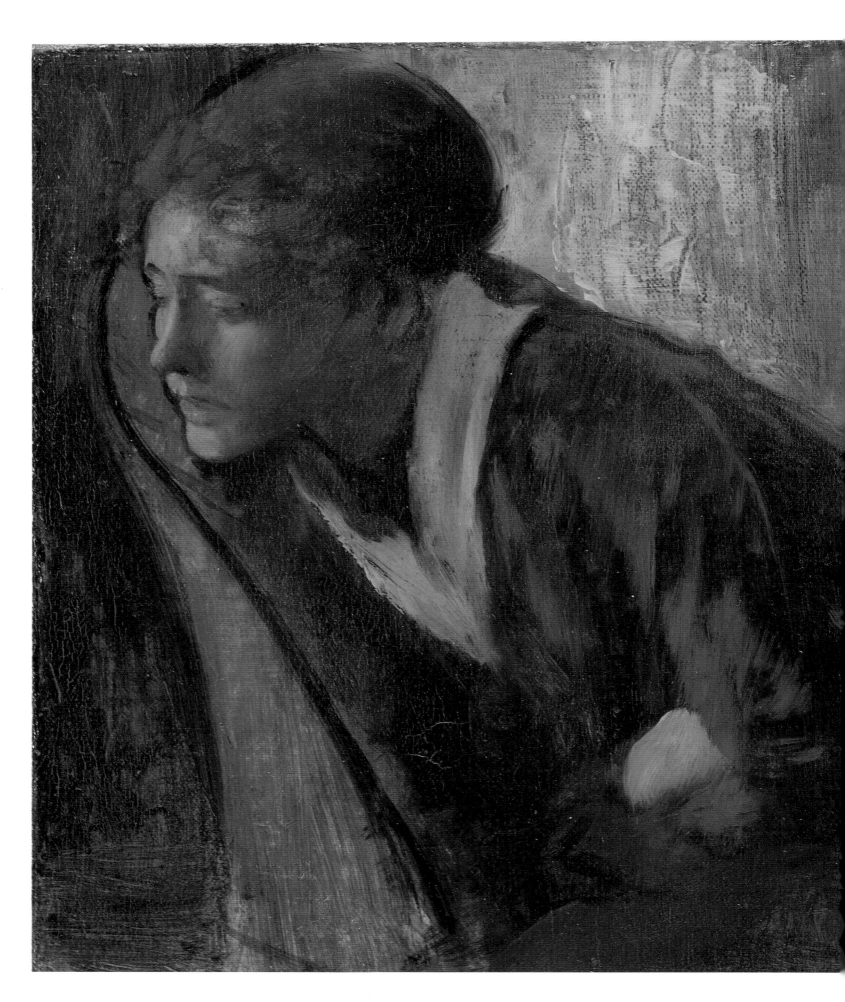

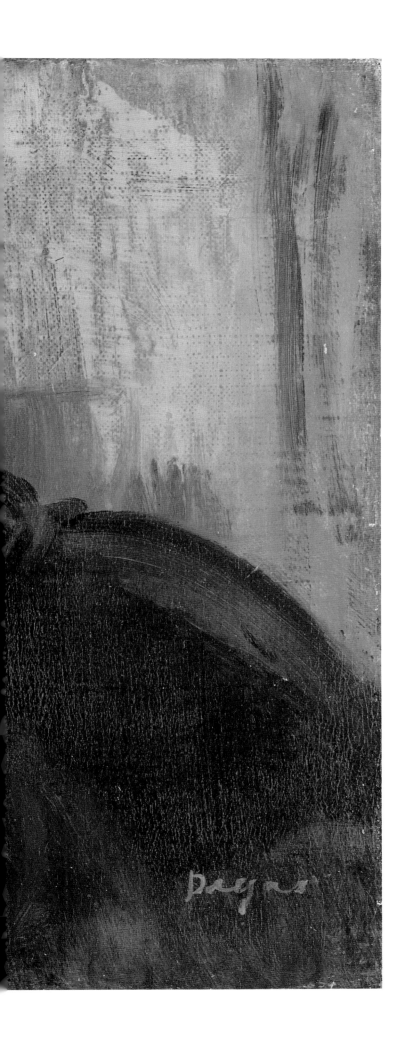

Degas *Melancholy* c.1874

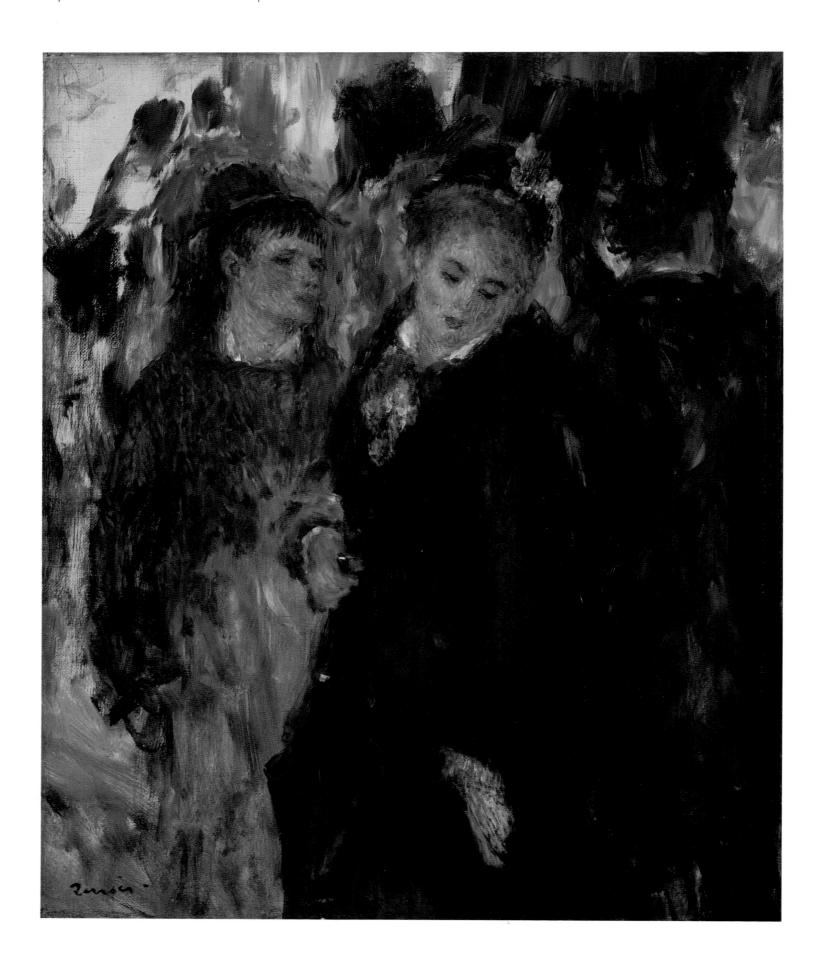

Renoir *In the Street* c.1877

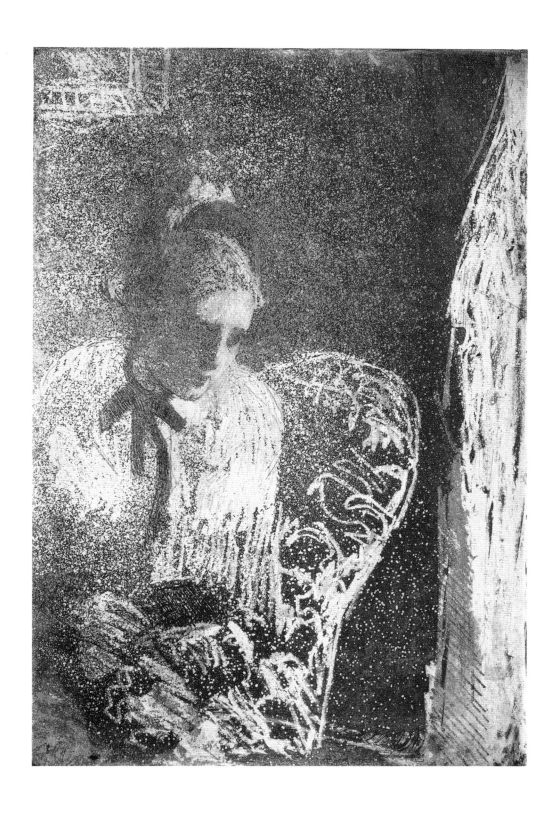

Cassatt *Waiting* 1880

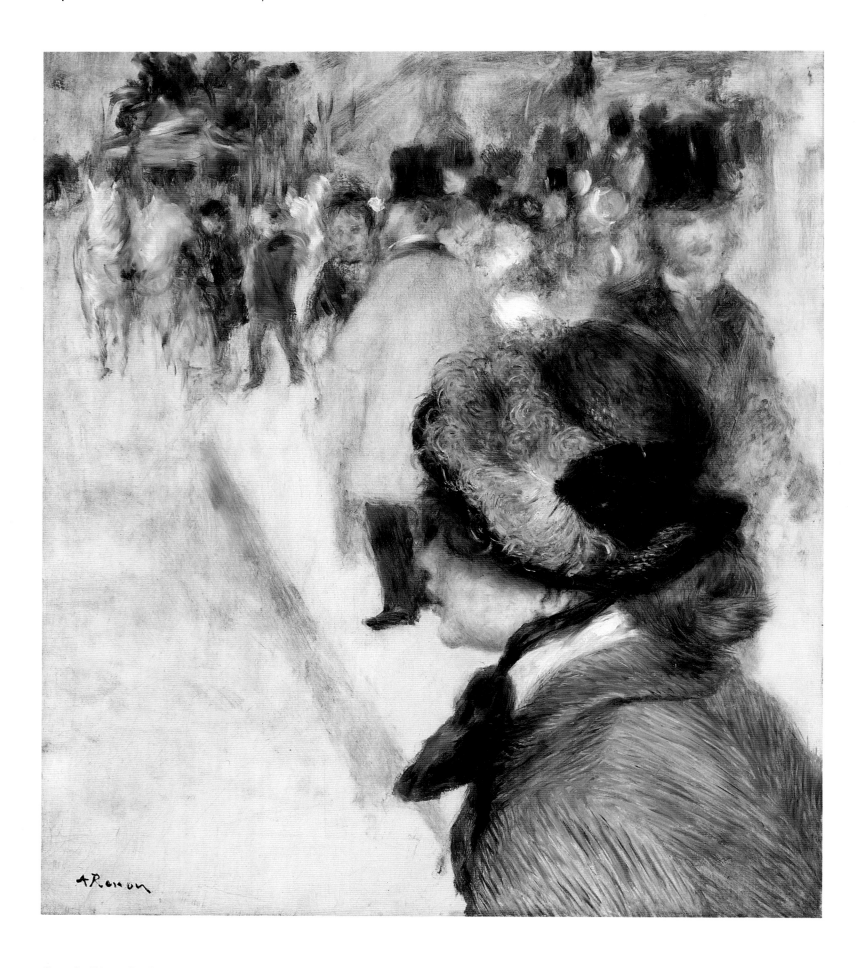

Renoir *Place Clichy* 1880

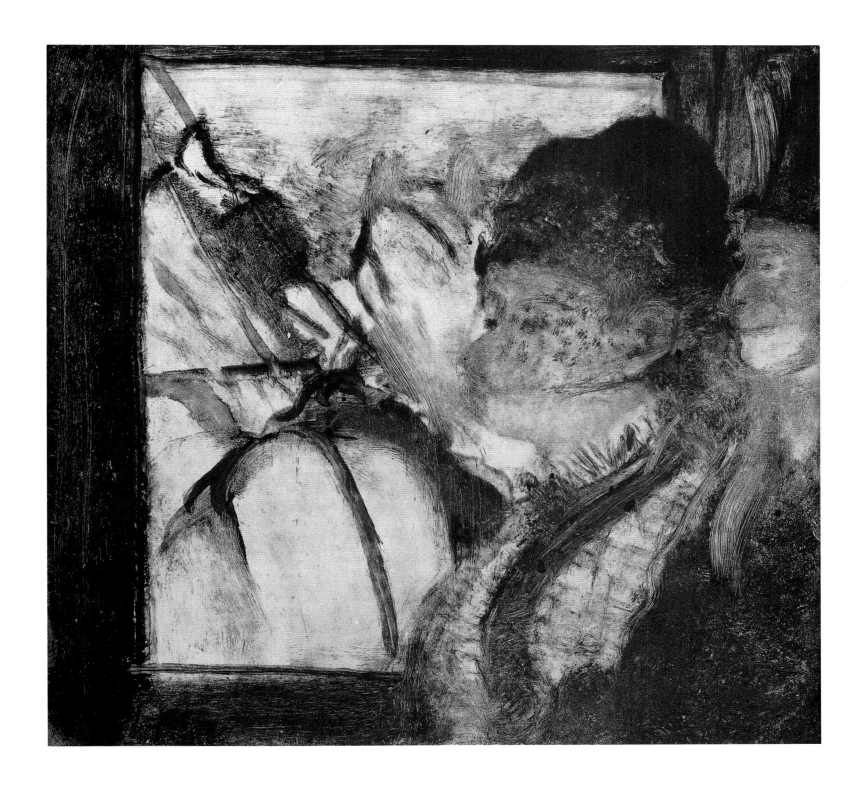

Degas *In the Omnibus* 1877–8

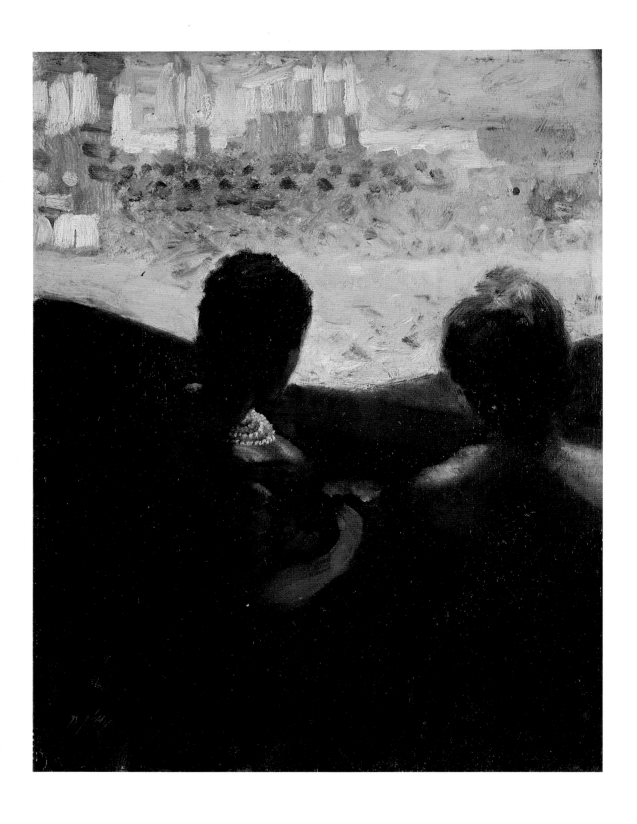

De Nittis *In the Opera Box* c.1876

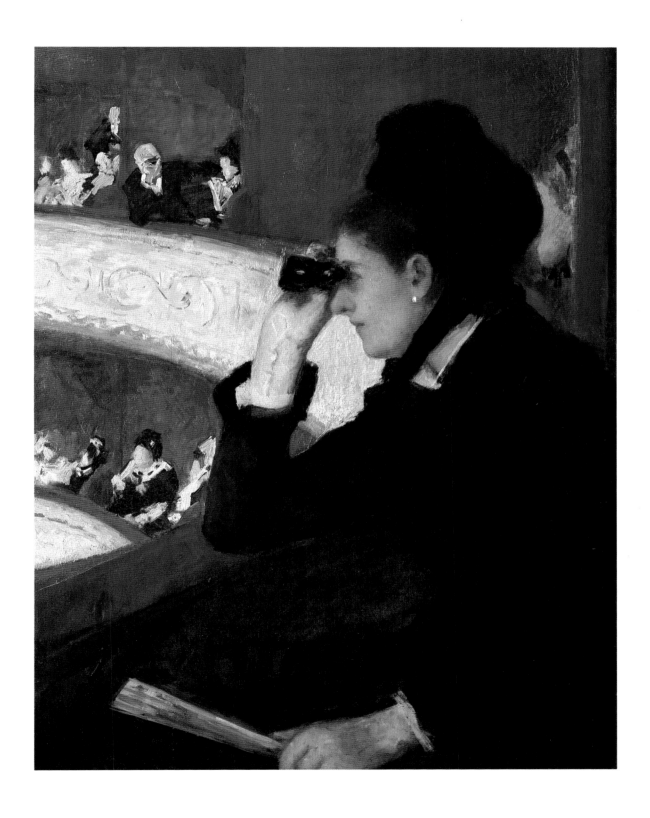

Cassatt *At the Opera* 1880

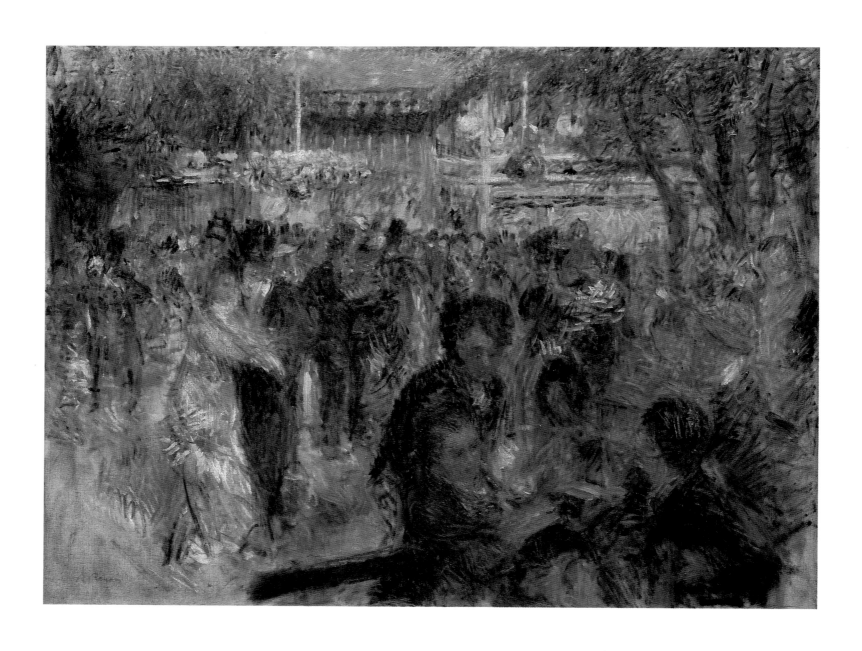

Renoir Sketch for *Le Moulin de la Galette* 1876

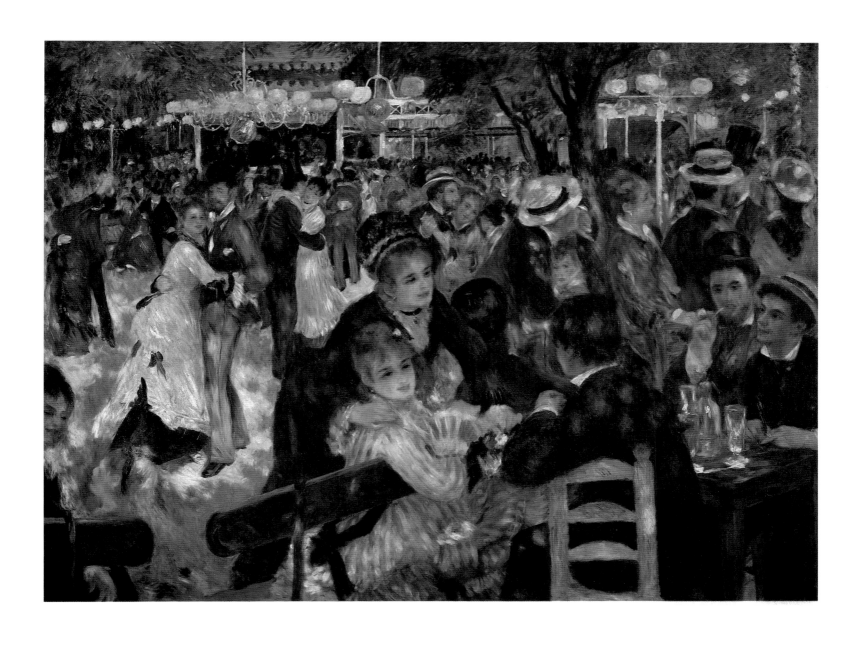

Renoir *Le Moulin de la Galette* 1876

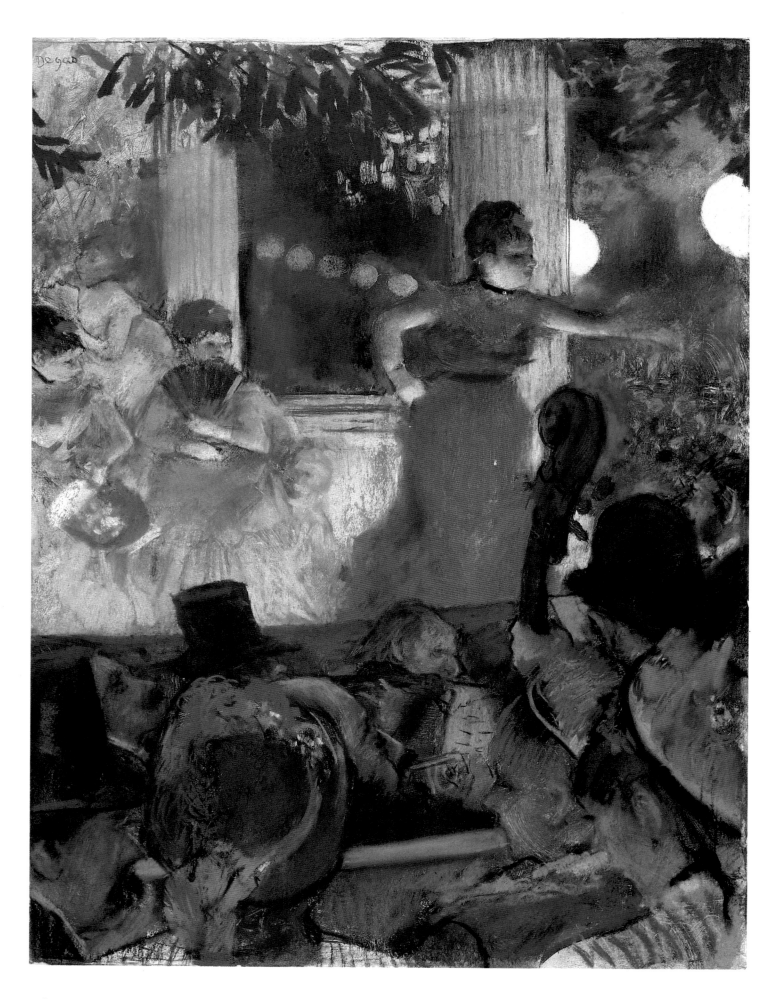

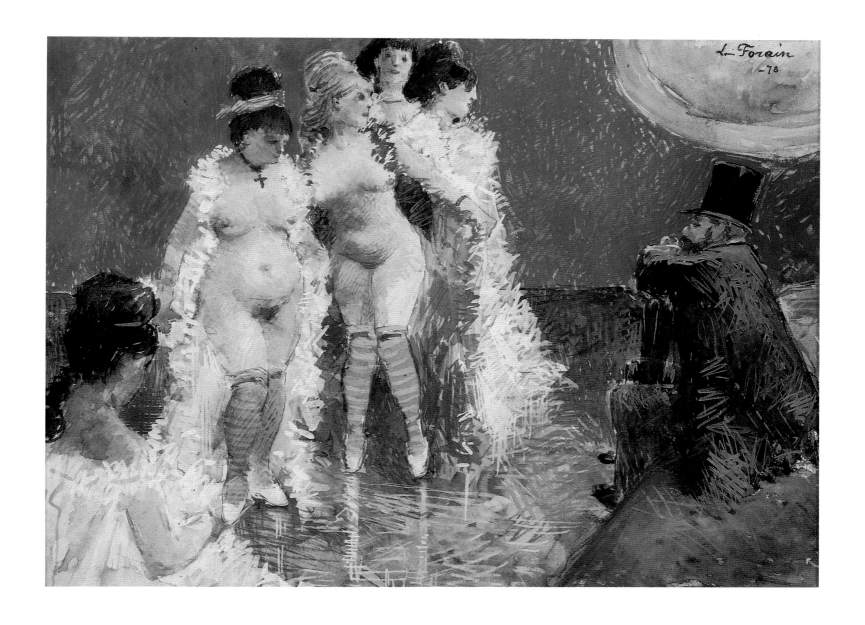

Degas *Café-concert aux Ambassadeurs* 1877

Forain *The Client* 1878

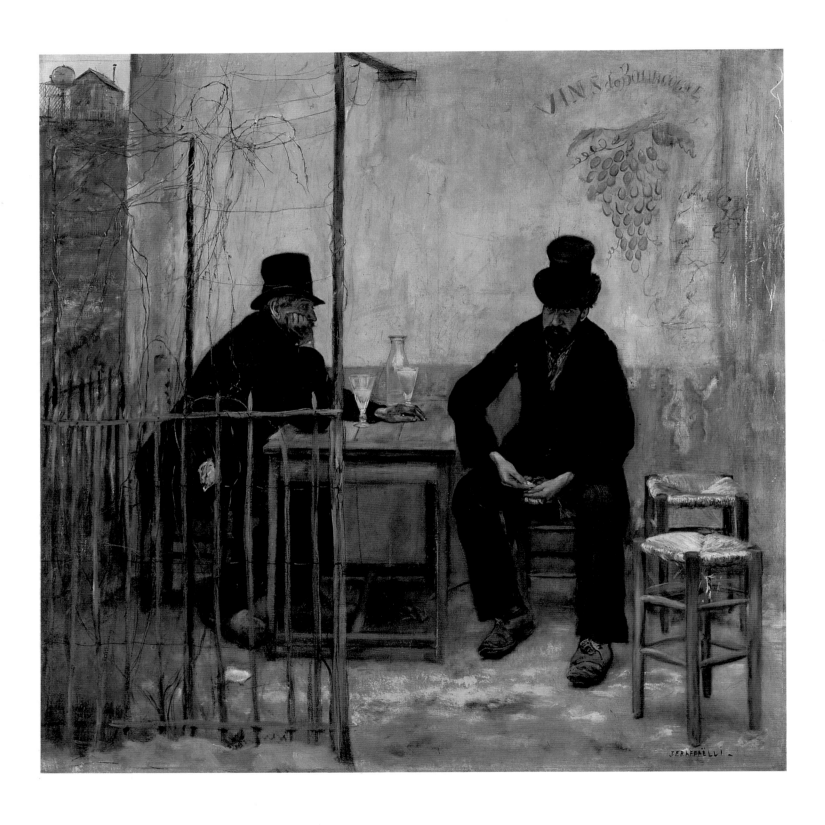

Raffaëlli *The Absinthe Drinkers* 1881

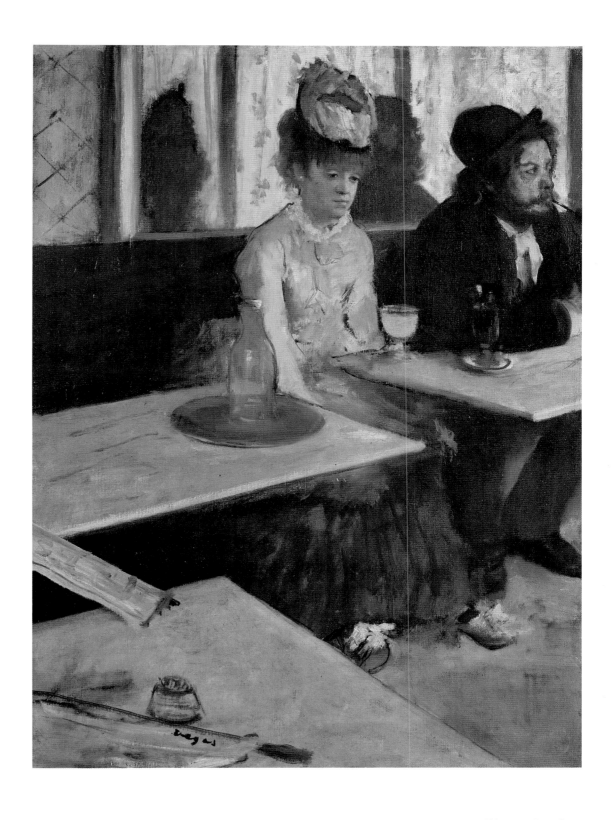

Degas *L'Absinthe* 1874

III: The Independent Masters 1880–1890

1882 saw the collapse of the Paris stock market: the brief period of prosperity was over, and although Durand-Ruel struggled through, times were once again uncertain. The level of internal dissent between the individual members of the Impressionist circle was now too great to be overcome and Durand-Ruel decided to concentrate upon one-person shows as a means of exhibiting his artists. He also began to seek out new markets and held exhibitions in Boston, Amsterdam, Berlin and London. Other dealers were entering the field. Georges Petit, Durand-Ruel's arch-rival, started showing Monet and Renoir in 1882.

Increasingly, the individual concerns of the artists within the Impressionist circle during the 1880s threatened the very existence of the exhibiting body. Apart from the continuing battles with the Degas-led faction, personal ambition caused the artists to look for other means of forwarding their careers. In addition, there was a general dissatisfaction with the various technical procedures adopted during the previous decade. The immediacy and spontaneity of the works and their casual subject matter were found to be wanting: in 1881 Gauguin was complaining to Pissarro that Sisley and Monet were 'churning out pictures at top speed ... we can't flood the place with rowing boats and endless views of Chatou – we'll be disgraced.' The artists began to search for a more structured way of organizing their visual sensations of nature; one that would equal other forms of artistic production in seriousness and ambition. In 1886 Pissarro could report, 'Impressionism is entering a completely new phase ... [a] totally different future ... is being prepared.'

Throughout the previous decade, the Impressionists had concentrated on colour and on the self-conscious preservation of an apparently spontaneous effect by the use of broken brushwork, which allowed the light ground of the canvas to play an important part in creating an impression of natural light. Their use of highly-visible and vigorous brushmarks to describe what they saw was in complete contrast to the academic practice of *le fini*, the highly-polished, licked surface characteristic of Salon painting of the time. At the later Impressionist shows, the exhibited works revealed a much more rigorous and controlled approach to nature, and styles that brought attention to the way the pictures were constructed were favoured – as in the regularized brushwork used by Cézanne in his *Mountains at l'Estaque*.

Discussions and disagreements continued apace, but in the late 1870s there was a change of venue – to the Café de la Nouvelle-Athènes in rue Pigalle, Montmartre. A number of young and ambitious artists sought inclusion in the group, artists who viewed the achievements of the early

1870s very much as stepping stones for a newer, more soph-
isticated art suitable for the times. The most important of
these were Paul Gauguin, Georges Seurat and Paul Signac.
Their challenging ideas and strong personalities exacer-
bated an already tense situation.

The older painters reacted differently to the change of
circumstances. Pissarro, true to character, was inclined to be
sympathetic to the newcomers, although he was continually
exasperated by Gauguin, who was 'always on the side of the
bastards!' Monet and Renoir, both highly ambitious and
jealous of their positions, were antagonistic to any change
and did not attempt to hide their disapproval; despite professional and personal differences, there remained a strong
bond between the two.

As always, Monet remained somewhat aloof from the
group and their discussions. He had a horror of theorizing
and, in any case, he had problems of his own. His wealthy
patron and friend Ernest Hoschedé was declared bankrupt
in the summer of 1877 and fled France, leaving his wife
Alice and five children with Claude and Camille Monet.
Two years later, Camille died after a prolonged and painful
illness. The extended Monet-Hoschedé family (Monet
eventually married Alice) and the artist's own love of comfort and fine food demanded a certain level of assured
income. Monet lived well when he could and did not flinch
from writing tough begging letters to his friends, dealers
and patrons. Despite being a successful artist and *bon viveur*,
Monet, along with all the other Impressionists, craved the
one thing his chosen occupation could not provide: security.
His domestic circumstances, and the problems involved in
exhibiting with artists with whom he felt he had little in
common, encouraged him to court success at the Salon.
Nevertheless, the ambition to paint nature was as strong as
ever and the 1880s saw him pursuing a more and more
independent manner of responding to the natural environment: 'When you go out to paint,' he told his American
friend Lilla Cabot Perry in 1890, 'try to forget what object
you have before you, a tree, a house, a field or whatever.
Merely think, here is a little square of blue, here an oblong
of pink, here a streak of yellow, and paint it just as it looks to
you, the exact colour and shape, until it gives your own
naive impression of the scene before you.'

Renoir had shown that it was possible to break into the
Salon and to attract rich and powerful patrons; indeed, he
had always been able to court the favours and interest of
such people. Travels to Italy had engendered a period of
research and opened to question all that he had discovered
in the previous decade. His attitude to his art underwent a
change, with a reaffirmation of his interest in people and in
the art of the past, particularly of the eighteenth century.

He developed a more academic style of painting by moving
away from the landscape and concentrating on the figure.

Both Renoir and Monet developed strong friendships
with Berthe Morisot and were often guests, along with the
poet Stéphane Mallarmé, Degas, Whistler and the painter
and collector Henri Lerolle, at Morisot's Thursday evening
soirées. She continued to paint the gardens of her homes,
the life of her family and landscapes with a powerful
sureness of touch and an exquisite sense of tone and colour.

The position of Alfred Sisley remains something of a
mystery: few of his letters survive and those that do suggest
a rather withdrawn and sensitive personality. He retired to
the relative isolation of Moret-sur-Loing, about fifteen
miles south-east of Paris, where he struggled with his com-
parative lack of success and produced landscapes of great
power, often imbued with an exquisite sense of melancholy.
Despite an exhibition at Durand-Ruel's Paris gallery in
1883 and a show in London, his financial situation
remained precarious and he did not receive the same critical
interest as his former associates. The critic Gustave Geffroy
reported seeing unsold canvases from the 1883 exhibition
stacked against the walls at Moret when he visited it in the
1890s.

Degas' technical brilliance was admired by all – one of
the main reasons that his peculiarities of character had been
tolerated for so long within the group – and his subject
matter had wide appeal although the reasons for his choices
were typically idiosyncratic: 'They call me a painter of dancers, not understanding that for me the dancer has been a
pretext for painting beautiful fabrics and rendering movement.' He followed his own path of obsessive experi-
mentation recognizing no boundaries across the repertoire
of visual expression.

Developing along lines parallel to Degas' researches,
Mary Cassatt's work explored images of women. The theme
of the mother and child remained the mainstay of her art,
which used asymmetrical arrangements and unusual view-
points to give a sense of immediacy and intimacy to her
images. Comparison with the work of her male contemporaries throws into relief the extraordinary degree of psycho-
logical insight with which she interpreted her chosen
subjects, untainted by any trace of sentimentality.

The last publicly-exhibited pictures Cézanne had shown
were at the Third Impressionist exhibition of 1877. Around
his home in the south of France he worked occasionally
with Renoir and once with Monet: Cézanne and Monet
admired each other's work although they saw each other
only rarely – Monet called Cézanne's *The Negro Scipio*,
which hung in his bedroom at Giverny, '*un morceau de
première force*.' Cézanne was an intimate friend of Camille

Pissarro, whose son Lucien recalls a 'sentence of great significance' during one of the discussions his father had with Cézanne and Piette: 'the important thing is not to paint a face or a figure, but to paint harmonies.' However, Cézanne spent more and more time alone at Aix. His financial reliance upon his family and his friends, especially Zola, came to an end in 1886, when his father, who had always opposed his son's choice of career, died leaving a substantial inheritance to the artist.

His friend Pissarro continued to have serious financial problems. At one stage in 1883 Caillebotte had to send money to support the painter and his family. In the same year, nineteen-year-old Lucien, the eldest of Pissarro's sons, was sent to London. This move initiated a correspondence that, in its humanity and insight, ranks with the writings of Delacroix and Van Gogh. Pissarro continued to live at Eragny, close to the peasant life of northern France and, like Renoir, was forced by circumstances and his own evolving ideas to abandon the style he had adopted in the 1870s.

Although by 1890 he had returned to a more fluid style reminiscent of his earlier work, Pissarro was the only one of the older artists to embrace Seurat's more 'scientific' and logical approach to painting. This highly complex technique had evolved from a study of academic sketching practice and the work of Delacroix grafted on to the ideas of the scientist Chevreul and on to contemporary technological advances in colour printing. Seurat rejected the informality of the typical Impressionist vision of city and country, although he adopted their working methods, and he aimed to paint works that would instil a sense of the classic into modern imagery. Instead of the open multi-directional brushwork of the older painters, he used small, dab-like strokes of pure colour. The result was a clean, luminous paint surface made up of the colours that would be optically mixed in the eye of the beholder rather than being combined, and thereby muddied, on the palette or canvas.

Equally important for the artists centred around Seurat was the ideological significance of their work. The political beliefs of the Impressionists were not expressed directly in their canvases, but for these younger artists the relationship between their private political beliefs and the public nature of their art was of great importance. To varying degrees they were involved with left-wing and anarchist activities, as well as being concerned with the ideas of the Symbolist writers, which pervaded the cultural life of the 1880s.

Ever the opportunist, Gauguin embraced such ideas wholeheartedly and, from being an ardent follower of Pissarro, shifted his interest to Cézanne. But by the end of the decade, as may be seen in works such as *Vision after the Sermon: Jacob Wrestling with the Angel*, he had rejected

Raffaëlli *The Workman c.*1888

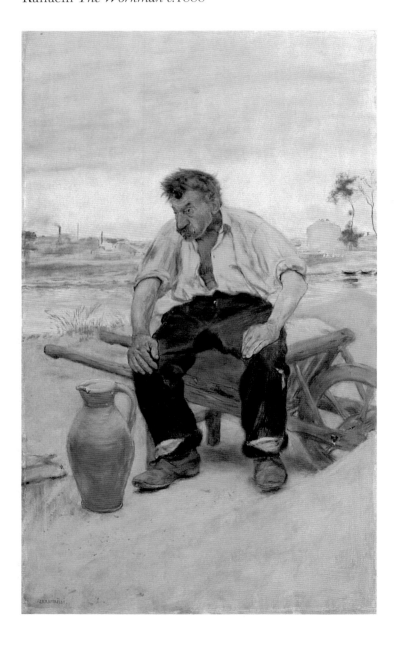

Neo-impressionism and embarked on other means in order to achieve his ambition to be the new leader of the avant-garde.

The tensions and challenges posed by the Neo-impressionists, the term used by critic Félix Fénéon to describe Seurat and his associates, were visible to all who visited the eighth, and final, Impressionist show in 1886. Monet, Sisley, Renoir and Caillebotte had refused to participate and among the works Degas sent in were ten pastels of women engaged in various aspects of their toilette, which caused a scandal in the Press. But it was the innovative works of the Neo-impressionists, shown together in a room dominated by Seurat's large *Sunday Afternoon on the Ile de la Grande Jatte*, which held the public's attention. The general reaction was one of mockery and ridicule, although there was a certain amount of sympathetic critical response.

By the late 1880s, the tide for the original members of the Impressionist group was beginning to turn. In 1889 Monet and the sculptor Auguste Rodin shared a retrospective exhibition at Durand-Ruel's Paris gallery which enjoyed enormous popular and critical acclaim. And it was this show, as much as anything, that marked Monet's rise to fame. By the turn of the century he was being acclaimed as the greatest living painter in France.

Gauguin *Vision After the Sermon* 1888

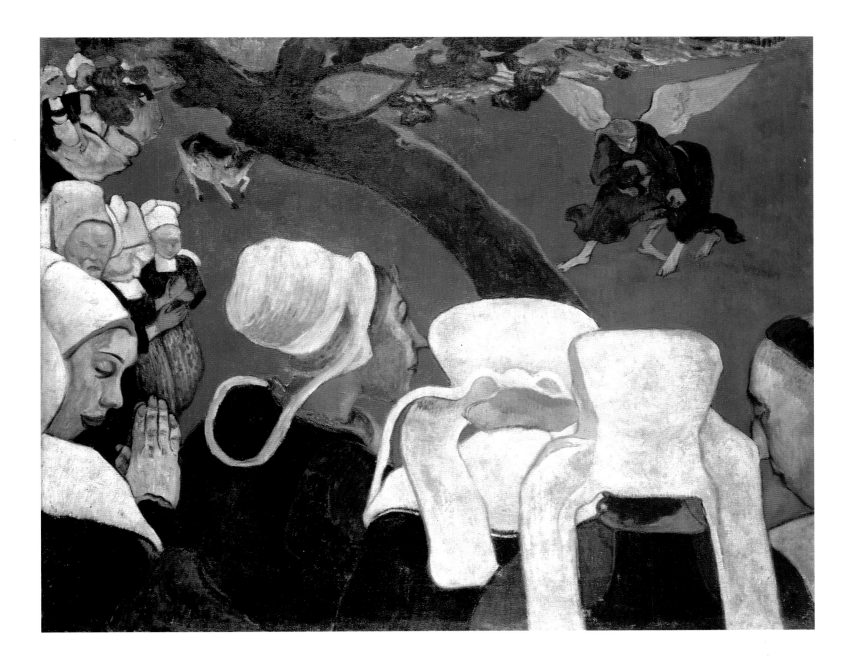

III: The Independent Masters 1880–1890

Divisions and Revisions

Claude Monet interviewed by T. Taboureaux in *La Vie moderne* (12 June 1880)

'... For some time my friends and I had been systematically rejected by the jury ...
What was to be done? Painting isn't everything, you've got to sell, you've got to live.
The dealers didn't want us. Nevertheless, we had to exhibit. But where? ... Nadar, that
wonderful Nadar, who is as good as the day is long, lent us a place to exhibit ...'

I interrupted:

'You're keeping to yourself now; I don't see your name any more in the
Impressionist showings.'

'Not at all; I am and I always will be an Impressionist. I'm the one who coined the
word, or at least, through a painting I had exhibited, furnished some reporter from *Le
Figaro* with the chance to launch this new insult. He had some success, as you know.
I say I'm an Impressionist; but I see my colleagues, men and women, only rarely. This
little church has become a banal school which opens its doors to every dabbler who
appears, so that the public, which began by laughing at what they considered an absurd
way of painting, now doesn't stop making fun of an exhibition, should it have the nerve
to call itself 'Impressionist', until they are back out in the street. That's the way it is!'

Gustave Caillebotte to Camille Pissarro

[Paris], *24 January 1881*

What is to become of our exhibitions? This is my well-considered opinion: we ought to
continue, and continue only in an artistic direction, the sole direction – in the final sense
– that is of interest to us all. I ask, therefore, that a show should be composed of all those
who have contributed real interest to the subject, that is, you, Monet, Renoir, Sisley,
Mme Morisot, Mlle Cassatt, Cézanne, Guillaumin; if you wish, Gauguin, perhaps Cordey,
and myself. That's all, since Degas refuses a show on such a basis.... Degas introduced
disunity into our midst....

He claims that he wanted to have Raffaëlli and the others because Monet and
Renoir had reneged and that there had to be someone. But for three years he has been
after Raffaëlli to join us, long before the defection of Monet, Renoir and even Sisley. He
claims that we must stick together and be able to count on each other (for God's sake!);
and whom does he bring us? Lepic, Legros, Maureau.... (Yet he didn't rage against the
defection of Lepic and Legros, and moreover, Lepic, heaven knows, has no talent. He has
forgiven him everything. No doubt since Sisley, Monet and Renoir have talent, he will
never forgive them.) In 1878 [he bought us] Zandomeneghi, Bracquemond, Mme
Bracquemond and in 1879 Raffaëlli ... and others. What a fighting squad in the great
cause of realism!!!! ...

[Degas] has cried out against all in whom he admits talent, in all periods of his life.

One could put together a volume from what he has said against Manet, Monet, you. . . .

To cap it all, the very one who has talked so much and wanted to do so much has always been the one who has personally contributed least. . . . All this depresses me deeply. If there had been only one subject of discussion among us, that of art, we would always have been in agreement.

I shall sum up: do you want an exclusively artistic exhibition? I don't know what we shall do in a year. Let us first see what we'll do in two months. If Degas wants to take part, let him, but without the crowd he drags along. The only ones of his friends who have any right are Rouart and Tillot. . . .

Edgar Degas to Gustave Caillebotte

24 January 1881

. . . Do you invite those people to your house?

Camille Pissarro to Gustave Caillebotte

[Paris], *27 January 1881*

You know me well enough to be sure that I would like nothing better than to have Monet and Renoir with us, but what I find extremely unfair is that, having left us in the lurch and not being concerned for a moment about exposing us to an unmitigated disaster, they now, having failed to succeed with the official Establishment, want to come back on their own terms as if they were the victors, when in all justice one ought to put up with fair punishment for sins committed. . . . I'm sorry, my dear Caillebotte, I cannot accept what you propose.

The only possible principle, as just as it is fair, is one of not abandoning colleagues, who have been accepted [in the past], rightly or wrongly, and who cannot be thrown out without ceremony . . . as for what you tell me of Degas, admit that if he has sinned by giving us some artists who do not fit the programme, nonetheless he has been lucky several times; [if you] remember that he has brought us Mlle Cassatt, Forain, and *you*, he will be pardoned!

Gustave Caillebotte to Camille Pissarro

Paris, 28 January 1881

. . . Will you allow me, however, to straighten out a few points? Renoir and Monet are not imposing any conditions, so far as I know. I am the only one to have spoken and only on my own, without being authorized or urged by anyone. Renoir and Monet, if you want to know, are completely unaware of what is going on.

I don't know what I shall do, I don't believe that an exhibition is possible this year. But I certainly shan't repeat the one held last year.

Paul Gauguin to Camille Pissarro

Paris, March 1881

We've taken premises in the Old England building, boulevard des Capucines; the place may be rather small but it's well lit and, more important, well located. Portier is now trying to get Belloir [a framer] to hurry up so that all our pictures will be ready by 2nd April. I was forgetting to tell you that the rent is 2,600, which is reasonable. It might be a good thing if you were to come soon and have a say in the organization of this exhibition since you are one of the main exhibitors. I am with Degas at the moment, and he says that as you're a friend of Caillebotte's it's *your job* to let him know that our exhibition is set up; he's welcome and we want to know if he'd like to exhibit with us as he has in the past. Need I tell you that no allusion must be made to any past unpleasantness. I know you have the necessary tact. . . .

Camille Pissarro to Esther Isaacson [his half-sister's daughter]

20 March 1881

. . . We are very pleased with the result [of 1881 exhibition], our reputation is affirmed more and more, we are taking our definitive place in the great movement of modern art.

Robert Cassatt to Alexander Cassatt [brothers of Mary Cassatt]

[Paris], *18 April 1881*

. . . I sent you some time ago a number of newspaper notices of Mame's [Mary Cassatt's] exposition and promised to send more – I have a lot of others but there has been so much of it that we all cry 'too much pudding'; so I spare you any further affliction, except the article from *Figaro* – a paper that has always been hostile to the *Indépendants*, & never before deigned to take any notice of Mame – Mame's success is certainly more marked this year than at any time previous. It is noticeable that of the three American papers published in Paris the *Parisian* is the only one that notices the Exposition – Mame keeps the *colony* at such a distance that she cannot expect any support from them. – The thing that pleases her most in this success is not the newspaper publicity, for that she despises as a rule – but the fact that artists of talent & reputation & other persons prominent in art matters ask to be introduced to her & compliment her on her work . . . She has sold all her pictures or can sell them if she chooses. – The things she painted last summer in the open air are those that have been most praised. . . .

. . . Well you must know in addition to the Pissaro [*sic*], of which she wrote you, she has bought for you a marine by Monet for 800 fcs – it is a beauty and you will see the day when you will have an offer of 8,000 for it. Degas still keeps promising to finish the picture you are to have & although it does not require more than two hours work it is still postponed. – However he said today that want of money would compel him to finish it at once. – You know he would not sell it to Mame, & she buys it from the dealer – who let's her have it as a favor and at less price than he would let it go for to anyone but an artist. – When you get these pictures you will probably be the only one in Phila[delphia] who owns specimens of either of the masters – Mame's friends the Elders [in New York] have a Degas & a Pissarro & Mame thinks that there are no others in America.

Paul Gauguin to Camille Pissarro

[Paris, August or September 1881]

I'm afraid you didn't make things quite clear to Degas last time you saw him. I had a very long discussion with that touchy individual yesterday evening from which it emerged that he thinks that Durand-Ruel is putting on the exhibition, that Renoir has not asked to show, but on the contrary has been pressurized by Durand-Ruel – in other words, Renoir is the star attraction, etc. . . . .

After a good deal of heated argument I managed to calm Degas down somewhat by saying that if it came to a *fight* with those characters (as he calls them) we would be a staunch and compact mass to resist them, etc. . . . .

We must give this matter serious thought, our future depends on it. Once we let the public fall into the habit of despising us the fight will be lost and we shall never be able to retrieve ourselves. This winter I hope we shall be able to hold a *general meeting* at which we can all air our views. When everyone has had his say, never fear, something will come out of it. We can't hope to create a movement outside the Ecole [des Beaux Arts] and the Salon unless there is mutual esteem among the exhibitors. You can explain to Caillebotte, who wants an *art show*, that if this art is to be different from the Academy's art, it cannot figure in the Academy's Salon.

Mlle Cassatt seems to be in the same boat and according to Degas is deeply despondent. I think all this needs to be cleared up. When you get back, please see to it. We must win *respect* and our movement will benefit. We'll achieve nothing, not even money, if we keep failing to pull together.

We must manage to live without Durand-Ruel if we have to. Did you know that the way things are going with Sisley and Monet, who are churning out pictures at top speed, he'll soon have 400 pictures on his hands that he won't be able to get rid of. Dammit, we can't flood the place with rowing-boats and endless views of Chatou – we'll be disgraced. Think it over, my dear Pissarro, let's not overdo it, you'd only make a fool of yourself. You who work seriously will be lumped together with the others and you know it. *A touch* of *plein air* is all very well but it does not add up to a complete *picture* . . .

Edouard Manet to Berthe Morisot

[Paris, Winter 1881–1882]

I have just had a visit from that terrible Pissarro who told me about your coming exhibition. These gentlemen don't appear to get on together . . . Gauguin acts as dictator. Sisley whom I also saw wants to know what Monet is going to do; as for Renoir, he has not yet returned to Paris. . . . Business is bad. Everyone is penniless as a result of the recent financial events and painting is feeling the effects.

Paul Gauguin to Camille Pissarro

Paris, 15 January 1882

Your letter is very puzzling. I don't understand what's going on at Pontoise. You think that you can retreat into your hole and come out later on, but you're wrong. Once you give up the struggle you've got to realize that it's all over. Degas can say what he likes, because he's certainly not retreating into his hole: he's made his reputation, he has his supporters and even the Academy, that he ridicules, would welcome him with open arms. He could, if he wanted, go to the Salon tomorrow, they'd fling open the doors and say: 'We told you you couldn't get anywhere with that lot.'

Go and see Caillebotte and arrange to exhibit *this year*; other years we'll try to do better.

If Caillebotte will have nothing to do with me, you have my full *permission* [to exhibit]. The main thing is that the *Impressionists* should exhibit since later on people will be able to see whom they want. It's up to you and you must not fade out just because of a few people who are glad to reap the profits without taking any of the hard knocks.

If you like we'll go and see Caillebotte together.

In any case *Degas has been wanting* to get out for two years, but the trouble is he didn't want to leave *alone*, he was determined to bring down everything with him.

Hold the exhibition with five people, if you like, *you, Guillaumin, Renoir, Monet and Caillebotte, but whatever you do, hold it! you know your future depends on it*; you'll see, the one in the worst mess isn't who one thinks it is. . . .

[P.S.] You can show my letter to Monsieur Caillebotte if you like.

Paul Gauguin to Camille Pissarro

Paris, 18 January 1882

. . . Something that does worry me is the exhibition. You're in Paris 2 days a month, so between now and March you'll be spending 2 days here and *quid novi* – nothing. Everything's gone quiet and we've landed ourselves with an outlay of 6,000 f, there's complete disunity among us and nothing's been settled. Guillaumin doesn't know whether to order *his frames* and has to decide now. He's not rich and it would be a great pity if he had unnecessary expense. You'll say that I'm always impetuous and eager to get ahead, but you'll admit that so far my calculations have proved right. If you know anything definite, drop me a line. Let me warn you that Raffaëlli is doing his best to go over to the Aquarellistes [a new society exhibiting watercolours and pastels], but he won't abandon our exhibition till he's certain of exhibiting somewhere else and just when we have to open. I'm convinced that Degas sees Raffaëlli simply as a pretext for breaking with us. There's something wrong-headed about the man and he's very destructive. Give this some thought, and for heaven's sake *let's do something.* . . .

There are already four societies of painters that have got together to exhibit, God knows how talented they are. All we manage to do is squabble. . . .

Pierre-Auguste Renoir to Paul Durand-Ruel

l'Estaque, Hôtel des Bains, Monday, 23 January 1882

L'Estaque, a small place like Asnières but on the seaside . . . I have met Cézanne here and we are going to work together.

Pierre-Auguste Renoir to Paul Durand-Ruel [rough draft]

[l'Estaque], *26 February 1882*

There are scarcely 15 art collectors in Paris capable of liking a painter without the backing of the Salon. There are eighty thousand of them who wouldn't buy a thing from a painter who is not in the Salon. Unfortunately I have one goal in life, and that is to increase the value of my canvases. The way I go about it may not be good, but I like it. For me to exhibit with Pissarro, Gauguin and Guillaumin would be like exhibiting with any socialist. The next thing you know Pissarro would invite the Russian Lavrof [the anarchist Pierre Lavroff] or some other revolutionary. The public doesn't like what smells of politics, and as for me, I don't want, at my age, to be a revolutionary. To exhibit with the Jew Pissarro means revolution.

Besides these gentlemen know that I have taken a big step because of the Salon. What they are doing is hurrying to make me lose what I have earned. They don't stop at anything for that, even if it means dropping me once I've fallen down. I don't want that. Get rid of those people and present me with artists like Monet, Sisley, Morisot, etc. and I'm your man, for that's not politics, it's pure art.

Pierre-Auguste Renoir to Paul Durand-Ruel

l'Estaque, 26 February 1882

This morning I sent you a telegram as follows: 'The paintings of mine that you have are your property, I can't prevent you from disposing of them, but I won't be the one who will exhibit.' ... This way I will not be an 'Indépendant' in spite of myself, unless I'm allowed to be so completely.... I am only defending our mutual interests, since I think that exhibiting there would make my canvases drop by 50%.

Pierre-Auguste Renoir to Paul Durand-Ruel

[l'Estaque, *27* or *28*] *February 1882*

I hope these gentlemen will give up the idiotic name 'Indépendant'. Please tell these gentlemen that I am not giving up the Salon. It is not a pleasure, but as I told you, this removes from me the revolutionary aspect, which scares me. I don't want to hold anything against anyone. It's a small weakness that I hope will be forgiven me. If I exhibit with Guillaumin, I might just as well exhibit with Carolus Duran [a successful portrait painter]. I don't much see the difference, but the important thing is that I don't share your illusion. As far as I'm concerned, no one knows anything about art, and only a medal can tip the scales. Delacroix used to say rightly that a painter ought to have all the honours at any price. The more decorations you have, the better known you are, and the less your painting is laughed at. The painting of an unknown or little-known man is lost forever because, I repeat, the public knows only a name and a decorated name. The painting of a well-known man is always rediscovered.

Pierre-Auguste Renoir to Victor Chocquet

l'Estaque, 2 March [1882]

I've just been sick and I'm convalescing. I can't tell you how kind Cézanne has been to me. He wanted to bring me his whole house. With his mother, we are having a big dinner at his place for our separation because he is going back to Paris while I stay somewhere in the South: strictly doctor's orders.... I'll probably go to Algiers for two weeks.... Cézanne ... will tell you all my suffering about that exhibition.

Pierre-Auguste Renoir to Paul Durand-Ruel

Algiers, [March] *1882*

I don't want to succumb to the mania of believing that something or other is bad just because of its place. In a word, I don't want to waste my time resenting the Salon. I don't even want to look as though I do. I think that one should do the best possible painting. That's all. Oh, if I were accused of neglecting my art, or of sacrificing my ideas out of stupid ambition, then I'd understand the criticisms. But there is nothing of the sort, they have nothing to say to me, quite the contrary.... I want to do some stunning painting for you that you will sell for a lot of money.... A little more patience, and soon I hope to give you some proofs that one can send things to the Salon and still do good painting.

I therefore beg you to plead my cause to my friends....

Eugène Manet to Berthe Morisot

[Paris], *1 March 1882*

I am writing this to you to give a brief account of what I have done about your exhibition [Morisot was in Nice].... Everyone was delighted to see me, especially because I had come for the purpose of exhibiting your works.... Your paintings will probably be placed on easels, for there is no place left to hang them.

... the rest of the day was devoted to your affairs.... Edouard seems improved. He is delighted about his decoration [Légion d'honneur]; but financial success does not seem to come to the rue St-Pétersbourg any more.

The Impressionists have all asked many questions about you and wanted to know whether you would come to see the exhibition ...

Eugène Manet to Berthe Morisot

[Paris, March 1882]

... I returned there this morning at eight o'clock. It is sure to be a success. Sisley is most fully represented and has made great strides.... Pissarro is more uneven ... Monet has some weak things side by side with some excellent ones ... Renoir's painting of boatmen looks very good. The views of Venice are detestable, real failures.... Caillebotte has some very boring figures done in blue ink, and some excellent small landscapes in pastel.

... Degas remains in the society, pays his dues, but does not exhibit. The society still uses the name of 'Indépendants' which he gave it.

All the upper part of the walls is hung with Gobelin tapestries which are very beautiful. The pictures are hung in three rows.

... Gustave [younger brother of Eugène and Edouard Manet] claims that it is your pictures that interest the public most.

Eugène Manet to Berthe Morisot

[Paris, March 1882]

... Pissarro asked Edouard to take part in the exhibition. I think he bitterly regrets his refusal. I have the impression that he hesitated a great deal ...

Berthe Morisot to Eugène Manet

[Nice, March 1882]

It is impossible to set up one's easel because of the wind. I have worked in my room too much ...

Am I not a failure at the exhibition? I have a feeling that I am, but I have become very philosophical. That sort of thing no longer depresses me as it did formerly ...

Eugène Manet to Berthe Morisot

[Paris, March 1882]

... The Impressionists, especially Renoir and Sisley, are doing well. Durand-Ruel gets 2,000 francs for a Sisley. Give me your prices. Edouard says one must ask high prices ...

Sisley *Geese*
(undated)

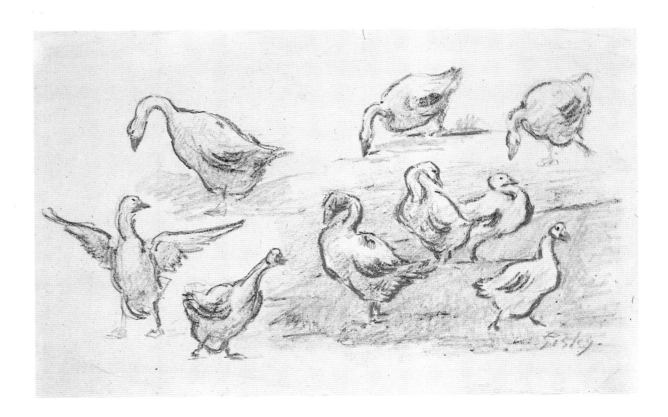

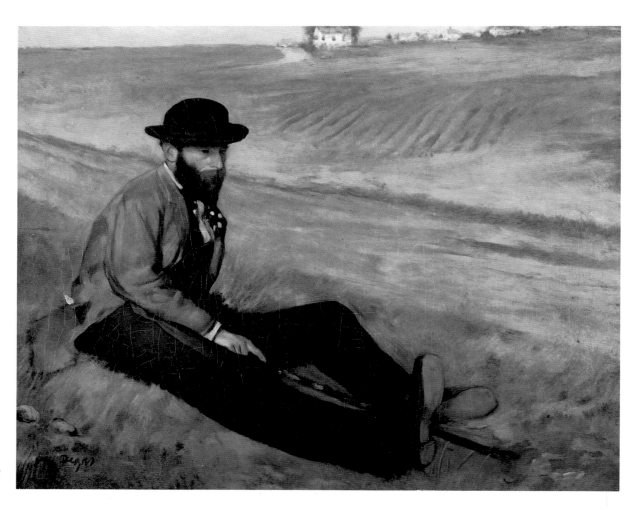

Degas
Portrait of Eugène Manet
1874

Berthe Morisot to Eugène Manet

[Nice, March 1882]

I received the newspapers last night and read them with great interest. Sisley and Pissarro seem to get all the glory. Why not Monet? This surprises me....

Have you met Mlle Cassatt? Why did she back out? ... Gauguin and I seem to play the part of the comic characters. Or am I mistaken? Do not be afraid to tell me, since being far away I am very philosophical.

Eugène Manet to Berthe Morisot

[Paris, March 1882]

Yesterday I met Mlle Cassatt at the exhibition. She seems to wish to be more intimate with us. She asks to do portraits of Bibi [daughter of Julie] and you. I said, yes, gladly, on condition of reciprocity....

The reasons for Degas' abstention is Gauguin's hostility towards him ...

Claude Monet to Paul Durand-Ruel

[Poissy], *10 November 1882*

... Following the conversation we had at your place the other day with Sisley ... I am not entirely of his opinion. My belief is that with collective exhibitions we have always held and too often repeated, we will finish up with public curiosity satiated and the press still against us. I do, however, agree with him about one-man shows: if each of us were to do our show in turn it would go on for ever; we will have to come to a decision, and it is above all up to you to decide what you think best for your own interests which are also our own. I will, for my part, do whatever you suggest, even though I dread exhibitions when not sufficiently prepared for them, as is my case ... without wishing to impose my own view of the matter, I believe that a one-man show would be far more beneficial for everyone concerned than a joint exhibition, particularly in the venue available which is small and intimate ...

The Death of Manet

Camille Pissarro to Lucien Pissarro

Paris, 29 March 1883

Our poor Manet is terribly sick. He has been completely poisoned by allopathic medicine. He has a gangrenous leg; this condition results from his having taken tremendous doses of spurred rye. We are losing a great painter and man of charm.

Edgar Degas to Paul-Albert Bartholomé [sculptor friend]

Wednesday, [Spring 1883]

... Manet is done for. That doctor Hureau is said to have poisoned him with too much diseased rye seed. Some papers, they say, have already taken care to announce his approaching end to him. His family will I hope have read them before he did. He is not in the least aware of his dangerous condition and he has a gangrenous foot.

Berthe Morisot to Edma Pontillon

[Paris, May 1883]

... These last days were very painful; poor Edouard suffered atrociously. His agony was horrible ... I am crushed. The expressions of sympathy have been intense and universal.... On the day of his funeral ... [it] seemed like one big family mourning for one of their own.

Camille Pissarro to Lucien Pissarro

Paris, 4 May 1883

You will see in *L'Intransigeant* the account of the burial of our lamented Manet. Antonin Proust said some words full of emotion; the newspaper, which is biased, called his speech undistinguished, but everybody said it perfectly expressed their feelings ...

Camille Pissarro to Lucien Pissarro

Osny, 28 December 1883

Manet's exhibition opens on 5th January. – Manet, great painter that he was, had a petty side, he was crazy to be recognized by the constituted authorities, he believed in success, he longed for honours. . . . He died without achieving his desire.

Berthe Morisot to Edma Pontillon

[Paris, January 1884]

Here I am again, sending you not the catalogue of the Beaux-Arts exhibition but of the auction at the Hôtel Drouot. Do you want to buy any pictures? I am sure that your husband will jump out of his chair at the idea, and even you will think that I have gone crazy, but too much wisdom and caution cause one to miss golden opportunities. In the old days Maman or Papa would never have dreamt of spending a thousand francs – or even five hundred – for a purchase of this kind. Faure is offered 20,000 francs for *The Dead Man* which he bought for a thousand ...

I think that everything would sell at very high prices were it not for the fact that we are in the middle of a recession.

Berthe Morisot to Edma Pontillon

[Paris, January 1884]

It's all over. It was a fiasco. Following on the victory at the Beaux-Arts, it was a complete failure ... I am broken hearted. The only consolation is that the works have gone to real art-lovers and artists.

In all the auction brought in 110,000 francs, whereas we had been counting on a minimum of 200,000. Times are bad, and it has been a severe blow. . . . Anyway, here I am with a whole gallery of pictures, our future inheritance from Madame Manet has been eaten into, but no matter; one can only laugh. . . .

Claude Monet to the Minister of Public Instruction, Armand Fallières

Paris, 7 February 1890

In the name of a group of subscribers, I have the honour of offering the *Olympia* by Edouard Manet to the State....

The controversy which Manet's paintings provoked, the attacks to which they were subjected, have now subsided. Had the war against such individuality continued we would have been no less convinced of the importance of Manet's *oeuvre* and of his ultimate triumph. One need only recall what happened to artists such as Delacroix, Corot, Courbet and Millet, to cite only a few famous names that were once decried, their isolated beginnings preceding certain glory after their deaths...

It seems to us, therefore, unacceptable that such a work should not have its place in our national collections, that a master should not be represented by the ceaseless activity of the art market, the competition created by America, the all-too predictable departure to another continent of countless works of art that are the joy and glory of France. We wanted to hold on to one of Edouard Manet's most characteristic paintings, one in which he is seen at the height of his glorious struggle, master of his vision and his craft....

Manet *L'Olympia* 1863

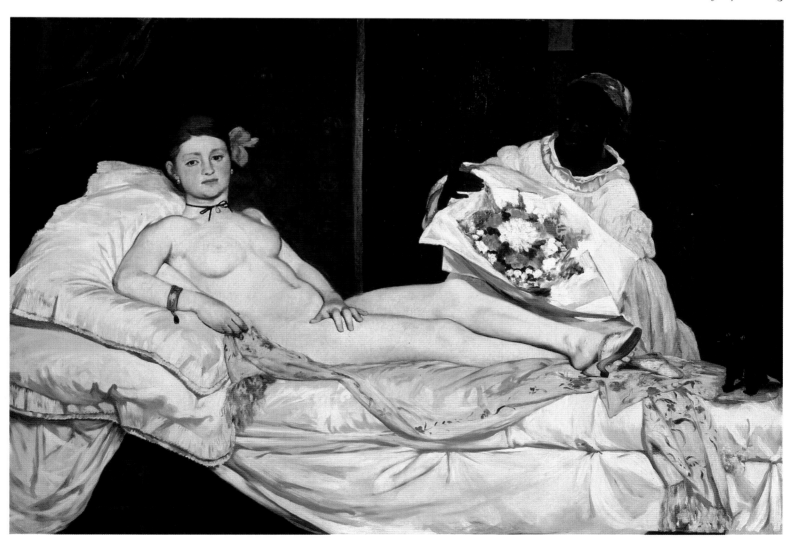

Pierre-Auguste Renoir to Paul Durand-Ruel

May 1884

The help I can give you at this moment doesn't amount to much, but if you need me, please consider me all yours, no matter what may happen. I will always be at your service ... As for paintings, if you are forced [by the crash of 1882 and subsequent economic crises] to make sacrifices, don't feel sorry about it, since I will do others for you and better ones.

Camille Pissarro to Claude Monet

7 December 1885

For some time there has been much talk about a show, it is discussed on every side. I paid a visit to Mlle Cassatt. From the very first we spoke about the show. Can't we come to an understanding about it? All of us, Degas, Caillebotte, Guillaumin, Berthe Morisot, Mlle Cassatt and two or three others would make an excellent nucleus for a show. The difficulty is in coming to an agreement.

Claude Monet to Paul Durand-Ruel

Giverny, 22 January 1886

... I have looked at all my paintings and it's no use, there aren't any, as far as I can see, which could be said to be finished and good as they are: no doubt there are some interesting ones but they're too unfinished for the average collector. But do you really need quite so many paintings for America? Surely you already have a fair number? You do, it's true, keep them cleverly hidden, since they are never on display, which in my opinion is a mistake: what's the point of us painting pictures if the public never gets to see them?

It's not that I don't want to give you any – there would be some I could give you, and I wouldn't be too angry if you actually displayed them. You think only of America, while here we are forgotten, since every new painting you get you hide away. Look at my paintings of Italy which have a special place among all I've done; who has seen them and what has become of them? If you take them away to America it will be I who lose out over here....

Camille Pissarro to Lucien Pissarro

Paris, [5 March 1886]

The exhibition is completely blocked. If we do not settle the whole thing in the next four or five days, it will be dropped altogether. Degas doesn't care, he doesn't have to sell, he will always have Mlle Cassatt and not a few exhibitors outside our group, artists like Lepic. If they have some success he will be satisfied. But what we need is money ... to spend money exhibiting at the same time as the official Salon is to run the risk of selling nothing. Mlle Cassatt and Degas say that this is no objection, but it's easy to talk that way when you don't have to wonder where your next meal will come from!

Camille Pissarro to Lucien Pissarro

Paris, [March 1886]

Because of Degas I missed the post last night. We went in a body to meet him to determine the number of paintings each would be allowed to exhibit. As usual, he arrived at an impossible hour. We had to stand in the street discussing the matter. Things are going well.

I went to dinner with the Impressionists. This time a great many came: Duret brought Burty, an influential critic, Moore, the English [*sic*] novelist, the poet Mallarmé, Huysmans, M. Deudon, and M. Berard; it was a real gathering. Monet had been in Holland, – he arrived from The Hague at eight o'clock, just in time for dinner. – I had a long discussion with Huysmans, he is very conversant with the new art and is anxious to break a lance for us. We spoke of the novel *L'Oeuvre* [Zola's novel about artists, containing a bitter depiction of Cézanne]. He is decidedly of my opinion. It seems that he had a quarrel with Zola, who is very worried. . . .

From *Claude Monet, sa vie, son oeuvre* by Gustave Geffroy (1922)

These dinners [at the Café Riche] were usually attended by Claude Monet, Camille Pissarro, Auguste Renoir, Alfred Sisley, Gustave Caillebotte, Dr de Bellio, Théodore Duret, Octave Mirbeau, and sometimes Stéphane Mallarmé.

They were evenings dedicated to talk and conversation, in which the happenings of the day were discussed in that freedom of spirit which was peculiar to artists who were free from any contact with official organizations. It must be admitted that the Impressionists' table was a very lively and noisy one, and that these men, relaxing after a day's work, were rather like children just let out of school. The discussions sometimes got quite heated, especially between Renoir and Caillebotte. The former, nervous and sarcastic, with his mocking voice, and a kind of Mephistophelism which marked with irony and a strange mirth his face already ravaged by his illness, took a mischievous delight in irritating Caillebotte, a choleric and irascible man whose face would change in colour from red to violet, and even to black when his opinions were contradicted with that sprightly flow of words which Renoir loved to employ against them. He would then display a fierceness which turned to anger, though that was inoffensive enough. . . . Renoir kept himself abreast by buying an encyclopaedia, out of which he culled arguments 'to floor Caillebotte'. . . .

Pissarro and Monet were also devotees of literature, both of them possessed of a sure and refined taste. I well remember a real duel for and against Victor Hugo . . . On other occasions, too, the arguments sometimes continued outside on the boulevard, and I am sure that there were some which were never resolved. . . .

Pierre-Auguste Renoir from *Renoir* by Denis Rouart (1954)

'Without actually falling out with them, I have had to break with many good friends. They could never be on time, never go home to bed, and held forth on art far too eloquently. I have no use for that nonsense.'

Pierre-Auguste Renoir from *Renoir* by Albert André (1919)

'They held against Corot his reworking his landscapes in the studio. They found Ingres revolting. I used to let them talk. I thought Corot was right . . .'

Camille Pissarro to [the journalist] Hugues Leroux [rough draft]

[May 1886]

The exhibition is, I assure you, very interesting this year. Impressionism is entering a completely new phase and you would have the advantage of being the first to glimpse the totally different future that is being prepared . . .

Camille Pissarro to Lucien Pissarro

Paris, [14 May 1887]

I have been wanting to write to you for three days, but lacked the three sous for postage.

I am very glad that I decided in favour of exhibiting; it was an experience I needed. Who knows, I may never again be able to show with the old group of the Impressionists, and I have every reason to be satisfied. You will see for yourself how wide is the divergence. It is an altogether different art, it is of course not understood, but it is seen, for it is so different, so clearly distinct; at a great distance this is recognized, and you would be amazed at the luminosity and simplicity of my works.

[Are] Monet's things a little too dark? I do not know whether I am correct in this, but these works seem to lack luminosity, by which I mean the light that bathes bodies in the shade as well as those in the sun. The effect is certainly decorative, but there is little finesse and crudities are prominent; I do not know if it belongs to our vision which while being not decoration is yet decorative.

As for Renoir, again the same hiatus. I do understand what he is trying to do, it is proper not to want to stand still, but he chose to concentrate on the line, his figures are all separate entities, detached from one another without regard for colour, the result is something unintelligible. Renoir, without the gift for drawing, and without his former instinctive feeling for beautiful colours, becomes incoherent. As for Sisley, he has not changed, he is adroit, delicate enough, but absolutely false . . .

Madame Berthe Morisot has some excellent things.

Camille Pissarro to Lucien Pissarro

Paris, [15 May 1887]

[The dealer] Petit has undertaken to push Monet and Sisley, hence it hardly matters to him whether or not I get anywhere; he has his faithful collectors who recruit buyers here and there. I observed these gentlemen several times propagandizing exclusively for Monet and Sisley. The placement of paintings was done in advance, the grouping was calculated, I know that; talking with Sisley I got what practically amounts to an admission. So you see my canvases were scattered to give them less importance. I let them get away with it this year, I don't want to say anything; besides I was afraid that my canvases would not show well with the others. This was unnecessary modesty on my part: grouped around my *Apple Eaters*, my show would have been much superior.

Yesterday I saw Bracquemond ... he was rather critical of Renoir, though he thought some parts of the large painting very well drawn – I am of his opinion as to the parts. – It is the ensemble, the synthesis which is faulty, and this they refuse to understand! – He also noted the crude execution in some of the Monets, particularly in one of the Holland canvases, in which the impasto is so thick that an unnatural light is added to the canvas, you can hardly conceive how objectionable it is to me, – even worse is the swept and meagre sky – no, I cannot accept this approach to art. ... As for Sisley, I just can't enjoy his work, it is commonplace, forced, disordered; Sisley has a good eye, and his work will certainly charm all those whose artistic sense is not very refined. – Madame Morisot is doing good work, she has neither advanced nor fallen back, she is a fine artist ... Seurat, Signac, Fénéon and all our young friends, like only my works and Madame Morisot's a little; naturally they are motivated by our common struggle. But Seurat, who is colder, more logical and more moderate, does not hesitate for a moment to declare that we have the right position, and that the Impressionists are even more retarded than before.

Pissarro *Les Lavandières* 1895

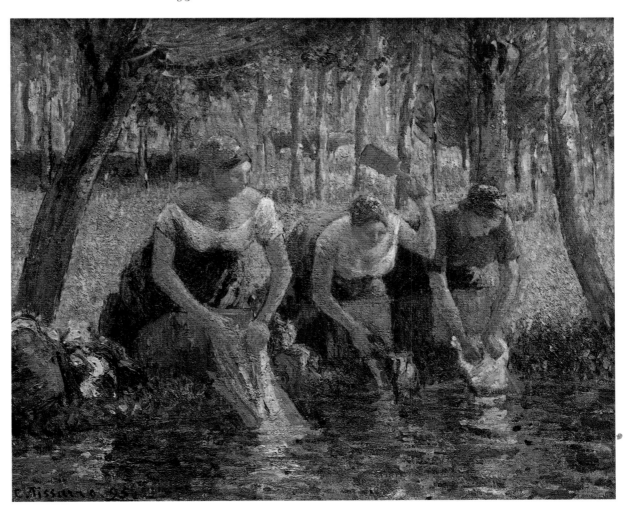

The Gauguin-Seurat Dilemma

Paul Gauguin to Camille Pissarro

Paris, [May or June] *1882*

... I would gladly have come to see you at Pontoise, but my Sundays are now very precious. I have so little time, and despite the weather over which I have no control and which makes a point of being variable on Sunday, if I don't make use of the day I feel badly about wasted time all week.

I can't resign myself to spending all my life as a financier and an amateur painter; I got it into my head that I'd become a painter. As soon as I see my way to earning my living with my painting I shall go all out. It makes my blood boil to think that my fragmented existence is the cause of all my trouble.

As things are now, we ought to triumph, you older men at the top and Guillaumin and myself in moderately good shape, whereas he and I carry less weight than a mere maid. The main thing is to put the hand to the plough. ...

Camille Pissarro to Lucien Pissarro

Rouen, 31 October 1883

... Yesterday I received a letter from Gauguin, who probably heard from Durand that I did some good work here. He is going to look me up and study the place's possibilities from the point of view of art and practicality. He is naive enough to think that since the people in Rouen are very wealthy, they can be easily induced to buy some paintings ... Gauguin disturbs me very much, he is so deeply commercial, at least he gives that impression. I haven't the heart to point out to him how false and unpromising is his attitude; true, his needs are great, his family being used to luxury, just the same his attitude can only hurt him. Not that I think we ought not try to sell, but I regard it a waste of time to think *only* of selling, one forgets one's art and exaggerates one's value. It is better to get low prices for a while, and even easier, particularly when your work is strong and original, and to go ahead bit by bit, as we do.

What will Gauguin think when I tell him about my talk with Monet who is completely opposed to another exhibition in Paris? This is also Renoir's position. – The people of Paris are fed up: let's not start anything. And truly, I think we have had enough exhibitions. But what will Gauguin not say! – The fact is he has his reputation to make! – I really don't know what to say to him, yet I think it absurd to weary anyone with our affairs, and then I have made up my mind to bide my time ...

Camille Pissarro to Lucien Pissarro

Rouen, 20 November 1883

... [Gauguin] is always on the side of the bastards! – he is more naive than I thought. ...

Camille Pissarro to Lucien Pissarro

Paris, [March 1886]

... Yesterday I had a violent run-in with M. Eugène Manet on the subject of Seurat and Signac. The latter was present, as was Guillaumin. You may be sure I rated Manet roundly. – Which will not please Renoir. – But anyhow, this is the point, I explained to M. Manet, who probably didn't understand anything I said, that Seurat has something new to contribute which these gentlemen, despite their talent, are unable to appreciate, that I am personally convinced of the progressive character of his art and certain that in no time it will yield extraordinary results ... I do not accept the snobbish judgements of 'romantic impressionists' in whose interest it is to combat new tendencies. I accept the challenge, that's all.

But before anything is done they want to stack the cards and ruin the exhibition – Monsieur Manet was beside himself! I didn't calm down. – They are all underhanded, but I won't give in.

Degas is a hundred times more loyal – I told him that Seurat's painting was very interesting. 'I would have noted that myself, Pissarro, except that the painting is so big!' Very well – if Degas sees nothing in it so much the worse for him. This simply means that there is something precious that escapes him. We shall see. Monsieur Manet would have also liked to prevent Seurat from showing his figure painting. I protested against this telling Manet that in such a case we would make no concessions, that we were willing, if space were lacking, to *limit our paintings* ourselves, but that we should fight anyone who tried to impose his choice upon us ...

Seurat *Un dimanche à la Grande Jatte* 1884

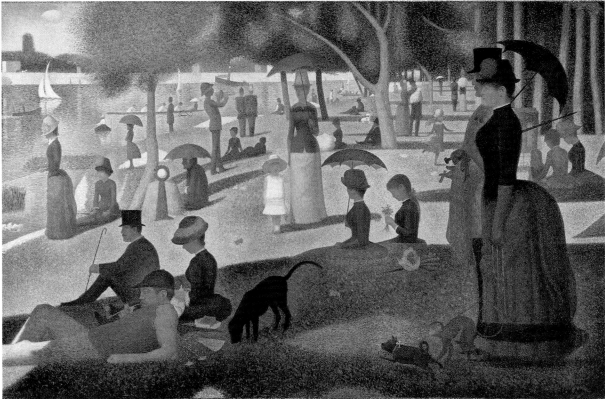

Georges Seurat to Paul Signac

Paris, Saturday, 19 June 1886

Yesterday, without letting me know, Gauguin went to your place to make the drawing for his woodcut which is with Pissarro's pictures. I don't know what you'll make of this behaviour. I heard about it in the evening at La Nouvelle-Athènes from Pissarro, who said it was a damn cheek. The same thing will happen again today and I thought I should warn you. I must protect myself. It's all very tricky – I don't know if you take it the same way as I do. Maybe you find it perfectly natural, but in any case I had to let you know. . . .

Camille Pissarro to Paul Durand-Ruel

[Eragny], 6 November 1886

I want it well understood that it is M. Seurat, an artist of great worth, who was the first to have the idea and to apply the scientific theory after having studied it profoundly. Like my other colleagues, Signac and Dubois-Pillet, I only followed the example given by Seurat. . . .

Theory

To seek a modern synthesis of methods based on science, that is based on M. Chevreul's theory of colour and on the experiments of Maxwell and the measurements of N. O. Rood.

To substitute optical mixture for mixture of pigments. In other words: the breaking up of tones into their constituents. For optical mixture stirs up more intense luminosities than does mixture of pigments.

As far as execution is concerned, we regard it as of little importance: art, as we see it, does not reside in the execution: originality depends only on the character of the drawing and the vision peculiar to each artist.

Camille Pissarro to Lucien Pissarro

Paris, 3 December 1886

Lately I have been going along with Seurat, Signac and Dubois-Pillet to La Nouvelle-Athènes; entering one evening, we saw Guillaumin, Gauguin, Zandomeneghi. – Guillaumin refused to shake hands with Signac, so did Gauguin; there was some explanation; impossible to understand a word of it; it appears that the cause was that affair in Signac's studio, a misunderstanding. Nevertheless Gauguin left abruptly without saying goodbye to me or to Signac. – Guillaumin came over to shake hands and asked whether I was going to dine with the Impressionists on Thursday. Much surprised, I replied that this was the first time I'd heard of the dinner. You can be sure that I won't spend thirteen to fifteen francs for dinner; I have three francs in my pocket, and besides we no longer understand each other. . . .

Camille Pissarro to Lucien Pissarro

Paris, 20 April 1891

I do not reproach Gauguin for having included a vermilion background, or two wrestling warriors and the Breton peasants in the foreground. I reproach him for pinching these elements from the Japanese, from the Byzantine painters and others, I reproach him for not applying his synthesis to our modern philosophy which is absolutely social, anti-authoritarian and anti-mystic. – This is the serious part of the question. It's a step backwards. Gauguin is not a seer, he's a schemer who has sensed a reaction among the bourgeoisie away from the great idea of solidarity that is germinating among the masses – an unconscious idea, but a fruitful one, the only idea that is legitimate! The same is true of the Symbolists! Don't you think so? This is why we must fight them like the plague!

Camille Pissarro to Lucien Pissarro

Paris, 13 May 1891

… We are fighting against terribly ambitious 'men of genius' who are concerned only to crush whoever stands in their path. It is sickening. If you knew how shamelessly Gauguin behaved in order to get himself elected (that is the word) man of genius, and how skilfully he went about it. We were left with no choice except to smooth the way for him. … De Bellio, who had been obstinately cold to Gauguin, confessed to me that he had changed his view of Gauguin's work, that he now considered him to have great talent, although not in sculpture. Why? … It is a sign of the times, my dear. The bourgeoisie frightened, astonished by the immense clamour of the disinherited masses, by the insistent demands of the people, feel that it is necessary to restore to the people their superstitious beliefs. Hence the bustling of religious symbolists, religious socialists, idealist art, occultism, Buddhism, etc., etc. Gauguin has sensed the tendency. … The Impressionists have the true position, they stand for a robust art based on sensation, and that is an honest stand. …

… everyone is devoting much more time to intrigue than to art … It is necessary to escape from this milieu.

Camille Pissarro to Lucien Pissarro

Eragny, [31 May 1887]

… If you happen to see Seurat or if you write to Signac, tell them that I have tried the mixture of cadmium … with red, white and Veronese green. It becomes black in four or five days from Veronese green. Even blacker than the yellow mixture.

Camille Pissarro to Lucien Pissarro

Paris, 6 September 1888

... I think continually of some way of painting without the dot. I hope to achieve this but I have not been able to solve the problem of dividing the pure tone without harshness ... How can one combine the purity and simplicity of the dot with the fullness, suppleness, liberty and spontaneity and freshness of sensation postulated by our Impressionist art? This is the question that preoccupies me, for the dot is meagre, lacking in body, diaphanous, more monstrous than simple, even in the Seurats, particularly in the Seurats ... I'm constantly pondering this question, I shall go to the Louvre to look at certain painters who are interesting from this point of view. Isn't it senseless that there are no Turners [here]?

Dialogues with Morisot

Berthe Morisot to Edma Pontillon

[Paris, 1884]

Degas is always the same, witty and paradoxical. I am beginning to develop close friendships with my colleagues, the Impressionists. Monet insists on offering me a panel for my drawing room....

Claude Monet to Berthe Morisot

Giverny, 5 August 1885

I came to Paris yesterday hoping to be able to pay you a visit, but unexpected errands deprived me of that pleasure ... come and spend a day at Giverny, with M. Manet and your lovely girl.

Your panel is almost finished ...

Berthe Morisot to Edma Pontillon

[Paris], *1886*

I'm working with the prospect of having an exhibition this year: everything I have done for a long time seems to me so horribly bad that I should like to have new, and above all better, things to show the public. The project is very much up in the air. Degas' perversity makes it almost impossible to realize: there are clashes of vanity in this little group that make any understanding difficult. It seems to me that I am about the only one without any pettiness of character: this makes up for my inferiority as a painter.

Claude Monet to Berthe Morisot

Château de la Pinède, près d'Antibes, 10 March 1888

I'm working tremendously hard. I take a lot of trouble, but I can't say I'm satisfied yet, for another spell of bad weather would spoil everything I have begun, and then it is so difficult, so fragile and delicate, and I tend to be so brutal. Anyhow, I am really making a big effort....

Berthe Morisot to Claude Monet

14 March 1888

I envy you your sun, and many other things besides, even your brutality! You are hard to satisfy, but I can see you are in form and making delightful pictures. . . .

One doesn't know where to go. I tried a field. I had no sooner sat down than I had more that fifty boys and girls around me, shouting and gesticulating. It ended in a pitched battle. The owner of the field came and told me quite crossly that we ought to ask permission to work, when we are there we attract the local youngsters who do a lot of damage. . . . In a boat, the troubles are different. It rocks, there's the infernal lapping of the waves, you have the sun and the wind, the boats change place every minute, etc. From my window, it's very pretty to look at, but very ugly to paint; views from above are nearly always incomprehensible. The upshot is that I'm not doing much, and the little I do seems horrible. . . .

The other day . . . I saw pictures by Pissarro that are much less *pointillé*, and very beautiful; it seems to me that they might be liked. I went there to see the nudes of that fierce Degas, which are becoming more and more extraordinary.

We often talk about you with Mallarmé, who is very devoted and full of friendly feelings towards you.

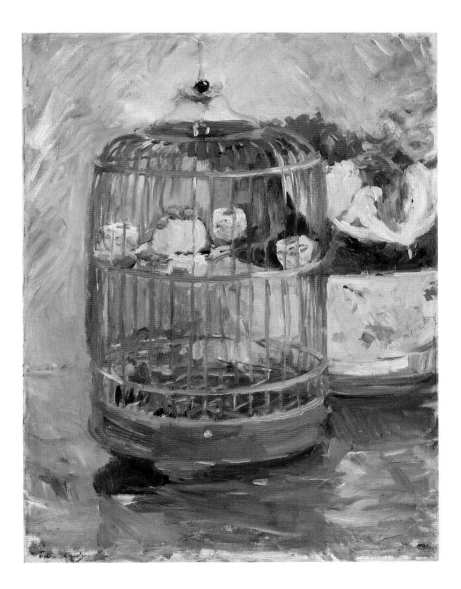

Morisot *The Birdcage* 1885

Berthe Morisot to Claude Monet

[Villa Ratti, Cimiez, Nice], *1889*

My dear Monet, may I drop the 'dear Sir', and treat you as a friend? ... I am working a great deal, but nothing comes of it. It is horribly difficult.

I know through Malarmé [*sic*] that you have marvels at [Théo] Van Gogh's, and indeed I regret that I am not there to see them ...

Claude Monet to Berthe Morisot

[the Creuse, 1889]

As you can see I am once more a little out of the way and at grips with the difficulties inherent in a change of surroundings. The place here is terribly wild; it reminds me of Belle-Île....

Berthe Morisot to Stéphane Mallarmé

[Mézy, near Meulan, 1890]

... I have worked a great deal to prepare a room for you; nonetheless, my dear friend, you are forewarned. Wednesday I shall go to Mlle Cassatt to see those marvellous Japanese prints at the Beaux-Arts with her....

Painting Out of Doors

From the notebooks of Berthe Morisot

My ambition is limited to the desire to capture something transient, and yet, this ambition is excessive.

... Degas claimed that study from nature was insignificant, painting being an art of convention, and that it would be infinitely better to learn how to draw from Holbein; Edouard [Manet] himself, ... a servile copyist of nature, was the most mannered painter in the world, never making a brushstroke without reference to the masters, for example, he never painted fingernails, because Frans Hals had never depicted them.

From *Degas: An Intimate Portrait* by Ambroise Vollard (1928)

I followed him into a little studio he had fixed up for himself in the grounds. He turned his back to the window and began work on one of his extraordinary out-of-door studies.

I could not get over my surprise at this method of doing a landscape indoors, and when I mentioned the fact, Degas replied:

'Just an occasional glance out of the window is enough when I am travelling. I can get along very well without even going out of my own house.'

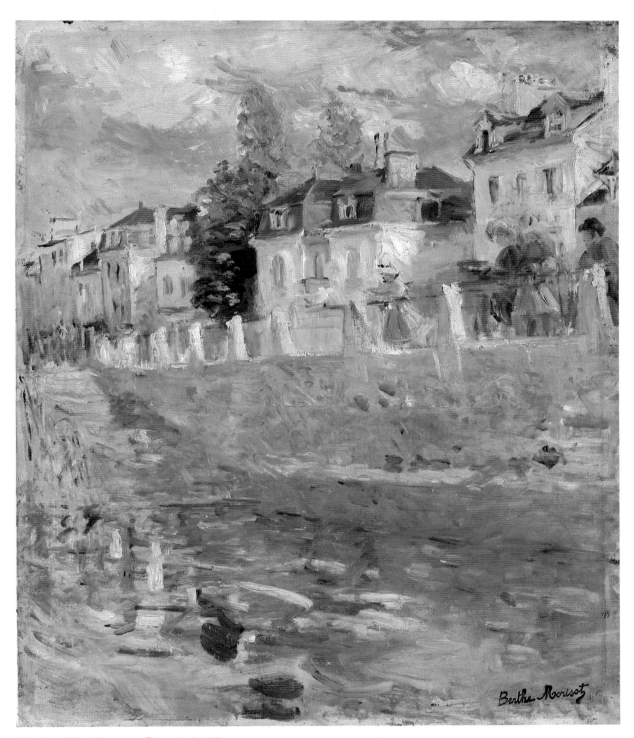

Morisot *The Quay at Bougival* 1883

Pierre-Auguste Renoir to Berthe Morisot

Summer 1891

I am resuming work in the studio while waiting for better things. A month has gone by during which I have done nothing but look at the sky ... It would have been delightful to work a little with you, but, but ... I am postponing this pleasure until better days. Forgive me if I do not take advantage of your kind hospitality. I am going to paint outdoor pictures in the studio.

From *En écoutant Cézanne, Degas et Renoir* by Ambroise Vollard (1938)

July 1909

'You know what I think of painters who work in the open,' [said Degas]. 'If I were the government I would have a company of police watching out for men who paint landscapes from nature. Oh, I don't wish for anybody's death; I should be quite content with a little buckshot to begin with.... Renoir, that's different, he can do what he likes.'

Pierre-Auguste Renoir from *Renoir et ses amis* by Georges Rivière (1921)

'Out of doors, one uses colours one would never think of in the weaker studio light. But landscape painting is a thankless job. You waste half the day for the sake of one hour's painting. You only finish one picture out of ten, because the weather keeps changing. You start work on a sunlight effect, and it comes on to rain – or you had a few clouds in the sky, and the wind blows them away. It's always the same story!'

Pierre-Auguste Renoir from *Renoir, My Father* by Jean Renoir (1962)

... a picture is meant to be looked at inside a house, where the windows let in a false light. So a little work must be done in the studio in addition to what one has done out of doors. You should get away from the intoxication of real light and digest your impressions in the reduced light of a room. Then you can get drunk on sunshine again. You go out and work, and you come back and work; and finally your picture begins to look like something.

Struggling On: Renoir

Pierre-Auguste Renoir to Théodore Duret

Paris, 15 October 1878

... The portrait of Mme Charpentier is entirely finished but I can't say what I think of it. I don't know at all. In a year I'll be able to judge it but not before....

Pierre-Auguste Renoir to Marguerite Charpentier [patron]

[early 1880s]

Do not wait for me, I will very probably have the sorrow of not being able to dine with you. I started a portrait this morning. I am starting another this evening, and afterwards I will probably go for a third. If I have to stay for dinner and go tomorrow, all these people are leaving soon and my head is completely upside down. As soon as I am a little freer, I will come to apologize to you and tell you about my likely failures or my most unlikely success.

Pierre-Auguste Renoir to Théodore Duret

[13 February] *1880*

I will be be completely recovered in about a week. I owe this fast recovery to Dr Terrier, he was marvellous. I am enjoying working with my left hand, it is very amusing and it's even better than what I would do with my right. I think it was a good thing to have broken my arm [caused by a fall from a bicycle], it made me make some progress. . . .

Pierre-Auguste Renoir to Paul Bérard [son of a patron]

[Chatou, Summer 1890]

I'm at Chatou . . . I'm doing a picture of boaters which I've been itching to do for a long time. I'm getting a little old and I didn't want to postpone this little party for which I wouldn't be able to meet the expenses later on, it's already very hard, I don't know if I'll finish it, but I told my misfortunes to Deudon [friend and patron], who agreed with me [that] even if the enormous expenses wouldn't let me finish the painting, it's still in progress; one must from time to time try things beyond one's strength.

Pierre-Auguste Renoir from *Renoir et ses amis* by Georges Rivière (1921)

'One day while I was painting a landscape in the neighbourhood of Algiers [in early 1882], I saw a man approaching who seemed to be dressed in purple and cloth-of-gold. He came down the path with great dignity, leaning on a stick; he looked like some magnificent prince out of the *Thousand and One Nights*. When the traveller reached me, my illusion vanished; my emir was nothing but a flea-bitten beggar. The sun, the divine sun, had enriched him with its light, and transformed his sordid rags into a royal robe. It's always the same in Algeria. The magic of the sun transmutes the palm trees into gold, the water seems full of diamonds and men become Kings from the East.'

Pierre-Auguste Renoir to Victor Chocquet

[Algiers, March or April 1882]

. . . I'm working a little. I will try to bring back some figures, but it's more and more difficult; too many painters in Algiers . . .

Pierre-Auguste Renoir to Paul Bérard

[Algiers, March or April 1882]

Women are so far unapproachable. I don't understand their jabber and they are so very fickle. I'm scared to death of starting something again and not finishing it. It's too bad, there are some pretty ones, but they don't want to pose.

Pierre-Auguste Renoir to Paul Durand-Ruel

Naples, 21 November 1881

I'm still afflicted with the malady of research. I don't like what I do, and I paint it out, and paint it out again. I hope that this mania will come to an end ...

I'm like a child at school. The white page must always be evenly written and slap! bang! there's a blot! I'm still blotting and I'm forty years old. I've been to see the Raphaels in Rome. They are very fine and I should have gone to see them sooner. They are full of knowledge and wisdom. Unlike me he didn't go in search of impossible things. But how fine it is. I prefer Ingres for oil painting. But Raphael's frescoes are admirable in their simplicity and grandeur.

Pierre-Auguste Renoir to Paul Bérard

[Paris], *October 1882*

It's not going well at the moment. I must begin Mme Clapisson's portrait all over again. It's a big flop. Durand, I believe, is not very pleased with his [portraits]. Well, all this takes a lot of thought, and with no exaggeration I must be careful if I don't want to slip in the public's esteem ...

I've been away a little too much. I must go back a little into my shell.

The day before yesterday I was packed to go and get some comfort at Vargemont [*sic*] and run away from Paris without telling anyone. I thought it over and I believe that I'm behaving more sensibly by not bringing my bad mood and by not getting angry with anyone. Now I'm delighted with what is happening to me. I'm going to get back on the right path and I'm going to enlist in Bonnat's studio. In a year or two I'll be able to make 30,000,000,000,000 francs a year. Don't talk to me any more about portraits in the sunlight. Nice black backgrounds, that's the real thing. . . .

Pierre-Auguste Renoir from *Renoir* by Ambroise Vollard (1920)

'About 1883 something like a break occurred in my work. I had reached the end of "Impressionism", and I had come to realize that I did not know how to paint or draw. In short, I found myself in a deadlock.'

Pierre-Auguste Renoir to Paul Durand-Ruel

[Genoa, December] *1883*

We [Monet and himself] are delighted with our trip. We've seen marvellous things, we'll probably bring back nothing or not much, because we've been mostly on the move, but what a trip! One has to stay much longer to do something. . . . . We've seen everything, or just about, between Marseilles and Genoa. Everything is superb. Vistas of which you have no idea. This evening the mountains were pink.

Hyères superb. St-Raphaël, Monte Carlo, and Bordighera are virgin stands of pine trees.

Pierre-Auguste Renoir to Paul Durand-Ruel

[La Rochelle, Summer] *1884*

I am stranded in La Rochelle. The last painting I saw by Corot had given me a mad desire to see this harbour, and I am astonished to see, in spite of the vague memory I have of the painting, the extraordinary reality of the tone.... This is the first trip that will have been of some use to me, and precisely because the weather is so bad that I have had to think and see rather than do any real work.... I've lost a lot by working in the studio in a space of 4 square metres. I would have gained ten years by doing a little of what Monet has done.

Pierre-Auguste Renoir to Paul Bérard

La Roche-Guyon, 17 August 1885

I'm involved in lots of things and not one of them is finished. I wipe out, I start over, I think the year will go by without one canvas, and that's why I turn down visits from painters, no matter who.... I stopped Durand-Ruel from coming to see me.... I WANT TO FIND WHAT I AM LOOKING FOR BEFORE GIVING UP. Let me look.... I have gone too deeply into the series of experiments to give up without regret.... Success may be at the end.

Renoir *Houses at la Roche-Guyon* 1885

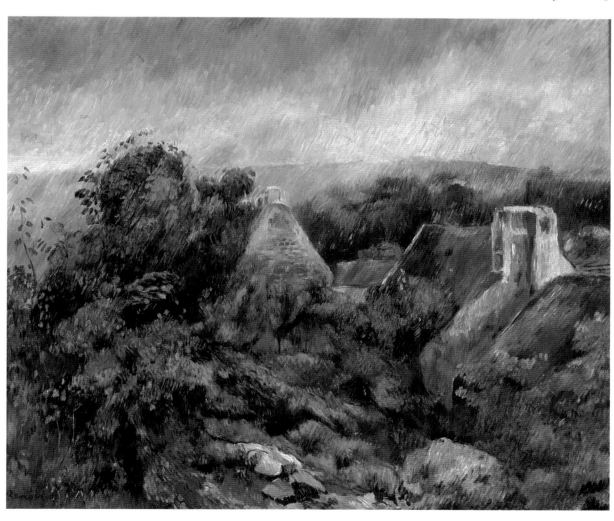

Pierre-Auguste Renoir to Paul Durand-Ruel

Essoyes, [September or October] *1885*

I think that this time you will be pleased. I've taken up again, and this time for good, the old sweet and light way of painting.... I'm making progress on each one.... It's nothing new, but it's a sequel to 18th-century paintings. I'm not speaking of good ones. This is to explain to you more or less my new, latest technique (Fragonard but not so good)....

Believe me, I'm not comparing myself to an 18th-century master. But I have to explain to you in what direction I'm working. These people who seem not to do nature knew more about it than we do.

Pierre-Auguste Renoir to Paul Bérard

[Paris, October] *1887*

I'm working ... since Durand keeps telling me canvases, canvases ... canvases, and the canvases don't come because I scraped everything off. Nevertheless I believe I'm going to beat Raphael and that people in the year 1887 are going to be amazed.

From the notebooks of Berthe Morisot

11 January 1886

[Renoir is a] master of line. All his preliminary studies should be shown to the public, who generally imagine that the Impressionists work with dashing recklessness. I don't think anyone could surpass him in rendering of form.

Renoir
Study for The Bathers
1884–7

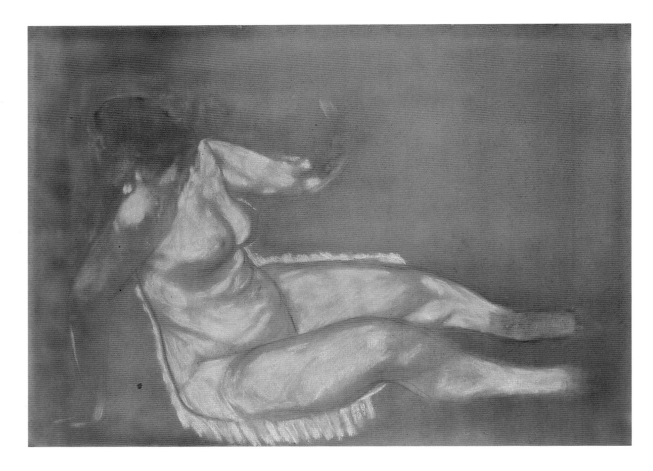

Camille Pissarro to Lucien Pissarro

Paris, 13 December 1888

I had a long conversation with Renoir. He admitted to me that everybody, Durand and his former collectors, attacked him, deploring his attempts to go beyond his romantic period. He seems to be very sensitive to what we think of his show; I told him that for us the search for unity was the end towards which every intelligent artist must bend his efforts, and that even with great faults it was more intelligent and more artistic to do this than to remain enclosed in romanticism. Well, now he doesn't get any more portraits to do.

From *Renoir* by François Fosca (1962)

One day when [Renoir] was visiting an exhibition, he stopped in front of his own portrait of M. Chocquet. 'Portrait of a lunatic — by a lunatic,' he muttered. The friend who was with him was somewhat taken aback; but Renoir explained that Chocquet was a 'delightful madman who went without in order to buy paintings he liked. My own form of madness', he added, 'has been to spend my whole life putting colour on canvas. Frankly, I don't think it has done anyone any harm.'

Renoir *The Bathers* 1887

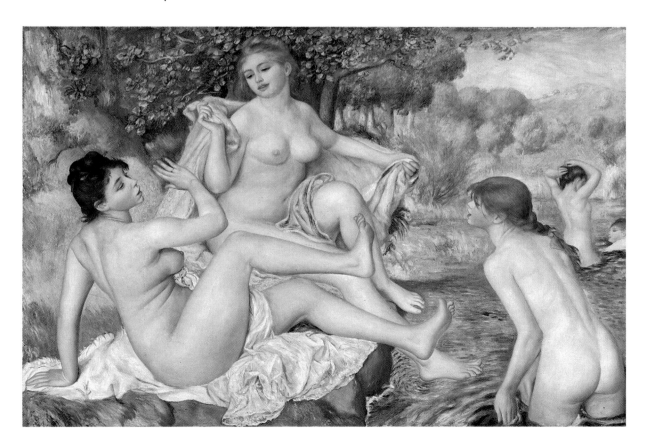

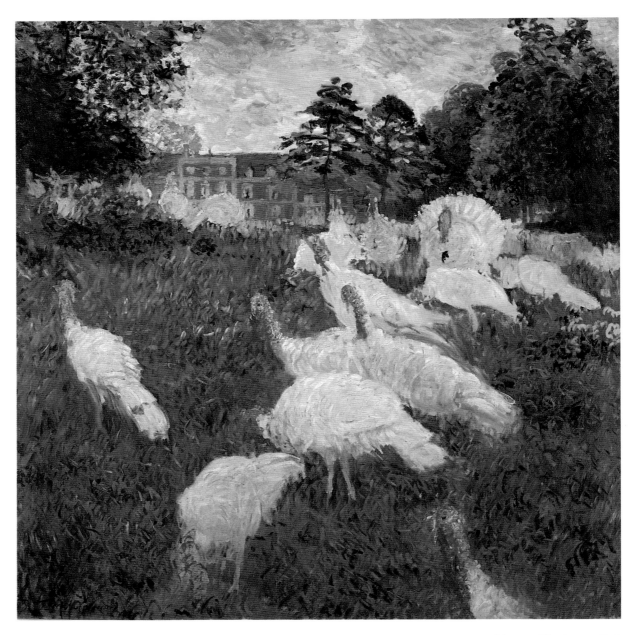

Monet *Turkeys* 1876

Struggling On: Monet

Claude Monet to Paul Durand-Ruel

[Pourville], *18 September 1882*

You will think I am wanting in courage, but I can't hold out any longer and am in a state of utter despair. After a few days of good weather, it's raining again and once again I have had to put the studies I started to one side. It's driving me to distraction and the unfortunate thing is that I take it out on my poor paintings. I destroyed a large picture of flowers which I'd just done along with three or four paintings which I not only scraped down but slashed. This is absurd, I know, but I feel the hour of my departure drawing near and I am witnessing a complete transformation taking place in nature, and my courage is failing... I'd like to be able to leave today so I wouldn't have to set my eyes on all those places I was unable to paint...

Claude Monet to Alice Hoschedé

Etretat, 1 February [1883]

... I've done an excellent day's work today, I'm very happy and what's more the weather is superb even though a little cold. I intend to do a large painting of the cliff at Etretat, although it is terribly bold of me to do so after Courbet has painted it so admirably, but I will try to do it in a different way ...

Claude Monet to Paul Durand-Ruel

Giverny, [12 January 1884]

... I would also ask you to set aside 500 francs for *Wednesday* which I will pick up when in Paris, since I've decided to leave for Italy straightaway. I want to spend a month in Bordighera, one of the most beautiful places we saw on our trip. From there I have great hopes of bringing you back a whole new series of things.

But I would ask you not to mention this trip to *anyone*, not because I want to make a secret out of it, but because I insist upon *doing it alone.* Much as I enjoyed making the trip there with Renoir as a tourist, I'd find it hard to work there together. I have always worked better alone and from my own impressions. So keep the secret unless otherwise instructed. If he knew I was about to go, Renoir would doubtless want to join me and that would be equally disastrous for both of us ...

Claude Monet to Paul Durand-Ruel

Giverny, Sunday, [27 April 1884]

I will come as you wish tomorrow morning but with a very few paintings and only because I don't want to offend you, since every single one of my paintings is in need of some kind of revision and the finishing touches must be done with care, and this will mean more than a day's work. I need to look over it all in peace and quiet, in the right conditions. For three months I've been at work and have spared no efforts and as I'm never satisfied when working from nature, it's only since I've been here these last few days that I've seen what can be done with a certain number of the paintings that I did ...

Claude Monet to Alice Hoschedé

[Etretat], *Friday evening,* [27 November 1885]

After another rainy morning I was glad to find the weather slightly improved: despite a high wind blowing and a rough sea, or rather, because of it, I hoped for a fruitful session at the Manneporte; however an accident befell me. Don't alarm yourself now, I am safe and sound since I'm writing to you, although you nearly had no news and I would never have seen you again. I was hard at work beneath the cliff, well sheltered from the wind, in the spot which you visited with me; convinced that the tide was drawing out I took no notice of the waves which came and fell a few feet away from me. In short, absorbed as I was, I didn't see a huge wave coming; it threw me against the cliff and I was tossed about in its wake along with my materials! My immediate thought was that I was done for, as the water dragged me down, but in the end I managed to clamber out on all fours, but Lord, what a state I was in! My boots, my thick stockings and my coat were soaked through; the palette which I had kept a grip on had been knocked over my face and my beard was covered in blue, yellow etc. But anyway, now the excitement has passed and no harm's done, the worst of it was that I lost my painting which was very soon broken up, along with my easel, bag, etc.

Impossible to fish anything out. Besides everything was torn to shreds by the sea, that 'old hag' as your sister calls her. Anyway, I was lucky to escape, but how I raged when I found once I'd changed that I couldn't work, and when it dawned on me that the painting I had been counting on was done for, I was furious. Immediately I set about telegraphing Troisgros to send me what's missing and an easel will be ready tomorrow...

To think I might never have seen you again.

From 'La Vie d'un Paysagiste' by Guy de Maupassant in *Gil Blas* (28 November 1886)

Off [Monet] went, followed by children carrying his canvases, five or six canvases representing the same subject at different times of day and with different light effects. He picked them up and put them down in turn, according to the changing weather....

Camille Pissarro to Lucien Pissarro

Paris, [9 January 1887]

... Monet has been to Durand's, he brought the paintings he did this year; he has one painted in bright sunlight, it is an incomprehensible fantasy; M. Caseburne [Durand-Ruel's cashier] himself admitted to me that it is absolutely incoherent, blobs of white mixed with Veronese green and yellows, and the drawing is completely lost.... I assure you I would not be afraid to show my work with Monet's. Durand says that Monet pities me because of the course I have taken. So! ... Perhaps he does, now ... but wait. You must realize that eventually we shall have all those who are not haunted by romanticism, who feel simple, naive nature, which does not exclude character and science, like the primitives.... Monet plays his salesman's game, and it serves him; but it is not in my character to do likewise, nor is it to my interest, and it would be in contradiction above all to my conception of art. I am not a romantic! ...

Camille Pissarro to Lucien Pissarro

Paris, 10 July 1888

I told you that Monet's recent paintings did not impress me as more advanced than his other works; almost all painters take this view. Degas is even more severe, he considers these paintings have been made to sell. Besides he always maintains that Monet made nothing but beautiful decorations. But the recent works are, as Fénéon says, more vulgar than ever. Renoir also finds them retrograde. Durand's son, too, is of this opinion; but of course his attitude is governed by the fact that he is a rival dealer.

I ran into Monet at Durand-Ruel's. For some reason or other he always seems to have a sly look. I happened to be reading an article which criticized his work in the most idiotic way, presenting arguments so stupid I couldn't help calling them to his attention;

the things said in his favour were equally idiotic. Other than this we did not discuss painting – what would be the point? – he cannot understand me. After all he may be right, for each of us must remain faithful to his own capacities! . . .

Claude Monet to Alice Hoschedé

Fresselines, Wednesday, 8 May [1889]

. . . I'm going to offer fifty francs to my landlord to see if I can have the oak tree's leaves removed, if I can't I'm done for since it appears in five paintings and plays a leading part in three, but I fear it won't do any good as he's an unfriendly old moneybags who's already tried to prevent access to one of his fields, and it was only because the priest intervened that I was able to carry on going there. Anyway, therein lies the only hope of salvation for these pictures.

Claude Monet to Alice Hoschedé

Fresselines, Wednesday, 8 May [1889]

I'm overjoyed, having unexpectedly been granted permission to remove the leaves from my fine oak tree! It was quite a business bringing along sufficiently long ladders into the ravine. Anyway it's done now, two men having worked on it since yesterday. Isn't it the final straw to be finishing a winter landscape at this time of year? . . .

Claude Monet to Gustave Geffroy

[Giverny], *22 June 1890*

I have once more taken up things that can't be done: water with grasses weaving on the bottom. . . . It's wonderful to see, but it's maddening to try to paint it. But I'm always tackling that sort of thing!

Claude Monet to Gustave Geffroy

[Giverny], *7 October 1890*

. . . I'm hard at it, working stubbornly on a series of different effects (grain stacks), but at this time of the year the sun sets so fast that it's impossible to keep up with it . . . I'm getting so slow at my work it makes me despair, but the further I get, the more I see that a lot of work has to be done in order to render what I'm looking for: 'instantaneity', the 'envelope' above all, the same light spread over everything, and more than ever I'm disgusted by easy things that come in one go. Anyway, I'm increasingly obsessed by the need to render what I experience, and I'm praying that I'll have a few more good years left to me because I think I may make some progress in that direction . . .

Cézanne *Provençal Landscape:*
*The Copse c.*1888

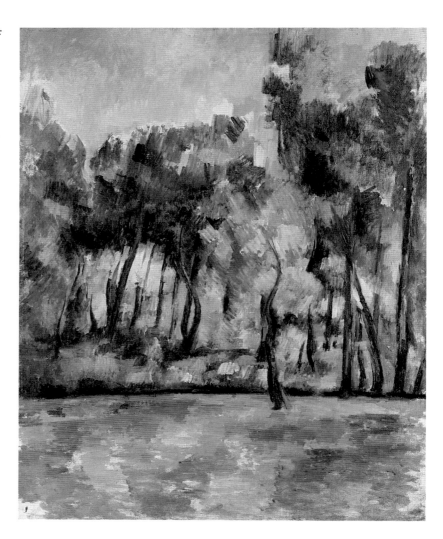

Struggling On: Cézanne

Paul Cézanne to Emile Zola

Gardanne, 4 April 1886

I've just received *L'Oeuvre* which you were kind enough to send to me. I would like to thank the author of *Les Rougon-Macquart* for this token of remembrance, and I ask permission to shake his hand in memory of years gone by.

Paul Cézanne to Emile Zola

[Aix], *Jas de Bouffan, 25 August 1885*

The comedy begins. I wrote to La Roche-Guyon the same day I was dropping you a line to thank you for thinking of me. I haven't had any news since; anyway, my isolation here is complete. The brothel in town . . . but nothing apart from that. I fork out – dirty phrase – but I need relaxation, and at that price I ought to have it.

I shall ask you, then, not to reply – my letter must have arrived in its own time.

I give you my thanks and beg you to bear with me.

I'm beginning to do some painting, but [only] because I'm more or less free of troubles. Every day I go to Gardanne, and in the evenings I come back to the country at Aix. If I'd only had a family who were indifferent – everything would have been so much better.

From *En écoutant Cézanne, Degas et Renoir* by Ambroise Vollard (1938)

[Cézanne] did not like people to watch him when he was painting. Renoir told me just how touchy he was. During a stay at Jas de Bouffan, Renoir accompanied Cézanne to his motif. An old woman was in the habit of sitting down with her knitting a few yards away. She only had to be near for Cézanne to be beside himself. As soon as he noticed her – and with his keen, penetrating eyes he caught sight of her from afar – he cried out: 'The old bitch is coming!' and despite all Renoir's efforts to stop him, he packed up his things in a rage and away he went.

Paul Cézanne to Emile Bernard

[1880s]

Isolation, that's all I'm good for. At least, that way, no one tries to take over my life for me.

Struggling On: Pissarro

Paul Gauguin to Camille Pissarro

Paris, July 1881

My dear Master, I have heard you put forward the theory that a painter must live in Paris in order to keep alive his ideas. How can you say such a thing at a time when we poor devils are sweltering at La Nouvelle-Athènes and all you choose to do is live like a hermit in his hermitage. I hope to see you here one of these days. . . .

Has Monsieur Cesanne [*sic*] found the exact *formula* for a work that will be accepted by all? If he has found a way of compressing the extravagant expression of all his sensations into one single process, I beg you to get him to talk about it in his sleep; ply him with one of those mysterious homeopathic drugs and come straight to Paris to share the information. . . .

Paul Gauguin to Camille Pissarro

Paris, 18 January 1882

I received your most extraordinary letter this morning. It seems that the fog is affecting your morale and that your mood is very black – I thought you had given up that colour. All the same I'm not too worried about you; I know that it's always a long and difficult task to finish anything however one goes about it, but you usually have the perseverance to get there in the end. . . .

Camille Pissarro to Théodore Duret

[Pontoise], *13 May 1882*

I am not rolling in money, as the romantics say . . . I am enjoying the fruits of a moderate but regular sale. I ask only one thing; that this continue. I dread a return to the past.

Camille Pissarro to Esther Isaacson

[Pontoise], *Summer 1882*

Durand-Ruel, one of the great dealers in Paris, came to see me and has taken a large part of my canvases and watercolours, and proposes to take everything that I do – it means tranquillity for some time, and the means of doing some important works . . .

Camille Pissarro to Lucien Pissarro

[1883]

I am very much disturbed by my unpolished and rough execution. I should like to develop a smooth technique which, by retaining the old fierceness, would be rid of those jarring notes which make it difficult to see my canvases clearly except when the light falls on them from the front. . . .

Camille Pissarro to Lucien Pissarro

Osny, 28 February 1883

. . . How I regret not having seen the Whistler show . . . he is even a bit too *pretentious* for me, aside from this I should say that for the room white and yellow is a charming combination. The fact is that we ourselves made the first experiments with colours: the room in which we showed was lilac, bordered with canary yellow. But we poor little rejected painters lack the means to carry out our concepts of decoration. As for urging Durand-Ruel to hold an exhibition in a hall decorated by us, it would, I think, be wasted breath. You saw how we had to fight with him for white frames, and finally I had to abandon the idea. . . .

Camille Pissarro to Lucien Pissarro

Osny, 13 June 1883

I mentioned to Degas that you are thinking of taking Legros' course in drawing. Degas says that there is one way of escaping Legros' influence, the method is simply this: it is to reproduce, in your own place from memory, the drawing you made in class. . . . a moment will come when you will be astonished by the ease with which you retain forms, and, curiously enough, the observations you make from memory will have far more power and be much more original than those you owe to direct contact with nature. The drawing will have art – it will be your own – this is a good way of escaping slavish imitation.

Camille Pissarro to Lucien Pissarro

Paris, July 1883

While you have the time – time should not be wasted – make drawings; it will do you more good than you can imagine. If you just made copies of bas-reliefs or Egyptian statues, but did them with scrupulous care, you would make progress. It is best to select simple things like a sphinx, some oxen, etc., there must be good things of this type at the Kensington Museum, not photographs, the originals themselves. Thus you will get the most perfect insight into the problem of simplification. The primitives aren't bad for this either, on the contrary: Holbein, *and do not neglect nature*.

Camille Pissarro to Lucien Pissarro

Rouen, 20 November 1883

. . . my works offend English taste. – Remember that I have the temperament of a peasant, I am melancholy, harsh and savage in my works, it is only in the long run that I can expect to please, provided those who look at my pictures have a grain of indulgence; but the eye of the passer-by is too hasty and sees only the surface.

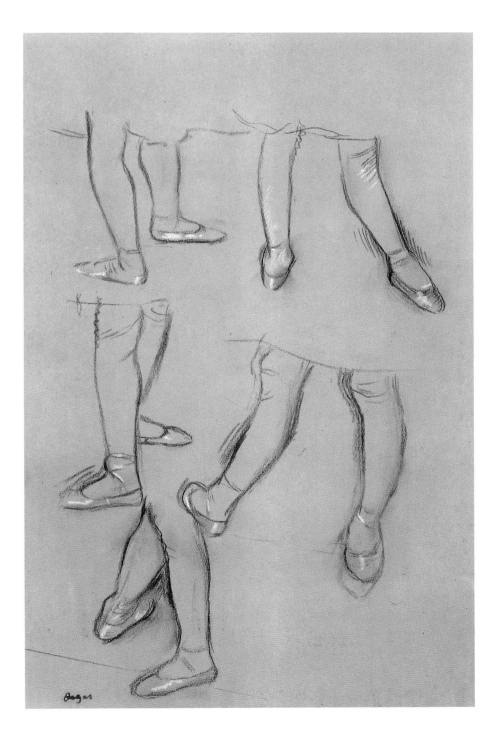

Degas
Studies for the Little Fourteen-Year-Old Dancer
1878–80

Paul Gauguin to Camille Pissarro

[Rouen, October 1884]

... I'm passionately interested in reading character from handwriting; if you have a letter from someone whom you know well and I don't know, it would amuse me to read his character and see if I'm right.

Your handwriting shows that you are:

Simple, open, not very tactful.

A thinker – well-balanced, more poet than logician, not very receptive to new ideas – keenly intelligent – very enthusiastic.

Very ambitious. At the same time stubborn and gentle.

Lazy – sometimes awkward and greedy for money.

Stingy – sometimes selfish and unloving.

You don't deviate from your chosen path.

Extremely wary.

Rather whimsical.

Well-shaped letter. You have a feeling for art, but not *aesthetics.*

Your spelling, which is often your own, shows that you're inclined to reject one detail in order to think up another. *All in all, a very complex character.*

This is what your writing shows. . . .

Camille Pissarro to Lucien Pissarro

Paris, [January 1886]

[I am] going to Durand's to see if anything has turned up. – Yesterday evening he had nothing to give me, not even twenty francs, it's very embarrassing! Things must be very bad. Everything is at a standstill.

I know that Monet, Sisley and Renoir get no more than I do. Monet particularly must be up against it, for Petit, too, is in dire straits, much worse off than even Durand . . .

Camille Pissarro to Lucien Pissarro

Paris, 30 July 1886

... Durand likes my paintings, but not the style of execution. His son, the one who went to New York with him, saw them but has not said a word to me. – Durand prefers the old execution, however he grants that my recent paintings have more light – in short, he isn't very keen. My *Grey Weather* doesn't please him; his son and Caseburne also dislike it. What kills art in France is that they only appreciate works that are easy to sell. It appears that the subject is unpopular. They object to the red roof and backyard, just what gave character to the painting which has the stamp of a *modern primitive,* and they dislike brick houses, precisely what inspired me.

Camille Pissarro to Lucien Pissarro

Paris, 3 December 1886

[M. Pillet] was delighted with my fans; he told me that my work was in no way unclear, and that many people up till now opposed to Impressionism have been struck with the clarity and strength of the drawing, and he felt that I had conquered the monotony which the desire to be sober and harmonious often brings. – Goodness! . . .

Camille Pissarro to Lucien Pissarro

Eragny, [23 February 1887]

. . . This morning I received a letter from de Bellio. He writes that he does not believe scientific research into the nature of colour and light can help the artist, neither can anatomy nor the laws of optics. . . .

But surely it is clear that we could not pursue our studies of light with much assurance if we did not have as a guide the discoveries of Chevreul and other scientists. I would not have distinguished between local colour and light if science had not given us the hint; the same holds true for complementary colours, contrasting colours, etc. 'Yes,' he will tell me, 'but these have always been taken into account, look at Monet.' It is at this point that the question becomes serious!

Pissarro *View from my Window* 1886

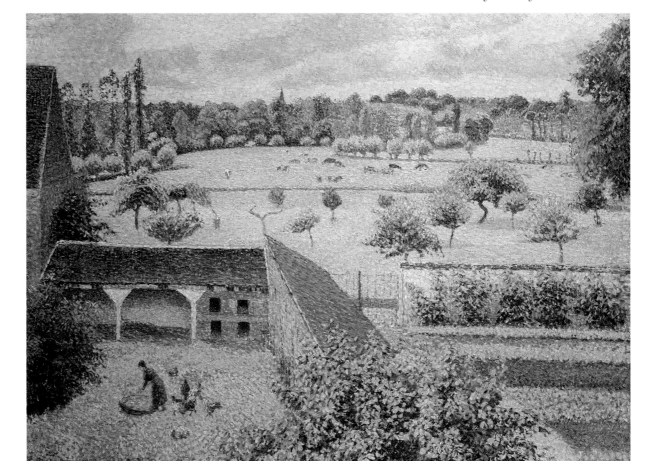

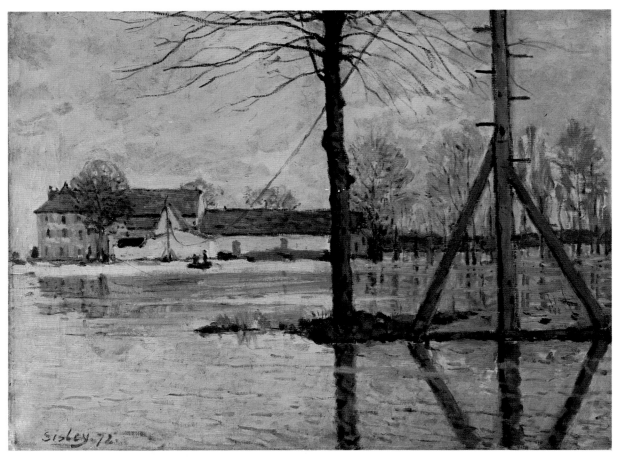

Sisley *Flood at Port Marly* 1872

Struggling On: Sisley

Alfred Sisley to Georges Charpentier

28 March 1879

After all the proofs of sympathy that you have given me, it is no secret I betray in explaining my unfortunate position. Since I decided to exhibit at the Salon I find myself more isolated than ever. You are my only hope.

I am forced to leave Sèvres and without resources. I do not know where to turn. I need 600 francs. But as it is a rather large sum I only ask you to advance me half of it. A week from today I may be able to find some rest. Perhaps among your friends there may be someone who, to do me a kindness, would advance me the sum in return for something of mine.

If I am hung, the Salon will help. I hope I shall be. In any case you will have contributed to getting me out of the most disastrous position in which I have yet found myself. I shall be very grateful. I should like to see you one of these days.

Alfred Sisley to Paul Durand-Ruel

[Moret-sur-Loing], *17 November 1885*

I have received the 200 francs. This will pay a bill which falls due on the 20th of this month and a few small debts. But afterwards? . . . I shall be again without a sou. However I must give something to my butcher and my grocer; to one I have paid nothing for six months and to the other nothing for a year. I also need some money for myself at the start of winter. There are certain things I must have, and I would like to think that I can depend upon a little calm in order to work. I am completely in pieces. Tomorrow or afterwards I shall send you three canvases. It is the only finished work I have.

Alfred Sisley to Alphonse Tavernier [friend]

[1880s]

. . . To give life to the work of art is certainly one of the most necessary tasks of the true artist. Everything must serve this end: form, colour, surface. The artist's impression is the life-giving factor.

Although the landscape painter must always be the master of his brush and his subject, the manner of painting must be capable of expressing the emotions of the artist. You see I am in favour of differing techniques within the same picture. This is not the general opinion at present, but I think I am right, especially when it is a question of light.

The sunlight in softening the outlines of one part of a scene will exalt others and these effects of light which seem nearly material in a landscape ought to be interpreted in a material way on canvas. . . .

The sky is not simply a background: its planes give depth (for the sky has planes as well as solid ground), and the shapes of clouds give movement to a picture. What is more beautiful indeed than the summer sky, with its wispy clouds idly floating across the blue? What movement and grace! Don't you agree? They are like waves on the sea; one is uplifted and carried away. But there is another aspect – the evening sky. Clouds grow thin, like furrowed fields, like eddies of water frozen in the air, and then gradually fade away in the light of the setting sun. Solemnity and melancholy – the sad moment of departure which I find especially moving.

Alfred Sisley to Paul Durand-Ruel

25 November 1885

You are better placed than I to know what will please the collectors. Therefore return to me the two canvases you think less saleable. I will replace them on my next trip. The situation here remains unchanged.

Struggling On: Degas

Edgar Degas to Albert Hecht [banker and ballet-enthusiast]

19 bis rue Fontaine St-Georges, Tuesday morning, [1880s]

Have you the *power* to get the Opéra to give me a pass for the day of the *dance examination*, which, so I have been told, is to be on Thursday?

I have done so many of these dance examinations without having seen them that I am a little ashamed of it.

Pierre-Auguste Renoir from *En écoutant Cézanne, Degas et Renoir* by Ambroise Vollard (1920)

'... look at [Degas'] pastels!... When you think that with difficult stuff to handle he has managed to achieve the colouring of frescoes! When I saw his extraordinary exhibition at Durand-Ruel's in '85, I was in the thick of experimenting, trying to get the quality of frescoes in oil painting; you can imagine how stunned I was when I saw his show!'

Edgar Degas to Henri Lerolle [painter and musician]

[Paris], *4 December 1883*

My dear Lerolle, go at once to hear Thérésa at the [café-concert] Alcazar, rue de Faubourg-Poissonière.

It is near the conservatoire and it is better. I have already said, a long time ago – I do not know what man of taste said it – that she should be put on to Gluck. ... It is the right moment to go and hear this admirable artist.

She opens her large mouth and there emerges the most roughly, the most delicately, the most spiritually tender voice imaginable. And the soul, and the good taste, where could one find better? It is admirable.

Edgar Degas to Henri Lerolle

21 August 1884

... If you were single, fifty years old (for the last month), you would know similar moments when a door shuts inside one ... I have made too many plans, here I am, blocked, impotent. And then I have lost the thread of things. I thought there would always be enough time. ...

Edgar Degas from 'Degas' by Walter Sickert, in *The Burlington Magazine* (November 1917)

'I have always tried to persuade my colleagues to look for more combinations in the direction of drawing, which I consider a more promising field than colour. But they paid no attention, and took the other path.'

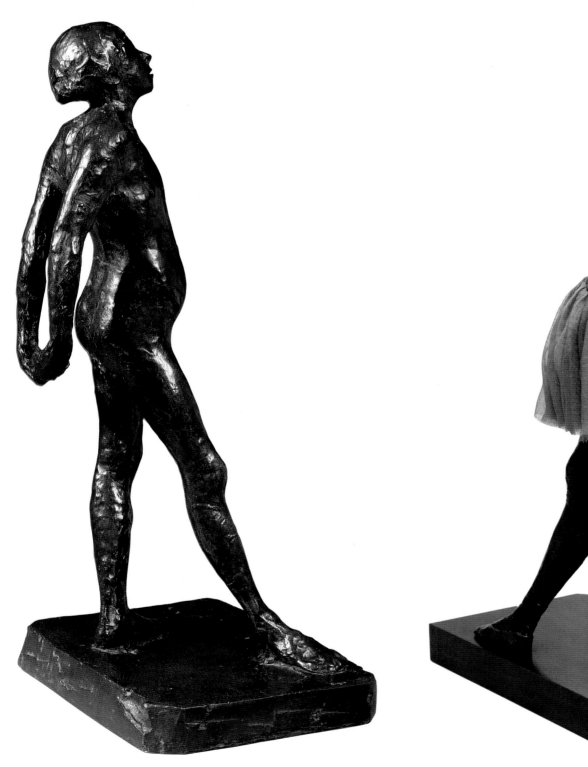
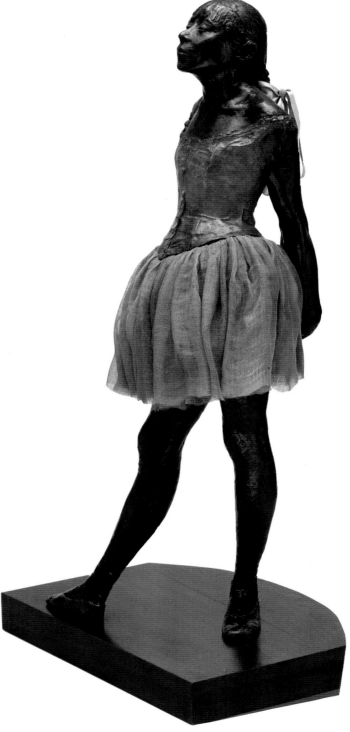

Degas *Nude Modello for Little Fourteen-Year-Old Dancer* c.1878–9

Degas *Little Fourteen-Year-Old Dancer* 1881

Pierre-Auguste Renoir from *Renoir* by François Fosca (1962)

'Degas is always doing his utmost to condemn colour. The truth of the matter is, he's a colourist himself but he just doesn't like it in other people.'

Pierre-Auguste Renoir from *Renoir, My Father* by Jean Renoir (1962)

... Since Chartres there has been only one sculptor, in my view that is Degas... Those who worked on the cathedrals succeeded in giving us an idea of eternity. That was the great preoccupation of their time. Degas found a way of expressing the malady of our contemporaries: I mean movement. Nowadays we all have the itch to move. Even Degas' jockeys and horses 'move'. But before he came along, only the Chinese had discovered the secret of movement. That is Degas' greatness: movement in the French style.
... Movement can be as eternal as immobility so long as it is in harmony with nature: if it expresses a natural human function. The flight of the swallow is as eternal as the tranquillity of the *Seated Scribe* in the Louvre. The statues in the Luxembourg are over-active for intellectual reasons, for literary reasons. A swallow speeds through the air to catch a gnat and to satisfy its hunger: not to verify a principle.'

Edgar Degas to Paul-Albert Bartholomé (sculptor)

Naples, 17 January 1886

... It is essential to do the same subject over again, ten times, a hundred times. In art nothing must appear accidental; not even movement.

Edgar Degas to Henri Rouart

Paris, Thursday, 1886

... One must continue to look at everything, the small and the large boats, the stir of people on the water and on the dry land too. It is the movement of people and things that distracts and even consoles if there is still consolation to be had for one so unhappy. If the leaves of the trees did not move, how sad the trees would be and we too! There is a tree in the garden of the neighbouring house which moves at each breath of wind. ...
I say to myself that this tree is delightful...

From the diaries of Daniel Halévy

30 December 1890

But my grandmother insisted, 'If someone said that you had lost your mind you know you wouldn't like it!'
   'If someone said I had lost my mind,' Degas replied, 'don't you think I'd be pleased? What use is my mind? Granted that it enables me to hail a bus and pay my fare. But once I am inside my studio, what use is my mind? I have my model, my pencil, my paper, my paints. My mind doesn't interest me.'

From 'Memoirs of Degas' in *The Burlington Magazine* by George Moore (1918)

[Degas]: '*La bête humaine qui s'occupe d'elle-même; un chat qui se lèche*... the nude has always been represented in poses which presuppose an audience, but these women of mine are honest, simple folk, unconcerned by any other interests than those involved in their physical condition ... It is as though you looked through a key-hole.'

Pierre-Auguste Renoir from *En écoutant Cézanne, Degas et Renoir* by Ambroise Vollard (1938)

'When one paints a brothel, it is often pornographic, but always desperately sad. Only Degas can give such subjects a joyful air together with the austerity of an Egyptian bas-relief. It is this near-religious and so chaste aspect of his work that makes it so great, and it is even more marked when he paints a prostitute.'

From *Degas, Dance, Drawing* by Paul Valéry (1937)

... [Degas] told me that, dining one day at Berthe Morisot's along with Mallarmé, he gave vent to his feelings about the agonies of poetic composition. 'What a business!' he lamented. 'My whole day gone on a blasted sonnet, without getting an inch further ... All the same, it isn't ideas I'm short of ... I'm full of them ... I've got too many ...'

'But Degas,' rejoined Mallarmé, with his gentle profundity, 'you can't make a poem with ideas ... *You make it with words.*'

Edgar Degas to Lorenz Frölich [Danish painter]
De Gas Brothers, New Orleans, [27 November 1872]
... nothing but a long stay can reveal the customs of a people, that is to say their charm. – Instantaneousness is photography, nothing more ...

From *Renoir, My Father* by Jean Renoir (1962)

In the hope of putting his adversary [Degas] in his place, Nadar had said, 'Don't forget that I too am a painter.' Deliberately affecting the accent of a roughneck, which made comic contrast to his conventional appearance, Degas replied, *'Va donc, ah, faux artiste, faux peintre, faux...tographe!'*

From *Growing Up With the Impressionists: the diary of Julie Manet*
[c.1896]
Monsieur Degas can think of nothing but photography. He has invited us all to dinner next week and he'll take our photograph by artificial light: the only thing is you have to pose for three minutes. He wanted to see if we would make good models and made M. Renoir pose, but he started laughing....

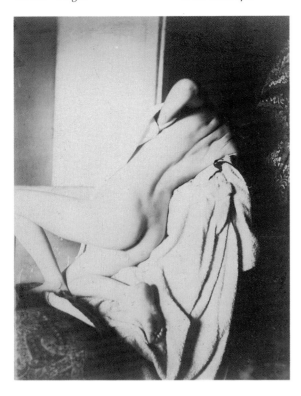

Degas Photograph, *Woman Drying Herself* 1896

Degas *After the Bath – Woman Drying Herself* 1896

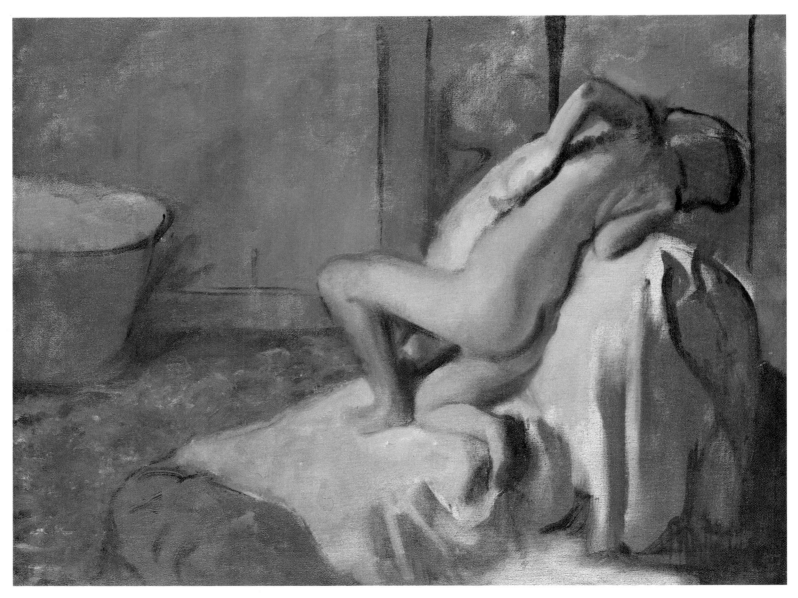

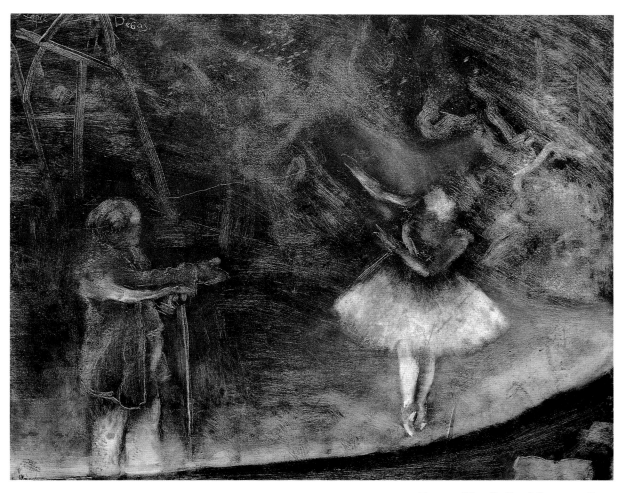

Degas *The Ballet Master* c.1874

Printmaking and the Japanese influence

Marcellin Desboutin to Joseph de Nittis

Dijon, 18 July 1876

Degas ... is no longer a friend, a man, an artist! He's a zinc or copper plate blackened with printer's ink, and plate and man are flattened together by his printing press whose mechanism has swallowed him completely! The man's crazes are out of this world. He is now in the metallurgic phase of reproducing his drawings with a roller and is running all over Paris, in the heat wave – trying to find the legion of specialists who will realize his obsession. He is a real poem! He talks only of metallurgists, lead-casters, lithographers, planishers!

Edgar Degas to Evariste de Valernes [painter]

[Paris], *6 December 1891*

... Ah! Sight! Sight! Sight! ... the difficulty of seeing makes me feel numb. ... I dream nevertheless of enterprises; I am hoping to do a suite of lithographs, a first series on nude women at their toilette and a second one on nude dancers. In this way one continues to the last day figuring things out. It is very fortunate that it should be so.

Camille Pissarro to Lucien Pissarro

Paris, 3 April 1891

It is absolutely necessary, while what I saw yesterday at Mlle Cassatt's is still fresh in my mind, to tell you about the coloured engravings she is to show at Durand-Ruel's ...

    You remember the effects you strove for at Eragny? Well, Mlle Cassatt has achieved just such effects, and admirably: the tone even, subtle, delicate, without stains on the seams, adorable blues, fresh rose etc. Then what must we have to succeed? ... money, yes, just a little money. We had to have copper plates, a *boîte à grain*, this was a bit of a nuisance but it is absolutely necessary to have uniform and imperceptible grains and a good printer. But the result is admirable, as beautiful as Japanese work, and it's done with printer's ink!

Cassatt *The Letter* 1891

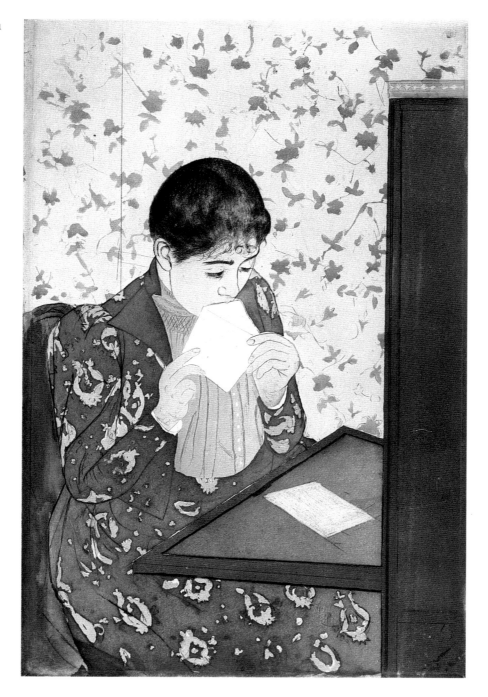

Claude Monet from *Les Peintres impressionnistes* by Théodore Duret (1878)

'We needed the arrival of Japanese albums in our midst before anyone dared to sit down on a river bank, and juxtapose on a canvas a roof which was bright red, a wall which was white, a green poplar, a yellow road and blue water. Before the example given by the Japanese this was impossible, the painter always lied. Nature with its boldest colours blinded him; all one ever saw on a canvas were subdued colours, drowning in a half-tone...'

Pierre-Auguste Renoir from *Renoir, My Father* by Jean Renoir (1962)

'There isn't a person, a landscape or a subject that doesn't possess at least some interest — although sometimes more or less hidden. When a painter discovers this hidden treasure, other people immediately exclaim at its beauty. Old Corot opened our eyes to the beauty of the Loing, which is a river like any other; and I am sure that the Japanese landscape is no more beautiful than other landscapes. But the point is that Japanese painters knew how to bring out their hidden treasure.'

Camille Pissarro to Lucien Pissarro

Paris, 2 February 1893

... I have been in Paris since yesterday ... we met M. and Mme Mirbeau at the railway station in Poissy and in the course of conversation the latter spoke to us with great enthusiasm of the Japanese exhibition (Utamaro and Hiroshige) organized by Bing at Durand's. We took the train to go and see it: a little room of faded rose and pistachio-green, it is exquisite, and the prints ... wonderful. It is an artistic event ...

I saw Monet at the Japanese exhibition. Damn it all, if this show doesn't justify us! There are grey sunsets that are the most striking instances of Impressionism.

Camille Pissarro to Lucien Pissarro

Paris, February 1893

... Went to the Impressionists' dinner yesterday with Titi [son], who became very annoyed in the company of the old gang.... Admirable, the Japanese exhibition. Hiroshige is a marvellous Impressionist. Monet, Renoir and I are full of enthusiasm for it. I'm pleased with my effects of snows and floods; these Japanese artists confirm my belief in our vision.

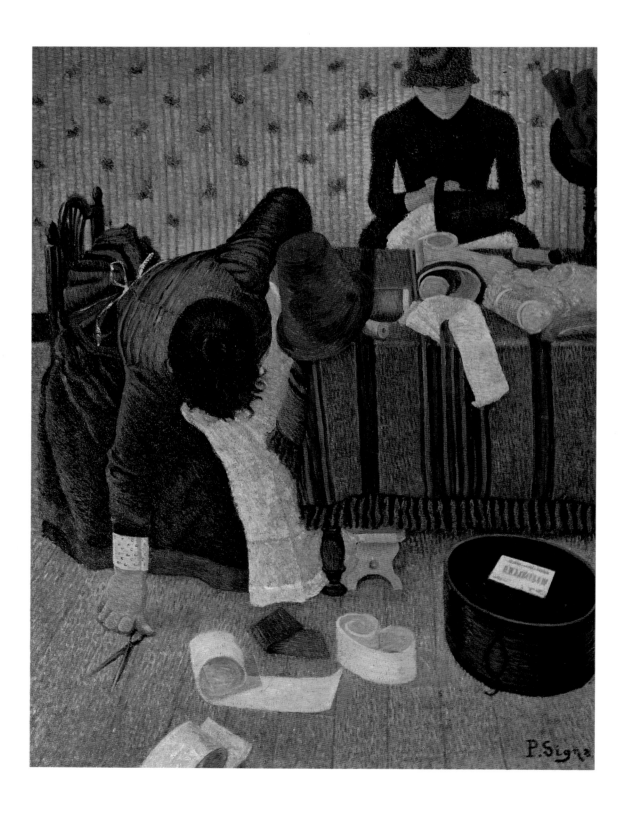

Signac *The Milliners* 1885–6

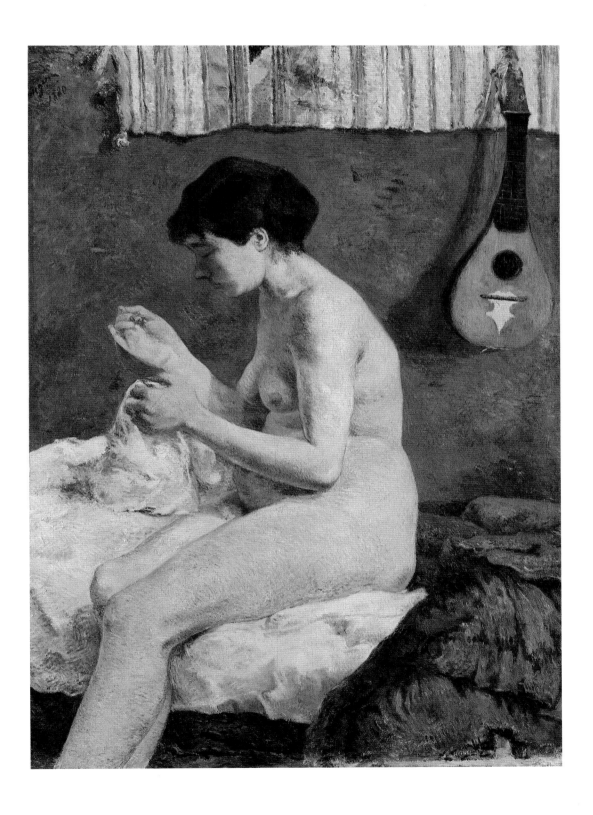

Gauguin *Nude* 1880

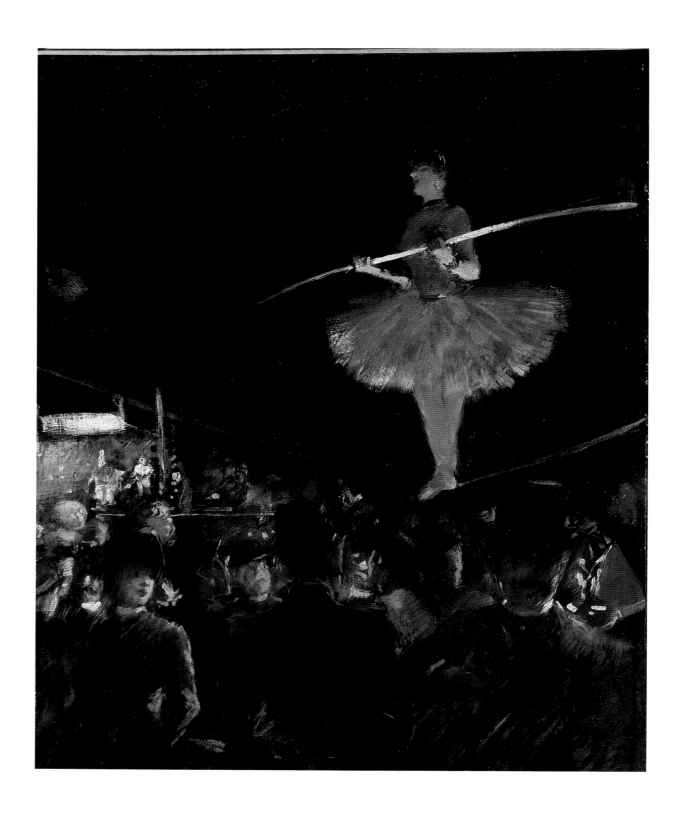

Forain *The Tightrope Walker* c.1880

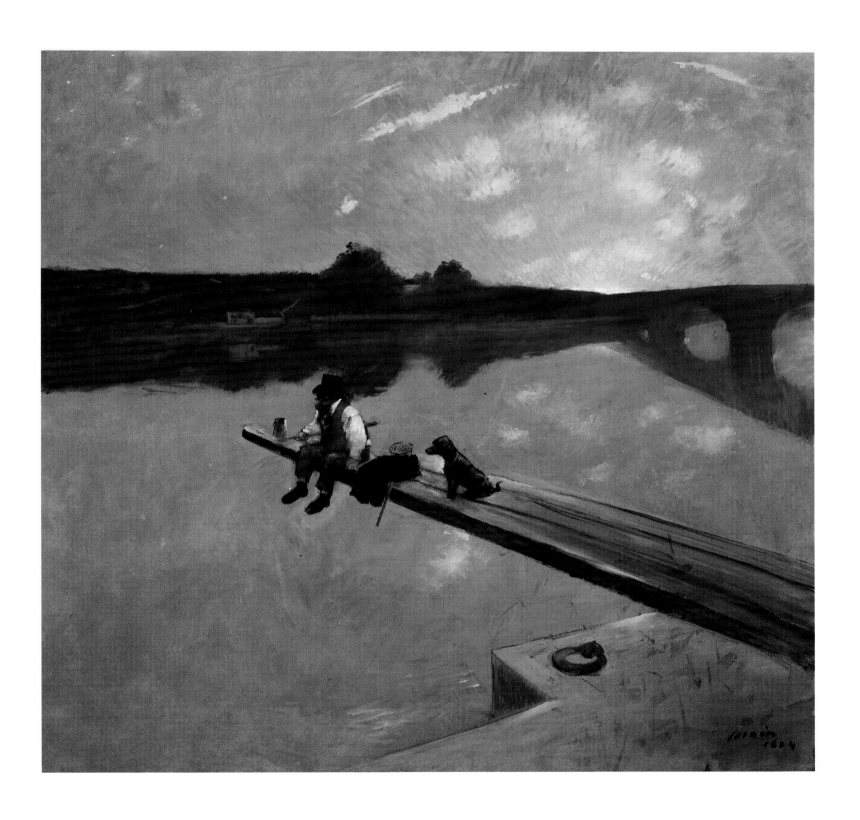

Forain *The Fisherman* 1884

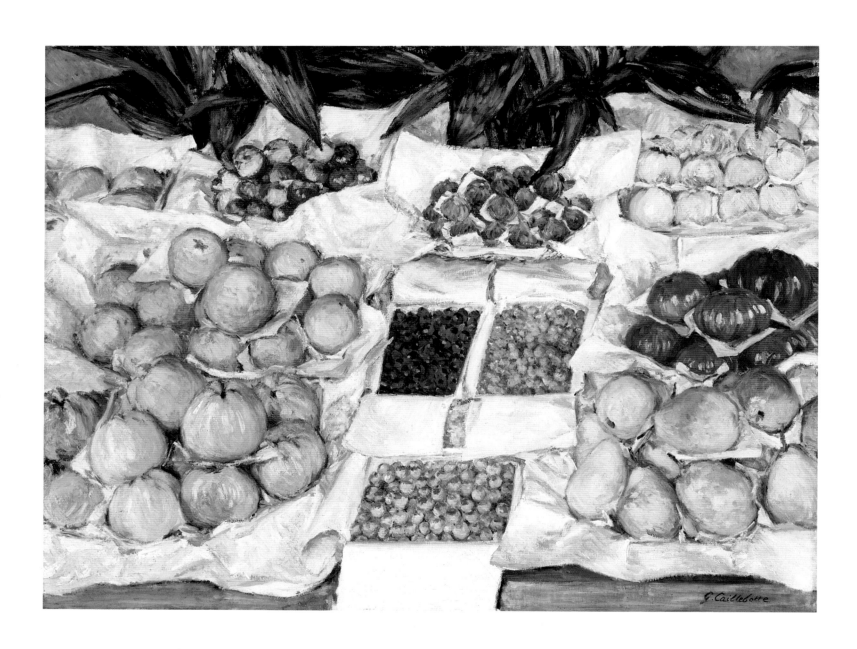

Caillebotte *Fruit Displayed on a Stand c.*1881–2

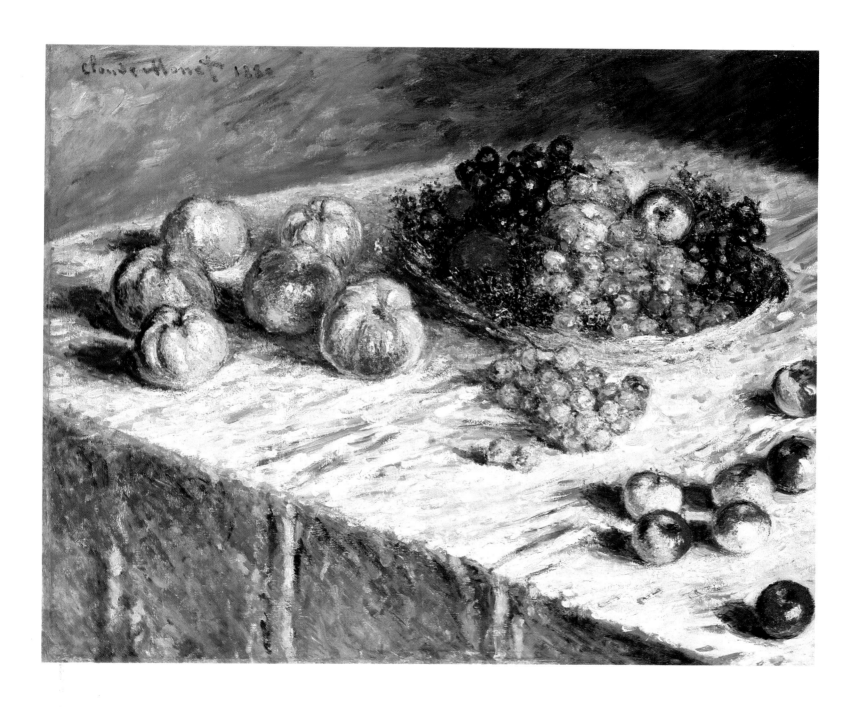

Monet *Still-Life: Apples and Grapes* 1800

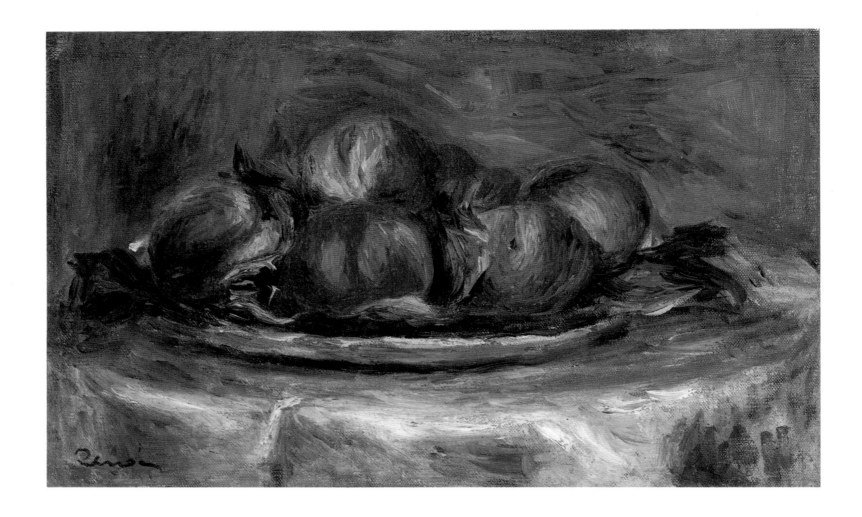

Renoir *Peaches on a Plate* 1902–5

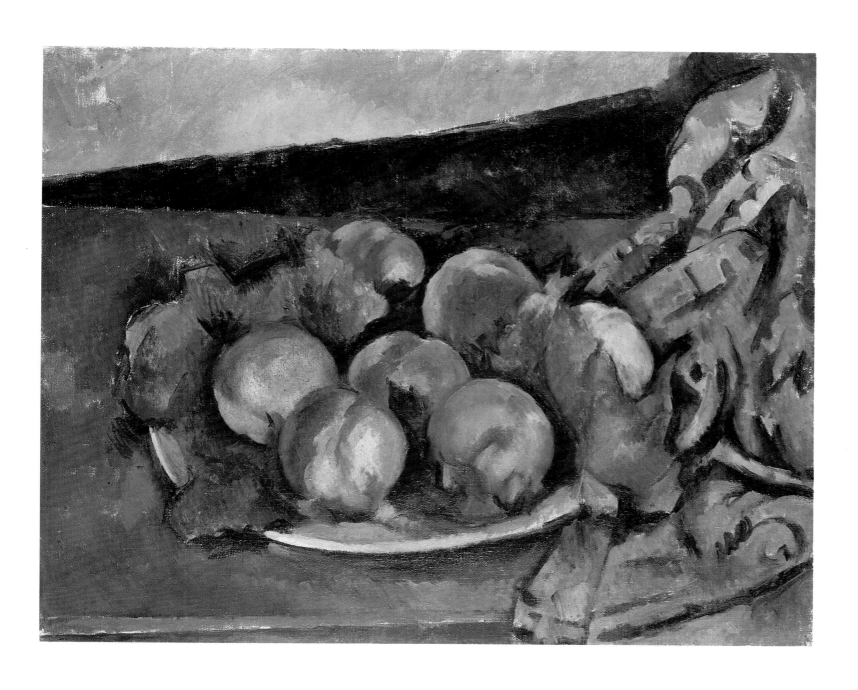

Cézanne *Dish of Peaches* c.1890–4

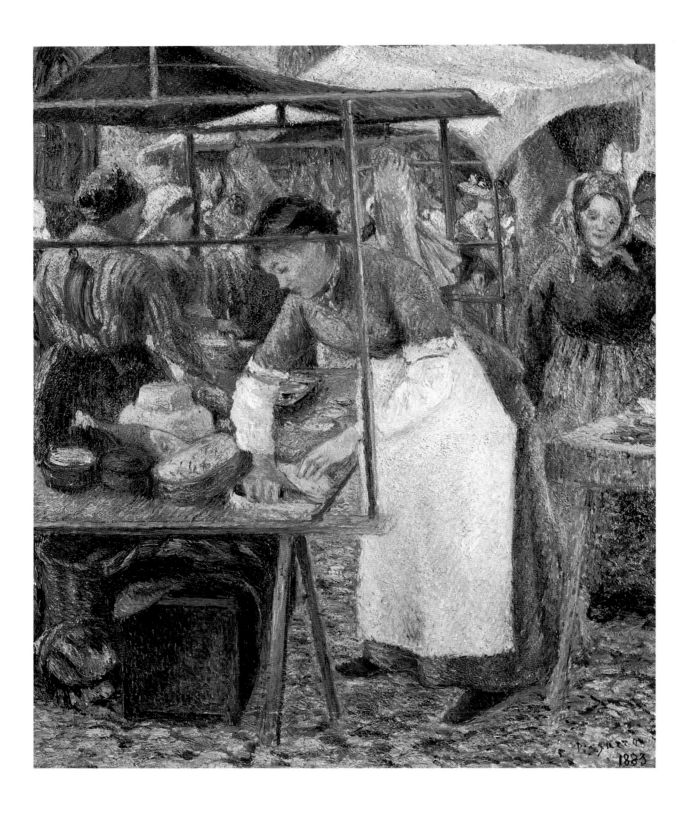

Pissarro *The Pork Butcher* 1883

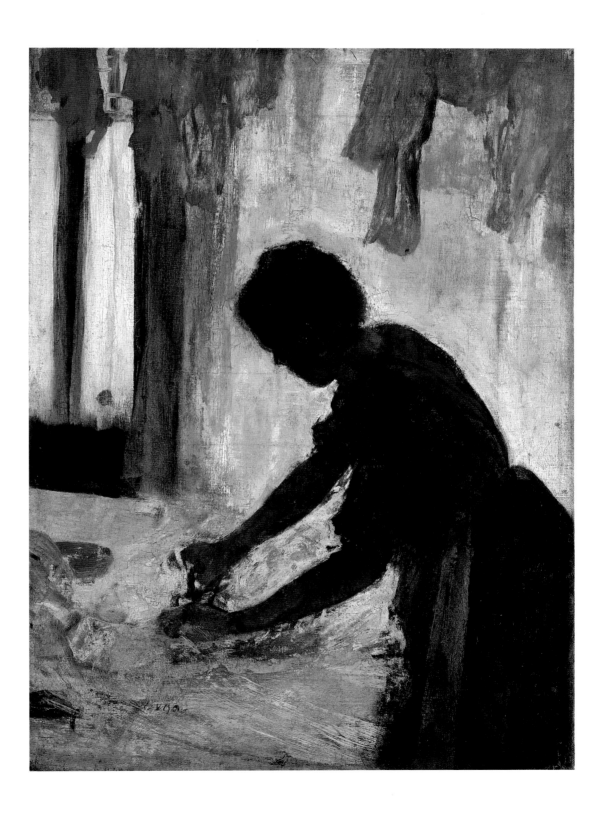

Degas *A Woman Ironing* 1873

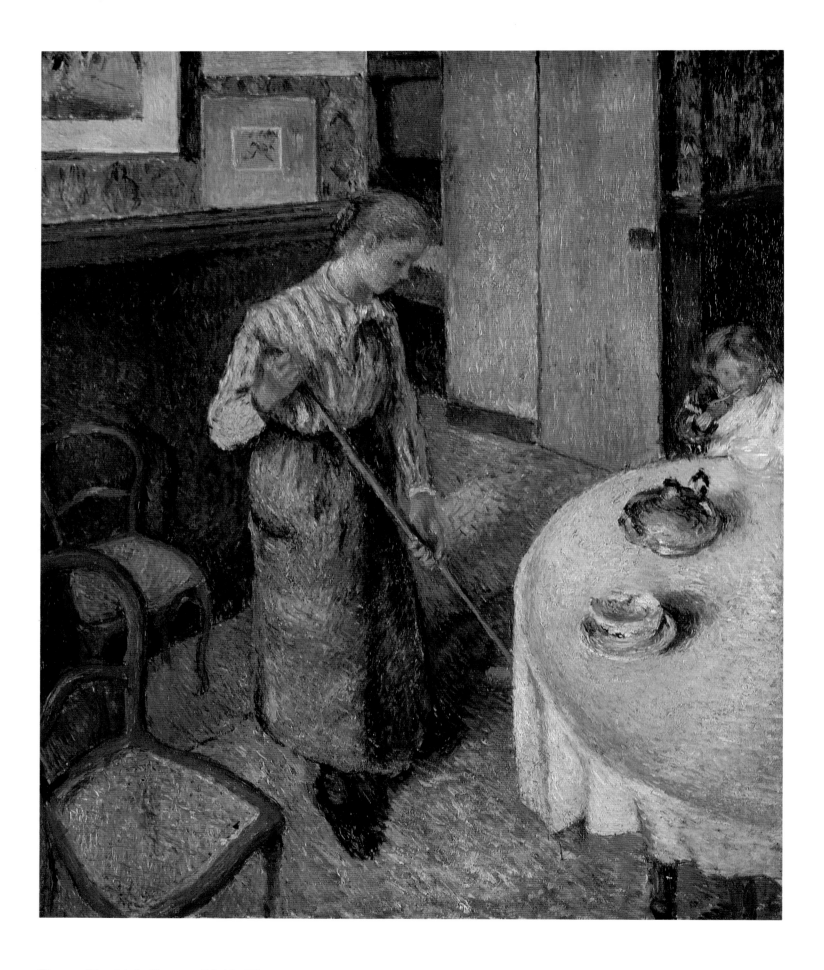

Pissaro *The Little Country Maid* 1882

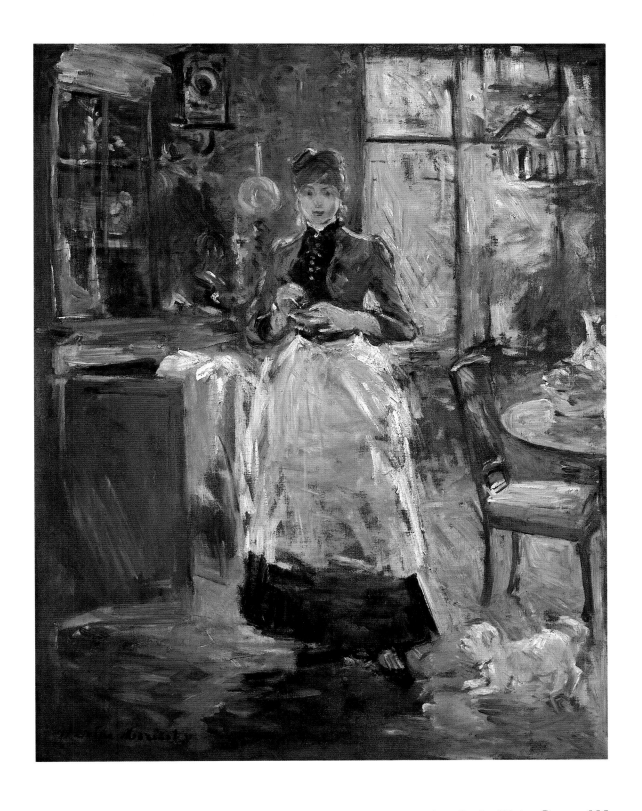

Morisot *In the Dining Room* 1886

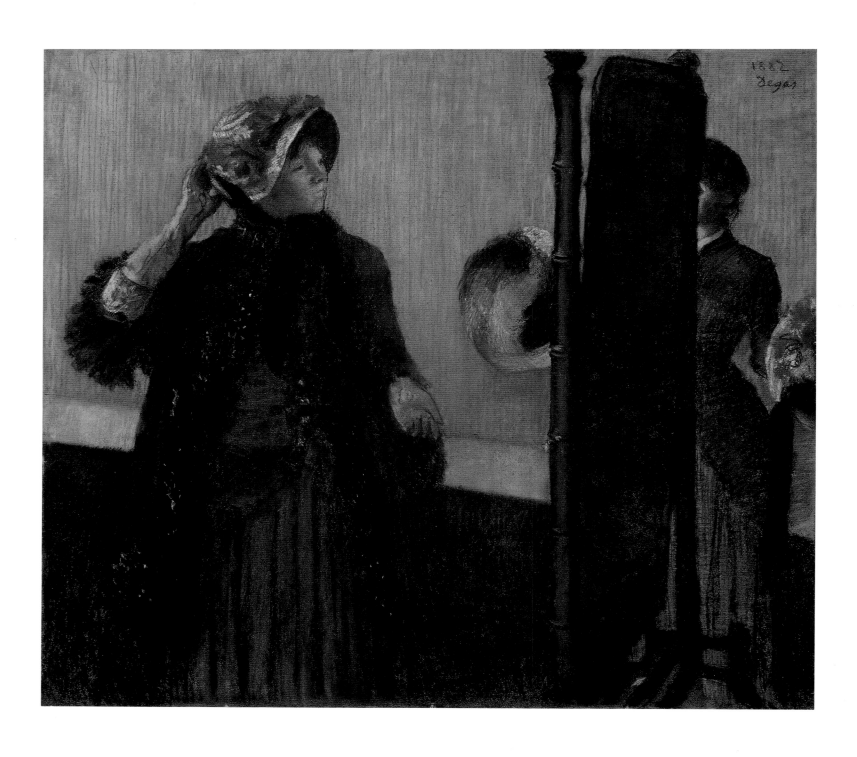

Degas *At the Milliner's* 1882

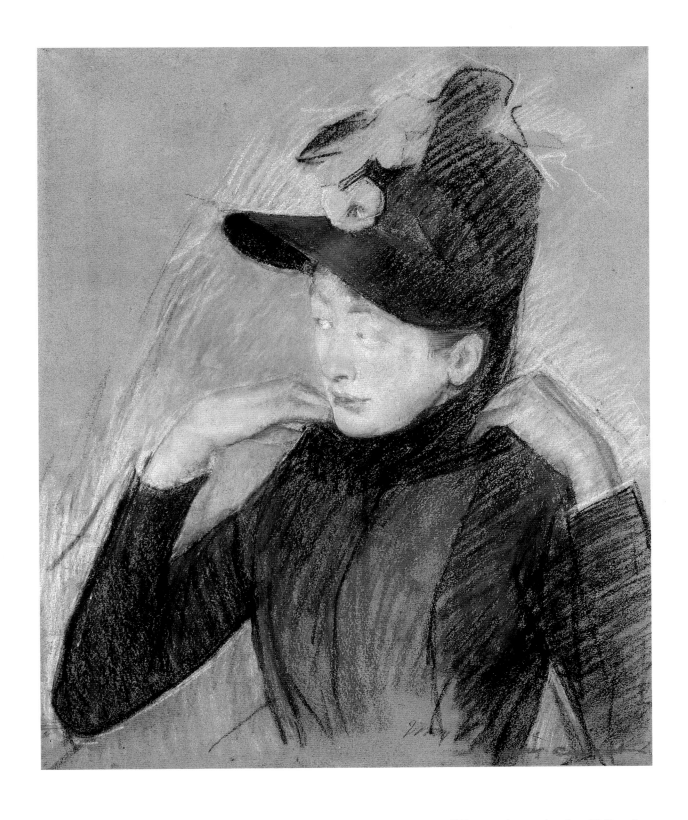

Cassatt *Woman Arranging her Veil* c.1890

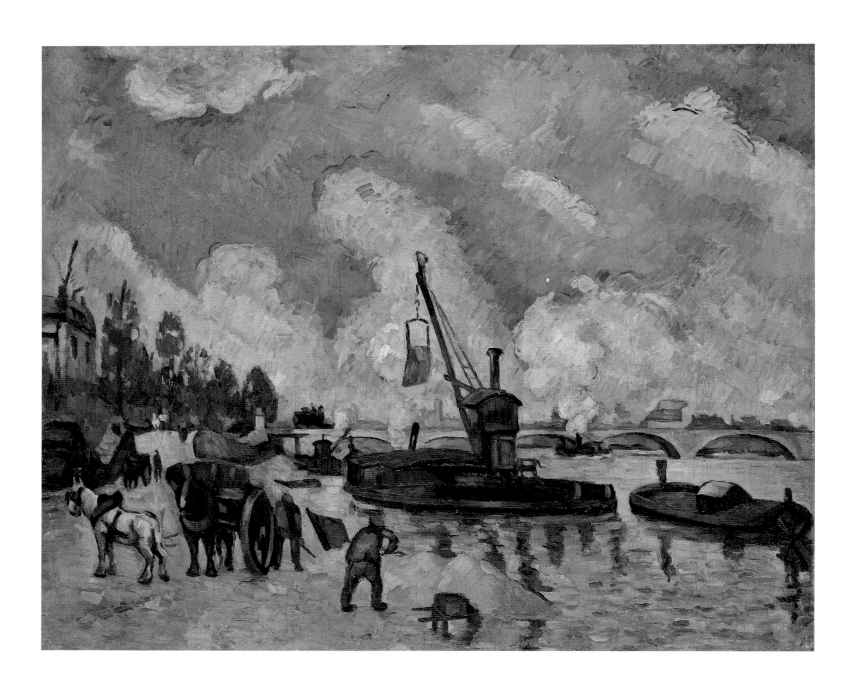

Cézanne *The Seine at Bercy* 1876–8

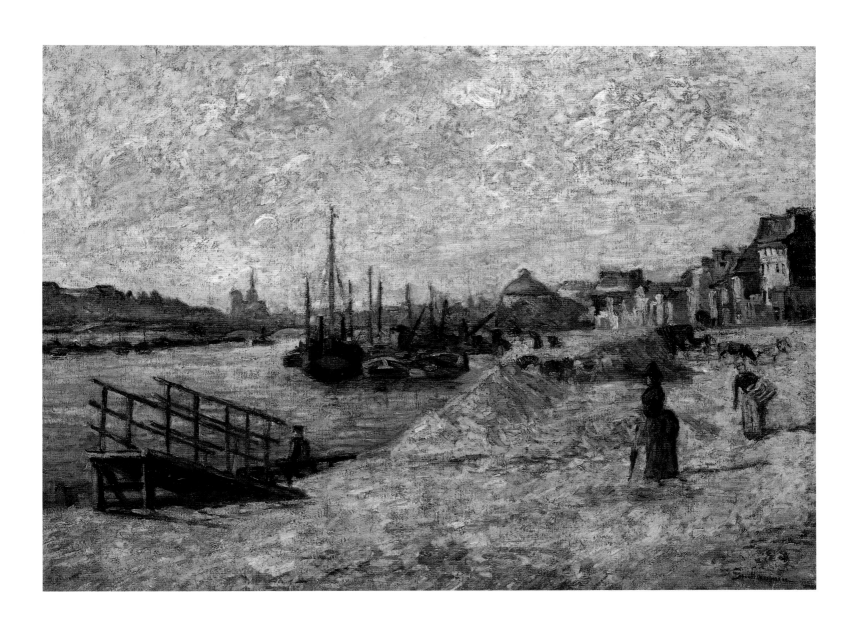

Guillaumin *Le Quai de Bercy* 1881

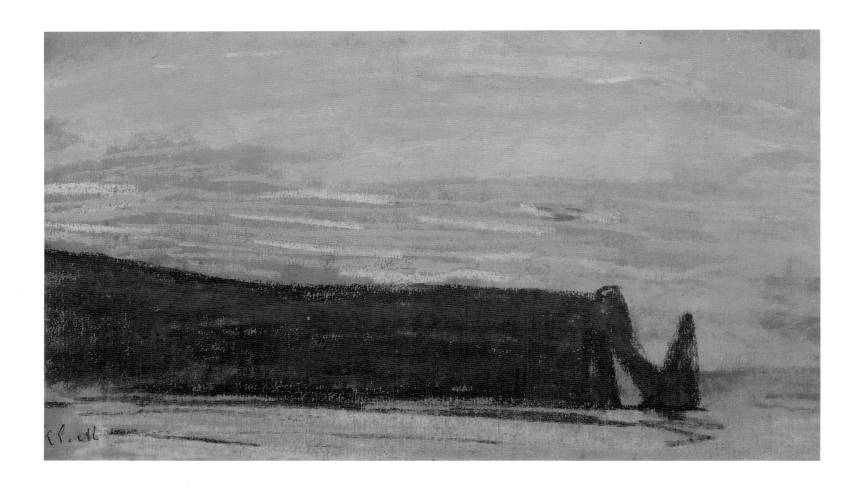

Monet *The Cliffs at Etretat* 1885

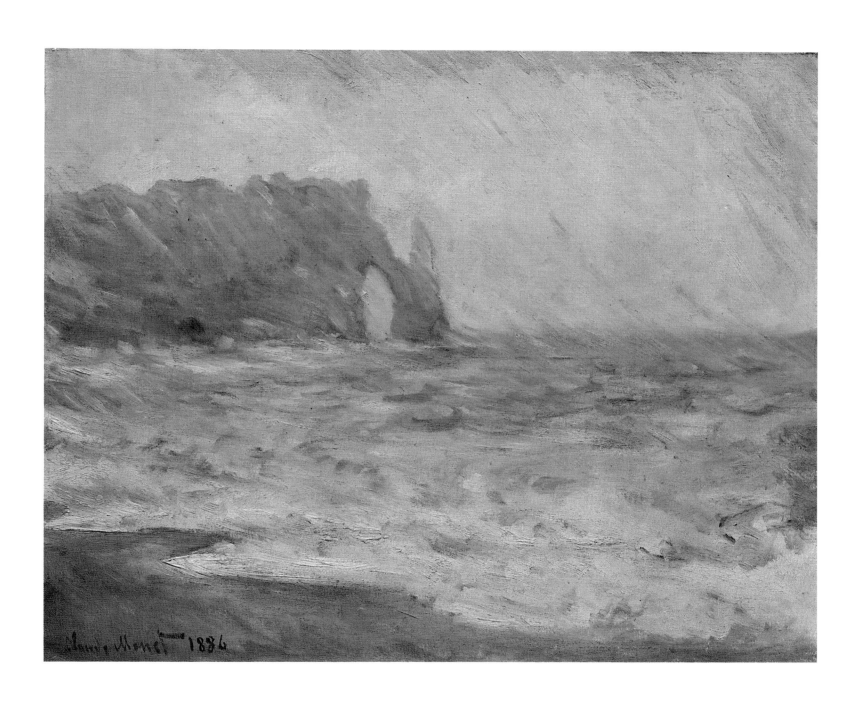

Monet *Rain, Etretat* 1886

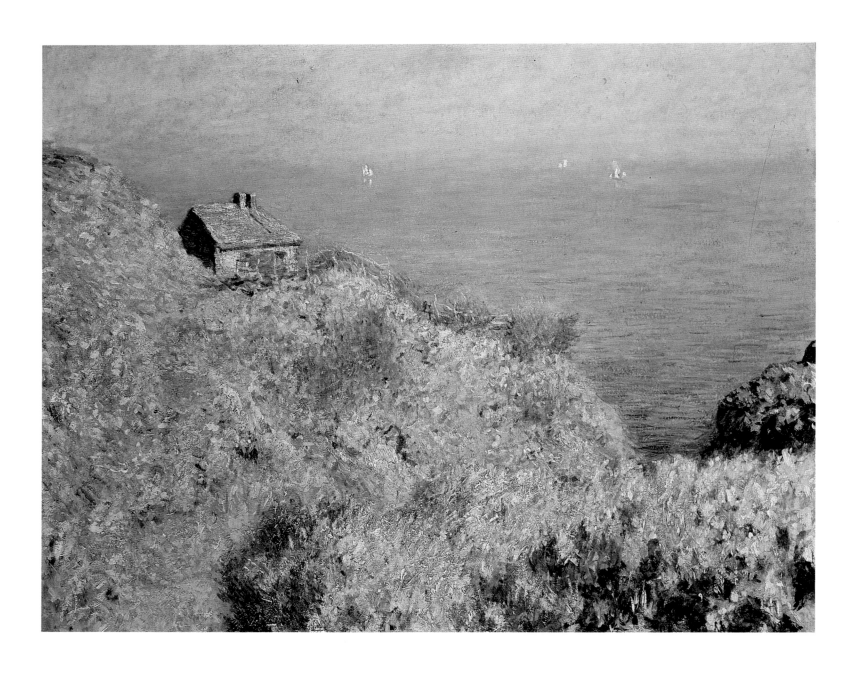

Monet *The Customs Officer's Cottage near Varengeville* 1882

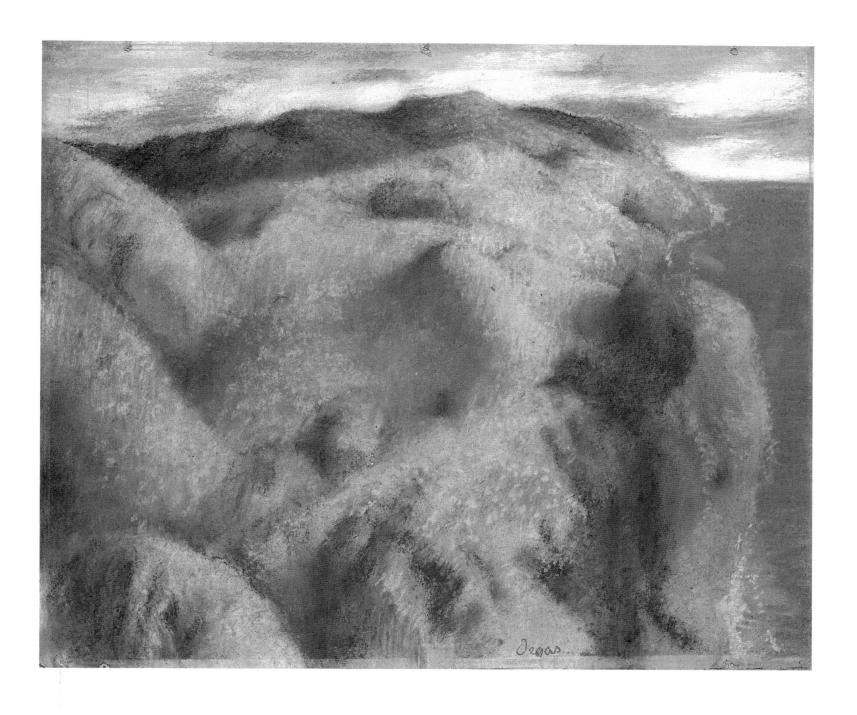

Degas *Landscape* c.1892

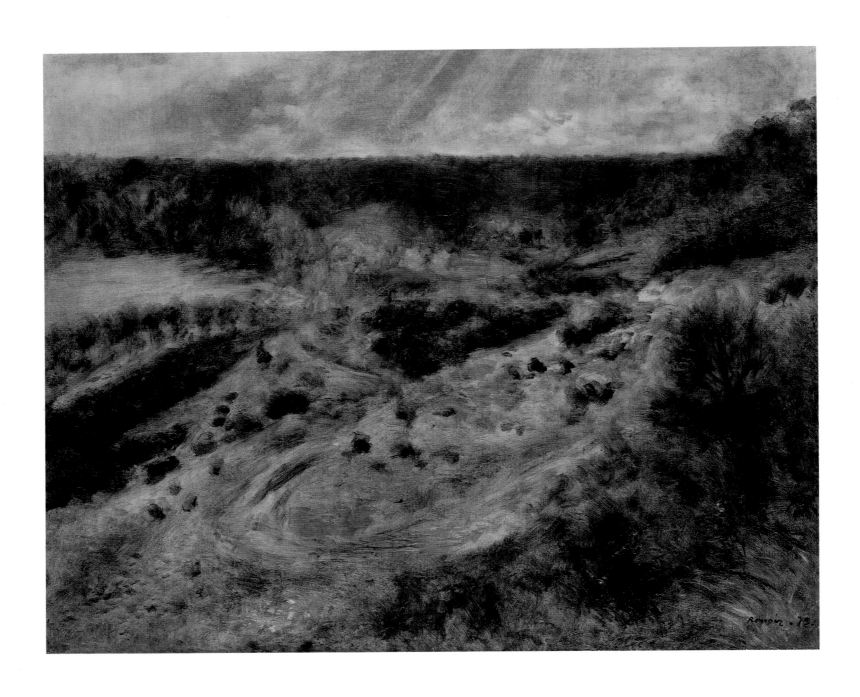

Renoir *Landscape at Wagremont* 1879

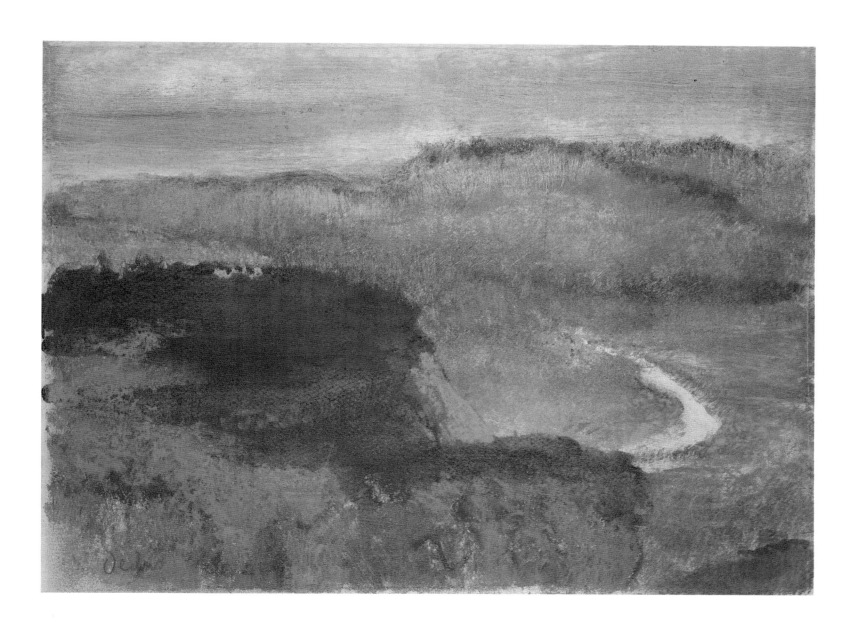

Degas *Landscape* 1890–3

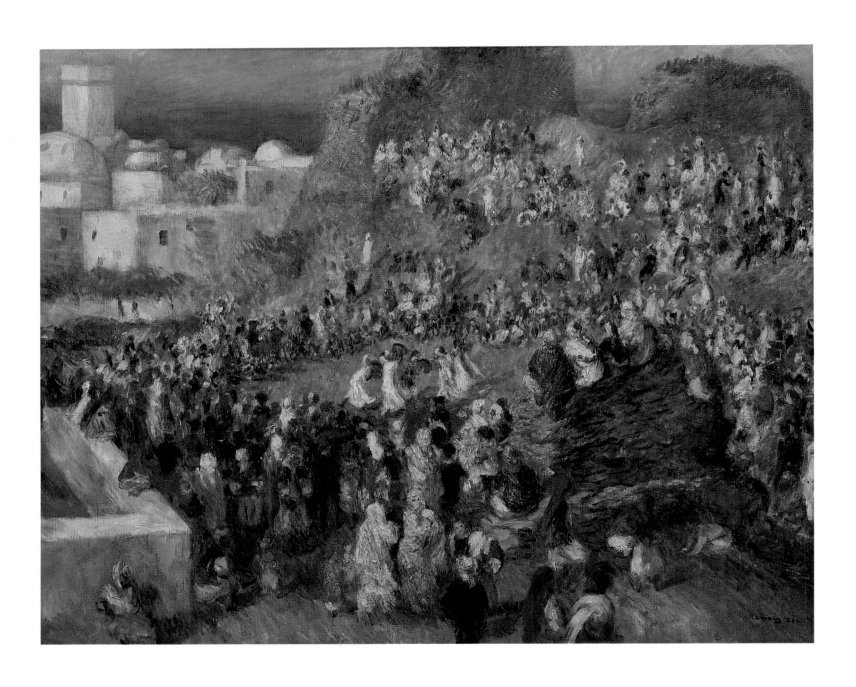

Renoir *Fête arabe à Alger* 1881

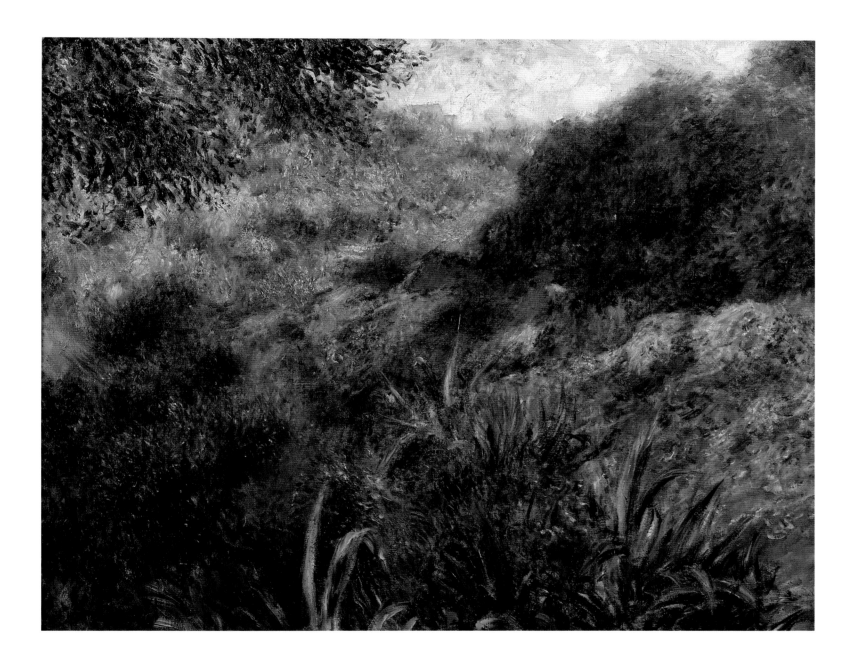

Renoir *Algerian Landscape* 1881

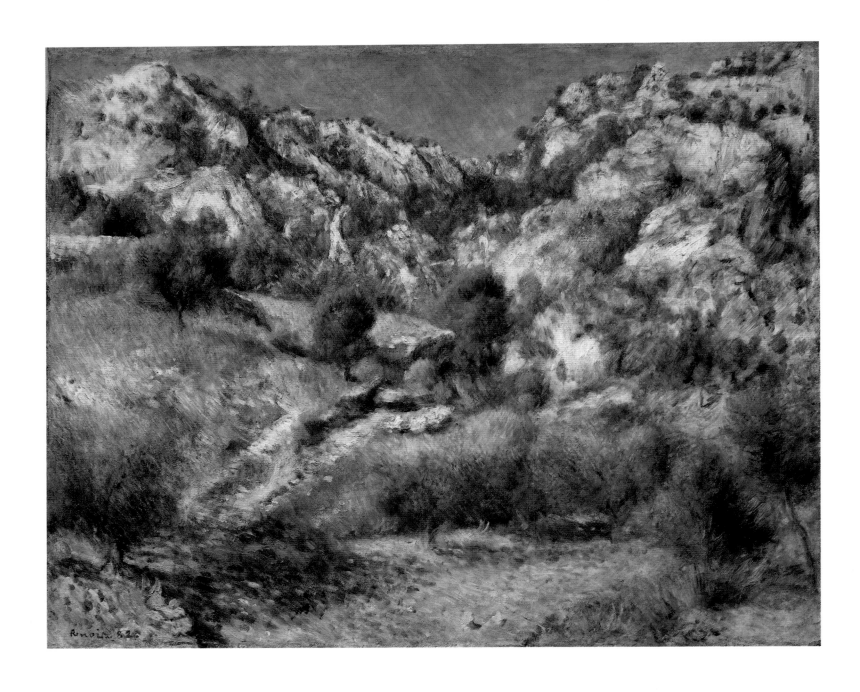

Renoir *Rocky Crags at L'Estaque* 1882

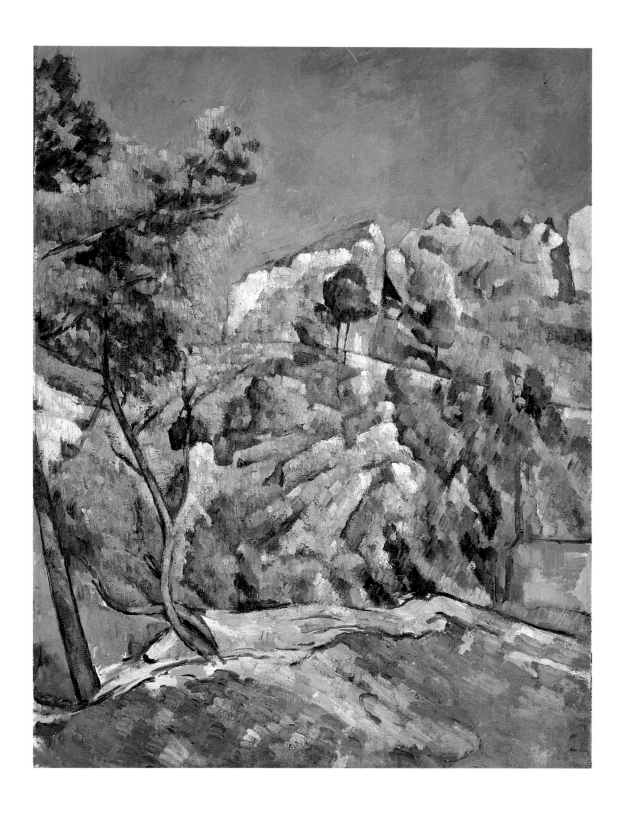

Cézanne *Bottom of the Ravine* 1878–80

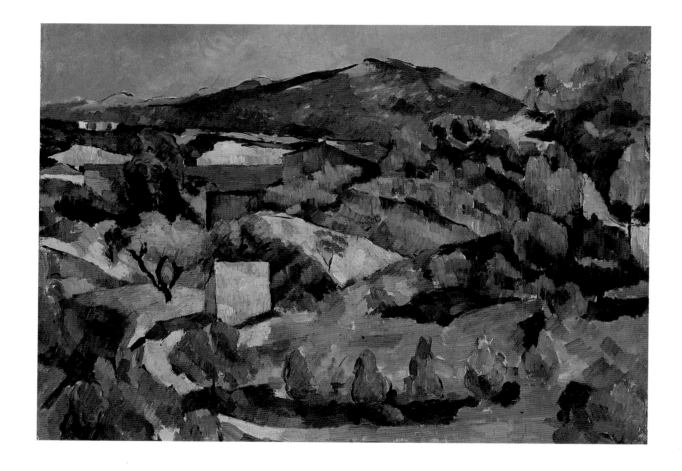

Cézanne *Mountains at L'Estaque* 1878–80

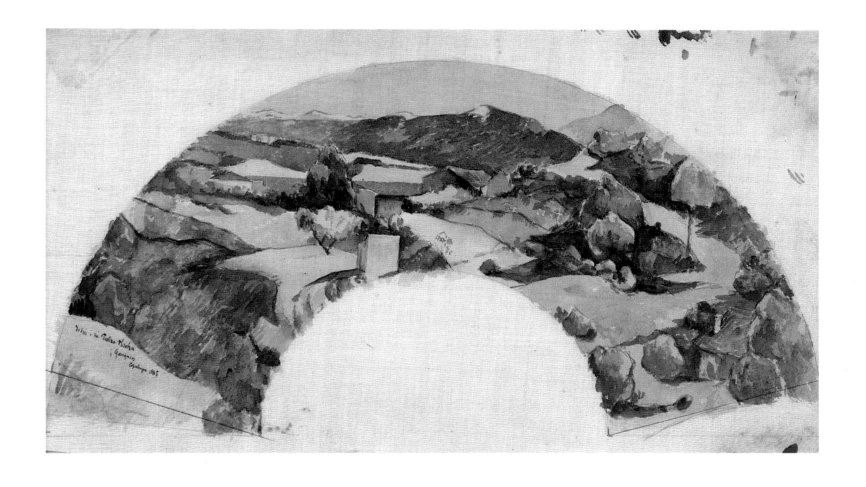

Gauguin *Provençal Landscape after Cézanne* Before 1885

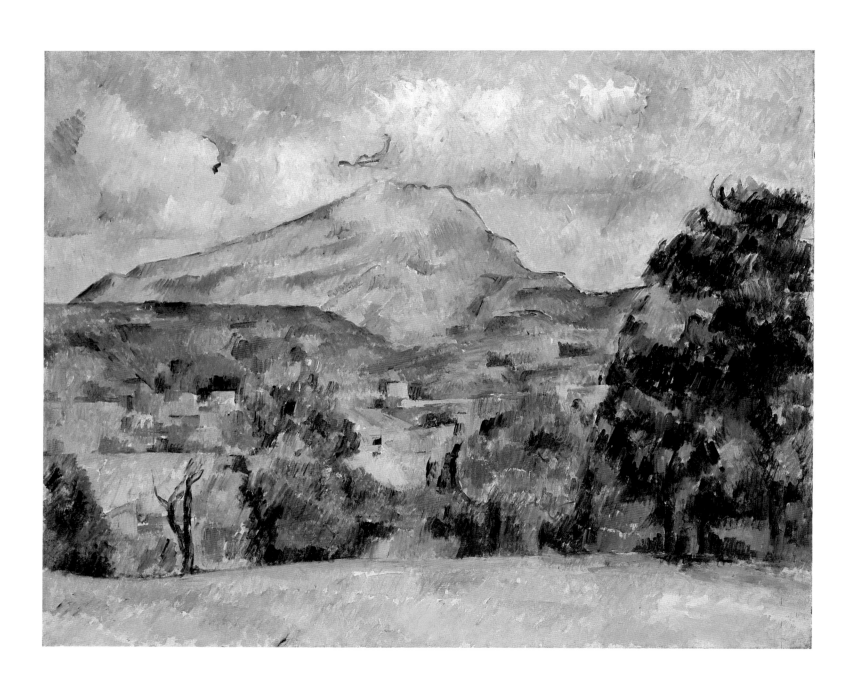

Cézanne *Mont Ste-Victoire* 1888–90

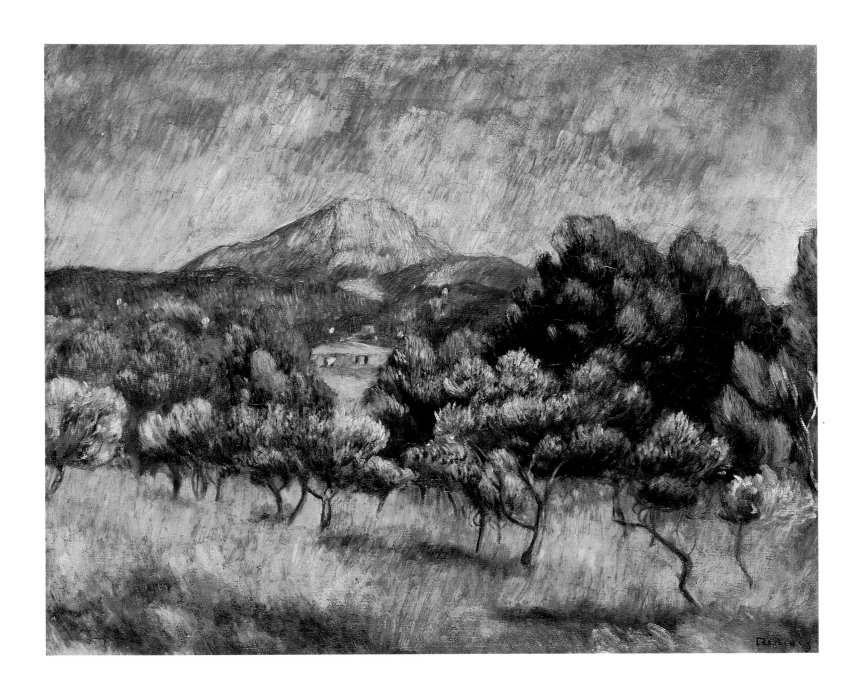

Renoir *Mont Ste-Victoire c.*1888–9

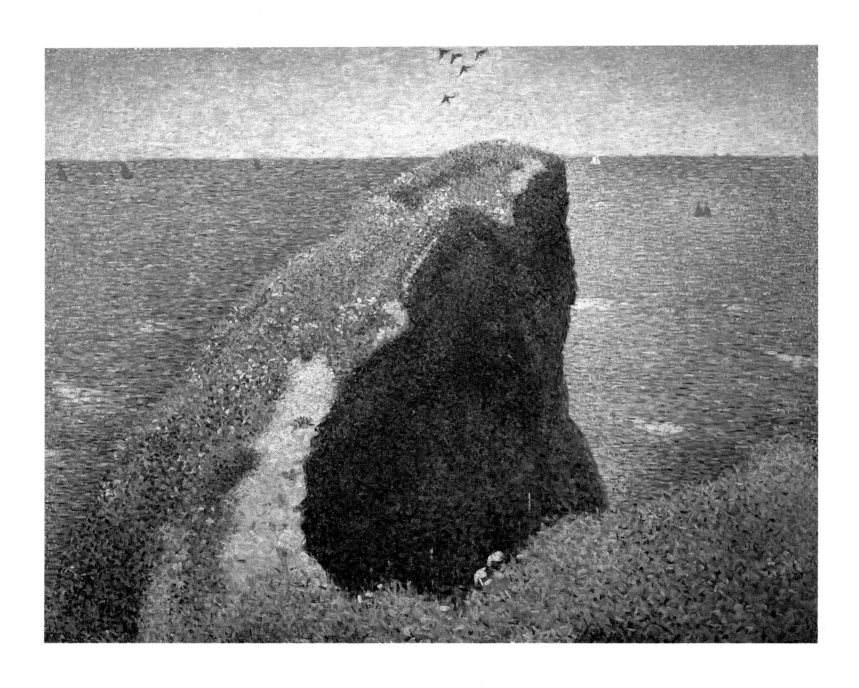

Seurat *Le Bec du Hoc* 1885

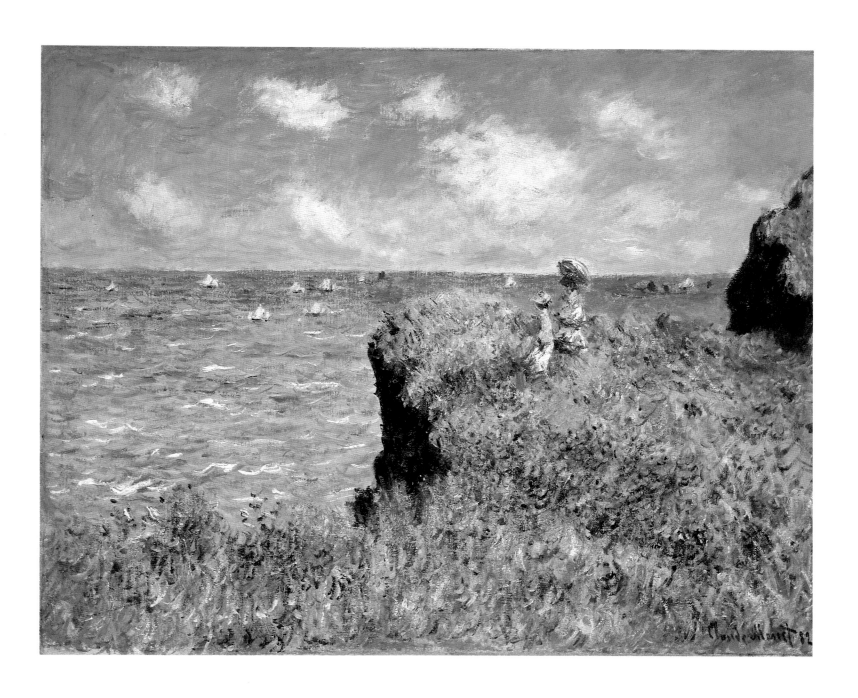

Monet *Cliff Walk at Pourville* 1882

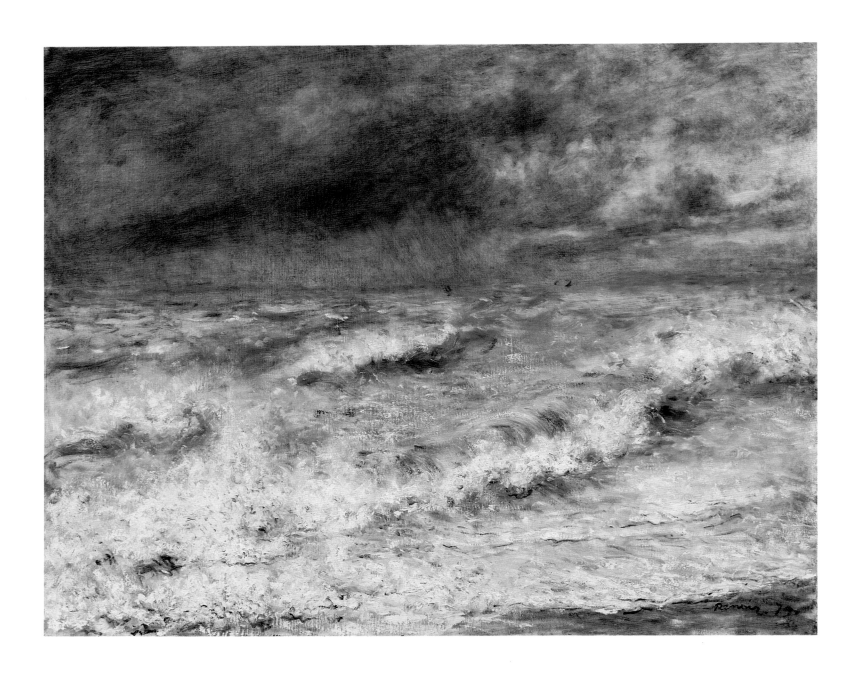

Renoir *The Wave* 1879

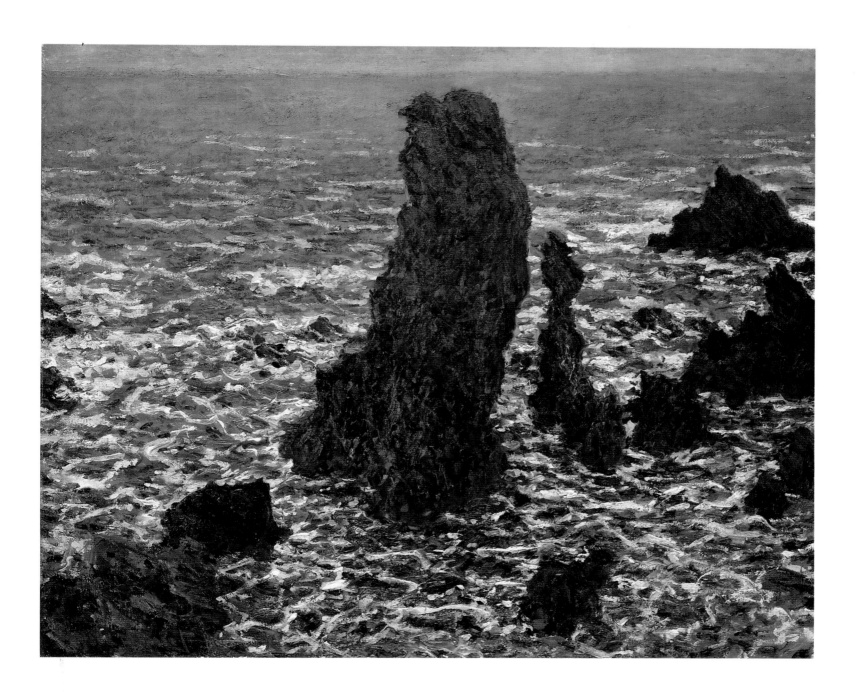

Monet *'Pyramids' at Port-Coton* 1886

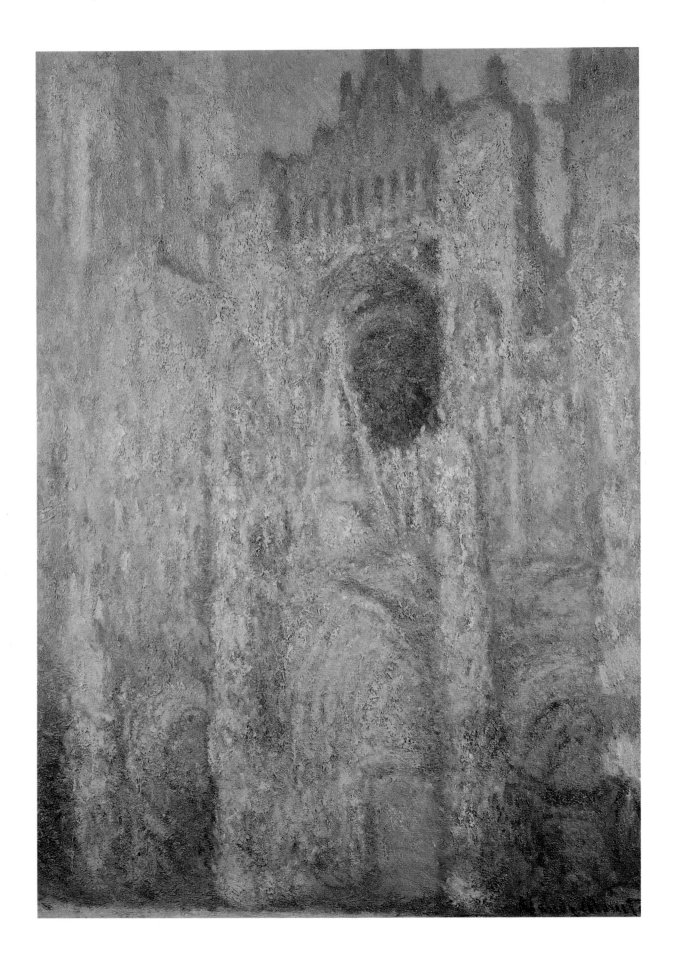

Monet *Rouen Cathedral* 1892–4

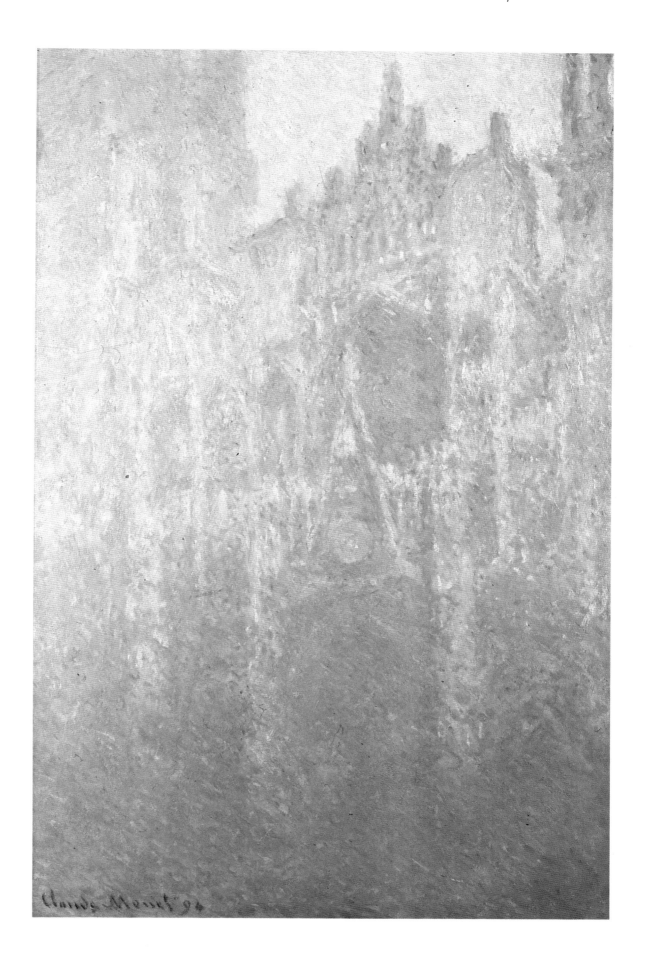

Monet *Rouen Cathedral* 1892–4

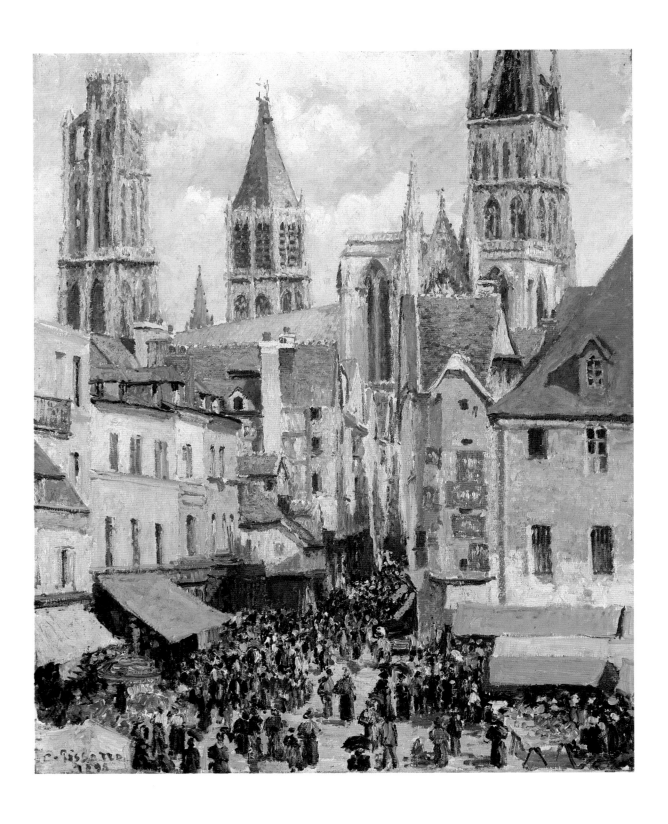

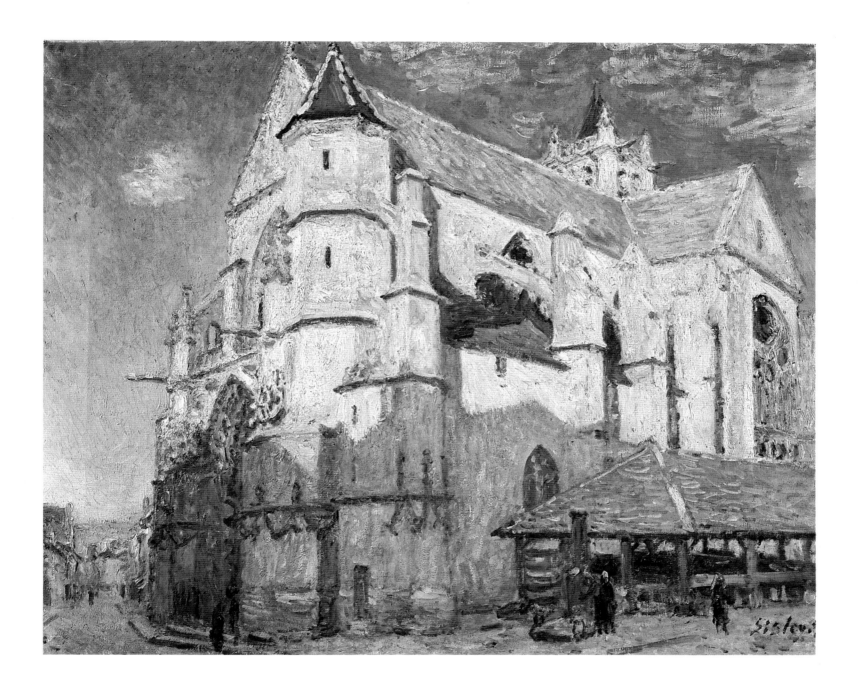

Pissarro *Rue de l'Epercie, Rouen* 1898

Sisley *Church at Moret* 1893

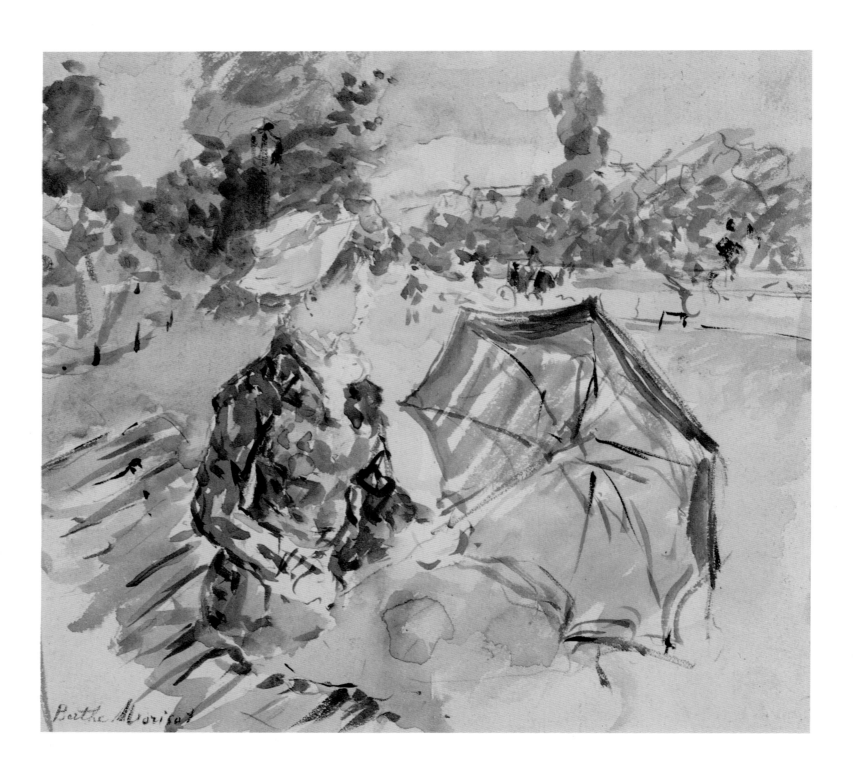

Morisot *Lady with a Parasol sitting in a Park* 1885

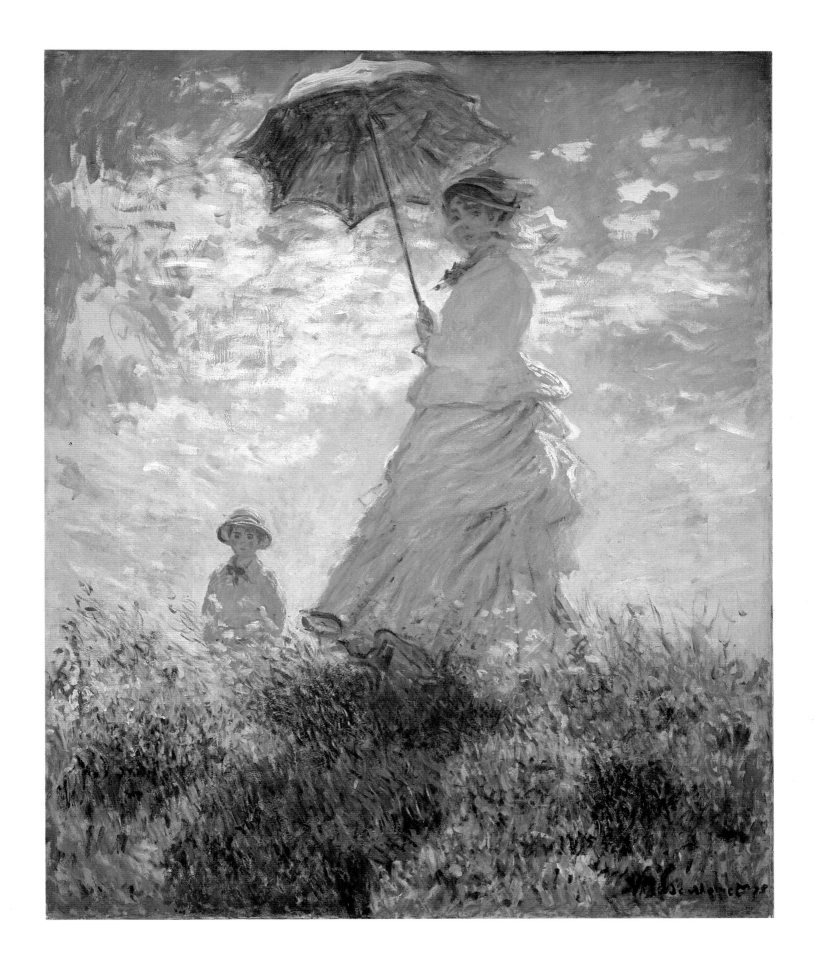

Monet *Woman with a Parasol – Mme Monet and her Son* 1875

IV: Growing Old 1890–1924

Morisot *Self-Portrait* 1885

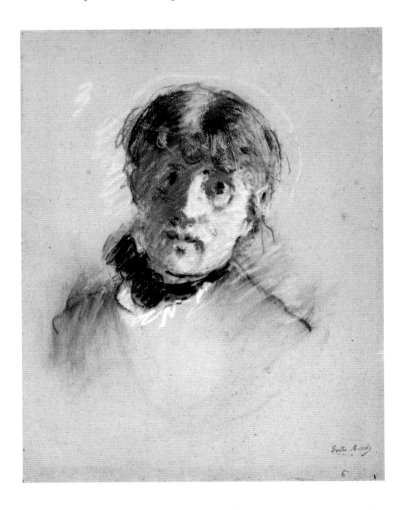

The late work of the Impressionist painters was produced at a time of continuing social, political and artistic upheaval. It was a period of financial crises and government scandals, of fears concerning the supposed threats of anarchism and socialism. The country was split in two by the Dreyfus affair, when in 1894 a Jewish army officer was wrongfully convicted of treason and endured a retrial before being exonerated in 1906. The effects were felt throughout French society for many years. It touched everyone: Pissarro and Monet were staunchly pro-Dreyfus, along with Emile Zola who had intervened in the scandal with his famous article, *J'accuse.* Cézanne, Renoir, Degas, Forain and Guillaumin were on the side of the army, the anti-Semites and the Establishment.

It was during these years, albeit with great difficulty, that the work of the Impressionist painters was finally accepted at both popular and institutional level, although some, like Sisley, were to die without receiving the benefits of public acclaim.

The enormous success of the exhibitions of Monet's *Haystacks, Poplars* and, above all, *Rouen Cathedral* series was counterbalanced by the fiasco of the Caillebotte bequest, which revived all the old hostilities towards Impressionism. Gustave Caillebotte, who died in March 1894, bequeathed his substantial art collection to the State on the condition that the works would be kept on permanent view. After a year of acrimonious discussions, agreement was finally reached: the French Government accepted thirty-eight works with little enthusiasm – all seven Degas were selected, but only two out of the five Cézannes – and twenty-seven pictures remained with Caillebotte's heirs.

The artists were growing old; their correspondence abounds with references to their health. Renoir, in particular, was stricken with a variety of terrible problems. Crippled with arthritis, he was able to paint only by having his brushes, the handles wrapped in cloth, placed into his deformed hands. He, Cassatt, Pissarro, Monet and Degas had recurrent problems with their eyesight: it is a matter of speculation how this affected their art.

As if to compensate, honours and public recognition began to arrive at their doors. Mary Cassatt was commissioned to paint a large decorative scheme at the Hall of the Columbian World's Exposition in Chicago in 1893 (to the probable annoyance of Degas, who is recorded as having commented once: 'It's been my lifelong dream to paint on walls'), and Renoir was appointed a Chevalier de la Légion d'honneur in July 1900.

Berthe Morisot's death in March 1895 and the retrospective exhibition of her work held a year later played a large part in patching up the old alliances, even though Degas remained as enigmatic and distant as ever. Monet had always remained friendly with Cézanne, although they did not meet after 1894, and he renewed his acquaintance with Mary Cassatt and Pissarro.

Cassatt and Pissarro had been friends since they had worked with Degas on the abortive project for a print journal in the late 1870s, and together they conspired to out-manoeuvre Durand-Ruel's near monopoly on the selling of their works. Cassatt corresponded with such luminaries as Samuel J. Avery, the president of trustees at New York's Metropolitan Museum, and Sarah Hallowell, who represented several American museums in Paris, in order to find outlets and recognition for their work in the United States. Monet's unabated success with his buyers contrasted markedly with Renoir's and Pissarro's continuing battles for financial security, a contrast Pissarro frequently referred to in his correspondence with his son. Towards the end of the century, through working with other dealers, prosperity gradually returned to the Pissarro household. And although plagued by family problems and tragedies, his retrospective of 1892, held at Durand-Ruel's gallery, was a success, earning him the status almost of an old master. By this time he was sixty-two years old.

By the end of the century the basic tenets of Impressionism were being questioned by artists espousing other means of artistic expression, the seeds of which, as the letters show, were an integral part of Impressionist practice. Seurat had died in 1891, leaving Neo-impressionism in the hands of Paul Signac and others, but the major avant-garde challenge came from those artists who, influenced by the Symbolists, had created an art that appeared to speak of higher things than the mundane realities the Impressionists took as their subject matter. Artists such as Van Gogh and Gauguin made it clear in their work and writings that they considered the earlier style to be a passing phase in the development of a more significant manner of painting.

A milestone was reached in 1895, when the young dealer Ambroise Vollard gave a show of Cézanne's work. It created a great stir among painters and a reassessment of the Provençal as one of the great figures of avant-garde art. Cézanne, who had not exhibited in Paris since 1877, had been working in relative isolation in the countryside around his home in Aix-en-Provence, where he remained until his death in 1906. His obsessive reworkings of the landscape, of themes and motifs taken from the masters, his large complicated figure groups and extraordinary still lifes were immediately recognized as being brilliant if deeply problematic. Vollard marketed his work shrewdly, and the 'Hermit of Aix' began to be sought out by a new generation of painters, such as Charles Camoin and Emile Bernard, and greatly influenced Henri Matisse and the Cubist painters.

The late work of Degas, Monet and Renoir was as ambitious as any of their earlier projects, but enriched by startling experiments with colour and extended forays in the direction of generalization and ambiguity. Degas died first, in 1917: 'I do not want any funeral orations! ... Yes! Forain, you can deliver one; you shall say, "He really loved drawing." ' In his last years, Renoir created a rich dream of opulent women who bask in a gloriously fecund landscape that seems as sexually charged as themselves. Monet, at the instigation of his friend and admirer, Prime Minister Georges Clemenceau, decided to donate to the nation a decorative scheme based on his *Nymphéas* to mark the end of the First World War. The installation, designed by the artist, in the Orangerie in Paris, was opened on 12 April 1922. Monet died five years later; Pablo Picasso was in his mid-forties.

Comparison of the early and late works of the Impressionists allows the viewer to wonder at the diversity and splendour of their achievements. Despite appearances to the contrary, as their correspondence reveals, their seemingly effortless art was the result of determined and concentrated effort and an absolute dedication to the business of making art.

IV: Growing Old 1890–1924

In Sickness and in Health

Camille Pissarro to Lucien Pissarro

Paris, 30 March 1891

Terrible news to report: Seurat died after a very brief illness. I heard the terrible news only this morning. He had been in bed for three days with a throat infection. Improperly treated, the illness developed with ruinous speed. It is my impression that the malady was the very one de Bellio told me about some time ago: diphtheria. The funeral takes place tomorrow. You can conceive the grief of all those who followed him or were interested in his artistic researches. It is a great loss for art ...

There is a splendid exhibition of [paintings by] the unfortunate Seurat; some marines, as delicate as ever, somewhat weak in colouration, but very artistic, and a large canvas, a *Circus*, which is excellently composed; ... the work as a whole has the stamp of an original artist, it is *something*! All his pictures are framed in chromatic colours and the ensemble gives the effect of an intense blue and violet stain; I find this disagreeable and discordant, it is not unlike the effect of plush!

Camille Pissarro to Lucien Pissarro

Paris, 1 April 1891

... Yesterday I went to Seurat's funeral. I saw Signac who was deeply moved by this great misfortune. I believe you are right, pointillism is finished, but I think it will have consequences which later on will be of the utmost importance for art. Seurat really added something.

Camille Pissarro to Lucien Pissarro

Paris, 3 April 1891

... This is a bad moment for me, Durand doesn't take my paintings. Mlle Cassatt was much surprised to hear that he no longer buys my work, it seems that he sells a great deal. – But for the moment people want nothing but Monets, apparently he can't paint enough pictures to meet the demand. Worst of all they all want *Sheaves in the Setting Sun*! Always the same story, everything he does goes to America at prices of four, five and six thousand francs. All this comes, as Durand remarked to me, from not shocking the collectors! True enough! What do you want? I replied. One has to build that way, advice is useless. But while waiting we have to eat and pay our debts. Life is hard!

Camille Pissarro to Lucien Pissarro

Paris, 13 April 1891

... Yesterday I met Sisley whom I had not seen for at least two years. He is quite happy as long as he is adrift. He said that Durand was our worst enemy; he had tried to beat down Monet, who unhesitatingly turned to Théo Van Gogh ... Durand then became as soft as felt, formerly ferocious he became tender as a lamb. I turned to Van Gogh too late, I might have had the same luck!

Since Durand is unable to support all the Impressionists, it is in his interest to let them fall by the wayside after he has obtained enough of their work, for he knows their pictures will not sell until much later. The lower the prices, the better for him – he can leave his canvases to his children. He behaves like a modern speculator for all his angelic soft spokenness. ... If I could find some base of support, I would certainly frustrate his hyena-like calculations – but my work is not understood, particularly since the death of Théo Van Gogh. Such is the influence of a man who believes! ... Perhaps I am out of date, or my art may conflict and not be reconcilable with the general trend which seems to have gone mystical. It must be that only another generation, free from all religious, mystical, unclear conceptions, a generation which would again turn in the direction of the most modern ideas, could have the qualities necessary to admire this approach. I firmly believe that something of our ideas, born as they are from anarchist philosophy, passes into our works which are thus antipathetic to the current trend. Certainly I feel that there is a sympathy for us among certain free spirits, but the one I can't understand is Degas, for he loves Gauguin and flatters me so. Friendliness and no more? ... How to understand him ... such an anarchist! in art, of course, and without realizing it!

Camille Pissarro to Lucien Pissarro

Eragny, 2 May 1891

... I leave Sunday, that is, tomorrow, for Paris, I will go to see Parentau who will probably operate on my eye. I was penniless and didn't know how I could leave here. As a last resort I wrote to Monet who promptly sent me a thousand francs. I will be able to ... pay the rent, put a little aside for the house, and make the trip to Paris. Good, but when will I sell something? ...

Mrs Cassatt to Alexander Cassatt

Bachvilliers par Chaumont-en-Vexin, 23 July 1891

... Mary is at work again, intent on fame and money she says ... After all a woman who is not married is lucky if she has a decided love for work of any kind and the more absorbing the better. ...

Claude Monet to Gustave Caillebotte

Giverny, 14 September 1891

Your boat would be a big help to me just now. I'm painting a lot of pictures on the river Epte and am very uncomfortable in my Norwegian rowing boat. If you don't really need it, send it to me either by steamer to Vernon or Port-Villé lock, or by rail. Rail would be the most practical, I think. Drop me a line anyway.

Alfred Sisley to Octave Mirbeau

Moret, 1 June 1892

An article on the Salon that appeared in *Le Figaro* on the 25th of last May, in which you devoted a few rather unfriendly lines to me, has been brought to my notice.

I have never replied to criticism made in good faith, I always, on the contrary, try to profit from it. But there the intention to do injury is so evident that you must allow me to defend myself.

You have made yourself a champion of a coterie which would be happy to see me in the dust. It will not have this pleasure, and you will gain nothing by your unjust and perfidious criticism.

There! Do you think I was right to reply?

From *My Friend Degas* by Daniel Halévy (1966)

Cavé, who lunched with me today, had recently gone to a velocipede competition to which Degas had summoned him to see two dancers from the Opéra doing stunts on tricycles. And Cavé told us how funny Degas' attitude was towards these creatures, and their attitude towards him. He finds them all charming, treats them as though they were his own children, makes excuses for anything they do, and laughs at everything they say. On the other hand, they absolutely venerate him and the most insignificant little 'rat' would give a good deal to please Degas.

From the diaries of Daniel Halévy

September 1892

After dinner the conversation turned to the *Thousand and One Nights* and Degas asked me if I had any news of the English edition. I told him that it was in fifteen volumes and cost nine hundred francs . . .

'I'll buy this translation with my money, my nine hundred francs. What difference does it make to me? I'll do two more pastels and they'll pay for it.' . . . But he asked Elie to find him a set at a reduced price in London, and this calmed him a little. 'But I could pay for them,' he said. 'I have twenty-one landscapes.'

We all protested. 'Twenty-one landscapes? But you have never done any! Not twenty-one?'

'Yes, twenty-one landscapes.'

'But how did you happen to do them?'

'They are the fruit of my travels this summer. I would stand at the door of my coach and as the train went along I could see things vaguely. That gave me the idea of doing landscapes. There are twenty-one.'

'What kind are they? Vague things?'

'Perhaps.'

'Reflections of your soul?' my father asked. 'Amiel said, "A landscape is a reflection of the soul." Do you like that definition?'

'A reflection of my eyesight,' Degas replied. 'We painters do not use such pretentious language.' . . .

October 1892

Degas came but little this winter. Did he see his other friends more? I think that at the moment he is keeping very much to himself. His eyes are getting worse and worse and he wears special glasses which greatly embarrass him; all that saddens him and I suspect he remains alone to hide from our eyes the melancholia against which he has striven so hard.

Last month he must have stopped work completely to get accustomed to his new glasses. He went all alone to Belgium for a week, without reading a single word, not even the railway guides.

Camille Pissarro to Lucien Pissarro

Paris, 2 October 1892

Speaking about Mlle Cassatt's decoration, I wish you could have heard the conversation I had with Degas on what is known as 'decoration'. I am wholly of his opinion; for him it is an ornament that should be made with a view to its place in an ensemble, it requires the collaboration of architect and painter. The decorative picture is an absurdity, a picture complete in itself is not a decoration. It seems that even the [decorative paintings of] Puvis de Chavannes don't go well in Lyons, etc.

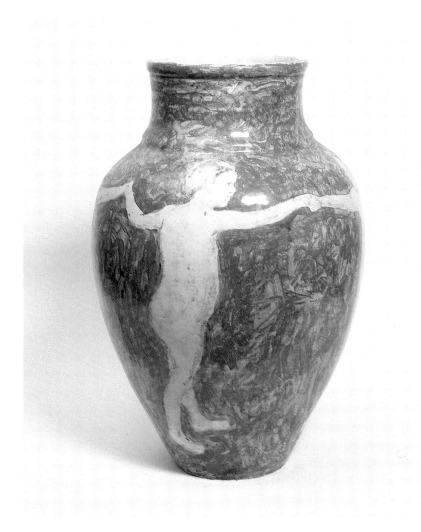

Cassatt *Ceramic Vase* 1901

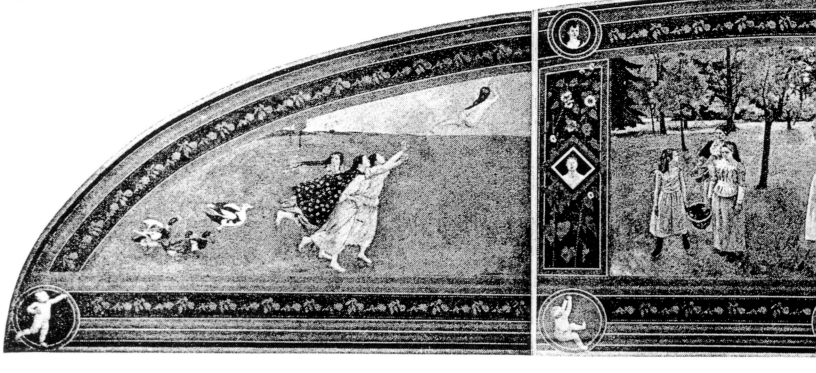

Cassatt
Modern Woman 1893: mural – decoration
of South Tympanum of Woman's Building,
World's Colombian Exposition, Chicago

Cassatt *Modern Woman* 1893: detail

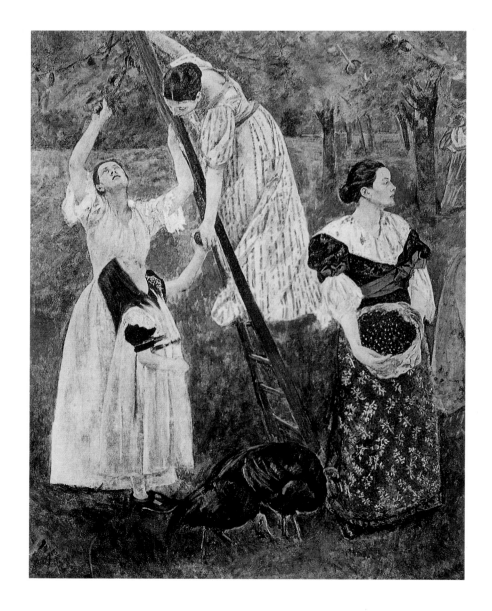

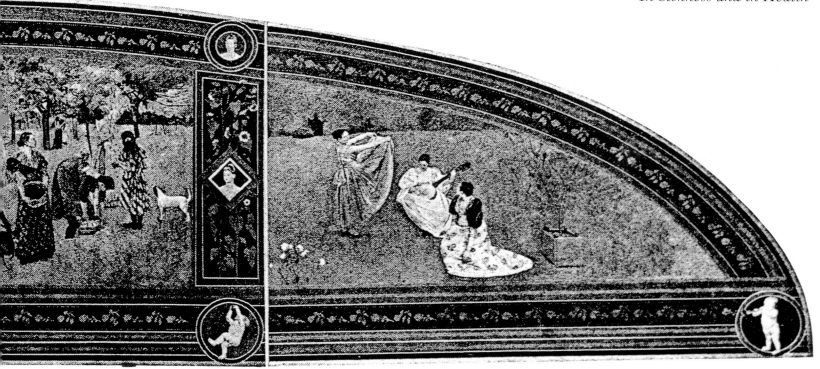

Mary Cassatt to Mrs Potter Palmer [Chicago collector]

Bachvilliers, 11 October [1892]

... Mr Avery sent me an article from one of the New York papers this summer in which the writer, referring to the order given to me, said my subject [for the mural at the 1893 Chicago Exposition] was to be the 'Modern Woman as glorified by Worth'! That would hardly describe my idea, of course I have tried to express the modern woman in the fashions of our day and have tried to represent those fashions as accurately & as much in detail as possible. I took for the subject of the central & largest composition Young Women plucking the fruits of knowledge & science – that enabled me to place my figures out of doors & allowed for brilliancy of color. I have tried to make the general [effect] as bright, as gay, as amusing as possible. The occasion is one of rejoicing, a great national fête. I reserved all the seriousness for the execution, for the drawing & painting. My ideal would have been one of those admirable old tapestries, brilliant yet soft. My figures are rather under life size although they seem as life. I could not imagine women in modern dress eight or nine feet high. An American friend asked me in rather a huffy tone the other day 'Then this is woman apart from her relations to man?' I told him it was. Men, I have no doubt, are painted in all their vigor on the walls of other buildings; ... the sweetness of childhood, the charm of womanhood, if I have not conveyed some sense of that charm, in one word if I have not been absolutely feminine, then I have failed. My central panel I hope to finish in a few days ... I will still have place on the side for two compositions, one, which I shall begin immediately, is young girls pursuing fame. This seems to me very modern & besides will give me an opportunity for some figures in clinging draperies. The other panel will represent the Arts, Music (nothing of St Cecilia) Dancing & all treated in the most modern way ... I think, my dear Mrs Palmer, that if you were here & I could take you out to my studio & show you what I have done that you would be most pleased indeed. . . . When the work reaches Chicago, when it is dragged up 48 feet & you will have to stretch your neck to get sight of it, at all, whether you like it then, is another question. . . .

Mary Cassatt to Mrs Potter Palmer

Bachvilliers, 1 December [1892]

... I have been shut up here so long now with one idea, that I am no longer capable of judging what I have done. I have been half a dozen times on the point of asking Degas [to] come and see my work, but if he happens to be in the mood he would demolish me so completely that I could never pick myself up in time to finish for the exposition ...

Mary Cassatt to Sarah Hallowell [American acquaintance]

[Paris], *1893*

... After all give me France. Women do not have to fight for recognition here if they do serious work. I suppose it is Mrs Potter's French blood which gives her organizing powers and determination that women should be *someone* and not *something*.

Claude Monet to Alice Monet

[Rouen], *Wednesday, 22 February 1893*

What terrible unsettled weather! I carry on regardless without a break. I'm feeling better but, dear God, this cursed cathedral is hard to do! Since I've been here, a week tomorrow, I've worked every day on the same two paintings and can't get what I want; well, it will come in the end, with a hard struggle. I'm glad I decided to come back, it's better like this ...

Camille Pissarro to Lucien Pissarro

Eragny, 26 July 1893

I have looked for the recipe for painting with cheese. The preparation that John L. Brown [a painter] uses is the following: a mixture of casein with borax solution (100 parts of casein to 10–12 parts of borax). You will find it in London. I advise you to have the mixture prepared by a pharmacist. You have to use powdered colours with it and work while the mixture is still lukewarm. I found it preferable not to pulverize certain colours too much – the result is then exactly like pastel....

Georges [one of Pissarro's sons] tells me that Epping is not very beautiful. Bah! one can make such beautiful things with so little. The motifs that are too beautiful sometimes appear even theatrical – just look at Switzerland. Old Corot, didn't he make some beautiful little paintings in Gisors, two willows, a little stream, a bridge, like the painting at the Universal Exhibition? What a masterpiece! Happy are those who see beauty in the modest spots where others see nothing. Everything is beautiful, the whole secret lies in knowing how to interpret. And from your description, the place must be very interesting....

Camille Pissarro to Lucien Pissarro

Eragny, 18 September 1893

... The weather is frightful today, rain and wind. It must be the same at Epping, it's a pity. It has been so beautiful lately and I was beginning to work regularly from nature.

It is maddening, for this is the most favourable time, September and October.
I can't endure the summer any more, with its thick, monotonous green, its dry distances,
where everything is clearly outlined, its tormenting heat, depression, somnolence. The
sensations necessary to art revive in September and October ... whereupon there is wind
and rain!

From *Men and Memories* by William Rothenstein (1932)

[Degas] spoke with particular admiration of Manet, regretting that he had not
appreciated him enough during his lifetime. Whistler habitually belittled Manet's work,
disliking to hear us praise it. Like Whistler, Degas had no great opinion of Cézanne as an
artist.

Degas was a confirmed bachelor of simple habits. He occupied two apartments,
one above the other, in the rue Massé, over which a devoted servant ruled and guarded
the painter against intruders. The walls of the lower flat were adorned with his beloved
French masters, while upstairs he kept his own works. Degas was then making studies
of laundresses ironing, and of women tubbing or at their toilettes. Some of these were
redrawn again and again on tracing paper pinned over the drawing already made;
this practice allowed for correction and simplification, and was common with artists in
France. Degas rarely painted from nature. He spoke of Monet's dependence in this
respect; 'I feel no need to faint in the presence of nature,' he mocked.

Degas complained much of his eyesight. Young people today who prefer the later
work of Degas and Renoir hardly realize how much of its character was due to failing sight.

Camille Pissarro to Lucien Pissarro

Paris, 1 March 1894

... We have just lost still another sincere and devoted friend: Caillebotte died suddenly of
cerebral paralysis. And he is one we can really mourn, he was good and generous, and a
painter of talent to boot.

Camille Pissarro to Lucien Pissarro

Paris, 29 May 1894

... I am broke, completely broke. ... The problem is to go on, and despite these hardly
encouraging prospects, make works full of sensation, wholly uncommercial, satisfactory
to both artist and collector; I should really like to see how the young Symbolists cried up
by the young poet Mauclair would deal with such a situation. ... He has a horror of
painters who see in art nothing but impasto and cabbages. What would the Gothic artists
say, who so loved cabbages and artichokes and knew how to make of them such natural
and symbolic ornaments? Words, words ... and they control everything. Gauguin is
behind this. *Farceur* and trickster!

Claude Monet to Alice Monet

Christiania [now Oslo, Norway], *13 February 1895*

... I can see that it's very cold where you are, but it's nothing compared to here; your night temperatures are our day ones. I can well understand how happy the skaters are, but I dread what's happening to the garden, the bulbs. Is the ice on the pond being watched carefully? It would be very sad if everything planted there were to die. ... I very much regret not being in Giverny, where I might have taken advantage of the fine sights to be seen there at this time of the year ...

Camille Pissarro to Lucien Pissarro

Paris, 24 February 1895

I received a letter from Dresden announcing that the exhibition will close in the first week of March: ... people found my work *interesting*...! Small comfort!... Why should people there be interested in my painting when even in Paris where I am known, known by everybody, people scorn or don't understand them. Moreover, as a result of this incomprehension I myself am ending up by wondering whether my work isn't poor and empty, without a hint of talent. It is said that money is scarce, but that is only relatively true; doesn't Monet sell his work, and at very high prices, don't Renoir and Degas sell? No, like Sisley, I remain in the rear of the Impressionist line.

Camille Pissarro to Lucien Pissarro

[Paris], *28 February 1895*

... What you write about the progress of the Impressionists abroad is only too true; evidently we were dropped before arriving! But I remark this, a consoling fact, there has been a great and real change. The Symbolists are finished. Gauguin, who is their foremost figure, has just had a serious setback; his sale was very poor. Without Degas, who purchased several canvases, it would have been still worse. Speaking of Gauguin, I discussed him with Degas lately. Degas made this characteristic remark:

'My dear fellow, I have a certain liking for what he does, although I am not blind to his tricks.'

'Well,' I said, 'I, too, know Gauguin has talent. Didn't I tell you long ago? But don't you grant that he is too much of a trickster?'

Incidently, this was once Degas' opinion.

Curiously enough, [Gauguin's] own pupils are beginning to drop him and returning to good and simple nature ... I feel – do I deceive myself? – that I am seriously understood by some of the young artists, and it is interesting to note that neither Monet nor Renoir are followed. Their work is counter to French Gothic art.

From *Growing Up With the Impressionists: the diary of Julie Manet*

Wednesday, 17 April 1895

Oh sorrow! Since last I wrote I have lost Maman. She died at half-past-ten on Saturday 2nd March. I cannot describe the enormity of my grief, the depth of my sadness. In three years my parents have left me and now I am an orphan.

Poor Maman, she suffered so much to have to leave me; she saw the end coming and didn't want me to go into her room to have such a sad memory of her. Her illness was short but painful; the sore throat was frightful and she could no longer breathe. Oh! Never, never would I have believed that such a terrible thing could happen. On Saturday morning she was still laughing; she was able to see my cousin Gabriel; how pretty she was then; she was her usual self; she was fine.

At 3 o'clock I spoke to Maman for the last time. At seven Dr Ganne came, I went into Maman's room, but it was impossible to stay – I couldn't bear to see her suffering like that, unable to breathe. I could see her dying and I thought she would be cured. I thought we had already had enough misfortune. About 10 o'clock Dr Ganne came back accompanied by a short doctor in evening dress, whom I only saw for a second and who will remain forever in my mind as a figure from a nightmare. (Oh! If only it were just a nightmare). But, no, alas, it's reality . . .

[note added to diary in 1962]

[Renoir was] in the midst of painting alongside Cézanne when he learned of Maman's death; he closed his paintbox and took the train – I have never forgotten the way he came into my room on the rue Weber and took me in his arms – I can still see his white flowing necktie with red polka dots. . .

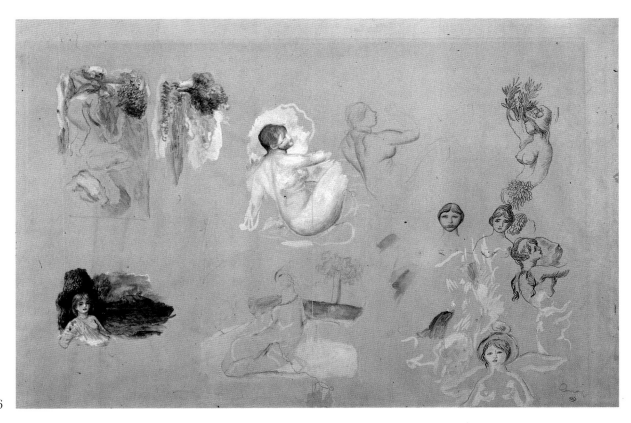

Renoir
Study of Bathers c.1885–6

Camille Pissarro to Lucien Pissarro

Paris, 6 March 1895

Still in Paris, because I want to attend the funeral of our old comrade Berthe Morisot, who died after an attack of influenza. You can hardly conceive how surprised we all were and how moved, too, by the disappearance of this distinguished woman, who had such a splendid feminine talent and who brought honour to our Impressionist group which is vanishing – like all things. Poor Mme Morisot, the public hardly knows her! It is just speculation that makes reputations and gives one glory, fortune sometimes, but often poverty....

Claude Monet from an article by François Thiébault-Sisson in *Le Temps* (1927)

'... having stopped one day in Vernon, I found the silhouette of the church so strange that I undertook to render it. It was early summer and the weather was still a little crisp. Cool foggy mornings were followed by sudden bursts of sunshine whose rays, warm as they were, succeeded only in slowly dissolving the mists clinging to all the rough surfaces of the building and which put an ideally vaporous envelope around the stone that time had turned golden. This observation was the starting point for my series of *Cathedrals*. I told myself it wouldn't be a bad idea to study the same subject at different times of the day and note the effects of light that modified the appearance and colours of the building in such a tangible way from one hour to the next. I didn't follow up the idea at the time, but little by little it germinated in my brain.'

Camille Pissarro to Lucien Pissarro

Eragny, 11 May 1895

Monet's exhibition opened yesterday, he is showing twenty *cathedrals of Rouen!* forty canvases in all. This will be the *great attraction*. It will run till the end of the month....

Camille Pissarro to Lucien Pissarro

Paris, 26 May 1895

I hope you receive the letter in time to make a trip with the little one. If only you could get here before Monet's show closes; his *Cathedrals* will be scattered everywhere, and particularly ought to be seen in a group. They have been attacked by the young painters and even by Monet's admirers. I am carried away by their extraordinary deftness. Cézanne, whom I met yesterday at Durand-Ruel's, is in complete agreement with my view that this is the work of a well-balanced but impulsive artist who pursues the intangible nuances of effects that are realized by no other painter....

Camille Pissarro to Esther Isaacson

Paris, 15 November 1895

At Vollard's there is a very complete exhibition of Cézanne's works. Still-lifes of astonishing perfection, and some unfinished work, really extraordinary for their fierceness and character. I don't imagine they will be understood. . . .

Camille Pissarro to Lucien Pissarro

Paris, 21 November 1895

How rarely do you come across true painters, who know how to balance two tones. . . . I also thought of Cézanne's show in which there were exquisite things, still-lifes of irreproachable perfection, others *much worked on* and yet unfinished, of even greater beauty, landscapes, nudes and heads that are unfinished but yet grandiose, and *so* painted, so supple . . . Why? Sensation is there! . . .

Curiously enough, while I was admiring this strange, disconcerting aspect of Cézanne, familiar to me for many years, Renoir arrived. But my enthusiasm was nothing compared with Renoir's. Degas himself is seduced by the charm of this refined savage, Monet, all of us. . . . Are we mistaken? I don't think so. . . . As Renoir said so well, these paintings have something of the quality of the things of Pompeii, so crude and so admirable! . . . Degas and Monet have bought some marvellous Cézannes, I exchanged a poor sketch of Louveciennes for an admirable small canvas of bathers and one of his self-portraits.

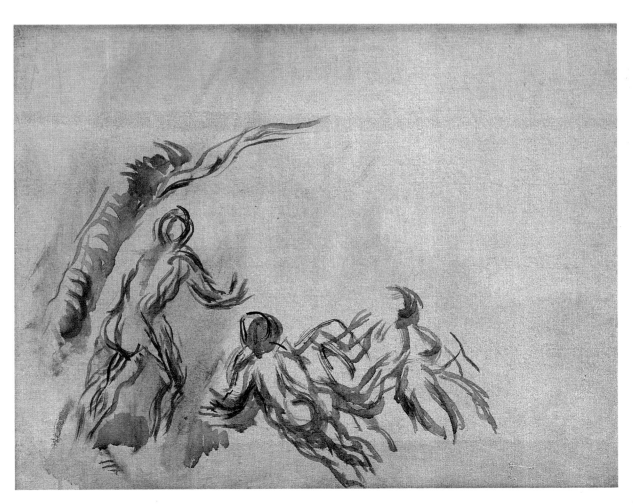

Cézanne
Study for Bathers
*c.*1900–6

Camille Pissarro to Lucien Pissarro

[Paris], 22 November 1895

... Mauclair has published an article [on Cézanne] which I am sending you. You will see that he is ill-informed like most of those critics who understand nothing. People forget that Cézanne was first influenced by Delacroix, Courbet, Manet and even Legros, like all of us; he was influenced by me at Pontoise, and I by him. You may remember the sallies of Zola and Béliard in this regard. They imagined that artists are the sole inventors of their styles and that to resemble someone else is to be unoriginal. Curiously enough, in Cézanne's show at Vollard's there are certain landscapes of Auvers and Pontoise [painted in 1871–1874] that are similar to mine. Naturally, we were always together! But what cannot be denied is that each of us kept the only thing that counts, the unique 'sensation'! – This could easily be shown.

From *Growing Up With the Impressionists: the diary of Julie Manet*

[Paris, November 1895]

... After dinner M. Renoir told us that M. Zandomeneghi was at loggerheads with him because, although Renoir often visited him. as he lived in the same building, he never bothered to return his calls. M. Renoir did a marvellous imitation of him, with his Italian accent, showing his paintings. Monsieur Renoir, who always found them frightful, said: 'It's very nice, but there's a blue in the background that I think is a bit bright.'

'It's precisely because of that blue', replied M. Zandomeneghi, 'that I did this picture,' and promptly took it to M. Durand-Ruel's. There, all the staff made fun of his blue and he was obliged to go home and cover it up. Monsieur Renoir told us lots of other stories about him, but they wouldn't have the same charm if told other than by M. Renoir with the Italian painter's nasal accent.

Wednesday, 20 November [1895]

In [Degas'] house the paintings are hung up anywhere or simply put on the floor. His dining-room is decorated with yellow handkerchiefs and above it are some Ingres drawings. Rumour has it that he always serves the same dinner – *rillettes de pays*, chicken, salad and preserves, all prepared by Zoë, who serves while making conversation and seems to be a very good soul. 'Zoë, you should make more crust,' M. Degas says to her. 'Another time I'll put more on, etc., etc....

Monday, 2 March 1896

Going into the Durand-Ruel gallery [to prepare for the Morisot memorial exhibition], the paintings spread out on the floor gave me the feeling of brightness (just as the white azalea had done).... M. Monet was already there. He kissed me tenderly and I was very pleased to see him again; it was very kind of him to come running over here like that, abandoning his work. M. Degas was busy with the hanging; then Renoir arrived, not looking well. Among other tasks, M. Mallarmé had to go to the printers for the catalogue.

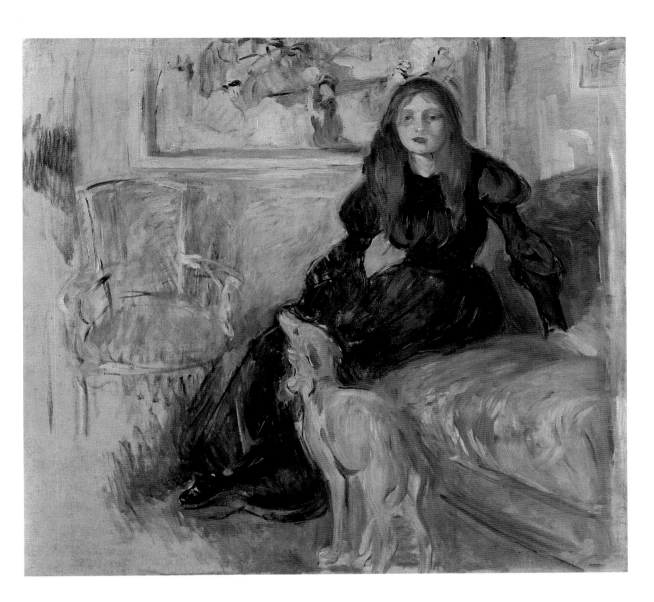

Morisot
Julie with Laertes 1893

Wednesday, 4 March to Friday, 6 March 1896

Went on to Durand-Ruel's with Aunt Edma and Blanche and took the bust [of Julie Manet by Morisot] with us. We found M. Degas all by himself putting up drawings in the room at the far end. He kept repeating constantly that he would have nothing to do with the public, those people who go around with wide eyes, looking at paintings, or more precisely, standing before them without seeing anything while declaring, 'Oh how beautiful! How very beautiful!'

M. Monet chose the painting Maman left to him; he took the one of me and Laërtes which I like very much and I'm very happy M. Monet has it now. He gave me a good-natured kiss saying, 'She's so sweet!', and he's invited us to go to Giverny....

At the end of the day we were asking ourselves how on earth everything was going to be ready by the next day, and we arranged to meet in the morning; but a decision had to be made as to whether the screen should be put with the drawings and watercolours in the middle of the big gallery or in the one at the end.

M. Degas was the only one who wanted the screen to remain in the big gallery where it cut the room in two and prevented one being able to view the large paintings ... in proper perspective, as well as other smaller ones whose tones look so harmonious next to each other when seen from a distance. M. Degas wouldn't hear a word about the general effect: 'There's no such thing as the general effect,' he said. 'Only imbeciles see a general effect. What on earth is it supposed to mean when one writes in a newspaper that the general impression of this year's Salon is much better than that of last year's?'

Towards 6 o'clock, night began to fall, only the paintings retaining a few rays of light which illuminated them; all those portraits of young girls seeming more and more alive and the screen even more of a barrier than ever. M. Monet asked M. Degas if he wouldn't mind trying the infamous screen in the end gallery the next day, but M. Degas claimed that the drawings on it wouldn't be visible – 'Those drawings are superb, I think more of them than all the paintings.'

'The screen in the gallery full of drawings would give it an intimate, quite charming atmosphere,' said M. Mallarmé. 'It will confuse the public to see drawings in the middle of the paintings.'

'Do I care a jot about the public?' shouted M. Degas. 'They see nothing – it's for myself, for ourselves, that we are mounting this exhibition; you can't honestly mean that you want to teach the public to see?'

'Certainly I do,' replied M. Monet, 'We want to try. If we put on this exhibition just for ourselves, it won't be worth going to the trouble of hanging all these paintings; we could quite simply look at them on the floor.'

During this discussion M. Renoir told us that what he wanted to do was put the couch in the middle of the room; in fact it would indeed be rather pleasant to be able to sit down while viewing but M. Degas wouldn't hear of it. 'I would stay on my feet for thirteen hours at a time if I had to,' he shouted.

It was dark by then, and, as he spoke, M. Degas paced back and forth in his great hooded cape and top hat, his silhouette looking very comical; M. Monet, also on his feet, was beginning to shout; M. Mallarmé was trying to smooth things over; M. Renoir, exhausted, was stranded on a chair. The Durand-Ruel men were laughing, and declared, 'He'll never give in.' Mlle Blanche, Jeannie, and I were just listening.

'You want me to remove this screen which I *adore*,' M. Degas said, emphasizing the last word.

'We adore Mme Manet,' retorted M. Monet. 'It's not a question of the screen, but one of Mme Manet's exhibition. Let's have it understood that we'll try the screen in the other room tomorrow.'

'If you can assure me that in your opinion the room is better without it.'

'Yes, that is my opinion!' stated Monet.

But that wasn't the end of it and the argument started up all over again. All of a sudden M. Degas shook hands with Jeannie and me and went towards the door. M. Monet held him back and they both shook hands; but M. Mallarmé hazarded the word 'couch' and, like a bolt of lightning, M. Degas rushed off into the narrow corridor. We heard the door slam and he'd gone. We left one another that evening a bit dumbfounded to say the least.

[The next morning] I arrived at Durand-Ruel's at 9 o'clock, but the only people there were the men sweeping the floors. I continued with my job of numbering the paintings and soon after M. Monet and M. Renoir arrived.

'You can bet Degas won't be coming,' said M. Renoir. 'He'll be here later in the day up a ladder hammering away and will say, "Can't we put a cord across the door to prevent people from getting in?" I know him too well.'

Sure enough, no M. Degas all morning. It was decided to put the screen in the end gallery and the watercolours and drawings were hung on it. At last everything was ready and beautifully arranged; the exhibition looked marvellous.

From the diaries of Daniel Halévy

21 January 1896

The Ingres are bought. I went to his [Degas'] house this morning to spend ten minutes hearing about them. He insisted on keeping me there for three hours. We strolled along the rue Laffitte announcing the victory to the dealers...

[Degas:] 'Yes, I shall give the Ingres portraits to the country; and then I shall go and sit in front of them and look at them and think about what a noble deed I have done.'

Camille Pissarro to Lucien Pissarro

Hôtel de Paris, 51 Quai de Paris, [Rouen, December 1895 or January 1896]
... Before leaving Paris I saw our friend [François] Oller, who told me some of the extraordinary things that befell him with Cézanne and that indicate that the latter is really a bit touched. It would take too long to tell you.... After numerous tokens of affection in this very southern expansiveness, Oller was confident that he could follow his friend Cézanne to Aix-en-Provence; a rendezvous was made for the next day for the P.L.M. train. '3rd-class,' said friend Cézanne. So the next day, Oller on the platform, strains his eyes, looking in all directions. No sign of Cézanne! The trains pass, no one!!! Finally, Oller says to himself, 'He has gone, thinking I left already,' makes up his mind and leaves. Arriving in Lyons he has 500 francs stolen from his wallet at the hotel. Not knowing what to do, he sends a telegram to Cézanne just in case; and Cézanne was, indeed, at home, had travelled first class! ... Oller receives one of those letters that you have to read to form an idea of what they are like. [Cézanne] forbade him the house, asked if he took him for an imbecile, etc. In short, an atrocious letter. My word, it is a variation of what happened to Renoir. It seems he is furious with all of us.

'Pissarro is an old fool, Monet too clever by half; they are no good [*ils n'ont rien dans la ventre*].... only I have temperament, only I understand how to paint a red! ...'

Aguiard has been present at scenes of this kind; speaking as a doctor, he assured Oller that Cézanne was sick, that the incident couldn't be taken seriously since he was not responsible. Is it not sad and a pity that a man endowed with such a beautiful temperament should have so little balance?

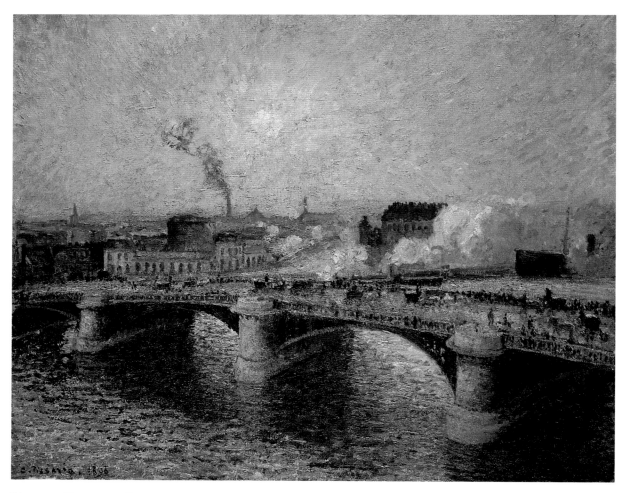

Pissarro *Boieldieu Bridge, Rouen, Sunset* 1896

Camille Pissarro to Lucien Pissarro

Rouen, 26 February 1896

... I have effects of fog and mist, of rain, of the setting sun and of grey weather, motifs of bridges seen from every angle, quays with boats; but what interests me especially is a motif of the iron bridge in the wet, with much traffic, carriages, pedestrians, workers on the quays, boats, smoke, mist in the distance, the whole scene fraught with animation and life. The picture is pretty well advanced, I am waiting for a little rain to put it in order. I hope these pictures won't be too bad, for the moment I see only their defects; at times I have fits of hope that they will be good.

I think I shall stay here until the end of March, for I have found a really uncommon motif in a room in a hotel facing north, ice-cold and without a fireplace. Just conceive for yourself: the whole of old Rouen seen from above the roofs, with the Cathedral, St-Ouen's church, and the fantastic roofs, really amazing turrets. Can you picture a canvas about 36 x 28 inches in size filled with old, grey, worm-eaten roofs? It is extraordinary!

Camille Pissarro to Lucien Pissarro

Rouen, 13 March 1896

. . . You will remember that the *Cathedrals* of Monet were all done with veiled effects which gave a certain mysterious charm to the edifice. My *Roofs of Old Rouen* with the cathedral in the background was done in grey weather and is clearly outlined against the sky; I liked it well enough, it pleased me to see the cathedral firm, grey and clear on a uniform sky in wet weather. Well then, Dépaux doesn't care for the sky! I think I shall keep the picture for us.

Paul Cézanne to Joachim Gasquet

Aix, 30 April 1896

My whole life, I've worked in order to earn my own living, but I thought one could produce well-made paintings without drawing people's attention to one's private existence. Undoubtedly, an artist wants to raise himself as far as possible intellectually, but the man must remain hidden. The pleasure should reside in the work. If it had been granted to me to achieve such a thing, I would have stayed in my corner with the few studio-companions with whom we used to go out drinking. I still have one stout friend [?Achille Emperaire – a painter friend] from those days; well, he didn't get there, in spite of the fact that he's a damn sight more of a painter than all the other triflers with their medals and decorations – it makes you mad. And you expect me, at my age, still to believe in something! Anyway, I'm as good as dead. You're young, and I understand that you want to succeed. But as far as I'm concerned, what's left for me to do in my position is to knuckle under, and were it not for the fact that I love so very much the configuration of the land in my part of the world, I wouldn't be here.

Paul Cézanne to Joachim Gasquet

Talloires, 21 July 1896

You, who are always so vigorous, should with your magnificent intellectual capacity be working on and on and without too much fatigue. I'm too distant from you, both in age and in the knowledge that you acquire from day to day; nonetheless, I come to commend myself to you and your kind remembrance so that the links that keep me bound to this old native soil – so vibrant, so harsh and reflecting the light with a brilliance that makes one blink one's eyelids and that casts a spell over the repository of one's feelings – don't snap and detach me, as it were, from the earth where I've felt so deeply, even without realizing it.

Camille Pissarro to Lucien Pissarro

Rouen, 6 November 1896

Yesterday evening I received your letter and also the very beautiful engraving for *L'Image*, it is truly superb and truly ours. It makes me think of the things we once tried to do, Monet in his large canvases and I myself in the big picture I was working on in 1868–1869, the one in which you posed with poor Minette in our garden at Louveciennes. . . .

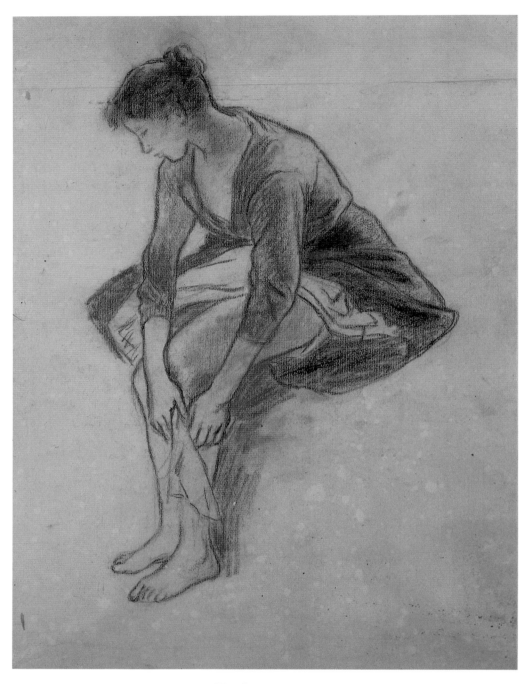

Pissarro *Young Woman Bathing Her Legs c.*1895

Camille Pissarro to Lucien Pissarro

Paris, 5 March 1897

In connection with the Caillebotte collection at the Luxembourg we can be satisfied with the quality of the works: Renoir has his *Bal au Moulin de la Galette*, which is a masterpiece; Degas has some very beautiful things; Monet has his *Railway Station*; Sisley's things are perhaps not his most careful works, but they are interesting enough. I have two of the best thing I did in 1877, as good as those in your mother's collection.

Only they're hung stupidly and very vilely framed, that's all. The young artists and some of the good collectors have paid me the highest compliments.... Real painters and people who understand them are very scarce. Haven't had time to go there but Degas told me all about it ... *L'Eclair* publishes an interview with Gérôme (the Institut has protested to the Ministers of the Fine Arts), he takes Renoir to task and says he should not be confused with Renouard [a slick Salon painter and printmaker], for the latter can draw and has talent! ... you may be sure that all this will do us a lot of good, this protest has been a sensation and things won't stop there.

From *Journal Inédit de Paul Signac*

11 February 1898

When you compare the old age [of Pissarro], all activity and work, with the senile and dull decay of the old *rentiers* or retired people, we see the importance art has for us.

Camille Pissarro to Lucien Pissarro

Paris, November 1898

I haven't had time to write about what I felt when I looked at the admirable works of Rembrandt. The thought that struck me after I had seen not only the Rembrandts, but the works of Frans Hals, Vermeer and so many other great artists, was that we modern painters, we are unassailably correct to seek where they did not or rather to feel differently from the way they did, since different we are, and their works are so definitely of their time that it would be absurd to follow them. And then as I have so often said, I am suspicious of those adroit painters who know how to make pastiches of the old masters. I have not as much respect for these artful ones as I have for painters who are incapable of masterpieces, yet look with their own eyes. But how can I describe Rembrandt's portraits to you? The paintings by Hals, and the *View of Delft* by Vermeer, are masterpieces akin to the works of the Impressionists. I returned from Holland more persuaded than ever to love Monet, Degas, Renoir, Sisley....

From *En écountant Cézanne, Degas et Renoir* by Ambroise Vollard (1938)

... [Cézanne] broke into a nervous laugh and, returning to the subject of Gustave Moreau, went on: 'If that distinguished aesthete paints nothing but rubbish, it is because his dreams of art are suggested not by the inspirations of nature, but by what he has seen in the museums, and still more by a philosophical cast of mind derived from too close an acquaintance with the masters whom he admires. I should like to have that good man under my wing, to point out to him the doctrine of a development of art by contact with nature. It's so sane, so comforting, the only just conception of art.... Pissarro had the right idea; but he went a little too far when he said that they ought to burn all the necropolises of art.

From *Sisley* by Gustave Geffroy (1923)

Sisley was already in delicate health when he invited me to make the easy journey to Moret. We were admirably entertained by Sisley, his wife and daughter in their home which was both bourgeois and rustic. There I became better acquainted with the master's paintings. I had admired his work at an exhibition in 1883. Alas, many of those same paintings were still against the wall, piled in corners. The vogue for Sisley's work had not yet come as it was beginning to do for Monet. And it did not take long to sense the sadness that lay beneath his resigned outward appearance and lively conversation.

... Everything was magnificent and harmonious. We spent the morning in the studio and after lunch everyone took charabancs to Moret, the banks of the Loing, and the forest of Fontainebleau where Sisley, acting as master of ceremonies, spoke with unforgettable charm ...

Alfred Sisley to Dr Veau [a friend]

[Moret-sur-Loing], *28 November 1898*

I am better than I would have believed possible after the last haemorrhage, and although ridiculously thin my strength is gradually returning. I am using dressing of arsenate of soda. I have rinses, and massage with Ponds extract and eau-de-Cologne for my back and legs. It is doing me more good than I dared hope, so you see, my dear friend, that I am recovering little by little.

Alfred Sisley to Dr Veau

[Moret-sur-Loing, Winter 1898–1899]

I cannot fight any longer, my dear friend, I am at the end of my tether. I can hardly sit long enough in a chair for my bed to be made, and the swelling in my throat, neck and ears makes it impossible for me to move my head. I think it will not be long now. If you know a good doctor, though, who would not want more than 100 or 200 francs, I will see him. If you could tell me the date and the time he would come, I would send a cab to the station.

Affectionately, and very sadly, I bid you farewell. . . .

Alfred Sisley to Dr Veau

[Moret-sur-Loing], *13 January 1898*

I am collapsing with pain and with a weakness which I no longer have the strength to fight.

From *Growing Up With the Impressionists: the diary of Julie Manet*

15 January 1898

In Renoir's studio there was talk of the Dreyfus affair, and against the Jews.

'They [the Jews] come to France to make money and then, if there is any trouble they run behind a tree,' said M. Renoir. 'There's a lot of them in the army because the Jews love to strut around in fancy uniforms. They have been hounded from all other countries and there must be a reason for it. They shouldn't be allowed to occupy a prominent place in France. People say that the Dreyfus case must be brought out into the open, but there are some things which can't be said and people refuse to understand that.'

M. Renoir started off on the subject of Pissarro, a 'Jew' whose children have no country of their own and who do no military service whatever ...

Camille Pissarro to Lucien Pissarro

204 rue de Rivoli, Paris, 22 January 1898

... I have heard that Sisley is desperately ill. He is a great painter and in my opinion ranks among the masters. I have seen paintings done by him of the most unusual vision and beauty, among others a *Flood*, which is a masterpiece.

About the drawing you are beginning: I think you ought to keep working on it. You must understand that adroitness is not indispensable. Didn't Renoir paint ravishing pictures with his left hand when he broke his right arm? ...

The Dreyfus case is not progressing too quickly, but it is not going too badly either. The Chamber of Deputies voted against the reactionaries by big majorities several times in a row ... The anti-Semites and the Esterhazyites are already beginning to be ridiculous, and that is always fatal!

From *Growing Up With the Impressionists: the diary of Julie Manet*

30 January 1898

[Renoir] spoke of the appeal that is currently being signed by Jews, anarchists and writers for a review of the Dreyfus case ... He refused, of course ...

22 April 1899

We spoke afterwards of Sisley and of the withdrawn manner in which he lived his last years at Moret, believing that everyone had it in for him. When he re-met M. Renoir – with whom he had lived – he would cross the street in order not to speak to him. He made himself very unhappy. M. Renoir told me that when I went to Valvins with Maman we had met him one day on a visit to Moret. Maman invited him to visit her at Valvins, he accepted. Then, after saying goodbye, he ran after her saying, 'After all, no. I shan't come to see you.'

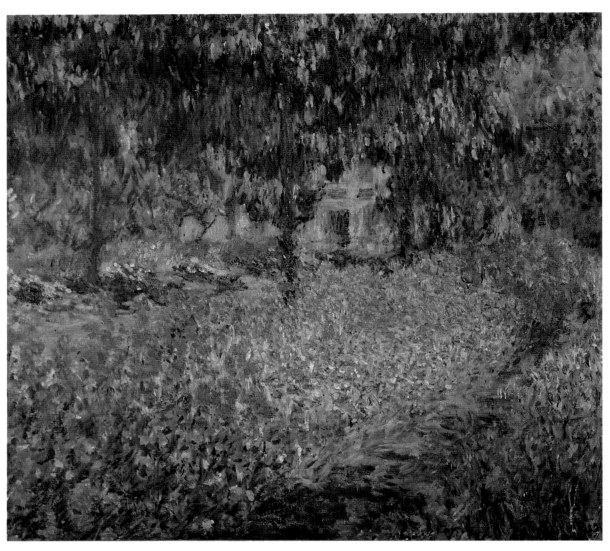

Monet *Artist's Garden at Giverny* 1900

The Final Years

Claude Monet to his gardener

Giverny, [February 1900]

Sowing: around 300 pots Poppies – 60 Sweet peas – around 60 pots white Agrimony – 30 yellow Agrimony – Blue sage – Blue Water-lilies in beds (greenhouse) – Dahlias – Iris Kaempferi. – From the 15th to the 25th, lay the dahlias down to root; plant out those with shoots before I get back. – Don't forget the lily bulbs. – Should the Japanese peonies arrive plant them immediately if weather permits, taking care initially to protect buds from the cold, as much as from the heat of the sun. Get down to pruning: rose trees not too long, except for the thorny varieties. In March sow the grass seeds, plant out the little nasturtiums, keep a close eye on the gloxinia, orchids etc., in the greenhouse, as well as the plants under frames. Trim the borders as arranged; put wires in for the clematis and climbing roses as soon as Picard has done the necessary. If the weather's bad, make some straw matting, but lighter than previously. Plant cuttings from the rose trees at the pond around manure in the hen huts. Don't delay work on tarring the planks and plant the *Helianthus latiflorus* in good clumps right away....

Claude Monet to Alice Monet

London, Monday, 19 March 1900, noon

Darling, I am in a state of utter despair and it wouldn't take much for me to drop everything on the spot and go tonight, and leave all my paintings... I was up at six and was appalled to see the roofs covered in snow; I was hoping that by the time I'd got dressed, it would melt away, but it became terribly foggy, so much so that we were in total darkness, and I had to have the lights on until half-past ten; then I thought I'd be able to work but I've never seen such changeable conditions and I had over 15 canvases under way, going from one to the other and back again, and it was never quite right; a few unfortunate brush strokes and in the end I lost my nerve and in a temper I packed everything away in crates with no further desire to look out of the window, knowing full well that in this mood I'd only mess things up and all the paintings I'd done were awful, and perhaps they are, more than I suppose. .... To have gone to all this trouble to get to this is just too stupid! Outside there's brilliant sunshine but I don't feel up to looking at it ...

Pierre-Auguste Renoir to Ambroise Vollard

Aix-les-Bains, 3 May 1900

I've come back to my little Hôtel de la Paix, where I am alone and very coddled. They make me little gourmet meals that that glutton Vollard would be very happy to taste. In short, since I didn't know what to do, I said to myself, let's write to Vollard, but what can I say to him since I have done nothing interesting!!! Bright idea, let's ask him for money. I know he loves that. 500 francs, in case the burglars should penetrate his sanctuary, that much at least would be saved, and that's why I thought of you, my dear Vollard.

Pierre-Auguste Renoir to Claude Monet

Louveciennes, 20 August 1900

I let them decorate me. Be assured that I am not letting you know to tell you whether I am wrong or right, but so that this little piece of ribbon does not become an obstacle to our old friendship. So call me dirty names, the most unpleasant words, it's all right with me, but no joking, whether I made a fool of myself or not. I want your friendship; as for the others, I don't give a damn.

Pierre-Auguste Renoir to Paul Durand-Ruel

[Louveciennes], *20 August 1900*

Yes, my dear Durand-Ruel, I am the culprit. So I hope that the firm of Durand-Ruel will take up a collection and buy me an honorary potty-chair. ....

Paul Cézanne from *Cézanne* by Joachim Gasquet (1926)

'... I would like to see them here, that crowd who write about us, here in front of this
face ... and with me clutching my paint tubes and brushes ... they're miles away ...
They don't even suspect how, by blending a finely-shaded green into a red, you can
make a mouth look sad or make a cheek smile. You yourself are aware that in every one
of my brush strokes there is something of my blood mixed with a little of your father's
[Henri Gasquet, who was sitting for Cézanne] – in the sun, the light, the colours; and
that there is a mysterious exchange between his soul, which he is unaware of, and my
eye which recreates it, and through which he will recognize himself ... if I were a
painter, a great painter! ... There, on my canvas, every stroke must correspond to a
breath taken by the world, to the brightness there on his whiskers, on his cheeks. We
must live in harmony together, my model, my colours and I, blending with every passing
moment. ...

'Painting is damned difficult ... You always think you've got it, but you haven't ...
Take your portrait – it's a fragment, and you know how hard you have to work on a face
to produce eyes which can see and a mouth which speaks ... You never fully know your
craft ... I could paint for a hundred years, a thousand years without stopping and
I would still feel as though I knew nothing ...

'God knows how the old masters got through those acres of work ... As for me,
I exhaust myself, work myself to death trying to cover fifty centimetres of canvas ...
No matter ... that's life ... I want to die painting ...'

Paul Cézanne to Charles Camoin [a young painter]

Aix, 3 February, 1902

Since you're there in Paris, and since the masters at the Louvre attract you, and if you
feel like it, do some studies after the great decorative masters, Veronese and Rubens, but
as you would if you were doing them from nature – which is something I've only ever
managed to do imperfectly. – But it's good, above all, that you should work from nature.
... I sincerely congratulate you on being so close to *Madame votre mère* – in moments of
sadness and low spirits, she will be for you the surest point of moral support, and the
liveliest source from which you can draw a fresh resolve to work at your art, which is
something you will have to try to succeed in doing, not without resilience and feebly,
but in a calm and sustained fashion, which cannot fail to bring with it a state of clear-
sightedness, very useful in guiding you with firmness in life. ...

From *Racontars de Rapin* by Paul Gauguin (1902)

You say: 'Cézanne is monochrome.' You might just as well say polychrome or polyphonic.
A matter of the eye and the ear! ... 'Cézanne stems from no one; he is content to be
Cézanne!' There's some mistake, otherwise he would not be the painter he is ... He
knows Virgil, he has looked understandingly at Rembrandt and Poussin.

Paul Cézanne to Joachim Gasquet

Aix, 8 July 1902

I despise all living painters, apart from Monet and Renoir, and I want to succeed by work.

Paul Cézanne to Charles Camoin

Aix, 11 March 1902

Since you left, the Bernheims and a second dealer have been to see me. My son did some business with them. But I remain faithful to Vollard, and am rather sorry my son has let him believe I could take my canvases to anyone else.

... Vollard, I have no doubt, will continue to be my intermediary with the public. He's a man of great flair and determination, and who knows how to go about things.

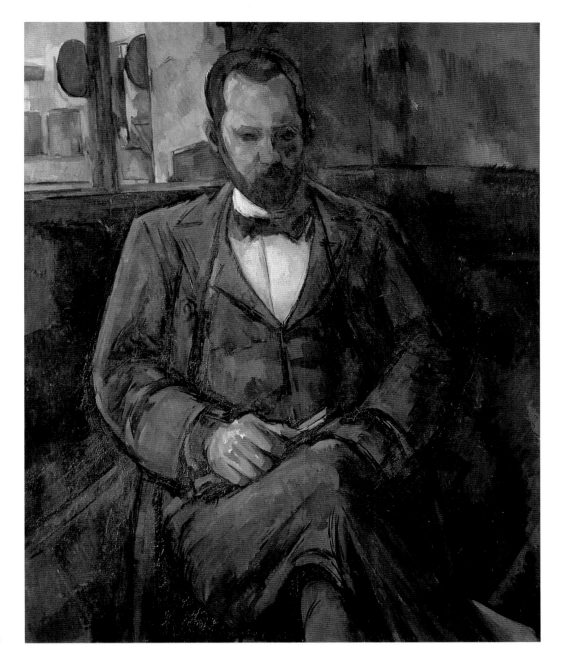

Cézanne *Portait of Vollard* c.1899

Paul Cézanne to Ambroise Vollard

Aix, 9 January 1903

I'm working stubbornly, I glimpse the promised land. Will I be like the great leader of the Hebrews or may I actually be able to enter in? . . .

I've made some progress. Why so late and so painfully? Is it that Art is, in fact, a priesthood, which requires those who are pure and who belong wholly to it? I'm sorry that such a distance separates us, for more than once I would turn to you to give me a little bit of moral support . . . If I'm still alive, we'll speak again about all this. Thank you for so kindly remembering me.

Claude Monet to Paul Durand-Ruel

Giverny, 23 March 1903

. . . I can't send you a single *London* painting since for this kind of work I need to be able to see them all, and quite honestly none of them are completely finished. I'm working on them all, or on a number of them anyway, and don't yet know how many I'll be able to exhibit, since what I'm doing is very delicate. One day I'm satisfied and the next everything looks bad, but anyway there'll be a few good ones at least . . .

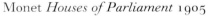

Monet *Houses of Parliament* 1905

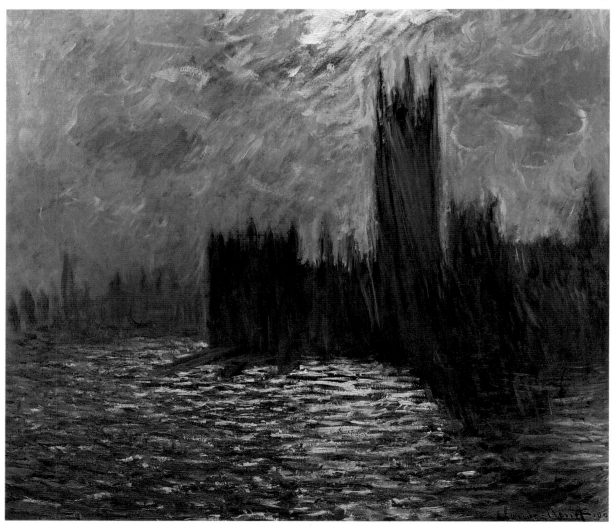

Claude Monet to Gustave Geffroy

Giverny, 15 April 1903

... You ask me when the exhibition of my poor old *London* pictures is due to begin.
I promised it would be ready by early May, but I'm afraid they'll all be ruined by then.
You tell me calmly to frame them and exhibit them as they are; that I won't, it would be
stupid to invite people to look at sketches which are far too incomplete. Where I went
wrong was to insist on adding finishing touches to them; a good impression is lost so
quickly; I very much regret it and it sickens me because it shows how powerless I am. If
I had left them as they were and had not planned to sell them, people could have done
what they liked with them after my death. Then, these essays, these preliminary studies,
could be shown as they are; now that I've had a go at every single one of them, I have to
see them through, for better or worse, to some kind of conclusion, but you have no idea
what a state of nerves and despair I'm in! So please excuse me.

Claude Monet to François Thiébault-Sisson [journalist]

[1903]

... The water flowers are far from being the whole scene; really, they are just the
accompaniment. The essence of the motif is the mirror of water whose appearance alters
at every moment, thanks to the patches of sky which are reflected in it, and which give it
its light and movement. . . .

Camille Pissarro to Lucien Pissarro

Le Havre, 10 July 1903

Honfleur is a pretty little town, completely flooded by villas, which are everywhere
along the coast, alas! But the harbour is very interesting, there are hotels which are quite
accessible, that is, charge no more than seven or eight francs a day. We slept at the
famous Hôtel St-Siméon, at which all the painters since 1830 have stayed. Formerly it
was a farmhouse, with apple trees in the green fields and a view of the sea; Boudin,
Corot, Daubigny, Monet, Jongkind stayed there, but nothing remains of those glorious
days. These idiotic new proprietors have put the place in 'good order'. It is horribly
painted up and polished, there are rectilinear gravel paths, one can get a view of the sea
only from the dining halls, from the front windows you can't even get a glimpse of the
sea now, in short, it is arranged to suit the taste of the English ladies who abound. It is
heartbreaking!

Edgar Degas to Henri Rouart

Sunday, [October 1903]

So [Pissarro] has died, the poor old wandering Jew. He will walk no more, and if one had
been warned, one would certainly have walked a little behind him. What has he been
thinking since the nasty affair, what did he think of the embarrassment one felt, in spite
of oneself, in his company? ... Did he think only of going back to the times when we
were pretty nearly unaware of his terrible race?

Paul Cézanne to Jules Borély [archaeologist]

1902

... As for old Pissarro, he was a father to me. He was the kind of man you would consult, a bit like 'the good Lord' himself.

Paul Cézanne to Emile Bernard

Aix, 15 April 1904

Let me repeat what I was telling you here: deal with nature in the cylinder, the sphere, the cone, with everything put into perspective, or so that each side of an object, of a surface, is directed towards a central point. The parallel lines at the horizon give the sense of breadth, either a section of nature or, if you prefer, of the spectacle that the *Pater Omnipotens Aeterne Deus* spreads out before our eyes. The perpendicular lines at the horizon give the sense of depth. Now, nature, for us men, is more a matter of depth than of surface, hence the need to introduce into our shimmering light, represented by reds and yellows, a sufficient amount of bluish tones to make one feel the air.

Let me tell you I've had another look at the study you did from the ground floor of the studio – it's good. You need only, I think, continue along this path. You have a natural understanding of what needs to be done, and you'll soon be able to turn your back on the Gauguins and [Van] Goghs.

Paul Cézanne to Emile Bernard

Aix, 12 May 1904

My dedication to work and my advanced age will sufficiently explain to you the delay I have shown in answering you.

... I've already said this to you, but Redon's talent gives me a great pleasure and I'm absolutely one with him in his feeling for and admiration of Delacroix. I'm not sure if my indifferent health will ever permit me to achieve my dream of painting his apotheosis.

I proceed very slowly, nature offering itself to me in a very complex light; and the progress still to be made is endless. One has to look hard at one's model and feel it very accurately; and then express oneself distinctively and forcefully.

Taste is the best judge. It is rare. Art only addresses itself to an exceedingly restricted number of individuals.

The artist must disdain any opinion that is not based on the intelligent observation of character.

He must be wary of the literary spirit, which so often makes the painter turn from his true path – the concrete study of nature – and lose himself for too long amidst intangible speculations.

Paul Cézanne from *Cézanne* by Joachim Gasquet (1926)

'I have my *motif* ... If I pass too high or too low, everything is ruined. There mustn't be one single stitch which is too loosely woven, not one gap through which emotion, light, truth might escape. You see, I develop my whole canvas at once, as a unity. Everything disparate I bring together in one outburst, one act of faith ... All that we see dissipates, moves on. Nature is always the same, but nothing of her remains, nothing of what appears before us. Our art must provide some fleeting sense of her permanence, with the essence, the appearance of her changeability.

'It must give us an awareness of her eternal qualities. What lies below her? Nothing, perhaps. Perhaps everything. Everything, do you see? And so I join her roaming hands.'

Claude Monet to Paul Durand-Ruel

Giverny, 4 October 1904

I've been having a few days' rest and I was planning to invite you to lunch some time soon but I've just decided to put a long-cherished plan of mine into practice: to go to Madrid to see the Velázquez. We are leaving by car on Friday morning for about three weeks ...

Paul Cézanne to Roger Marx [art historian]

[Aix], 23 January 1905

To my way of thinking, one does not substitute oneself for the past, one simply adds another link to it. With a painter's temperament and an ideal of art, this is to say, a conception of nature, one would have needed means of expression that were sufficient to make one intelligible to ordinary members of the public and to win one a fitting place in the history of art.

Paul Cézanne to an unknown young artist

[undated]

Perhaps I came too soon. I was more the painter of your generation that of my own ... You are young, full of vitality, you will impress your art with an animation that only those who feel deeply can give it. As for me, I grow old. I shan't have the time to express myself ... To work ...

The reading of the model and its expression is sometimes very slow in coming.

Claude Monet to Georges Durand-Ruel

Giverny, [3 July] 1905

... As for the paints I use, is it really as interesting as all that? I don't think so, considering that one could do something even more luminous and better with another palette. The point is to know how to use the colours, the choice of which is, when all's said and done, a matter of habit. Anyway I use flake white, cadmium yellow, vermilion, deep madder, cobalt blue, emerald green and that's all.

Paul Cézanne to his son Paul

Aix, Sunday, 26 August 1906

I continue working with pleasure and yet, sometimes, there is such a filthy light that nature seems ugly to me. One must, therefore, make a choice.

Paul Cézanne to his son Paul

Aix, 8 September 1906

Anyway, I must tell you that I am becoming, as a painter, more perceptive before nature, but that with me, to realize my sensations is always painfully hard. I can't capture the intensity that unfolds itself to my senses. I haven't got that magnificent richness of coloration which animates nature. Here, on the river bank, motifs abound, the same subject seen from a different angle offers a subject of study of the most vital interest, and so varied I believe I could keep myself busy for months on end without changing my position, simply leaning now a little to the right, now a little to the left.

Paul Cézanne to Emile Bernard

Aix, 21 September 1906

Will I reach the goal I've so much sought after and so long pursued? I hope so, but while it is not attained, a vague state of unease continues, which will only disappear when I have reached the port, or have achieved something that turns out better than in the past... And so I carry on with my work....

I continue my studies of nature, and it seems to me that I am making slow progress. I would have liked to have you near me, for solitude always weighs one down a bit. But I'm old, ill, and I swore to myself that I would die painting, rather than sink into that degrading dotage which threatens all old people who allow themselves to be dominated [by] passions that stupefy their senses.

...I believe in the logical development of that which we see and feel through the study of nature, at the risk of having to worry later about problems of technique; technique being for us no more than a means by which we succeed in making the public feel what we ourselves feel so deeply and of winning people's indulgence. The great figures [of the past] whom we admire can only have done that.

Paul Cézanne to his son Paul

Aix, 15 October 1906

I continue to work with difficulty, but still, at least it's something. It's the important thing, I believe. Sensations being what my life's essentially been about, I reckon I'm impervious....

My dear Paul, to give you news as satisfactory as you want it to be, I'd have to be twenty years younger. – I repeat, I eat well, and a little moral satisfaction – but, as for that, it is only work that can give it to me – would do a lot for me. – All my compatriots are arseholes compared to me... I think the young painters are a lot more intelligent than the others, all the old ones can see in me is a disastrous rival.

Marie Cézanne [the artist's sister] to the young Paul Cézanne

[Aix], *20 October 1906*

Your father has been ill since Monday ... He stayed out in the rain for several hours, he was brought back on a laundry cart; and the two men had to carry him up to his bed. The next day, very early in the morning, he went out into the garden to do some work on a portrait of Vallier, underneath the lime-tree, he came back a dying man.

Claude Monet to Gustave Geffroy

[Giverny], *11 August 1908*

... You must know I'm entirely absorbed in my work. These landscapes of water and reflections have become an obsession. It's quite beyond my powers at my age, and yet I want to succeed in expressing what I feel. I've destroyed some ... I start others ... and I hope that something will come out of so much effort ...

Monet *Waterlilies c.*1914–7

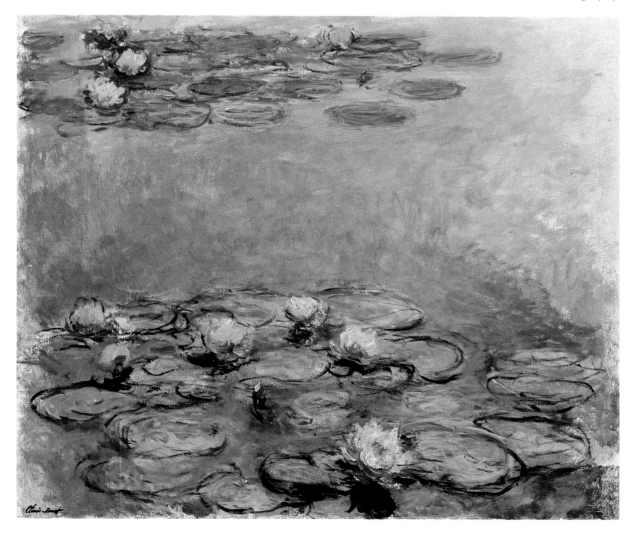

Claude Monet to Gustave Geffroy

[1909]

I was tempted to use the theme of the *Nymphéas* for the decoration of a salon: carried along the walls, its unity enfolding all the panels, it was to produce the illusion of an endless whole, a wave without horizon and without a shore; nerves strained by work would relax in its presence, following the reposing example of its stagnant waters, and for him who would live in it, this room would offer an asylum of peaceful meditation in the midst of a flowering aquarium . . .

I have painted for half a century and will soon have passed my sixty-ninth year, but far from decreasing, my sensitivity has sharpened with age. As long as constant commerce with the outside world can maintain the ardour of my curiosity, and my hand remains the prompt and faithful servant of my perception, I have nothing to fear from old age. I have no other wish than a close fusion with nature, and I desire no other fate than (according to Goethe's precept) to have worked and lived in harmony with her laws. Beside her grandeur, her power, and her immortality, the human creature seems but a miserable atom.

From *Degas and his Model* by Alice Michel (1919)

'I am always thinking of death. Whether it be day or night-time, it is always before my eyes . . . Oh! How sad it is to be old! You, my girl, have no idea what it is, you with your mere twenty-five years.'

He collapsed into the armchair and covered his eyes.

Torn between annoyance and pity the young girl looked down at him. Her robust youth was both offended and amazed by these lamentations which were repeated nearly every day in terms which hardly ever varied. Knowing that he liked to be consoled, however, she said:

'Come now, M. Degas, why are you always talking about death? You are only seventy-six; you have plenty of time to think about it . . . I bet you'll live longer than Harpignies who's in his nineties now.'

'Ha ha! Old Harpignies! It's true, he's still around and isn't ready to snuff it yet.'

From *Renoir, My Father* by Jean Renoir (1962)

[Renoir, aged 70, *c.*1911]: What struck outsiders coming into his presence for the first time were his eyes and hands. His eyes were light brown, verging on yellow. Often he would point out to us on the horizon a bird of prey flying over the valley of the Cagne . . . His hands were terribly deformed. Rheumatism had cracked the joints, bending the thumb towards the palm, and the other fingers towards the wrist. Visitors' . . . reaction, which they dared not express was 'It's not possible. With those hands he can't paint these pictures. There's a mystery.' The mystery was Renoir himself . . . His hands with the fingers curved inwards could no longer pick up anything. . . . The truth is that Renoir's skin had become so tender that contact with the wooden handle of the brush injured it.

To avoid this difficulty he had a little piece of cloth inserted into the hollow of his hand. His twisted fingers gripped rather than held the brush. But until his death his arm remained as steady as that of a young man.

Claude Monet to Gustave Geffroy

Giverny, 7 June 1912

Heartfelt thanks for your two fine articles which I'm very proud of. No, I'm not a great painter. Neither am I a great poet. I only know that I do what I can to convey what I experience before nature and that most often, in order to succeed in conveying what I feel, I totally forget the most elementary rules of painting, if they exist that is. In short, I let a good many mistakes show through when fixing my sensations. It will always be the same and this is what makes me despair. . . .

Claude Monet to [G. or J.] Bernheim-Jeune [dealer]

Giverny, 5 August 1912

. . . I've been plagued by an endless succession of troubles and anxieties. . . . I can only see with one eye. I've got a cataract (I wasn't mistaken when I complained about my eyesight). So I'm following a course of treatment in order to delay, and if possible avoid, an operation. The operation is nothing, but my sight will be totally altered after it, and that's what matters most to me. . . .

More than ever and despite my poor sight, I need to paint and paint unceasingly . . .

Mary Cassatt to an unknown recipient

[between January 1913 and February 1914]

I must take some of your nuts to Renoir, who suffers at times greatly (senile gangrene of the foot) . . . His wife I dislike and now that she has got rid of his nurse and model, she is always there. He is doing the most awful pictures of enormously fat red women with very small heads. Vollard persuades himself they are fine. J. Durand-Ruel knows better.

From *Renoir, My Father* by Jean Renoir (1962)

The pleasure he got out of life as a man coincided with the pleasure he felt as a painter. Once, towards the end of his life [around 1914], I heard him make the following rejoinder to a journalist who seemed to be astonished by his crippled hands:

'With such hands how do you paint?' the man asked, crudely.

'With my prick,' replied Renoir, really vulgar for once.

It took place in the dining-room at Les Collettes. There were a half-dozen or so visitors. No one laughed at his quip. For what he said was a striking expression of the truth; one of those rare testimonies, so seldom expressed in the history of the world, to the miracle of transformation of matter into spirit.

Pierre-Auguste Renoir to Georges Durand-Ruel

Cagnes, 30 August 1917

I have received a letter and a telegram informing me of Degas' death. It's fortunate for him and for the people around him. Any conceivable death is better than living the way he was.

Claude Monet to Georges Clemenceau

[Giverny], *12 November 1918*

I am on the verge of finishing two decorative panels which I want to sign on Victory Day and am writing to ask you if they could be offered to the State with you acting as intermediary. It's little enough, but it's the only way I have of taking part in the victory. I'd like the panels to be placed in the Musée des Arts Décoratifs and would be delighted if you were to select them.

Pierre-Auguste Renoir to Georges Rivière [friend]

[July 1919]

I feel I am still making some progress. I am beginning to get to know how to paint. It has taken me fifty years of work to get this far – and there's still more to do. . . .

Claude Monet to Georges Clemenceau

[Giverny], *10 November 1919*

. . . I'm very much afraid that an operation might be fatal, that once the bad eye has been suppressed the other eye will follow. So I prefer to make the best of my bad sight, such as it is, and give up painting if I have to, but at least be able to see something of the things I love, sky, water and trees, not to mention my nearest and dearest . . .

From an article by Félix Fénéon in *Le Bulletin des Artistes* (15 December 1919)

In the course of his illness, [Renoir] alluded, but without self-pity, to his probable end. 'I'm finished,' he said . . . On 30th November, he was still painting; he had begun a little still-life of two apples. Then his last illness overtook him. He was attended by two doctors from Nice: Prat (a surgeon) and Duthil. Dr Duthil had recently killed two woodcocks, and had told the painter about this exploit; the birds, associated with thoughts of his painting, kept coming back to his mind in his delirium, and were his last preoccupation.

'Give me that palette . . . those two woodcocks . . . turn this one's head to the left . . . give me back my palette . . . I can't paint that beak . . . Quick, some paint . . . change the position of those woodcocks . . .'

He died at two o'clock in the morning on Wednesday 3rd December.

Claude Monet to Félix Fénéon

[Giverny, mid-December 1919]

... You can imagine how painful the loss of Renoir has been to me: with him goes part of my own life. All I've been able to do these last three days has been to go back over our early years of struggle and hope ... It's hard to be alone, though no doubt it won't be for long as I'm feeling my age increasingly as each day goes by, despite what people say ...

Claude Monet to Georges Clemenceau

[Giverny, c.1920]

... Ever since I entered my sixties I had had the idea of setting about a kind of 'synthesis' in each of the successive categories of themes that held my attention — of summing up in one canvas, sometimes in two, my earlier impressions and sensations. I had given up the notion. It would have meant travelling a good deal, and for a long time revisiting one by one all the places through which my life as a painter had taken me, and verifying my emotions. I said to myself, as I made sketches, that a series of general impressions captured at the times of the day when I had the best chances of seeing correctly would not be without interest. I waited for the idea to consolidate, for the grouping and composition to settle in my brain, little by little, of their own accord, and the day when I felt I had enough cards to try my luck with real hope of success, I determined to pass to action and did so.

Claude Monet to Dr Charles Coutela [opthalmologist]

Giverny, 9 April 1924

... For months I've been slaving away and achieved nothing worthwhile. Is it my age or faulty sight? Both no doubt, but my sight most of all. I have recovered my perception of black and white, for reading and writing in other words, and I'm grateful for that of course, but my vision as a painter has, alas, gone as I'd thought and it's not your fault.

I tell you this in complete confidence. I hide it as much as possible, but I'm feeling terribly saddened and discouraged. Life is a torture to me. I don't know what to say. You know that I am surrounded by care and affection. Perhaps it's fatigue, but apart from near sight, there's no doubt that I see with increasing difficulty. The first spectacles are the only ones I'm satisfied with in artificial light, and the odd thing is that I accidentally put them on in daylight and no longer noticed those yellows and blues which made you choose tinted lenses. So what's to be done and what hope is there? ...

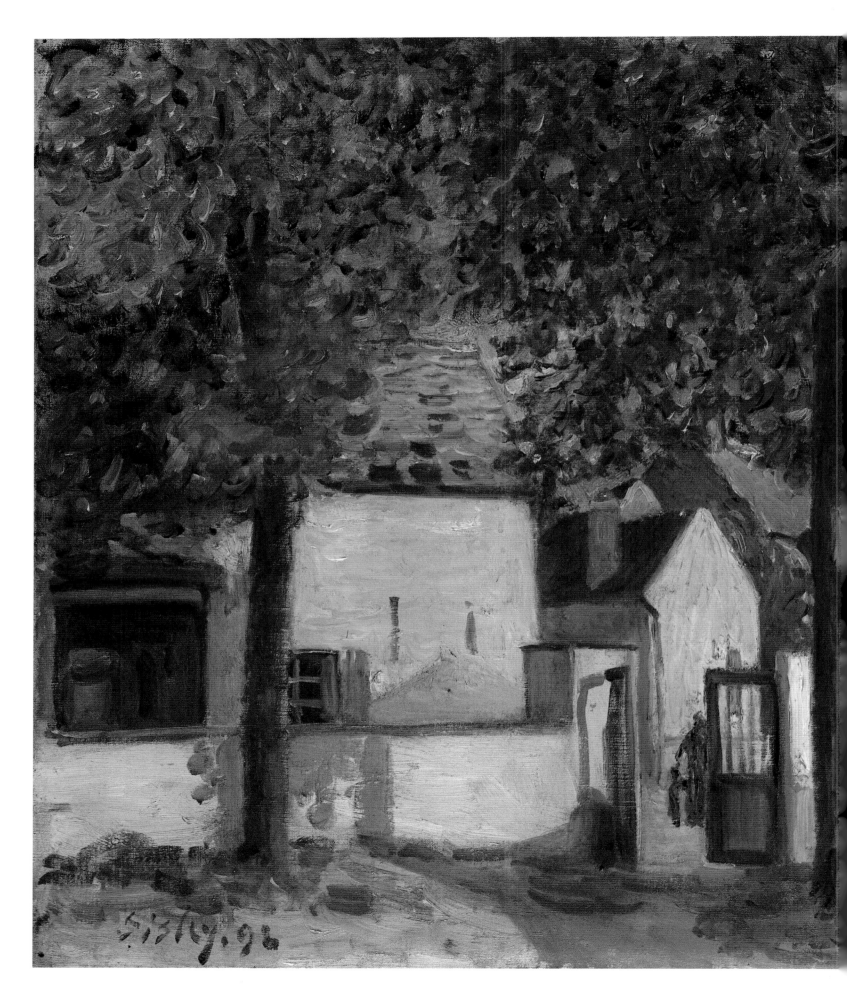

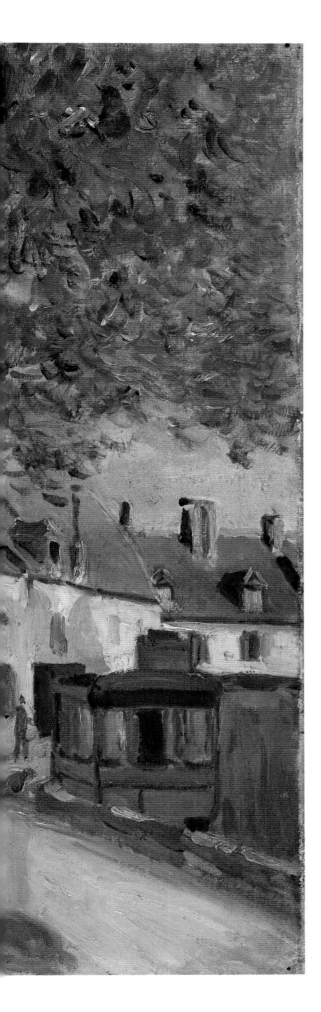

Sisley *View of the Village of Moret* 1892

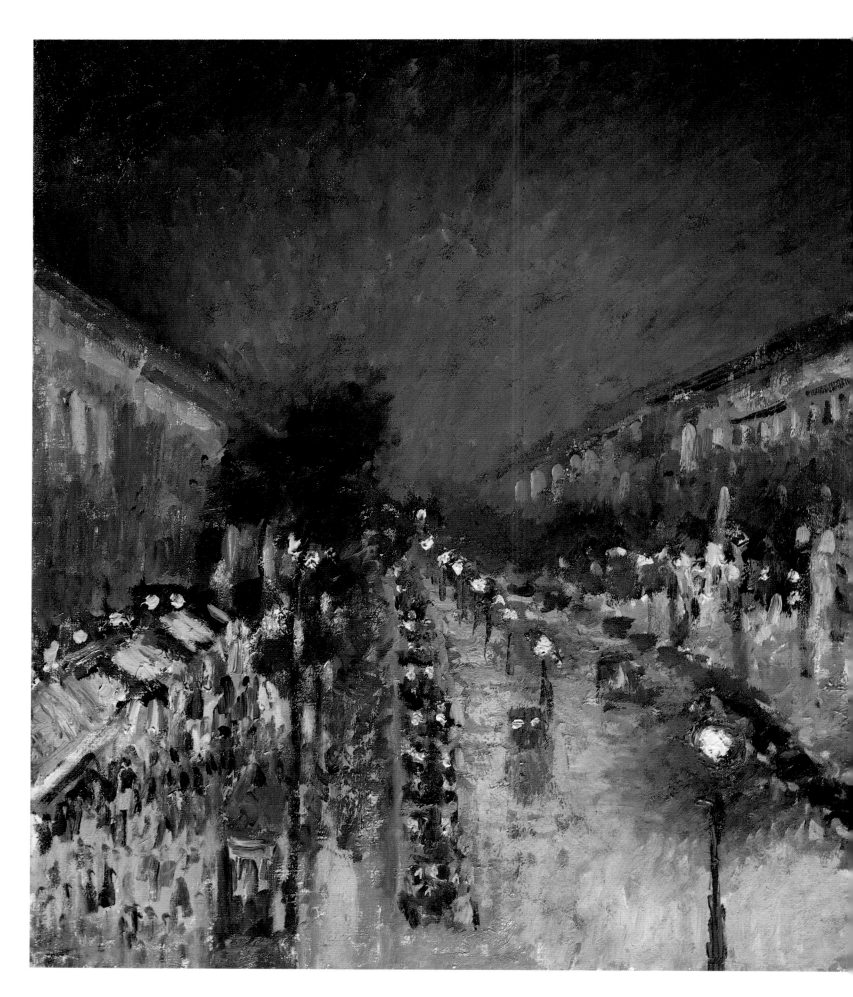

Pissarro *Boulevard Montmartre, Night Effect* 1897

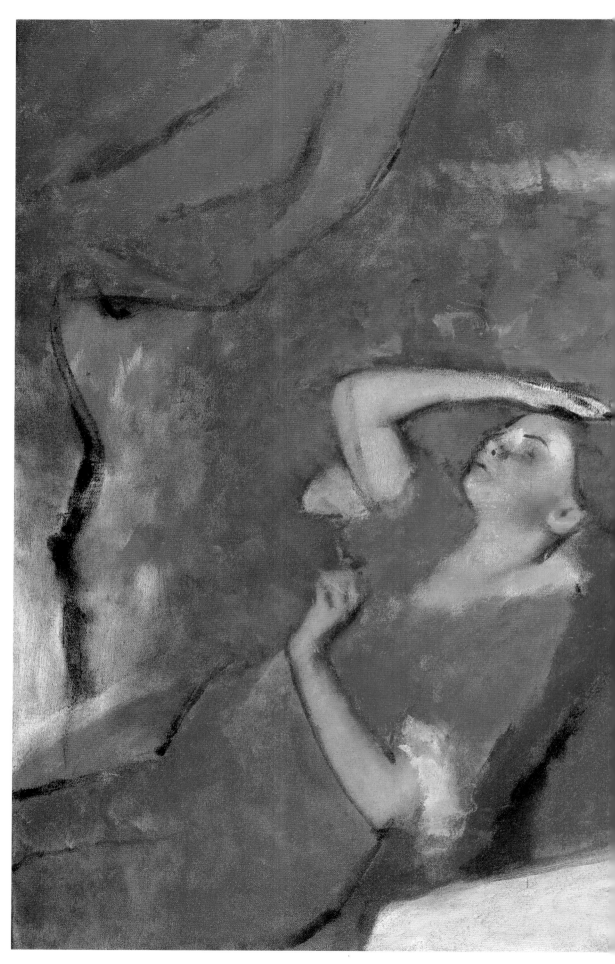

Degas *Combing the Hair* c.1892–5

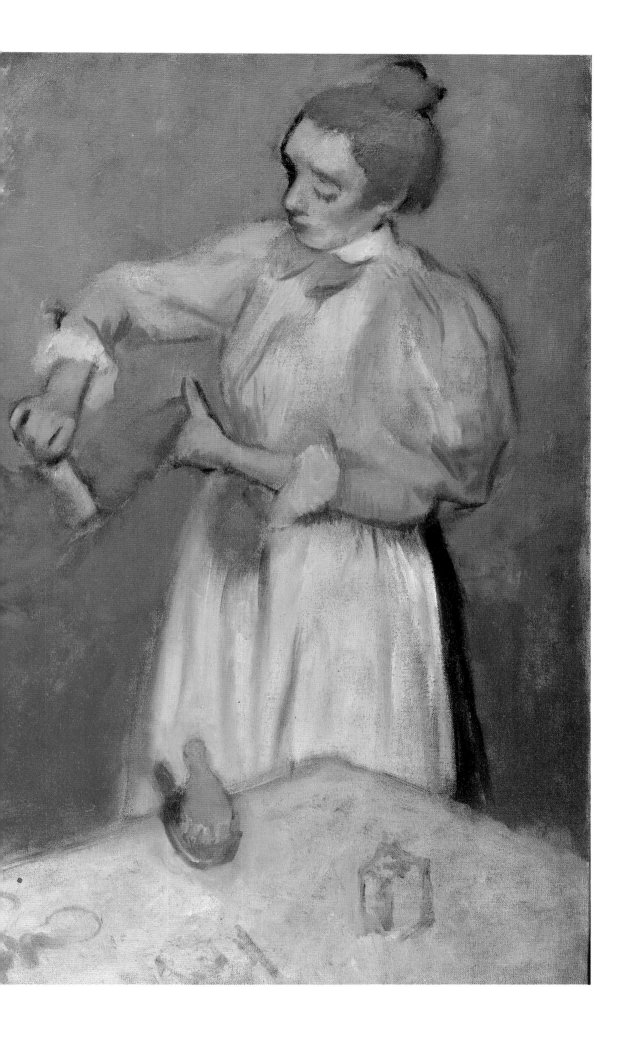

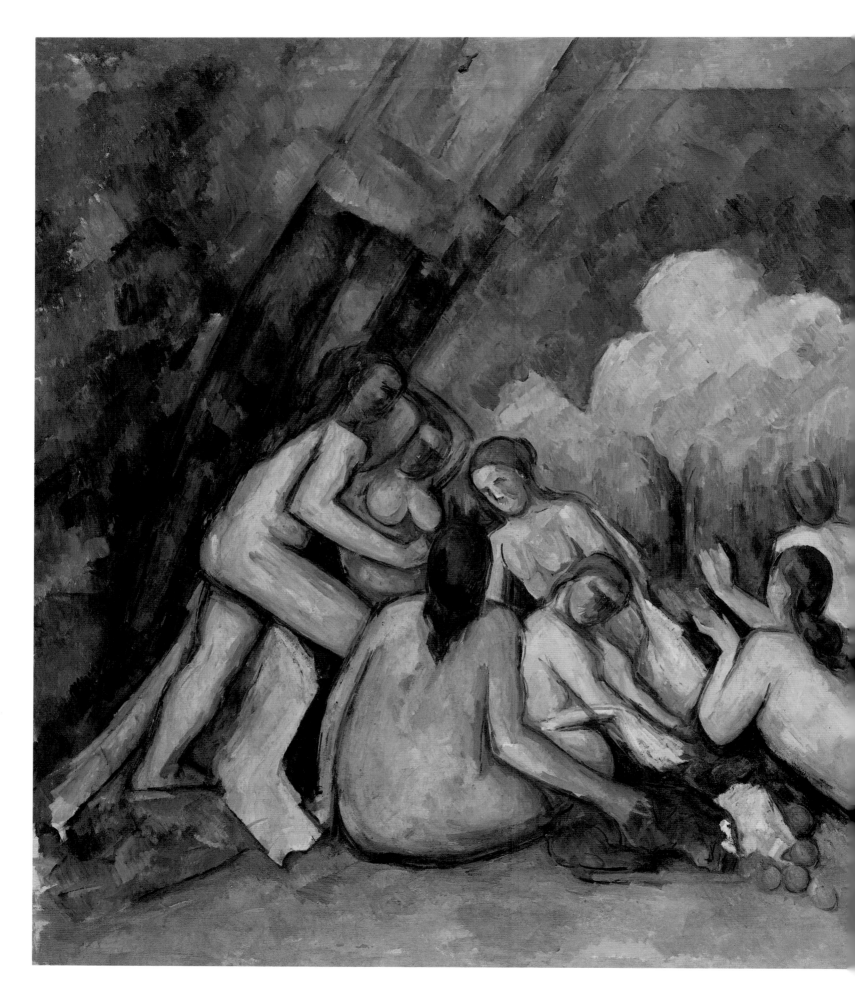

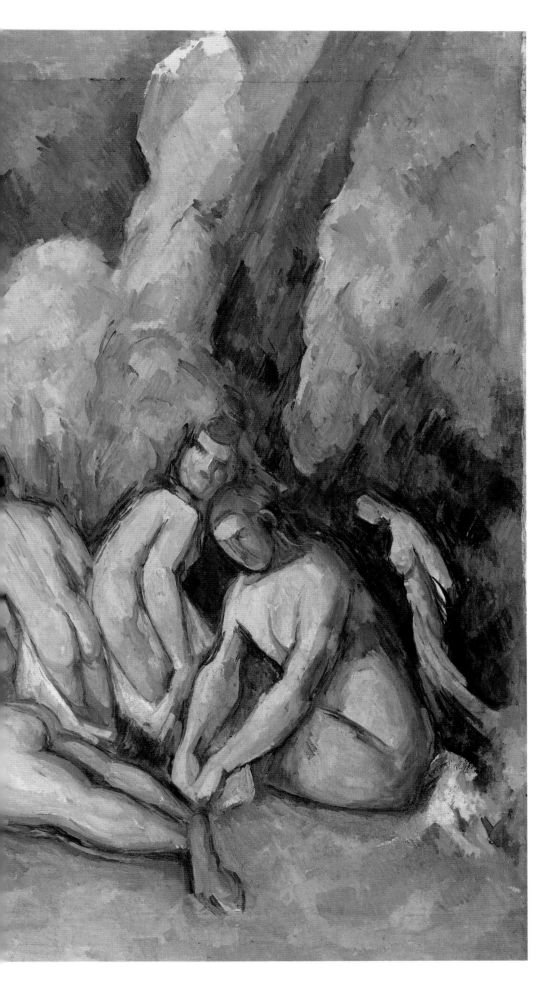

Cézanne *Les grandes baigneuses*
Begun 1895

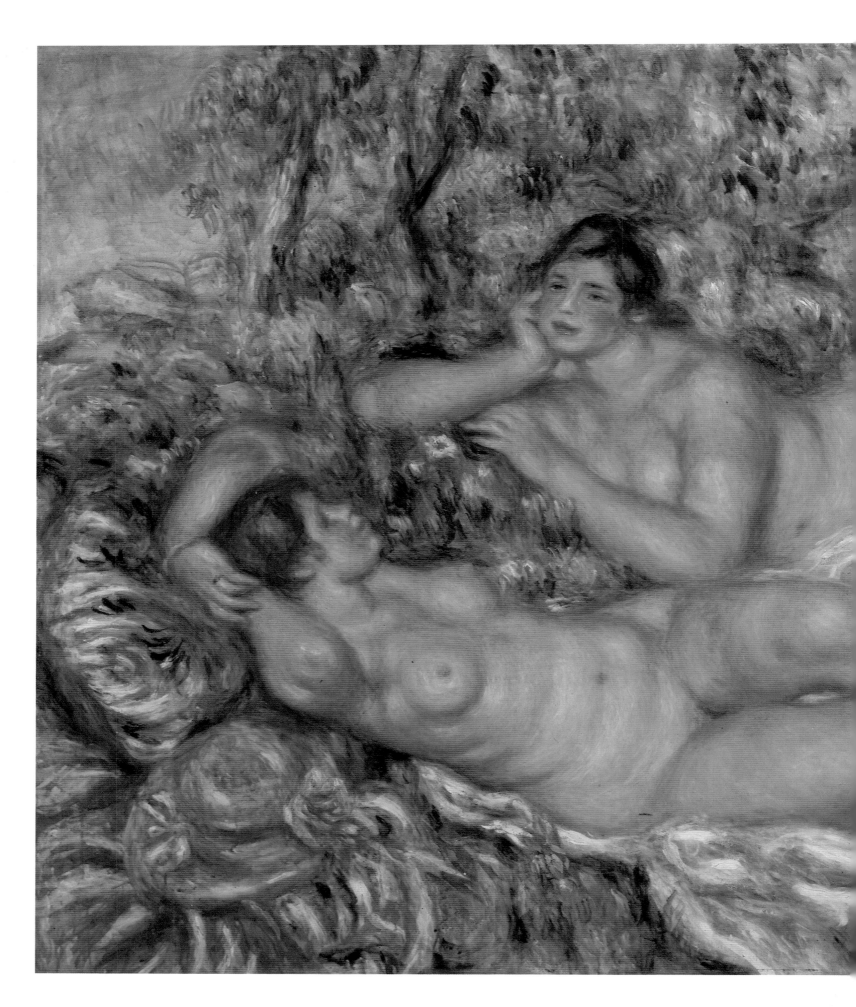

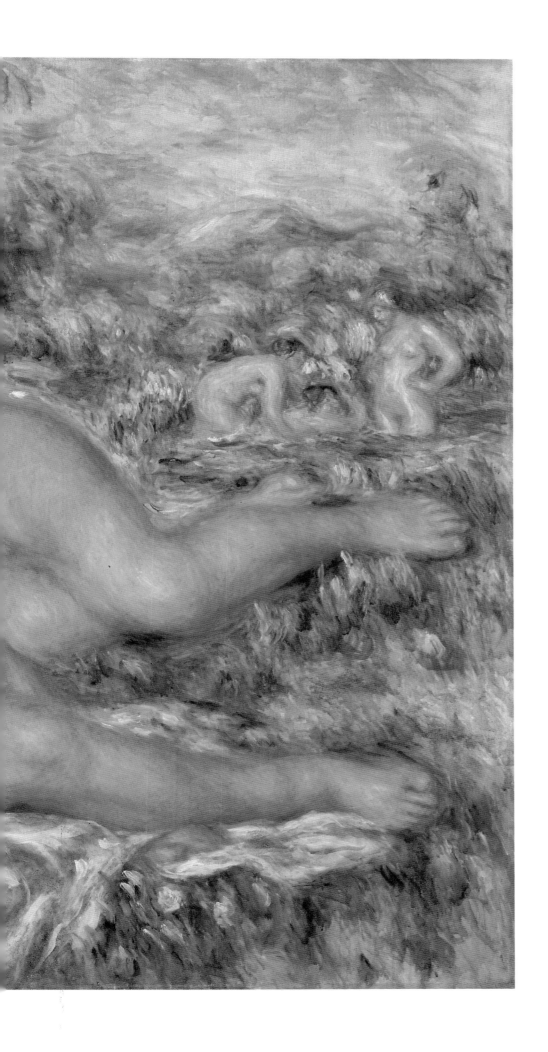

Renoir *Les grandes baigneuses* 1918–19

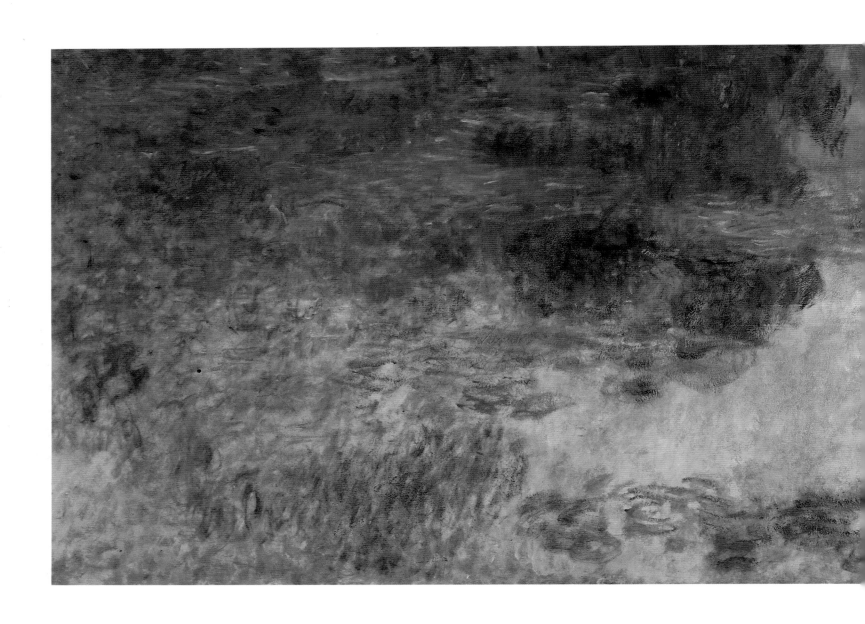

Monet *Waterlilies, Evening* 1916–22

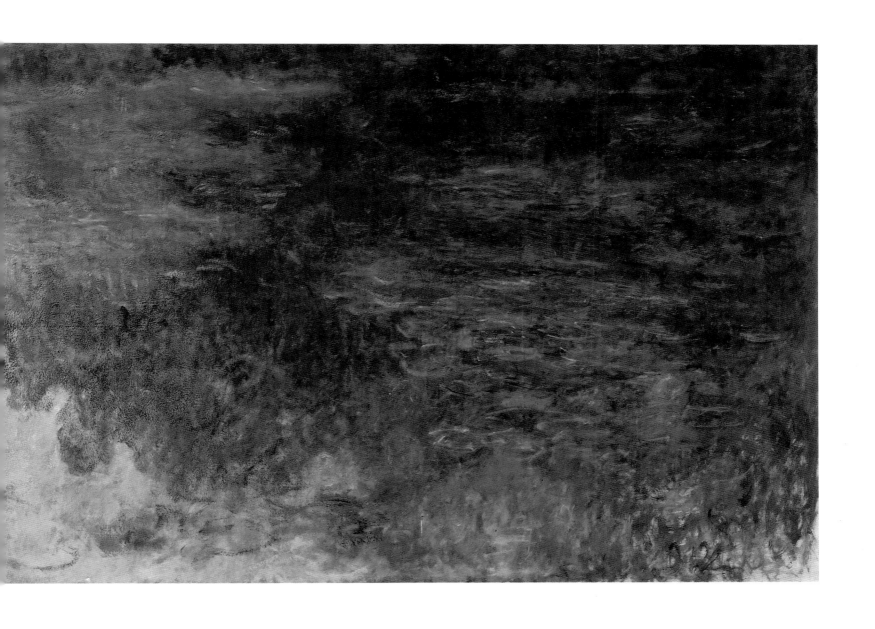

List of Plates

263 Woman with a Parasol – Madame Monet and her Son, 1875
Claude Monet
Oil on canvas, 100 × 81 cm
National Gallery of Art, Washington;
Collection of Mr and Mrs Paul Mellon

264 Bathers, Guernsey, c.1882
Pierre-Auguste Renoir
Oil on canvas, 54 × 65 cm
Ny Carlsberg Glyptotek, Copenhagen

265 Women Bathing, 1885
Paul Gauguin
Oil on canvas, 38.1 × 46.2 cm
National Museum of Western Art, Tokyo

266 Self-Portrait, 1885
Berthe Morisot
Pastel on blue laid paper, 47.5 × 37.5 cm
The Art Insitute of Chicago;
Regenstein Collection

271 Ceramic Vase, 1901
Mary Cassatt
Ceramic with decorated green and pink glaze
Ville de Paris, Musée du Petit Palais

272/3 Modern Woman, 1893
Mary Cassatt
Mural decoration of South Tympanum of
Woman's building, World's Columbian
Exposition, Chicago. Presumed lost.

277 Study of Bathers, c.1885–6
Pierre-Auguste Renoir
Watercolour, pencil and pen, 32.5 × 49.5 cm
Musée du Louvre, Paris

279 Study for Bathers, c.1900–6
Paul Cézanne
Oil on canvas, 33 × 40.9 cm
Christie's, London

281 Julie with Laertes, 1893
Berthe Morisot
Oil on canvas, 73 × 80 cm
Musée Marmottan, Paris

284 Boieldieu Bridge, Rouen, Sunset, 1896
Camille Pissarro
Oil on canvas, 72.4 × 91.4 cm
Birmingham Museum and Art Gallery

286 Young Woman Bathing Her Legs, c.1895
Camille Pissarro
Coloured chalks highlighted with pastel,
53.1 × 39.1 cm
Ashmolean Museum, Oxford

290 Monet's Garden at Giverny, 1900
Claude Monet
Oil on canvas, 81 × 92 cm
Musée d'Orsay, Paris

293 Portrait of Vollard, c.1899
Paul Cézanne
Oil on canvas, 100 × 81 cm
Ville de Paris, Musée du Petit Palais

294 Houses of Parliament, 1905
Claude Monet
Oil on canvas, 81 × 92 cm
Musée Marmottan, Paris

299 Waterlilies, c.1914–7
Claude Monet
Oil on canvas, 130.5 × 49.8 cm
Christie's, London

304/5 View of the Village of Moret, 1892
Alfred Sisley
Oil on canvas, 38.1 × 47 cm
National Museum of Wales, Cardiff

306/7 Boulevard Montmartre Night Effect, 1897
Camille Pissarro
Oil on canvas, 53.3 × 64.8 cm
The National Gallery, London

308/9 Combing the Hair, c.1892–5
Edgar Degas
Oil on canvas, 114.3 × 146.1 cm
The National Gallery, London

310/11 Les grandes baigneuses,
begun 1895
Paul Cézanne
Oil on canvas, 127.2 × 196.1 cm
The National Gallery, London

312/13 Les grandes baigneuses, 1918–19
Pierre-Auguste Renoir
Oil on canvas, 110 × 160 cm
Musée d'Orsay, Paris

314/15 Waterlilies, Evening, 1916–22
Claude Monet
Oil on canvas, 200 × 300 cm
Kunsthaus, Zürich

Picture acknowledgements

The publishers would like to thank the museums, galleries and collections credited in the *List of Plates* for permission to reproduce the works in this book. Transparencies were kindly supplied by the collections concerned and by the following:

Artothek, 12, 140, 220; Bridgeman Art Library 50, 66/67, 73, 78, 176, 240, 258; Chicago Historical Society 272/3; Christie's Colour Library 88, 108, 196, 211 left, 279, 299; E.T. Archive 94, 161; Giraudon 52, 56, 60; Studio Lourmel 114, 117, 238, 281, 294; Photothèque des musées de la ville de Paris 271, 293; RMN 10, 21, 24, 25, 30, 37, 42, 51, 54, 57, 58, 59, 82, 95, 98, 120, 121, 122, 123, 124, 127, 132, 133, 142, 146, 153, 157, 159, 163, 179, 198, 244, 245, 261, 277, 290, 312/313; Scala 145/154; Reproduced by kind permission of Sotheby's, London 96; Sotheby's, New York, 162.

Guide to the Principal Personalities mentioned in the text

Bazille, Frédéric (1841–1870)
The tragic death of Bazille, during the Franco-Prussian War, robbed the Impressionist movement of one of its most likeable and exciting talents. He was born into a wealthy family from Montpellier in the south of France; his friendship and financial support were of important help to Monet, Sisley and Renoir in their early years. He exhibited at the Salons of 1866, 1868, 1869 and 1870.

Bellio, Georges de (1828–1924)
The Romanian aristocrat and homeopathic physician de Bellio was an important collector of Impressionist paintings. In his professional capacity he gave free medical advice to his artist friends.

Bernheim-Jeune, Gaston (1870–1953)
One of the first dealers to take up the Impressionist cause was Bernheim-Jeune. His gallery became a major outlet for Impressionst paintings from the 1880s onwards.

Caillebotte, Gustave (1848–1894)
The wealthy bachelor and trained naval architect Caillebotte was also a highly-skilled artist and patron of the Impressionists. His entrepreneurial skills and financial assistance were equally important to their survival, and his ambitious paintings are as powerful and daring as those of his friends. In later years he became increasingly interested in flower-growing and yachting, eventually giving up art almost completely. His collection of major Impressionist canvases, donated to the nation, forms the backbone of the French state collection.

Cassatt, Mary Stevenson (1844–1926)
In 1871–2 Cassatt, a wealthy American expatriate, visited Italy, where she made a special study of Coreggio. In 1872 entries painted by her were accepted at the Paris Salon. Her work at the Salon of 1874 attracted the attention of Degas, who invited her to show with the Impressionists; this she first did in 1879. She was an assured and innovative painter and printmaker, and was instrumental in bringing the work of the Impressionists to the attention of collectors in the United States. She and Monet were the only members of the group to carry out works on a large scale. She featured in several of Degas' paintings, pastels and prints.

Cézanne, Paul (1839–1906)
Cézanne was born in Aix-en-Provence. Fiercely dedicated to his art, he began painting in the 1860s in a dramatic, forceful manner. Under the influence primarily of Camille Pissarro, he came to direct his efforts increasingly towards the interpretation of the landscape, still-life and the figure. Cézanne arrived in Paris in 1861 and met up with his childhood friend, the critic and novelist Emile Zola. In Paris he also met a wide circle of artists, including those from the Impressionist group. He divided his time between Paris and his home in Aix. He exhibited rarely; he showed with the Impressionists on only two occasions, in 1870 and 1874. In 1895 the young dealer Ambroise Vollard dedicated a one-man show to his work. Cézanne's compositions reflect his love of the natural landscape and reverence for the old masters.

Chocquet, Victor (1821–1898)
Chocquet, a customs inspector, was one of a small group of collectors of Impressionist paintings whose support for artists such as Cézanne, Renoir and Monet in the 1870s was crucial to the artists' financial and moral wellbeing.

Clemenceau, Georges (1841–1929)
The French statesman Clemenceau was passionately interested in art and became friendly with Monet in the 1890s. He was one of the most important political figures of his time, twice Prime Minister of the French Republic (in 1906–9 and 1917–20). In November 1918 he inspired Monet to donate to the nation his large decorative cycle, *The Waterlilies*. The cycle was completed just before Monet's death and installed in the Orangerie in Paris a year later on 17 May 1927.

Corot, Camille (1796–1875)
The landscape painter Corot was a key influence on the Impressionists. His *plein air* work had a great effect on the early paintings of Morisot, Pissarro, Monet and Renoir; his later work may well have had an effect upon Monet's paintings of the 1880s and 90s.

Courbet, Gustave (1819–1877)
Courbet was a major figure in the realist movement who in the 1860s, together with Manet, provided a focal point for young, independently-minded artists. He was born in Ornans in the southeast of France and moved to Paris in 1839. He exhibited at the Salon in the early 1840s, but he received his first significant notice only in 1849. His bravura techniques, unconventional compositions and subject matter shocked and puzzled the social and artistic Establishment of the 1850s and 60s. His political activity during the Commune in 1871 led to his persecution and imprisonment. In 1873 he went into voluntary exile in Switzerland.

Degas, Edgar (1834–1917)
One of Ingres' former pupils trained Degas in the academic tradition. The young artist – born in Paris into a wealthy banking family – made a personal pilgrimage to Italy in 1856–9. On his return to Paris he moved from doing ambitious history paintings to creating works that responded more exactly to his experience of modern urban life – the ballet, horse-racing, and scenes of high and low life. These he treated in a self-consciously modern way, though always with a deep awareness of the works of the past. He was obsessed by the technical aspects of his art and worked in a wide variety of media – sculpture, pastel and print. After 1870 he exhibited regularly with the Impressionists until 1886, after which he allowed his work to be handled by various dealers, especially Durand-Ruel. Like Monet and Pissarro, he suffered problems with his eyesight which may well have had an effect on his artistic practice.

Desboutin, Marcellin (1823–1902)
Degas' teetotal friend Desboutin was an etcher and habitué of the Café Guerbois. He features in *Au Café* – better known as *L'Absinthe* – by Degas (c.1876) in which he appears with the actress Ellen Andrée.

Durand-Ruel, Paul (1831–1892)
A major influence upon the Impressionists was the support they received from the dealer Paul Durand-Ruel. His father Jean had founded the Durand-Ruel gallery in 1862 and had supported among others Delacroix and Courbet; Paul continued this tradition by supporting the *Indépendants*. He had an extraordinary business sense and was responsible for realizing the potential of the American market. He played a key role in ensuring the survival of Impressionism, especially in the 1870s. His son Charles continued the family business and sustained its interest in the paintings of the Impressionists.

Duranty, Edmond (1833–1886)
A critic and novelist of the realist school, Duranty was also a friend of the Impressionists and one of the regulars at the Café Guerbois. He was the author of the pamphlet *La Nouvelle Peinture* which, with the work of Degas in mind, provided the rationale for a new school of painting based upon realist lines. He was the subject of a major portrait by Degas now in the Burrell Collection in Glasgow.

Duret, Théodore (1838–1927)
Duret was both a politician and an art critic. Like Duranty, he was on close terms with the *Indépendant* painters and sympathetic to their innovations. He was especially interested in their technical procedures. A portrait of Duret, now in the Petit Palais, Paris, was painted by Monet with whom he was particularly friendly.

Fantin-Latour, Henri (1836–1904)
Both Whistler and Degas were among Fantin-Latour's friends. He was invited to England by the American artist and found a commercial outlet for his work there. His early paintings are realist in character, but he later specialized in flower and fantasy pieces.

Forain, Jean-Louis (1852–1931)
The cathedral city of Rheims was Forain's birthplace, but he received his artistic education in Paris where he spent the rest of his life. In the 1870s he became friendly with the Impressionists and participated in their exhibitions in 1879 and 1881–6. Forain was a much admired caricaturist, illustrator and painter; Degas in particular held him in high regard. His oils and drawings show a fascination with those aspects of modern life that also attracted Manet and Degas.

Gachet, Paul (1828–1909)
Dr Gachet was one of the most eccentric members of the Impressionist circle. He was a homeopathic doctor, amateur etcher and enthusiastic member of the Society for Mutual Autopsy. His support for artists encompassed both their medical and personal needs. He was particularly friendly with Pissarro and Cézanne, and managed to interest the latter briefly in etching. Later he was to look after Vincent Van Gogh at the end of his life.

Gasquet, Joachim (1873–1921)
The young poet and journalist Gasquet befriended Cézanne in 1896 and their relationship was sustained for four years. In 1926 Gasquet wrote a rather florid account of his friendship with the artist.

Gauguin, Paul (1848–1903)
Although born in Paris, Gauguin spent most of the first six years of his life in Peru. When a young man he travelled widely as a merchant seaman and in the French Navy, before accepting a post in a successful firm of stockbrokers. He got to know the Impressionists and built up an impressive collection of their canvases. The financial crisis of 1883 precipitated a decision to become a full-time artist. He worked with both Pissarro and Cézanne and exhibited with the Impressionists from 1879 to 1886. By the early 1880s, however, he had become dissatisfied with what he saw as the limitations of Impressionism; this dissatisfaction revealed itself fully in his paintings of the latter part of the decade. He lived in Brittany in 1886, 1888 and 1889 and became the leader of the Pont-Aven group. He visited Martinique in 1887 and lived in Tahiti in 1891–3 and 1895–1901, before moving to the Marquesas Islands where he died.

Gogh, Théo Van (1857–1891)
Vincent Van Gogh's younger brother Théo was employed by Goupil's, the Paris-based art dealers. There he attempted to develop an interest among the firm's rather conservative clientele for avant-garde works, especially those of the Impressionists. He died, six months after the suicide of his artist brother.

Geffroy, Gustave (1855–1926)
In 1886, on Belle-Ile off Brittany, Geffroy met Monet and became one of the painter's staunchest supporters. Geffroy was an important writer and respected commentator on the arts. He later developed a passion for Cézanne's work, although Cézanne remained distant from him and never finished the portrait he began of the writer.

Gonzalès, Eva (1849–1883)
The daughter of a celebrated journalist and popular novelist, Eva Gonzalès left the atelier of her master Charles Chaplin to study with Eugène Manet, brother of Edouard. Berthe Morisot obviously regarded her as something of a rival, yet like Edouard Manet, Gonzalès never exhibited at any of the Impressionist exhibitions. She died a few months after Edouard Manet.

Guillaumin, Armand (1841–1927)
Only after winning a prize in the state lottery, in 1891, was Guillaumin able to become a full-time painter; until then he had worked in the Paris civil service. He was born at Moulins, but lived mainly in the capital. He was particularly friendly with Pissarro and Cézanne and showed at most of the Impressionist exhibitions. In the 1890s with his new-found wealth he helped the younger artists Gauguin, Seurat, Signac and Van Gogh.

Lepic, Vicomte Ludovic-Napoléon (1839–1889)
The aristocratic dog-breeder and amateur printmaker and pastelliste Lepic was represented in two Impressionist exhibitions. He also features prominently in Degas' painting *La Place de la Concorde*, which was destroyed during the Second World War. Lepic was a close friend of Degas and he is reputed to have introduced his friend to the art of the monotype in about 1874. Degas' monotype *The Ballet Master* was signed by both artists.

Mallarmé, Stéphane (1842–1898)
Mallarmé was a poet of the Symbolist school and a great friend and admirer of Manet, Morisot, Renoir and Monet. He wrote perceptively of their art and his poetry offers many intriguing parallels with the work of his friends.

Manet, Edouard (1832–1883)

Born in Paris into a wealthy family, Manet lived in the French capital all his life. He was trained by the historical painter Thomas Couture from 1850 to 1856, but was always drawn to the challenge of interpreting contemporary life. Throughout his career he considered the Salon as the correct exhibiting forum for artists. His work was the cause of many scandals during the 1860s and from this time onwards he had a major influence on the work of younger artists. He became a close friend of Monet in 1869 and his work started to show an interest in some of the Impressionists' techniques.

Monet, Alice (1844–1911)

Claude Monet's second wife Alice was first married to the enigmatic Ernest Hoschedé, who was a major patron of Monet's in the 1870s. As a result of one of the many financial crashes of the period, Hoschedé lost his money and effectively abandoned his family. Monet, already a widower with two sons, took in Alice's family of six daughters, of whom the eldest Blanche, married Monet's son Jean. The artist eventually married Alice in 1892 and she lived with him at Giverny until her death.

Monet, Camille (1847–1879)

Camille Doncieux posed for some of Monet's best-known canvases and shared the very real hardships of the early years of his career. They married in 1870, three years after the birth of their first son Jean and she died a year after the birth of their second son Michel.

Monet, Claude (1840–1926)

Although born in Paris, Monet was raised in Le Havre, where he was introduced to landscape painting by the artist Eugène Boudin. He moved to Paris in 1859, meeting Pissarro that same year and Renoir, Sisley and Bazille three years later while studying in the atelier of Charles Gleyre. He found some favour at the Salon in the 1860s, but from the 1870s exhibited mainly in group exhibitions and in the galleries of his dealers. In the 1870s he concentrated on painting modern urban scenes and the landscape around Paris and on the Normandy coast. In the 1880s he travelled around France painting a wide variety of landscapes. He eventually settled at Giverny where he spent the final years of his life exploring the artistic possibilities presented by his extensive garden.

Moreau, Gustave (1826–1856)

Moreau was a friend and mentor of Degas' early years. He had independant means and had been trained in the academic manner by François Picot. He travelled to Italy in 1841 and later in 1857–9, in the company of Degas. The masters of the Italian quattrocento had a lasting impact on his work. His elaborate allegorical compositions, usually of a mythological character, were in complete contrast to those of his erstwhile friend.

Morisot, Berthe (1841–1895)

One of the key forces that kept the Impressionist group together as an exhibiting body was Berthe Morisot, who showed at all but one of their exhibitions. Corot was a friend of the family and in the early 1860s he gave Berthe and her sister Edma lessons in *plein air* painting. Berthe rapidly developed a startlingly fresh and original style of her own which was highly regarded by her colleagues, although, like so many of her friends, she was plagued by debilitating attacks of self-doubt. She married Manet's brother Eugène in 1874 and her work had an influence on that of her brother-in-law from the late 1870s to his death in 1883.

Murer, Eugène (1845–1906)

Murer was a boyhood friend of Armand Guillaumin. He was also a novelist, poet, painter and *pâtissier*. He and his sister ran a *crèmerie* at 95 boulevard Voltaire and during the 1870s this establishment became a rendezvous for his painter friends on Wednesday nights. Murer was willing to exchange works of art in return for meals and in this way he built up an impressive collection of Impressionist paintings.

Nadar [Félix Tournachon] (1820–1910)

The most famous photographer of his day was also a caricaturist, novelist and balloonist. Nadar was as well known for his entrepreneurial skills as he was for his achievements in photography. He was one of the Café Guerbois circle and sympathetic to young talent. He allowed the *Société anonyme des peintres* to use his recently-vacated studio on the corner of the rue Daudon and the fashionable boulevard des Capucines as the venue for their first *Indépendant* exhibition.

Nittis, Joseph de (1846–1884)

The Italian painter de Nittis was associated with the Florentine *Macchiaoli* group of painters, whose chief apologist, Diego Martelli, was a frequent visitor to Paris and was painted by Degas. De Nittis was strongly influenced by the Impressionists and especially by Degas. He exhibited at several of the Impressionist exhibitions.

Pissarro, Camille (1830–1903)

The island of Saint Thomas in the Danish West Indies was Pissarro's birthplace; his parents were Jewish. He developed an interest in art and in 1855 made his way to Paris. He received some encouragement from Corot in the late 1850s and made his Salon debut in 1859. In the same year he met Monet and in 1861 Cézanne, for whom he developed a strong affection; they worked together many times, most significantly in the 1870s. He exhibited in the Salon in the 1860s, but after the 1870s he became one of the staunchest defenders of the *Indépendant* shows. After 1886–8 he was influenced by the work of Seurat and the Neo-impressionists, adopting a pointillist technique and expressing sympathy with their anarchist beliefs which were very much in tune with his own political outlook.

Pissarro, Lucien (1863–1944)

Camille Pissarro's eldest son, born in Paris, was a talented painter and printmaker. Lucien was initially taught painting by his father and, like him, was much influenced by Seurat and the Neo-impressionists. He exhibited in the 1886 Impressionist show and with the Belgian exhibiting group, Les Vingt. He went to live in England and this separation from the family initiated the famous correspondence with his father. He became associated with the Arts and Crafts movement and had some influence on British painters of the New English Art Club and later the Camden Town Group.

Puvis de Chavannes, Pierre (1824–1898)

An early friend and mentor of Berthe Morisot was the Lyons-born Puvis de Chavannes, whose works were a decisive presence in the French art world during this later part of the 19th century. He was especially revered for his large-scale decorative canvases, pale in colour and harmonious in composition. He decorated many official buildings in France including the Panthéon, Paris, the Longchamp Palace and the town halls at Amiens and Marseilles. His work was much criticized in his early career, but from the 1860s he was loaded with honours and prestigious government commissions, and was accepted by both avant-garde painters and the Establishment.

Raffaëlli, Jean-François (1850–1926)

Despite an Italian-sounding name, Raffaëlli was born and lived in Paris, where his father was a successful chemist and manufacturer of silk dyes. The young Raffaëlli supported himself as an actor and singer before enrolling at the studio of the historical painter Gérôme. His friendship with Duranty and other novelists of the Naturalist school was important to the development of his art. He was one of Degas' protegés and exhibited with the Impressionists in 1880–1. He had a special affinity with the working class and their environment. His prosaic, almost journalistic, manner of painting enjoyed critical success and in turn created a certain amount of tension within the Impressionist exhibiting group.

Renoir, Pierre-Auguste (1841–1919)
After an apprenticeship with the porcelain painters Frères Lèvy in the 1860s, Renoir began copying in the Louvre, where he was particularly interested in the painters of the 18th century. He later enrolled at Gleyre's atelier where he met Monet, Sisley and Bazille. During the late 60s and the 70s, he shared with Monet an interest in depicting scenes drawn from contemporary life. He was successful at the 1877 Salon and became increasingly wary of involving himself with the often dubious publicity that the Impressionist shows attracted. After a decisive trip to Italy in 1881 he began to feel a profound unease with what he saw as the limitations of Impressionism and sought an art that would be the equal of the art he had admired in the Louvre and at Pompeii. In 1886 his one-man show at Durand-Ruel's gallery brought him critical recognition and financial success. He increasingly produced works of an idyllic nature, usually depicting nude or near nude figures in imaginary landscape settings.

Rouart, Henri (1833–1912)
Close ties bound the wealthy industrialist and collector Henri Rouart to the Impressionist circle. He was a schoolfriend of Degas and remained close to the artist until his death. He was also an amateur artist who showed in several of the Impressionist exhibitions. One of his sons, Ernest, received some painting lessons from Degas and later married Berthe Morisot's daughter Julie Manet. Ernest's and Julie's son, Denis Rouart, was later to edit Berthe Morisot's correspondence.

Seurat, Georges (1859–1891)
From 1877 to 1879 Seurat underwent a formal art education at the Ecole des Beaux-Arts. He lived in Paris, his ambition being to interpret the life of the city on a momumental scale in a suitably modern manner. He was much influenced by Chevreul's book on the theory of colour. In 1885–6, after meeting with Paul Signac, he developed the pointillist or divisionist technique. He exhibited regularly with the *Indépendants* in Paris and from 1887 with Les Vingt in Brussels. His aesthetic ideas were still being formulated in his works at the time of his early death; his ideas were subsequently developed by followers and imitators.

Sickert, Walter Richard (1860–1942)
Sickert was an English painter of Danish descent. He met Whistler in 1879 and was profoundly influenced by his work and personality. In 1883, he was sent by Whistler to Paris, where he made the acquaintance of Degas, who replaced the American painter as the major influence on his painting.

Signac, Paul (1863–1935)
Paris was Signac's home until 1892 when he moved to St-Tropez. He was largely self-taught, and derived his style and subject matter from Impressionism. He met Seurat in 1884 and became an enthusiastic and vocal supporter of pointillism. In 1899 he published his book *De Delacroix au Néo-impressionisme* which set out his interpretation of the pointillist movement.

Sisley, Alfred (1839–1899)
Sisley was born in Paris of English parents. He entered the studio of Charles Gleyre in 1862 and there met Renoir, Bazille and Monet. Until 1870 he could rely upon his father's support and after Gleyre's studio closed, he let his friends spend the winter months in his own studio. As with Monet, landscape was his first love and he mainly painted the villages, small towns and countryside around Paris. He was supported by Durand-Ruel and collected by Duret and the famous baritone Jean-Baptiste Faure, who took him to England in 1874. He participated in the Impressionist shows but did not enjoy great success. In the late 1880s he and his family settled in the village of Moret-sur-Loing where he lived and worked until his death. From 1886 he exhibited at the Salon, but, despite the support of Durand-Ruel, his work was never taken up by collectors and he died a disappointed man, withdrawn from his former colleagues. His work was only to enjoy a popular success after his death.

Tissot, James (1836–1902)
Degas, Whistler and Fantin-Latour were among Tissot's friends. He was a painter who specialized in modish scenes of contemporary fashionable life. Despite the best endeavours of Degas, he refused to participate in the first Impressionist show. He settled in England after the Franco-Prussian War and enjoyed great artistic and financial success from his work.

Vollard, Ambroise (1867–1939)
The vivid and engaging memoirs by Vollard of the Impressionists and their circle are some of the most interesting accounts of the period that survive. Vollard was a brilliant salesman who opened his small gallery in the rue Laffitte in 1893 and gave Cézanne his first one-man show there two years later.

Whistler, James Abbott McNeill (1834–1903)
The American-born artist Whistler lived and worked in both France and England. Originally influenced by the work of Courbet, he later sought an art based upon a synthesis of Japanese and European models. His aesthetic ideas were very influential and his *Ten O'clock Lecture* was translated by Stéphane Mallarmé. It had a profound effect on a wide range of artists including Gauguin and Monet.

Zandomeneghi, Federigo (1841–1917)
Zandomeneghi was Venetian by birth and, like de Nittis, was in close contact with the Florentine group of artists known as the *Macchiaioli*. He lived in Paris from 1874 until his death. He frequently exhibited with the Impressionists; his work bears closest resemblance to that of Degas.

Zola, Emile (1840–1902)
Cézanne's childhood friend Zola became a major critic and novelist. He wrote supportive articles on Manet, Courbet and the Impressionists in the 1860s and 70s. In 1886 he published his novel *L'Oeuvre*, a *roman à clef* about the Parisian art scene which caused a certain amount of friction between him and his former friends. Cézanne refused to meet Zola again after reading the novel.

Index

Text Acknowledgements

Permission to reproduce letters, memoirs and writings has been generously granted by many people, institutions, publishers and dealers. The Editor of this volume has made every effort to contact all copyright holders, but those he has been unable to reach are invited to contact him so that acknowledgements can be made in subsequent editions. Grateful acknowledgements to the following:

Art Institute of Chicago; Archives of American Art, Smithsonian Institute, Washington; Ashmolean Museum of Art, Oxford, Pissarro Archives; Bernheim-Jeune Archives, Paris; Bibliothèque Nationale, Paris, Cabinet des Estampes; Brooklyn Museum, New York; Hôtel Drouot, Paris; Houston Museum of Fine Arts; Musée du Louvre, Paris, Départment des Arts Graphiques, Fonds Orsay; Musée Gustave Moreau, Paris.

The descendents of Alice Monet for permission to reproduce the following: W. 312, 1, 2, 1883; W. 651, 27, 11, 1885; W. 975, 8, 5, 1889; W. 976, 9, 5, 1889; W. 1179, 22, 2, 1893; W. 1268, 13, 2, 89; W. 1276, 1, 3, 1895; W. 1533, 19, 3, 1900 (according to the numbering system used in *Claude Monet, Biographie et catalogue raisonné* by D. Wildenstein, Lausanne and Paris, 1974–85).

Estate of Lois Cassatt Thayer for permission to quote from the letters of the Cassatt family.

Art Bulletin for 'Some Unpublished Letters by Edgar Degas', Vol LI, 3, Sept 1969, translated by T. Reff (to be included in forthcoming collected correspondence of Degas, ed. T. Reff).

La Bibliothèque des Arts for *Caillebotte, sa vie et son oeuvre* by M. Berhaut.

La Bibliothèque des Arts, Lausanne et Paris, and the Wildenstein Institute for *Claude Monet, Biographie et catalogue raisonné* by D. Wildenstein. David Carritt Ltd for Sisley exhibition catalogue by R. Nathanson.

Bruno Cassirer for *Degas Letters* edited by M. Guerin, translated by M. Kay.

Burlington Magazine for 'Renoir, Lise and the Le Coeur Family: A Study of Renoir's Early Development' by D. Cooper (May, September–October 1959), and for 'Degas' by W. Sickert (November 1917).

Crown Publishers for *Journal* by E. Delacroix, edited by W. Pach.

Durand-Ruel for *Archives de l'Impressionnisme* by L. Venturi, Copyright Durand-Ruel.

Editions Littéraires de Paris for *Renoir, ses amis, ses modèles* by J. Baudot.

Faber & Faber Ltd for *Men and Memories* by W. Rothenstein.

Fine Arts Museums of San Francisco for *The New Painting Impressionism, 1874–1886* by Charles S. Moffett *et al.* All rights reserved.

Bernard Grasset for *Correspondance* by P. Cézanne, ed. J. Rewald, for *Lettres impressionistes à Dr. Gachet et Eugène Murer*, and for *Degas Letters*, ed. Marcel Guerin, translated by M. Kay, Oxford; Cassirer 1947.

C. Klincksieck for *Journal (1893–1899)* by J. Manet.

Alfred A. Knopf Inc. for *Renoir: an Intimate Record* by A. Vollard, translated by H. L. Van Doren and R. T. Weaver, Copyright 1925, renewed 1953.

Samuel Josefowitz Collection for *Racontars d'un rapin*, original manuscript in possession of Samuel Josefowitz Collection.

Macdonald Orbis for *Cézanne by Himself, Degas by Himself, Monet by Himself* by R. Kendall.

Museum of Modern Art, New York for *History of Impressionism* by J. Rewald.

Oxford University Press for *Pages from the Goncourt Journal* by E. and J. Goncourt, translated and edited by R. Baldick, and for *Degas Notebooks* edited by T. Reff.

Pantheon Books Inc. for *Artists on Art: From the XIVth to the XXth Century* by R. Goldwater and M. Treves, and for *Letters to his Son, Lucien* by Camille Pissarro, edited by J. Rewald, translated by L. Abel.

Percy Lund Humphries for *Correspondence of Berthe Morisot* edited by D. Rouart, translated by B. W. Hubbard.

A. D. Peters and Co. and Little, Brown and Co. for *Renoir, My Father* by J. Renoir, translated by R. and D. Weaver, copyright Jean Renoir.

Princetown University Press for *Impressionism and its Sources* edited by B. E. White, translated by L. G. Slaughter.

Princetown University Press and Routledge, Kegan Paul for *Degas, Dance, Drawing* by P. Valéry, translated by D. Paul.

Quarto Group plc for *Techniques of the Impressionists* by A. Callen.

Quatre-Chemins Editart for *Correspondence de Berthe Morisot*, 1950.

Ralph E. Shikes and Paula Harper for *Pissarro, His Life and Works*, Horizon Press 1980.

Skira for *Renoir* by D. Rouart.

Sotheby's Publications, Philip Wilson Publishers, Rosalind de Boland Roberts and Jane Roberts for *Growing up with the Impressionists* by Julie Manet.

Thames and Hudson for *The Impressionists at First Hand* by B. Denvir, and for *Renoir* by F. Fosca, and for *Letters of Great Artists* edited by R. Friedenthal.

Editions Valhermeil and Association des Amis de Camille Pissarro, Pontoise for *Mon cher Pissarro: Lettres de Ludovic Piette à Camille Pissarro* edited by J. Bailly-Herzberg.

Wesleyan University Press and University Press of New England for *My Friend Degas* by D. Halévy, translated by M. Curtiss.

Barbara Ehrlich White for *Renoir: His Life, Art, and Letters*, Abrams, 1984, and for *Impressionism in Perspective*, Englewood Cliffs NJ, Prentice-Hall, translations by L. G. Slaughter (English translations © Barbara Ehrlich White).

Yale University Press for *Art into Nature* by J. House.

Select Bibliography

B. Bernard (ed.), *The Impressionist Revolution*, London, 1986.
A. Callen, *Techniques of the Impressionists*, London, 1982.
T. J. Clark, *The Painting of Modern Life: Paris in the Art of Manet and his Followers*, London, 1985.
T. Garb, *The Unknown Impressionists*, Oxford, 1988.
T. Garb, *Women Impressionists*, Oxford, 1986.
R. L. Herbert, *Impressionism: Art, Leisure and Parisian Society*, Yale, 1988.
Los Angeles, County Museum of Art, *A Day in the Country: Impressionism and the French Landscape*, exhibition catalogue by R. Bretell, S. Schaefer and S. Gache-Patin, 1984.
J. Rewald, *The History of Impressionism*, 4th edition, New York and London, 1973.
San Francisco, Fine Art Museums, *The New Painting, Impressionism, 1874–1886*, exhibition catalogue by C. S. Moffet and others, 1986.
B. E. White, *Renoir: His Life, Art and Letters*, New York, 1984.